Volume IV

The

ETHIOPIAN

BIBLE

The Prophets

Preface

It is with immense gratitude and a renewed sense of purpose that we present the fourth volume of The Ethiopian Bible. This volume continues the journey through the words of the prophets, unveiling the profound wisdom of ancient scriptures and their relevance to both present and future generations.

The Book of the Prophet Isaiah, which forms the core of this volume, invites readers to reflect on humanity's spiritual and moral challenges, showcasing the power of faith and redemption. The prophecies contained herein speak not only to their original audience but continue to resonate deeply, offering comfort, guidance, and hope to modern readers.

As the penultimate volume in this series, this text sets the stage for the conclusion, consolidating central themes while encouraging readers to engage deeply with the divine message. The structure and commentary in this edition aim to make these complex texts accessible, fostering meaningful dialogue and reflection.

We extend our heartfelt thanks to the collaborators and scholars who have made this work possible, providing a cohesive and enriching exploration of sacred writings. May this volume serve as a source of inspiration and contemplation, illuminating your path toward understanding and inner peace.

Exploring the Volume IV

The Prophets

A Divine Call to Reflection

The Ethiopian Bible's fourth volume, *The Prophets*, immerses readers in the profound and often challenging words of the ancient prophets. This collection unveils divine wisdom through visions, warnings, and promises of redemption, firmly rooted in a historical and theological framework. From the poetic declarations of Isaiah to the visionary insights of Ezekiel, this volume bridges the eternal divine message with the human experience across centuries.

The prophetic tradition in Ethiopia holds a unique position within its biblical canon. Unlike the segmented treatment in many Western canons, the Ethiopian approach integrates these texts with its broader theological and cultural heritage. The prophets' voices echo the concerns of justice, faith, and hope—concerns as relevant today as they were in ancient times.

Prophecy and Ethiopian Identity

Ethiopia's historical engagement with biblical prophecy extends beyond scripture into its cultural and political narratives. The prophets' messages, especially those found in Isaiah and Jeremiah, resonate deeply with Ethiopian Orthodox theology, which emphasizes God's active involvement in guiding nations and individuals toward righteousness.

- **Isaiah's Vision**: The Book of Isaiah, central to this volume, outlines a divine plan of redemption and hope amid turmoil. Themes such as the suffering servant and the promise of a renewed Zion have profound theological significance, both within Ethiopia's liturgical traditions and in its understanding of national identity.
- **Jeremiah's Warnings**: Jeremiah's laments over the faithlessness of Judah and the impending exile parallel Ethiopian interpretations of historical trials, offering lessons in divine justice and restoration.
- **Ezekiel's Symbols**: The vivid imagery of Ezekiel, including the vision of dry bones and the restoration of Israel, is often understood in Ethiopian traditions as metaphors for spiritual renewal and the hope of resurrection.

The Prophets' Unique Role in Ethiopian Theology

The Ethiopian Orthodox Tewahedo Church regards the prophets as integral mediators of God's covenant, bridging the Old and New Testaments. Their messages foreshadow the coming of Christ and provide moral and spiritual guidance. This theological continuity is reflected in Ethiopian worship, where prophetic readings often accompany celebrations of major liturgical feasts.

The Linguistic Beauty of Ge'ez in Prophetic Texts

The translation of the prophetic books into Ge'ez imbues them with a unique poetic and rhythmic quality, preserving their profound spiritual resonance. Phrases such as:

"የሚታይ አስተርእዮ እናቀርባለን።"
("We present the vision revealed.")

echo the majesty and mystery of divine revelation, capturing the awe-inspiring nature of prophetic messages. Ge'ez, as a sacred language, enriches the understanding of these texts, connecting the reader to their spiritual and historical roots.

Themes of Redemption, Judgment, and Hope

The prophetic writings in this volume traverse themes of divine judgment, human repentance, and ultimate redemption. They challenge readers to confront their failings while offering visions of divine mercy and hope for renewal.

- **Justice and Repentance**: The call to justice and the denunciation of hypocrisy in Isaiah 1:17—*"Learn to do right; seek justice. Defend the oppressed. Take up the cause of the fatherless; plead the case of the widow."*—underscore a timeless moral imperative.
- **Redemption and Covenant**: Jeremiah's assurance of a new covenant (Jeremiah 31:31-34) reflects a transformative promise that aligns closely with Ethiopian understandings of divine grace.

- **Hope in Restoration**: Ezekiel's vision of dry bones (Ezekiel 37) encapsulates the power of faith and God's promise to breathe new life into His people.

Relevance for Contemporary Readers

The prophetic books offer timeless lessons, urging reflection on personal and communal responsibility. Their emphasis on moral integrity, social justice, and unwavering faith resonates with contemporary challenges, providing spiritual guidance and hope.

As you delve into this volume, allow the prophets' voices to guide you in understanding the profound intersections of history, faith, and divine purpose. They are not just ancient words; they are living messages, calling each of us to reflect, repent, and renew our commitment to justice and faith.

TABLE OF CONTENTS

The Book of the Prophet Isaiah

1

1 The vision of Isaiah the son of Amoz, which he saw concerning Judah and Jerusalem, in the days of Uzziah, Jotham, Ahaz, and Hezekiah, kings of Judah. 2 Hear, heavens, and listen, earth; for Yahweh has spoken: "I have nourished and brought up children and they have rebelled against me. 3 The ox knows his owner, and the donkey his master's crib; but Israel doesn't know. My people don't consider." 4 Ah sinful nation, a people loaded with iniquity, offspring of evildoers, children who deal corruptly! They have forsaken Yahweh. They have despised the Holy One of Israel. They are estranged and backward. 5 Why should you be beaten more, that you revolt more and more? The whole head is sick, and the whole heart faint. 6 From the sole of the foot even to the head there is no soundness in it, but wounds, welts, and open sores. They haven't been closed, bandaged, or soothed with oil. 7 Your country is desolate. Your cities are burned with fire. Strangers devour your land in your presence and it is desolate, as overthrown by strangers. 8 The daughter of Zion is left like a shelter in a vineyard, like a hut in a field of melons, like a besieged city. 9 Unless Yahweh of Armies had left to us a very small remnant, we would have been as Sodom. We would have been like Gomorrah. 10 Hear Yahweh's word, you rulers of Sodom! Listen to the law of our God, you people of Gomorrah! 11"What are the multitude of your sacrifices to me?", says Yahweh. "I have had enough of the burnt offerings of rams and the fat of fed animals. I don't delight in the blood of bulls, or of lambs, or of male goats. 12 When you come to appear before me, who has required this at your hand, to trample my courts? 13 Bring no more vain offerings. Incense is an abomination to me. New moons, Sabbaths, and convocations— I can't stand evil assemblies. 14 My soul hates your New Moons and your appointed feasts. They are a burden to me. I am weary of bearing them. 15 When you spread out your hands, I will hide my eyes from you. Yes, when you make many prayers, I will not hear. Your hands are full of blood. 16 Wash yourselves. Make yourself clean. Put away the evil of your doings from before my eyes. Cease to do evil. 17 Learn to do well. Seek justice. Relieve the oppressed. Defend the fatherless. Plead for the widow." 18"Come now, and let's reason together," says Yahweh: "Though your sins are as scarlet, they shall be as white as snow. Though they are red like crimson, they shall be as wool. 19 If you are willing and obedient, you will eat

the good of the land; 20 but if you refuse and rebel, you will be devoured with the sword; for Yahweh's mouth has spoken it." 21 How the faithful city has become a prostitute! She was full of justice. Righteousness lodged in her, but now there are murderers. 22 Your silver has become dross, your wine mixed with water. 23 Your princes are rebellious and companions of thieves. Everyone loves bribes and follows after rewards. They don't defend the fatherless, neither does the cause of the widow come to them. 24 Therefore the Lord, Yahweh of Armies, the Mighty One of Israel, says: "Ah, I will get relief from my adversaries, and avenge myself on my enemies. 25 I will turn my hand on you, thoroughly purge away your dross, and will take away all your tin. 26 I will restore your judges as at the first, and your counselors as at the beginning. Afterward you shall be called 'The city of righteousness, a faithful town.' 27 Zion shall be redeemed with justice, and her converts with righteousness. 28 But the destruction of transgressors and sinners shall be together, and those who forsake Yahweh shall be consumed. 29 For they shall be ashamed of the oaks which you have desired, and you shall be confounded for the gardens that you have chosen. 30 For you shall be as an oak whose leaf fades, and as a garden that has no water. 31 The strong will be like tinder, and his work like a spark. They will both burn together, and no one will quench them."

2

1 This is what Isaiah the son of Amoz saw concerning Judah and Jerusalem. 2 It shall happen in the latter days, that the mountain of Yahweh's house shall be established on the top of the mountains, and shall be raised above the hills; and all nations shall flow to it. 3 Many peoples shall go and say, "Come, let's go up to the mountain of Yahweh, to the house of the God of Jacob; and he will teach us of his ways, and we will walk in his paths." For the law shall go out of Zion, and Yahweh's word from Jerusalem. 4 He will judge between the nations, and will decide concerning many peoples. They shall beat their swords into plowshares, and their spears into pruning hooks. Nation shall not lift up sword against nation, neither shall they learn war any more. 5 House of Jacob, come, and let's walk in the light of Yahweh. 6 For you have forsaken your people, the house of Jacob, because they are filled from the east, with those who practice divination like the Philistines, and they clasp hands with the children of foreigners. 7 Their land is full of silver and gold, neither is there any end of their treasures. Their land also is full of horses, neither is there any end of their chariots. 8 Their land also is full of idols. They worship

the work of their own hands, that which their own fingers have made. 9 Man is brought low, and mankind is humbled; therefore don't forgive them. 10 Enter into the rock, and hide in the dust, from before the terror of Yahweh, and from the glory of his majesty. 11 The lofty looks of man will be brought low, the arrogance of men will be bowed down, and Yahweh alone will be exalted in that day. 12 For there will be a day of Yahweh of Armies for all that is proud and arrogant, and for all that is lifted up, and it shall be brought low — 13 for all the cedars of Lebanon, that are high and lifted up, for all the oaks of Bashan, 14 for all the high mountains, for all the hills that are lifted up, 15 for every lofty tower, for every fortified wall, 16 for all the ships of Tarshish, and for all pleasant imagery. 17 The loftiness of man shall be bowed down, and the arrogance of men shall be brought low; and Yahweh alone shall be exalted in that day. 18 The idols shall utterly pass away. 19 Men shall go into the caves of the rocks, and into the holes of the earth, from before the terror of Yahweh, and from the glory of his majesty, when he arises to shake the earth mightily. 20 In that day, men shall cast away their idols of silver and their idols of gold, which have been made for themselves to worship, to the moles and to the bats, 21 to go into the caverns of the rocks, and into the clefts of the ragged rocks, from before the terror of Yahweh, and from the glory of his majesty, when he arises to shake the earth mightily. 22 Stop trusting in man, whose breath is in his nostrils; for of what account is he?

3

1 For, behold, the Lord, Yahweh of Armies, takes away from Jerusalem and from Judah supply and support, the whole supply of bread, and the whole supply of water; 2 the mighty man, the man of war, the judge, the prophet, the diviner, the elder, 3 the captain of fifty, the honorable man, the counselor, the skilled craftsman, and the clever enchanter. 4 I will give boys to be their princes, and children shall rule over them. 5 The people will be oppressed, everyone by another, and everyone by his neighbor. The child will behave himself proudly against the old man, and the wicked against the honorable. 6 Indeed a man shall take hold of his brother in the house of his father, saying, "You have clothing, you be our ruler, and let this ruin be under your hand." 7 In that day he will cry out, saying, "I will not be a healer; for in my house is neither bread nor clothing. You shall not make me ruler of the people." 8 For Jerusalem is ruined, and Judah is fallen; because their tongue and their doings are against Yahweh, to provoke the eyes of his glory. 9 The look of their faces testify against them. They parade their sin like Sodom. They don't hide it.

Woe to their soul! For they have brought disaster upon themselves. 10 Tell the righteous that it will be well with them, for they will eat the fruit of their deeds. 11 Woe to the wicked! Disaster is upon them, for the deeds of their hands will be paid back to them. 12 As for my people, children are their oppressors, and women rule over them. My people, those who lead you cause you to err, and destroy the way of your paths. 13 Yahweh stands up to contend, and stands to judge the peoples. 14 Yahweh will enter into judgment with the elders of his people and their leaders: "It is you who have eaten up the vineyard. The plunder of the poor is in your houses. 15 What do you mean that you crush my people, and grind the face of the poor?" says the Lord, Yahweh of Armies. 16 Moreover Yahweh said, "Because the daughters of Zion are arrogant, and walk with outstretched necks and flirting eyes, walking daintily as they go, jingling ornaments on their feet; 17 therefore the Lord brings sores on the crown of the head of the women of Zion, and Yahweh will make their scalps bald." 18 In that day the Lord will take away the beauty of their anklets, the headbands, the crescent necklaces, 19 the earrings, the bracelets, the veils, 20 the headdresses, the ankle chains, the sashes, the perfume containers, the charms, 21 the signet rings, the nose rings, 22 the fine robes, the capes, the cloaks, the purses, 23 the hand mirrors, the fine linen garments, the tiaras, and the shawls. 24 It shall happen that instead of sweet spices, there shall be rottenness; instead of a belt, a rope; instead of well set hair, baldness; instead of a robe, a wearing of sackcloth; and branding instead of beauty. 25 Your men shall fall by the sword, and your mighty in the war. 26 Her gates shall lament and mourn. She shall be desolate and sit on the ground.

4

1 Seven women shall take hold of one man in that day, saying, "We will eat our own bread, and wear our own clothing. Just let us be called by your name. Take away our reproach." 2 In that day, Yahweh's branch will be beautiful and glorious, and the fruit of the land will be the beauty and glory of the survivors of Israel. 3 It will happen that he who is left in Zion and he who remains in Jerusalem shall be called holy, even everyone who is written among the living in Jerusalem, 4 when the Lord shall have washed away the filth of the daughters of Zion, and shall have purged the blood of Jerusalem from within it, by the spirit of justice and by the spirit of burning. 5 Yahweh will create over the whole habitation of Mount Zion and over her assemblies, a cloud and smoke by day, and the shining of a flaming fire by night, for over

all the glory will be a canopy. 6 There will be a pavilion for a shade in the daytime from the heat, and for a refuge and for a shelter from storm and from rain.

5

1 Let me sing for my well beloved a song of my beloved about his vineyard. My beloved had a vineyard on a very fruitful hill. 2 He dug it up, gathered out its stones, planted it with the choicest vine, built a tower in the middle of it, and also cut out a wine press in it. He looked for it to yield grapes, but it yielded wild grapes. 3 "Now, inhabitants of Jerusalem and men of Judah, please judge between me and my vineyard. 4 What could have been done more to my vineyard, that I have not done in it? Why, when I looked for it to yield grapes, did it yield wild grapes? 5 Now I will tell you what I will do to my vineyard. I will take away its hedge, and it will be eaten up. I will break down its wall, and it will be trampled down. 6 I will lay it a wasteland. It won't be pruned or hoed, but it will grow briers and thorns. I will also command the clouds that they rain no rain on it." 7 For the vineyard of Yahweh of Armies is the house of Israel, and the men of Judah his pleasant plant. He looked for justice, but behold, oppression, for righteousness, but behold, a cry of distress. 8 Woe to those who join house to house, who lay field to field, until there is no room, and you are made to dwell alone in the middle of the land! 9 In my ears, Yahweh of Armies says: "Surely many houses will be desolate, even great and beautiful, unoccupied. 10 For ten acres of vineyard shall yield one bath, and a homer of seed shall yield an ephah." 11 Woe to those who rise up early in the morning, that they may follow strong drink, who stay late into the night, until wine inflames them! 12 The harp, lyre, tambourine, and flute, with wine, are at their feasts; but they don't respect the work of Yahweh, neither have they considered the operation of his hands. 13 Therefore my people go into captivity for lack of knowledge. Their honorable men are famished, and their multitudes are parched with thirst. 14 Therefore Sheol has enlarged its desire, and opened its mouth without measure; and their glory, their multitude, their pomp, and he who rejoices among them, descend into it. 15 So man is brought low, mankind is humbled, and the eyes of the arrogant ones are humbled; 16 but Yahweh of Armies is exalted in justice, and God the Holy One is sanctified in righteousness. 17 Then the lambs will graze as in their pasture, and strangers will eat the ruins of the rich. 18 Woe to those who draw iniquity with cords of falsehood, and wickedness as with cart rope, 19 who say, "Let him make

haste, let him hasten his work, that we may see it; let the counsel of the Holy One of Israel draw near and come, that we may know it!" 20 Woe to those who call evil good, and good evil; who put darkness for light, and light for darkness; who put bitter for sweet, and sweet for bitter! 21 Woe to those who are wise in their own eyes, and prudent in their own sight! 22 Woe to those who are mighty to drink wine, and champions at mixing strong drink; 23 who acquit the guilty for a bribe, but deny justice for the innocent! 24 Therefore as the tongue of fire devours the stubble, and as the dry grass sinks down in the flame, so their root shall be as rottenness, and their blossom shall go up as dust, because they have rejected the law of Yahweh of Armies, and despised the word of the Holy One of Israel. 25 Therefore Yahweh's anger burns against his people, and he has stretched out his hand against them and has struck them. The mountains tremble, and their dead bodies are as refuse in the middle of the streets. For all this, his anger is not turned away, but his hand is still stretched out. 26 He will lift up a banner to the nations from far away, and he will whistle for them from the end of the earth. Behold, they will come speedily and swiftly. 27 No one shall be weary nor stumble among them; no one shall slumber nor sleep, neither shall the belt of their waist be untied, nor the strap of their sandals be broken, 28 whose arrows are sharp, and all their bows bent. Their horses' hoofs will be like flint, and their wheels like a whirlwind. 29 Their roaring will be like a lioness. They will roar like young lions. Yes, they shall roar, and seize their prey and carry it off, and there will be no one to deliver. 30 They will roar against them in that day like the roaring of the sea. If one looks to the land, behold, darkness and distress. The light is darkened in its clouds.

6

1 In the year that King Uzziah died, I saw the Lord sitting on a throne, high and lifted up; and his train filled the temple. 2 Above him stood the seraphim. Each one had six wings. With two he covered his face. With two he covered his feet. With two he flew. 3 One called to another, and said, "Holy, holy, holy, is Yahweh of Armies! The whole earth is full of his glory!" 4 The foundations of the thresholds shook at the voice of him who called, and the house was filled with smoke. 5 Then I said, "Woe is me! For I am undone, because I am a man of unclean lips and I live among a people of unclean lips, for my eyes have seen the King, Yahweh of Armies!" 6 Then one of the seraphim flew to me, having a live coal in his hand, which he had taken with the tongs from off the altar. 7 He touched my mouth with it, and said,

"Behold, this has touched your lips; and your iniquity is taken away, and your sin forgiven." 8 I heard the Lord's voice, saying, "Whom shall I send, and who will go for us?" Then I said, "Here I am. Send me!" 9 He said, "Go, and tell this people, 'You hear indeed, but don't understand. You see indeed, but don't perceive.' 10 Make the heart of this people fat. Make their ears heavy, and shut their eyes; lest they see with their eyes, hear with their ears, understand with their heart, and turn again, and be healed." 11 Then I said, "Lord, how long?" He answered, "Until cities are waste without inhabitant, houses without man, the land becomes utterly waste, 12 and Yahweh has removed men far away, and the forsaken places are many within the land. 13 If there is a tenth left in it, that also will in turn be consumed, as a terebinth, and as an oak whose stump remains when they are cut down, so the holy seed is its stump."

7

1 In the days of Ahaz the son of Jotham, the son of Uzziah, king of Judah, Rezin the king of Syria and Pekah the son of Remaliah, king of Israel, went up to Jerusalem to war against it, but could not prevail against it. 2 David's house was told, "Syria is allied with Ephraim." His heart trembled, and the heart of his people, as the trees of the forest tremble with the wind. 3 Then Yahweh said to Isaiah, "Go out now to meet Ahaz, you, and Shearjashub your son, at the end of the conduit of the upper pool, on the highway of the fuller's field. 4 Tell him, 'Be careful, and keep calm. Don't be afraid, neither let your heart be faint because of these two tails of smoking torches, for the fierce anger of Rezin and Syria, and of the son of Remaliah. 5 Because Syria, Ephraim, and the son of Remaliah, have plotted evil against you, saying, 6 "Let's go up against Judah, and tear it apart, and let's divide it among ourselves, and set up a king within it, even the son of Tabeel." 7 This is what the Lord Yahweh says: "It shall not stand, neither shall it happen." 8 For the head of Syria is Damascus, and the head of Damascus is Rezin. Within sixty-five years Ephraim shall be broken in pieces, so that it shall not be a people. 9 The head of Ephraim is Samaria, and the head of Samaria is Remaliah's son. If you will not believe, surely you shall not be established.'" 10 Yahweh spoke again to Ahaz, saying, 11 "Ask a sign of Yahweh your God; ask it either in the depth, or in the height above." 12 But Ahaz said, "I won't ask. I won't tempt Yahweh." 13 He said, "Listen now, house of David. Is it not enough for you to try the patience of men, that you will try the patience of my God also? 14 Therefore the Lord himself will give you a sign. Behold, the virgin will

conceive, and bear a son, and shall call his name Immanuel. 15 He shall eat butter and honey when he knows to refuse the evil and choose the good. 16 For before the child knows to refuse the evil and choose the good, the land whose two kings you abhor shall be forsaken. 17 Yahweh will bring on you, on your people, and on your father's house days that have not come, from the day that Ephraim departed from Judah, even the king of Assyria. 18 It will happen in that day that Yahweh will whistle for the fly that is in the uttermost part of the rivers of Egypt, and for the bee that is in the land of Assyria. 19 They shall come, and shall all rest in the desolate valleys, in the clefts of the rocks, on all thorn hedges, and on all pastures. 20 In that day the Lord will shave with a razor that is hired in the parts beyond the River, even with the king of Assyria, the head and the hair of the feet; and it shall also consume the beard. 21 It shall happen in that day that a man shall keep alive a young cow, and two sheep. 22 It shall happen, that because of the abundance of milk which they shall give he shall eat butter, for everyone will eat butter and honey that is left within the land. 23 It will happen in that day that every place where there were a thousand vines worth a thousand silver shekels, will be for briers and thorns. 24 People will go there with arrows and with bow, because all the land will be briers and thorns. 25 All the hills that were cultivated with the hoe, you shall not come there for fear of briers and thorns; but it shall be for the sending out of oxen, and for sheep to tread on."

8

1 Yahweh said to me, "Take a large tablet, and write on it with a man's pen, 'For Maher Shalal Hash Baz'; 2 and I will take for myself faithful witnesses to testify: Uriah the priest, and Zechariah the son of Jeberechiah." 3 I went to the prophetess, and she conceived, and bore a son. Then Yahweh said to me, "Call his name 'Maher Shalal Hash Baz.' 4 For before the child knows how to say, 'My father' and 'My mother,' the riches of Damascus and the plunder of Samaria will be carried away by the king of Assyria." 5 Yahweh spoke to me yet again, saying, 6"Because this people has refused the waters of Shiloah that go softly, and rejoice in Rezin and Remaliah's son; 7 now therefore, behold, the Lord brings upon them the mighty flood waters of the River: the king of Assyria and all his glory. It will come up over all its channels, and go over all its banks. 8 It will sweep onward into Judah. It will overflow and pass through. It will reach even to the neck. The stretching out of its wings will fill the width of your land, O Immanuel. 9 Make an uproar, you peoples, and be broken in pieces! Listen, all you from far countries: dress for battle, and be

shattered! Dress for battle, and be shattered! ¹⁰ Take counsel together, and it will be brought to nothing; speak the word, and it will not stand, for God is with us." ¹¹ For Yahweh spoke this to me with a strong hand, and instructed me not to walk in the way of this people, saying, ¹²"Don't call a conspiracy all that this people call a conspiracy. Don't fear their threats or be terrorized. ¹³ Yahweh of Armies is who you must respect as holy. He is the one you must fear. He is the one you must dread. ¹⁴ He will be a sanctuary, but for both houses of Israel, he will be a stumbling stone and a rock that makes them fall. For the people of Jerusalem, he will be a trap and a snare. ¹⁵ Many will stumble over it, fall, be broken, be snared, and be captured." ¹⁶ Wrap up the covenant. Seal the law among my disciples. ¹⁷ I will wait for Yahweh, who hides his face from the house of Jacob, and I will look for him. ¹⁸ Behold, I and the children whom Yahweh has given me are for signs and for wonders in Israel from Yahweh of Armies, who dwells in Mount Zion. ¹⁹ When they tell you, "Consult with those who have familiar spirits and with the wizards, who chirp and who mutter," shouldn't a people consult with their God? Should they consult the dead on behalf of the living? ²⁰ Turn to the law and to the covenant! If they don't speak according to this word, surely there is no morning for them. ²¹ They will pass through it, very distressed and hungry. It will happen that when they are hungry, they will worry, and curse their king and their God. They will turn their faces upward, ²² then look to the earth and see distress, darkness, and the gloom of anguish. They will be driven into thick darkness.

9

¹ But there shall be no more gloom for her who was in anguish. In the former time, he brought into contempt the land of Zebulun and the land of Naphtali; but in the latter time he has made it glorious, by the way of the sea, beyond the Jordan, Galilee of the nations. ² The people who walked in darkness have seen a great light. The light has shined on those who lived in the land of the shadow of death. ³ You have multiplied the nation. You have increased their joy. They rejoice before you according to the joy in harvest, as men rejoice when they divide the plunder. ⁴ For the yoke of his burden, and the staff of his shoulder, the rod of his oppressor, you have broken as in the day of Midian. ⁵ For all the armor of the armed man in the noisy battle, and the garments rolled in blood, will be for burning, fuel for the fire. ⁶ For a child is born to us. A son is given to us; and the government will be on his shoulders. His name will be called Wonderful Counselor, Mighty God, Everlasting

Father, Prince of Peace. 7 Of the increase of his government and of peace there shall be no end, on David's throne, and on his kingdom, to establish it, and to uphold it with justice and with righteousness from that time on, even forever. The zeal of Yahweh of Armies will perform this. 8 The Lord sent a word into Jacob, and it falls on Israel. 9 All the people will know, including Ephraim and the inhabitants of Samaria, who say in pride and in arrogance of heart, 10"The bricks have fallen, but we will build with cut stone. The sycamore fig trees have been cut down, but we will put cedars in their place." 11 Therefore Yahweh will set up on high against him the adversaries of Rezin, and will stir up his enemies, 12 The Syrians in front, and the Philistines behind; and they will devour Israel with open mouth. For all this, his anger is not turned away, but his hand is stretched out still. 13 Yet the people have not turned to him who struck them, neither have they sought Yahweh of Armies. 14 Therefore Yahweh will cut off from Israel head and tail, palm branch and reed, in one day. 15 The elder and the honorable man is the head, and the prophet who teaches lies is the tail. 16 For those who lead this people lead them astray; and those who are led by them are destroyed. 17 Therefore the Lord will not rejoice over their young men, neither will he have compassion on their fatherless and widows; for everyone is profane and an evildoer, and every mouth speaks folly. For all this his anger is not turned away, but his hand is stretched out still. 18 For wickedness burns like a fire. It devours the briers and thorns; yes, it kindles in the thickets of the forest, and they roll upward in a column of smoke. 19 Through Yahweh of Armies' wrath, the land is burned up; and the people are the fuel for the fire. No one spares his brother. 20 One will devour on the right hand, and be hungry; and he will eat on the left hand, and they will not be satisfied. Everyone will eat the flesh of his own arm: 21 Manasseh eating Ephraim and Ephraim eating Manasseh, and they together will be against Judah. For all this his anger is not turned away, but his hand is stretched out still.

10

1 Woe to those who decree unrighteous decrees, and to the writers who write oppressive decrees 2 to deprive the needy of justice, and to rob the poor among my people of their rights, that widows may be their plunder, and that they may make the fatherless their prey! 3 What will you do in the day of visitation, and in the desolation which will come from afar? To whom will you flee for help? Where will you leave your wealth? 4 They will only bow down under the prisoners, and will fall under the slain. For all this his anger

is not turned away, but his hand is stretched out still. 5 Alas Assyrian, the rod of my anger, the staff in whose hand is my indignation! 6 I will send him against a profane nation, and against the people who anger me I will give him a command to take the plunder and to take the prey, and to tread them down like the mire of the streets. 7 However, he doesn't mean so, neither does his heart think so; but it is in his heart to destroy, and to cut off not a few nations. 8 For he says, "Aren't all of my princes kings? 9 Isn't Calno like Carchemish? Isn't Hamath like Arpad? Isn't Samaria like Damascus?" 10 As my hand has found the kingdoms of the idols, whose engraved images exceeded those of Jerusalem and of Samaria, 11 shall I not, as I have done to Samaria and her idols, so do to Jerusalem and her idols? 12 Therefore it will happen that when the Lord has performed his whole work on Mount Zion and on Jerusalem, I will punish the fruit of the willful proud heart of the king of Assyria, and the insolence of his arrogant looks. 13 For he has said, "By the strength of my hand I have done it, and by my wisdom, for I have understanding. I have removed the boundaries of the peoples, and have robbed their treasures. Like a valiant man I have brought down their rulers. 14 My hand has found the riches of the peoples like a nest, and like one gathers eggs that are abandoned, I have gathered all the earth. There was no one who moved their wing, or that opened their mouth, or chirped." 15 Should an ax brag against him who chops with it? Should a saw exalt itself above him who saws with it? As if a rod should lift those who lift it up, or as if a staff should lift up someone who is not wood. 16 Therefore the Lord, Yahweh of Armies, will send among his fat ones leanness; and under his glory a burning will be kindled like the burning of fire. 17 The light of Israel will be for a fire, and his Holy One for a flame; and it will burn and devour his thorns and his briers in one day. 18 He will consume the glory of his forest and of his fruitful field, both soul and body. It will be as when a standard bearer faints. 19 The remnant of the trees of his forest shall be few, so that a child could write their number. 20 It will come to pass in that day that the remnant of Israel, and those who have escaped from the house of Jacob will no more again lean on him who struck them, but shall lean on Yahweh, the Holy One of Israel, in truth. 21 A remnant will return, even the remnant of Jacob, to the mighty God. 22 For though your people, Israel, are like the sand of the sea, only a remnant of them will return. A destruction is determined, overflowing with righteousness. 23 For the Lord, Yahweh of Armies, will make a full end, and that determined, throughout all the earth. 24 Therefore the Lord, Yahweh of

Armies, says, "My people who dwell in Zion, don't be afraid of the Assyrian, though he strike you with the rod, and lift up his staff against you, as Egypt did. 25 For yet a very little while, and the indignation against you will be accomplished, and my anger will be directed to his destruction." 26 Yahweh of Armies will stir up a scourge against him, as in the slaughter of Midian at the rock of Oreb. His rod will be over the sea, and he will lift it up like he did against Egypt. 27 It will happen in that day that his burden will depart from off your shoulder, and his yoke from off your neck, and the yoke shall be destroyed because of the anointing oil. 28 He has come to Aiath. He has passed through Migron. At Michmash he stores his baggage. 29 They have gone over the pass. They have taken up their lodging at Geba. Ramah trembles. Gibeah of Saul has fled. 30 Cry aloud with your voice, daughter of Gallim! Listen, Laishah! You poor Anathoth! 31 Madmenah is a fugitive. The inhabitants of Gebim flee for safety. 32 This very day he will halt at Nob. He shakes his hand at the mountain of the daughter of Zion, the hill of Jerusalem. 33 Behold, the Lord, Yahweh of Armies, will lop the boughs with terror. The tall will be cut down, and the lofty will be brought low. 34 He will cut down the thickets of the forest with iron, and Lebanon will fall by the Mighty One.

11

1 A shoot will come out of the stock of Jesse, and a branch out of his roots will bear fruit. 2 Yahweh's Spirit will rest on him: the spirit of wisdom and understanding, the spirit of counsel and might, the spirit of knowledge and of the fear of Yahweh. 3 His delight will be in the fear of Yahweh. He will not judge by the sight of his eyes, neither decide by the hearing of his ears; 4 but he will judge the poor with righteousness, and decide with equity for the humble of the earth. He will strike the earth with the rod of his mouth; and with the breath of his lips he will kill the wicked. 5 Righteousness will be the belt around his waist, and faithfulness the belt around his waist. 6 The wolf will live with the lamb, and the leopard will lie down with the young goat, the calf, the young lion, and the fattened calf together; and a little child will lead them. 7 The cow and the bear will graze. Their young ones will lie down together. The lion will eat straw like the ox. 8 The nursing child will play near a cobra's hole, and the weaned child will put his hand on the viper's den. 9 They will not hurt nor destroy in all my holy mountain; for the earth will be full of the knowledge of Yahweh, as the waters cover the sea. 10 It will happen in that day that the nations will seek the root of Jesse, who stands as a banner of the peoples; and his resting place will be glorious. 11 It will happen

in that day that the Lord will set his hand again the second time to recover the remnant that is left of his people from Assyria, from Egypt, from Pathros, from Cush, from Elam, from Shinar, from Hamath, and from the islands of the sea. 12 He will set up a banner for the nations, and will assemble the outcasts of Israel, and gather together the dispersed of Judah from the four corners of the earth. 13 The envy also of Ephraim will depart, and those who persecute Judah will be cut off. Ephraim won't envy Judah, and Judah won't persecute Ephraim. 14 They will fly down on the shoulders of the Philistines on the west. Together they will plunder the children of the east. They will extend their power over Edom and Moab, and the children of Ammon will obey them. 15 Yahweh will utterly destroy the tongue of the Egyptian sea; and with his scorching wind he will wave his hand over the River, and will split it into seven streams, and cause men to march over in sandals. 16 There will be a highway for the remnant that is left of his people from Assyria, like there was for Israel in the day that he came up out of the land of Egypt.

12

1 In that day you will say, "I will give thanks to you, Yahweh; for though you were angry with me, your anger has turned away and you comfort me. 2 Behold, God is my salvation. I will trust, and will not be afraid; for Yah, Yahweh, is my strength and song; and he has become my salvation." 3 Therefore with joy you will draw water out of the wells of salvation. 4 In that day you will say, "Give thanks to Yahweh! Call on his name! Declare his doings among the peoples! Proclaim that his name is exalted! 5 Sing to Yahweh, for he has done excellent things! Let this be known in all the earth! 6 Cry aloud and shout, you inhabitant of Zion, for the Holy One of Israel is great among you!"

13

1 The burden of Babylon, which Isaiah the son of Amoz saw. 2 Set up a banner on the bare mountain! Lift up your voice to them! Wave your hand, that they may go into the gates of the nobles. 3 I have commanded my consecrated ones; yes, I have called my mighty men for my anger, even my proudly exulting ones. 4 The noise of a multitude is in the mountains, as of a great people; the noise of an uproar of the kingdoms of the nations gathered together! Yahweh of Armies is mustering the army for the battle. 5 They come from a far country, from the uttermost part of heaven, even Yahweh, and the weapons of his indignation, to destroy the whole land. 6 Wail, for

Yahweh's day is at hand! It will come as destruction from the Almighty. 7 Therefore all hands will be feeble, and everyone's heart will melt. 8 They will be dismayed. Pangs and sorrows will seize them. They will be in pain like a woman in labor. They will look in amazement one at another. Their faces will be faces of flame. 9 Behold, the day of Yahweh comes, cruel, with wrath and fierce anger; to make the land a desolation, and to destroy its sinners out of it. 10 For the stars of the sky and its constellations will not give their light. The sun will be darkened in its going out, and the moon will not cause its light to shine. 11 I will punish the world for their evil, and the wicked for their iniquity. I will cause the arrogance of the proud to cease, and will humble the arrogance of the terrible. 12 I will make people more rare than fine gold, even a person than the pure gold of Ophir. 13 Therefore I will make the heavens tremble, and the earth will be shaken out of its place in Yahweh of Armies' wrath, and in the day of his fierce anger. 14 It will happen that like a hunted gazelle and like sheep that no one gathers, they will each turn to their own people, and will each flee to their own land. 15 Everyone who is found will be thrust through. Everyone who is captured will fall by the sword. 16 Their infants also will be dashed in pieces before their eyes. Their houses will be ransacked, and their wives raped. 17 Behold, I will stir up the Medes against them, who will not value silver, and as for gold, they will not delight in it. 18 Their bows will dash the young men in pieces; and they shall have no pity on the fruit of the womb. Their eyes will not spare children. 19 Babylon, the glory of kingdoms, the beauty of the Chaldeans' pride, will be like when God overthrew Sodom and Gomorrah. 20 It will never be inhabited, neither will it be lived in from generation to generation. The Arabian will not pitch a tent there, neither will shepherds make their flocks lie down there. 21 But wild animals of the desert will lie there, and their houses will be full of jackals. Ostriches will dwell there, and wild goats will frolic there. 22 Hyenas will cry in their fortresses, and jackals in the pleasant palaces. Her time is near to come, and her days will not be prolonged.

14

1 For Yahweh will have compassion on Jacob, and will yet choose Israel, and set them in their own land. The foreigner will join himself with them, and they will unite with the house of Jacob. 2 The peoples will take them, and bring them to their place. The house of Israel will possess them in Yahweh's land for servants and for handmaids. They will take as captives those whose captives they were; and they shall rule over their oppressors. 3 It will happen

in the day that Yahweh will give you rest from your sorrow, from your trouble, and from the hard service in which you were made to serve, 4 that you will take up this parable against the king of Babylon, and say, "How the oppressor has ceased! The golden city has ceased!" 5 Yahweh has broken the staff of the wicked, the scepter of the rulers, 6 who struck the peoples in wrath with a continual stroke, who ruled the nations in anger, with a persecution that no one restrained. 7 The whole earth is at rest, and is quiet. They break out in song. 8 Yes, the cypress trees rejoice with you, with the cedars of Lebanon, saying, "Since you are humbled, no lumberjack has come up against us." 9 Sheol from beneath has moved for you to meet you at your coming. It stirs up the departed spirits for you, even all the rulers of the earth. It has raised up from their thrones all the kings of the nations. 10 They all will answer and ask you, "Have you also become as weak as we are? Have you become like us?" 11 Your pomp is brought down to Sheol, with the sound of your stringed instruments. Maggots are spread out under you, and worms cover you. 12 How you have fallen from heaven, shining one, son of the dawn! How you are cut down to the ground, who laid the nations low! 13 You said in your heart, "I will ascend into heaven! I will exalt my throne above the stars of God! I will sit on the mountain of assembly, in the far north! 14 I will ascend above the heights of the clouds! I will make myself like the Most High!" 15 Yet you shall be brought down to Sheol, to the depths of the pit. 16 Those who see you will stare at you. They will ponder you, saying, "Is this the man who made the earth to tremble, who shook kingdoms, 17 who made the world like a wilderness, and overthrew its cities, who didn't release his prisoners to their home?" 18 All the kings of the nations sleep in glory, everyone in his own house. 19 But you are cast away from your tomb like an abominable branch, clothed with the slain who are thrust through with the sword, who go down to the stones of the pit; like a dead body trodden under foot. 20 You will not join them in burial, because you have destroyed your land. You have killed your people. The offspring of evildoers will not be named forever. 21 Prepare for slaughter of his children because of the iniquity of their fathers, that they not rise up and possess the earth, and fill the surface of the world with cities. 22"I will rise up against them," says Yahweh of Armies, "and cut off from Babylon name and remnant, and son and son's son," says Yahweh. 23"I will also make it a possession for the porcupine, and pools of water. I will sweep it with the broom of destruction," says Yahweh of Armies. 24 Yahweh of Armies has sworn, saying, "Surely, as I have thought, so shall it happen; and as I have purposed, so shall it stand: 25 that I will break the Assyrian in my land, and tread him under foot on my mountains. Then his yoke will leave them, and his burden leave their shoulders. 26 This is the plan that is determined for the whole earth. This is the hand that is stretched out over all the nations. 27 For Yahweh of Armies has planned, and who can stop it? His hand is stretched out, and who can turn it back?" 28 This burden was in the year that King Ahaz died. 29 Don't rejoice, O Philistia, all of you, because the rod that struck you is broken; for out of the serpent's root an adder will emerge, and his fruit will be a fiery flying serpent. 30 The firstborn of the poor will eat, and the needy will lie down in safety; and I will kill your root with famine, and your remnant will be killed. 31 Howl, gate! Cry, city! You are melted away, Philistia, all of you; for smoke comes out of the north, and there is no straggler in his ranks. 32 What will they answer the messengers of the nation? That Yahweh has founded Zion, and in her the afflicted of his people will take refuge.

15

1 The burden of Moab. For in a night, Ar of Moab is laid waste, and brought to nothing. For in a night Kir of Moab is laid waste, and brought to nothing. 2 They have gone up to Bayith, and to Dibon, to the high places, to weep. Moab wails over Nebo and over Medeba. Baldness is on all of their heads. Every beard is cut off. 3 In their streets, they clothe themselves in sackcloth. In their streets and on their housetops, everyone wails, weeping abundantly. 4 Heshbon cries out with Elealeh. Their voice is heard even to Jahaz. Therefore the armed men of Moab cry aloud. Their souls tremble within them. 5 My heart cries out for Moab! Her nobles flee to Zoar, to Eglath Shelishiyah; for they go up by the ascent of Luhith with weeping; for on the way to Horonaim, they raise up a cry of destruction. 6 For the waters of Nimrim will be desolate; for the grass has withered away, the tender grass fails, there is no green thing. 7 Therefore they will carry away the abundance they have gotten, and that which they have stored up, over the brook of the willows. 8 For the cry has gone around the borders of Moab, its wailing to Eglaim, and its wailing to Beer Elim. 9 For the waters of Dimon are full of blood; for I will bring yet more on Dimon, a lion on those of Moab who escape, and on the remnant of the land.

16

1 Send the lambs for the ruler of the land from Selah to the wilderness, to the

mountain of the daughter of Zion. 2 For it will be that as wandering birds, as a scattered nest, so will the daughters of Moab be at the fords of the Arnon. 3 Give counsel! Execute justice! Make your shade like the night in the middle of the noonday! Hide the outcasts! Don't betray the fugitive! 4 Let my outcasts dwell with you! As for Moab, be a hiding place for him from the face of the destroyer. For the extortionist is brought to nothing. Destruction ceases. The oppressors are consumed out of the land. 5 A throne will be established in loving kindness. One will sit on it in truth, in the tent of David, judging, seeking justice, and swift to do righteousness. 6 We have heard of the pride of Moab, that he is very proud; even of his arrogance, his pride, and his wrath. His boastings are nothing. 7 Therefore Moab will wail for Moab. Everyone will wail. You will mourn for the raisin cakes of Kir Hareseth, utterly stricken. 8 For the fields of Heshbon languish with the vine of Sibmah. The lords of the nations have broken down its choice branches, which reached even to Jazer, which wandered into the wilderness. Its shoots were spread abroad. They passed over the sea. 9 Therefore I will weep with the weeping of Jazer for the vine of Sibmah. I will water you with my tears, Heshbon, and Elealeh: for on your summer fruits and on your harvest the battle shout has fallen. 10 Gladness is taken away, and joy out of the fruitful field; and in the vineyards there will be no singing, neither joyful noise. Nobody will tread out wine in the presses. I have made the shouting stop. 11 Therefore my heart sounds like a harp for Moab, and my inward parts for Kir Heres. 12 It will happen that when Moab presents himself, when he wearies himself on the high place, and comes to his sanctuary to pray, that he will not prevail. 13 This is the word that Yahweh spoke concerning Moab in time past. 14 But now Yahweh has spoken, saying, "Within three years, as a worker bound by contract would count them, the glory of Moab shall be brought into contempt, with all his great multitude; and the remnant will be very small and feeble."

17

1 The burden of Damascus. "Behold, Damascus is taken away from being a city, and it will be a ruinous heap. 2 The cities of Aroer are forsaken. They will be for flocks, which shall lie down, and no one shall make them afraid. 3 The fortress shall cease from Ephraim, and the kingdom from Damascus, and the remnant of Syria. They will be as the glory of the children of Israel," says Yahweh of Armies. 4"It will happen in that day that the glory of Jacob will be made thin, and the fatness of his flesh will become lean. 5 It will be like when

the harvester gathers the wheat, and his arm reaps the grain. Yes, it will be like when one gleans grain in the valley of Rephaim. 6 Yet gleanings will be left there, like the shaking of an olive tree, two or three olives in the top of the uppermost bough, four or five in the outermost branches of a fruitful tree," says Yahweh, the God of Israel. 7 In that day, people will look to their Maker, and their eyes will have respect for the Holy One of Israel. 8 They will not look to the altars, the work of their hands; neither shall they respect that which their fingers have made, either the Asherah poles or the incense altars. 9 In that day, their strong cities will be like the forsaken places in the woods and on the mountain top, which were forsaken from before the children of Israel; and it will be a desolation. 10 For you have forgotten the God of your salvation, and have not remembered the rock of your strength. Therefore you plant pleasant plants, and set out foreign seedlings. 11 In the day of your planting, you hedge it in. In the morning, you make your seed blossom, but the harvest flees away in the day of grief and of desperate sorrow. 12 Ah, the uproar of many peoples who roar like the roaring of the seas; and the rushing of nations that rush like the rushing of mighty waters! 13 The nations will rush like the rushing of many waters, but he will rebuke them, and they will flee far off, and will be chased like the chaff of the mountains before the wind, and like the whirling dust before the storm. 14 At evening, behold, terror! Before the morning, they are no more. This is the portion of those who plunder us, and the lot of those who rob us.

18

1 Ah, the land of the rustling of wings, which is beyond the rivers of Ethiopia; 2 that sends ambassadors by the sea, even in vessels of papyrus on the waters, saying, "Go, you swift messengers, to a nation tall and smooth, to a people awesome from their beginning onward, a nation that measures out and treads down, whose land the rivers divide!" 3 All you inhabitants of the world, and you dwellers on the earth, when a banner is lifted up on the mountains, look! When the trumpet is blown, listen! 4 For Yahweh said to me, "I will be still, and I will see in my dwelling place, like clear heat in sunshine, like a cloud of dew in the heat of harvest." 5 For before the harvest, when the blossom is over, and the flower becomes a ripening grape, he will cut off the sprigs with pruning hooks, and he will cut down and take away the spreading branches. 6 They will be left together for the ravenous birds of the mountains, and for the animals of the earth. The ravenous birds will eat them in the summer, and all the animals of the earth will eat them in the winter. 7 In

that time, a present will be brought to Yahweh of Armies from a people tall and smooth, even from a people awesome from their beginning onward, a nation that measures out and treads down, whose land the rivers divide, to the place of the name of Yahweh of Armies, Mount Zion.

19

1 The burden of Egypt. "Behold, Yahweh rides on a swift cloud, and comes to Egypt. The idols of Egypt will tremble at his presence; and the heart of Egypt will melt within it. 2 I will stir up the Egyptians against the Egyptians, and they will fight everyone against his brother, and everyone against his neighbor; city against city, and kingdom against kingdom. 3 The spirit of the Egyptians will fail within them. I will destroy their counsel. They will seek the idols, the charmers, those who have familiar spirits, and the wizards. 4 I will give over the Egyptians into the hand of a cruel lord. A fierce king will rule over them," says the Lord, Yahweh of Armies. 5 The waters will fail from the sea, and the river will be wasted and become dry. 6 The rivers will become foul. The streams of Egypt will be diminished and dried up. The reeds and flags will wither away. 7 The meadows by the Nile, by the brink of the Nile, and all the sown fields of the Nile, will become dry, be driven away, and be no more. 8 The fishermen will lament, and all those who fish in the Nile will mourn, and those who spread nets on the waters will languish. 9 Moreover those who work in combed flax, and those who weave white cloth, will be confounded. 10 The pillars will be broken in pieces. All those who work for hire will be grieved in soul. 11 The princes of Zoan are utterly foolish. The counsel of the wisest counselors of Pharaoh has become stupid. How do you say to Pharaoh, "I am the son of the wise, the son of ancient kings"? 12 Where then are your wise men? Let them tell you now; and let them know what Yahweh of Armies has purposed concerning Egypt. 13 The princes of Zoan have become fools. The princes of Memphis are deceived. They have caused Egypt to go astray, those who are the cornerstone of her tribes. 14 Yahweh has mixed a spirit of perverseness in the middle of her; and they have caused Egypt to go astray in all of its works, like a drunken man staggers in his vomit. 15 Neither shall there be any work for Egypt, which head or tail, palm branch or rush, may do. 16 In that day the Egyptians will be like women. They will tremble and fear because of the shaking of Yahweh of Armies's hand, which he shakes over them. 17 The land of Judah will become a terror to Egypt. Everyone to whom mention is made of it will be afraid, because of the plans of Yahweh of Armies, which he determines against it. 18

In that day, there will be five cities in the land of Egypt that speak the language of Canaan, and swear to Yahweh of Armies. One will be called "The city of destruction." 19 In that day, there will be an altar to Yahweh in the middle of the land of Egypt, and a pillar to Yahweh at its border. 20 It will be for a sign and for a witness to Yahweh of Armies in the land of Egypt; for they will cry to Yahweh because of oppressors, and he will send them a savior and a defender, and he will deliver them. 21 Yahweh will be known to Egypt, and the Egyptians will know Yahweh in that day. Yes, they will worship with sacrifice and offering, and will vow a vow to Yahweh, and will perform it. 22 Yahweh will strike Egypt, striking and healing. They will return to Yahweh, and he will be entreated by them, and will heal them. 23 In that day there will be a highway out of Egypt to Assyria, and the Assyrian shall come into Egypt, and the Egyptian into Assyria; and the Egyptians will worship with the Assyrians. 24 In that day, Israel will be the third with Egypt and with Assyria, a blessing within the earth; 25 because Yahweh of Armies has blessed them, saying, "Blessed be Egypt my people, Assyria the work of my hands, and Israel my inheritance."

20

1 In the year that Tartan came to Ashdod, when Sargon the king of Assyria sent him, and he fought against Ashdod and took it; 2 at that time Yahweh spoke by Isaiah the son of Amoz, saying, "Go, and loosen the sackcloth from off your waist, and take your sandals from off your feet." He did so, walking naked and barefoot. 3 Yahweh said, "As my servant Isaiah has walked naked and barefoot three years for a sign and a wonder concerning Egypt and concerning Ethiopia, 4 so the king of Assyria will lead away the captives of Egypt and the exiles of Ethiopia, young and old, naked and barefoot, and with buttocks uncovered, to the shame of Egypt. 5 They will be dismayed and confounded, because of Ethiopia their expectation, and of Egypt their glory. 6 The inhabitants of this coast land will say in that day, 'Behold, this is our expectation, where we fled for help to be delivered from the king of Assyria. And we, how will we escape?'"

21

1 The burden of the wilderness of the sea. As whirlwinds in the South sweep through, it comes from the wilderness, from an awesome land. 2 A grievous vision is declared to me. The treacherous man deals treacherously, and the destroyer destroys. Go up, Elam; attack! I have stopped all of Media's

sighing. 3 Therefore my thighs are filled with anguish. Pains have seized me, like the pains of a woman in labor. I am in so much pain that I can't hear. I am so dismayed that I can't see. 4 My heart flutters. Horror has frightened me. The twilight that I desired has been turned into trembling for me. 5 They prepare the table. They set the watch. They eat. They drink. Rise up, you princes, oil the shield! 6 For the Lord said to me, "Go, set a watchman. Let him declare what he sees. 7 When he sees a troop, horsemen in pairs, a troop of donkeys, a troop of camels, he shall listen diligently with great attentiveness." 8 He cried like a lion: "Lord, I stand continually on the watchtower in the daytime, and every night I stay at my post. 9 Behold, here comes a troop of men, horsemen in pairs." He answered, "Fallen, fallen is Babylon; and all the engraved images of her gods are broken to the ground. 10 You are my threshing, and the grain of my floor!" That which I have heard from Yahweh of Armies, the God of Israel, I have declared to you. 11 The burden of Dumah. One calls to me out of Seir, "Watchman, what of the night? Watchman, what of the night?" 12 The watchman said, "The morning comes, and also the night. If you will inquire, inquire. Come back again." 13 The burden on Arabia. You will lodge in the thickets in Arabia, you caravans of Dedanites. 14 They brought water to him who was thirsty. The inhabitants of the land of Tema met the fugitives with their bread. 15 For they fled away from the swords, from the drawn sword, from the bent bow, and from the heat of battle. 16 For the Lord said to me, "Within a year, as a worker bound by contract would count it, all the glory of Kedar will fail, 17 and the residue of the number of the archers, the mighty men of the children of Kedar, will be few; for Yahweh, the God of Israel, has spoken it."

22

1 The burden of the valley of vision. What ails you now, that you have all gone up to the housetops? 2 You that are full of shouting, a tumultuous city, a joyous town, your slain are not slain with the sword, neither are they dead in battle. 3 All your rulers fled away together. They were bound by the archers. All who were found by you were bound together. They fled far away. 4 Therefore I said, "Look away from me. I will weep bitterly. Don't labor to comfort me for the destruction of the daughter of my people. 5 For it is a day of confusion, and of treading down, and of perplexity from the Lord, Yahweh of Armies, in the valley of vision, a breaking down of the walls, and a crying to the mountains." 6 Elam carried his quiver, with chariots of men and horsemen; and Kir uncovered the shield. 7 Your choicest valleys were full of

chariots, and the horsemen set themselves in array at the gate. 8 He took away the covering of Judah; and you looked in that day to the armor in the house of the forest. 9 You saw the breaches of David's city, that they were many; and you gathered together the waters of the lower pool. 10 You counted the houses of Jerusalem, and you broke down the houses to fortify the wall. 11 You also made a reservoir between the two walls for the water of the old pool. But you didn't look to him who had done this, neither did you have respect for him who planned it long ago. 12 In that day, the Lord, Yahweh of Armies, called to weeping, to mourning, to baldness, and to dressing in sackcloth; 13 and behold, there is joy and gladness, killing cattle and killing sheep, eating meat and drinking wine: "Let's eat and drink, for tomorrow we will die." 14 Yahweh of Armies revealed himself in my ears, "Surely this iniquity will not be forgiven you until you die," says the Lord, Yahweh of Armies. 15 The Lord, Yahweh of Armies says, "Go, get yourself to this treasurer, even to Shebna, who is over the house, and say, 16'What are you doing here? Who has you here, that you have dug out a tomb here?' Cutting himself out a tomb on high, chiseling a habitation for himself in the rock!" 17 Behold, Yahweh will overcome you and hurl you away violently. Yes, he will grasp you firmly. 18 He will surely wind you around and around, and throw you like a ball into a large country. There you will die, and there the chariots of your glory will be, you disgrace of your lord's house. 19 I will thrust you from your office. You will be pulled down from your station. 20 It will happen in that day that I will call my servant Eliakim the son of Hilkiah, 21 and I will clothe him with your robe, and strengthen him with your belt. I will commit your government into his hand; and he will be a father to the inhabitants of Jerusalem, and to the house of Judah. 22 I will lay the key of David's house on his shoulder. He will open, and no one will shut. He will shut, and no one will open. 23 I will fasten him like a nail in a sure place. He will be for a throne of glory to his father's house. 24 They will hang on him all the glory of his father's house, the offspring and the issue, every small vessel, from the cups even to all the pitchers. 25" In that day," says Yahweh of Armies, "the nail that was fastened in a sure place will give way. It will be cut down and fall. The burden that was on it will be cut off, for Yahweh has spoken it."

23

1 The burden of Tyre. Howl, you ships of Tarshish! For it is laid waste, so that there is no house, no entering in. From the land of Kittim it is revealed to them. 2 Be still, you inhabitants of the coast, you whom the merchants of

Sidon that pass over the sea have replenished. ³ On great waters, the seed of the Shihor, the harvest of the Nile, was her revenue. She was the market of nations. ⁴ Be ashamed, Sidon; for the sea has spoken, the stronghold of the sea, saying, "I have not travailed, nor given birth, neither have I nourished young men, nor brought up virgins." ⁵ When the report comes to Egypt, they will be in anguish at the report of Tyre. ⁶ Pass over to Tarshish! Wail, you inhabitants of the coast! ⁷ Is this your joyous city, whose antiquity is of ancient days, whose feet carried her far away to travel? ⁸ Who has planned this against Tyre, the giver of crowns, whose merchants are princes, whose traders are the honorable of the earth? ⁹ Yahweh of Armies has planned it, to stain the pride of all glory, to bring into contempt all the honorable of the earth. ¹⁰ Pass through your land like the Nile, daughter of Tarshish. There is no restraint any more. ¹¹ He has stretched out his hand over the sea. He has shaken the kingdoms. Yahweh has ordered the destruction of Canaan's strongholds. ¹² He said, "You shall rejoice no more, you oppressed virgin daughter of Sidon. Arise, pass over to Kittim. Even there you will have no rest." ¹³ Behold, the land of the Chaldeans. This people didn't exist. The Assyrians founded it for those who dwell in the wilderness. They set up their towers. They overthrew its palaces. They made it a ruin. ¹⁴ Howl, you ships of Tarshish, for your stronghold is laid waste! ¹⁵ It will come to pass in that day that Tyre will be forgotten seventy years, according to the days of one king. After the end of seventy years it will be to Tyre like in the song of the prostitute. ¹⁶ Take a harp; go about the city, you prostitute that has been forgotten. Make sweet melody. Sing many songs, that you may be remembered. ¹⁷ It will happen after the end of seventy years that Yahweh will visit Tyre. She will return to her wages, and will play the prostitute with all the kingdoms of the world on the surface of the earth. ¹⁸ Her merchandise and her wages will be holiness to Yahweh. It will not be treasured nor laid up; for her merchandise will be for those who dwell before Yahweh, to eat sufficiently, and for durable clothing.

24

¹ Behold, Yahweh makes the earth empty, makes it waste, turns it upside down, and scatters its inhabitants. ² It will be as with the people, so with the priest; as with the servant, so with his master; as with the maid, so with her mistress; as with the buyer, so with the seller; as with the creditor, so with the debtor; as with the taker of interest, so with the giver of interest. ³ The earth will be utterly emptied and utterly laid waste; for Yahweh has spoken this

word. 4 The earth mourns and fades away. The world languishes and fades away. The lofty people of the earth languish. 5 The earth also is polluted under its inhabitants, because they have transgressed the laws, violated the statutes, and broken the everlasting covenant. 6 Therefore the curse has devoured the earth, and those who dwell therein are found guilty. Therefore the inhabitants of the earth are burned, and few men are left. 7 The new wine mourns. The vine languishes. All the merry-hearted sigh. 8 The mirth of tambourines ceases. The sound of those who rejoice ends. The joy of the harp ceases. 9 They will not drink wine with a song. Strong drink will be bitter to those who drink it. 10 The confused city is broken down. Every house is shut up, that no man may come in. 11 There is a crying in the streets because of the wine. All joy is darkened. The mirth of the land is gone. 12 The city is left in desolation, and the gate is struck with destruction. 13 For it will be so within the earth among the peoples, as the shaking of an olive tree, as the gleanings when the vintage is done. 14 These shall lift up their voice. They will shout for the majesty of Yahweh. They cry aloud from the sea. 15 Therefore glorify Yahweh in the east, even the name of Yahweh, the God of Israel, in the islands of the sea! 16 From the uttermost part of the earth have we heard songs. Glory to the righteous! But I said, "I pine away! I pine away! woe is me!" The treacherous have dealt treacherously. Yes, the treacherous have dealt very treacherously. 17 Fear, the pit, and the snare are on you who inhabit the earth. 18 It will happen that he who flees from the noise of the fear will fall into the pit; and he who comes up out of the middle of the pit will be taken in the snare; for the windows on high are opened, and the foundations of the earth tremble. 19 The earth is utterly broken. The earth is torn apart. The earth is shaken violently. 20 The earth will stagger like a drunken man, and will sway back and forth like a hammock. Its disobedience will be heavy on it, and it will fall and not rise again. 21 It will happen in that day that Yahweh will punish the army of the high ones on high, and the kings of the earth on the earth. 22 They will be gathered together, as prisoners are gathered in the pit, and will be shut up in the prison; and after many days they will be visited. 23 Then the moon will be confounded, and the sun ashamed; for Yahweh of Armies will reign on Mount Zion and in Jerusalem; and glory will be before his elders.

25

1 Yahweh, you are my God. I will exalt you! I will praise your name, for you have done wonderful things, things planned long ago, in complete

faithfulness and truth. 2 For you have made a city into a heap, a fortified city into a ruin, a palace of strangers to be no city. It will never be built. 3 Therefore a strong people will glorify you. A city of awesome nations will fear you. 4 For you have been a stronghold to the poor, a stronghold to the needy in his distress, a refuge from the storm, a shade from the heat, when the blast of the dreaded ones is like a storm against the wall. 5 As the heat in a dry place you will bring down the noise of strangers; as the heat by the shade of a cloud, the song of the dreaded ones will be brought low. 6 In this mountain, Yahweh of Armies will make all peoples a feast of choice meat, a feast of choice wines, of choice meat full of marrow, of well refined choice wines. 7 He will destroy in this mountain the surface of the covering that covers all peoples, and the veil that is spread over all nations. 8 He has swallowed up death forever! The Lord Yahweh will wipe away tears from off all faces. He will take the reproach of his people away from off all the earth, for Yahweh has spoken it. 9 It shall be said in that day, "Behold, this is our God! We have waited for him, and he will save us! This is Yahweh! We have waited for him. We will be glad and rejoice in his salvation!" 10 For Yahweh's hand will rest in this mountain. Moab will be trodden down in his place, even like straw is trodden down in the water of the dunghill. 11 He will spread out his hands in the middle of it, like one who swims spreads out hands to swim, but his pride will be humbled together with the craft of his hands. 12 He has brought the high fortress of your walls down, laid low, and brought to the ground, even to the dust.

26

1 In that day, this song will be sung in the land of Judah: "We have a strong city. God appoints salvation for walls and bulwarks. 2 Open the gates, that the righteous nation may enter: the one which keeps faith. 3 You will keep whoever's mind is steadfast in perfect peace, because he trusts in you. 4 Trust in Yahweh forever; for in Yah, Yahweh, is an everlasting Rock. 5 For he has brought down those who dwell on high, the lofty city. He lays it low. He lays it low even to the ground. He brings it even to the dust. 6 The foot shall tread it down, even the feet of the poor and the steps of the needy." 7 The way of the just is uprightness. You who are upright make the path of the righteous level. 8 Yes, in the way of your judgments, Yahweh, we have waited for you. Your name and your renown are the desire of our soul. 9 With my soul I have desired you in the night. Yes, with my spirit within me I will seek you earnestly; for when your judgments are in the earth, the inhabitants of the

world learn righteousness. ¹⁰ Let favor be shown to the wicked, yet he will not learn righteousness. In the land of uprightness he will deal wrongfully, and will not see Yahweh's majesty. ¹¹ Yahweh, your hand is lifted up, yet they don't see; but they will see your zeal for the people and be disappointed. Yes, fire will consume your adversaries. ¹² Yahweh, you will ordain peace for us, for you have also done all our work for us. ¹³ Yahweh our God, other lords besides you have had dominion over us, but we will only acknowledge your name. ¹⁴ The dead shall not live. The departed spirits shall not rise. Therefore you have visited and destroyed them, and caused all memory of them to perish. ¹⁵ You have increased the nation, O Yahweh. You have increased the nation! You are glorified! You have enlarged all the borders of the land. ¹⁶ Yahweh, in trouble they have visited you. They poured out a prayer when your chastening was on them. ¹⁷ Just as a woman with child, who draws near the time of her delivery, is in pain and cries out in her pangs, so we have been before you, Yahweh. ¹⁸ We have been with child. We have been in pain. We gave birth, it seems, only to wind. We have not worked any deliverance in the earth; neither have the inhabitants of the world fallen. ¹⁹ Your dead shall live. Their dead bodies shall arise. Awake and sing, you who dwell in the dust; for your dew is like the dew of herbs, and the earth will cast out the departed spirits. ²⁰ Come, my people, enter into your rooms, and shut your doors behind you. Hide yourself for a little moment, until the indignation is past. ²¹ For, behold, Yahweh comes out of his place to punish the inhabitants of the earth for their iniquity. The earth also will disclose her blood, and will no longer cover her slain.

27

¹ In that day, Yahweh with his hard and great and strong sword will punish leviathan, the fleeing serpent, and leviathan, the twisted serpent; and he will kill the dragon that is in the sea. ² In that day, sing to her, "A pleasant vineyard! ³ I, Yahweh, am its keeper. I will water it every moment. Lest anyone damage it, I will keep it night and day. ⁴ Wrath is not in me, but if I should find briers and thorns, I would do battle! I would march on them and I would burn them together. ⁵ Or else let him take hold of my strength, that he may make peace with me. Let him make peace with me." ⁶ In days to come, Jacob will take root. Israel will blossom and bud. They will fill the surface of the world with fruit. ⁷ Has he struck them as he struck those who struck them? Or are they killed like those who killed them were killed? ⁸ In measure, when you send them away, you contend with them. He has removed them with his

rough blast in the day of the east wind. 9 Therefore by this the iniquity of Jacob will be forgiven, and this is all the fruit of taking away his sin: that he makes all the stones of the altar as chalk stones that are beaten in pieces, so that the Asherah poles and the incense altars shall rise no more. 10 For the fortified city is solitary, a habitation deserted and forsaken, like the wilderness. The calf will feed there, and there he will lie down, and consume its branches. 11 When its boughs are withered, they will be broken off. The women will come and set them on fire, for they are a people of no understanding. Therefore he who made them will not have compassion on them, and he who formed them will show them no favor. 12 It will happen in that day that Yahweh will thresh from the flowing stream of the Euphrates to the brook of Egypt; and you will be gathered one by one, children of Israel. 13 It will happen in that day that a great trumpet will be blown; and those who were ready to perish in the land of Assyria, and those who were outcasts in the land of Egypt, shall come; and they will worship Yahweh in the holy mountain at Jerusalem.

28

1 Woe to the crown of pride of the drunkards of Ephraim, and to the fading flower of his glorious beauty, which is on the head of the fertile valley of those who are overcome with wine! 2 Behold, the Lord has one who is mighty and strong. Like a storm of hail, a destroying storm, and like a storm of mighty waters overflowing, he will cast them down to the earth with his hand. 3 The crown of pride of the drunkards of Ephraim will be trodden under foot. 4 The fading flower of his glorious beauty, which is on the head of the fertile valley, shall be like the first-ripe fig before the summer, which someone picks and eats as soon as he sees it. 5 In that day, Yahweh of Armies will become a crown of glory and a diadem of beauty to the residue of his people, 6 and a spirit of justice to him who sits in judgment, and strength to those who turn back the battle at the gate. 7 They also reel with wine, and stagger with strong drink. The priest and the prophet reel with strong drink. They are swallowed up by wine. They stagger with strong drink. They err in vision. They stumble in judgment. 8 For all tables are completely full of filthy vomit and filthiness. 9 Whom will he teach knowledge? To whom will he explain the message? Those who are weaned from the milk, and drawn from the breasts? 10 For it is precept on precept, precept on precept; line on line, line on line; here a little, there a little. 11 But he will speak to this nation with stammering lips and in another language, 12 to whom he said, "This is the

resting place. Give rest to the weary," and "This is the refreshing;" yet they would not hear. 13 Therefore Yahweh's word will be to them precept on precept, precept on precept; line on line, line on line; here a little, there a little; that they may go, fall backward, be broken, be snared, and be taken. 14 Therefore hear Yahweh's word, you scoffers, that rule this people in Jerusalem: 15"Because you have said, 'We have made a covenant with death, and we are in agreement with Sheol. When the overflowing scourge passes through, it won't come to us; for we have made lies our refuge, and we have hidden ourselves under falsehood.'" 16 Therefore the Lord Yahweh says, "Behold, I lay in Zion for a foundation a stone, a tried stone, a precious cornerstone of a sure foundation. He who believes shall not act hastily. 17 I will make justice the measuring line, and righteousness the plumb line. The hail will sweep away the refuge of lies, and the waters will overflow the hiding place. 18 Your covenant with death shall be annulled, and your agreement with Sheol shall not stand. When the overflowing scourge passes through, then you will be trampled down by it. 19 As often as it passes through, it will seize you; for morning by morning it will pass through, by day and by night; and it will be nothing but terror to understand the message." 20 For the bed is too short to stretch out on, and the blanket is too narrow to wrap oneself in. 21 For Yahweh will rise up as on Mount Perazim. He will be angry as in the valley of Gibeon; that he may do his work, his unusual work, and bring to pass his act, his extraordinary act. 22 Now therefore don't be scoffers, lest your bonds be made strong; for I have heard a decree of destruction from the Lord, Yahweh of Armies, on the whole earth. 23 Give ear, and hear my voice! Listen, and hear my speech! 24 Does he who plows to sow plow continually? Does he keep turning the soil and breaking the clods? 25 When he has leveled its surface, doesn't he plant the dill, and scatter the cumin seed, and put in the wheat in rows, the barley in the appointed place, and the spelt in its place? 26 For his God instructs him in right judgment and teaches him. 27 For the dill isn't threshed with a sharp instrument, neither is a cart wheel turned over the cumin; but the dill is beaten out with a stick, and the cumin with a rod. 28 Bread flour must be ground; so he will not always be threshing it. Although he drives the wheel of his threshing cart over it, his horses don't grind it. 29 This also comes out from Yahweh of Armies, who is wonderful in counsel, and excellent in wisdom.

29

1 Woe to Ariel! Ariel, the city where David encamped! Add year to year; let the feasts come around; 2 then I will distress Ariel, and there will be mourning and lamentation. She shall be to me as an altar hearth. 3 I will encamp against you all around you, and will lay siege against you with posted troops. I will raise siege works against you. 4 You will be brought down, and will speak out of the ground. Your speech will mumble out of the dust. Your voice will be as of one who has a familiar spirit, out of the ground, and your speech will whisper out of the dust. 5 But the multitude of your foes will be like fine dust, and the multitude of the ruthless ones like chaff that blows away. Yes, it will be in an instant, suddenly. 6 She will be visited by Yahweh of Armies with thunder, with earthquake, with great noise, with whirlwind and storm, and with the flame of a devouring fire. 7 The multitude of all the nations that fight against Ariel, even all who fight against her and her stronghold, and who distress her, will be like a dream, a vision of the night. 8 It will be like when a hungry man dreams, and behold, he eats; but he awakes, and his hunger isn't satisfied; or like when a thirsty man dreams, and behold, he drinks; but he awakes, and behold, he is faint, and he is still thirsty. The multitude of all the nations that fight against Mount Zion will be like that. 9 Pause and wonder! Blind yourselves and be blind! They are drunken, but not with wine; they stagger, but not with strong drink. 10 For Yahweh has poured out on you a spirit of deep sleep, and has closed your eyes, the prophets; and he has covered your heads, the seers. 11 All vision has become to you like the words of a book that is sealed, which men deliver to one who is educated, saying, "Read this, please;" and he says, "I can't, for it is sealed;" 12 and the book is delivered to one who is not educated, saying, "Read this, please;" and he says, "I can't read." 13 The Lord said, "Because this people draws near with their mouth and honors me with their lips, but they have removed their heart far from me, and their fear of me is a commandment of men which has been taught; 14 therefore, behold, I will proceed to do a marvelous work among this people, even a marvelous work and a wonder; and the wisdom of their wise men will perish, and the understanding of their prudent men will be hidden." 15 Woe to those who deeply hide their counsel from Yahweh, and whose deeds are in the dark, and who say, "Who sees us?" and "Who knows us?" 16 You turn things upside down! Should the potter be thought to be like clay, that the thing made should say about him who made it, "He didn't make me;" or the thing formed say of him who formed it, "He has no understanding"? 17 Isn't it yet a very little

while, and Lebanon will be turned into a fruitful field, and the fruitful field will be regarded as a forest? 18 In that day, the deaf will hear the words of the book, and the eyes of the blind will see out of obscurity and out of darkness. 19 The humble also will increase their joy in Yahweh, and the poor among men will rejoice in the Holy One of Israel. 20 For the ruthless is brought to nothing, and the scoffer ceases, and all those who are alert to do evil are cut off— 21 who cause a person to be indicted by a word, and lay a snare for one who reproves in the gate, and who deprive the innocent of justice with false testimony. 22 Therefore Yahweh, who redeemed Abraham, says concerning the house of Jacob: "Jacob shall no longer be ashamed, neither shall his face grow pale. 23 But when he sees his children, the work of my hands, in the middle of him, they will sanctify my name. Yes, they will sanctify the Holy One of Jacob, and will stand in awe of the God of Israel. 24 They also who err in spirit will come to understanding, and those who grumble will receive instruction."

30

1"Woe to the rebellious children", says Yahweh, "who take counsel, but not from me; and who make an alliance, but not with my Spirit, that they may add sin to sin; 2 who set out to go down into Egypt without asking for my advice, to strengthen themselves in the strength of Pharaoh, and to take refuge in the shadow of Egypt! 3 Therefore the strength of Pharaoh will be your shame, and the refuge in the shadow of Egypt your confusion. 4 For their princes are at Zoan, and their ambassadors have come to Hanes. 5 They shall all be ashamed because of a people that can't profit them, that are not a help nor profit, but a shame, and also a reproach." 6 The burden of the animals of the South. Through the land of trouble and anguish, of the lioness and the lion, the viper and fiery flying serpent, they carry their riches on the shoulders of young donkeys, and their treasures on the humps of camels, to an unprofitable people. 7 For Egypt helps in vain, and to no purpose; therefore I have called her Rahab who sits still. 8 Now go, write it before them on a tablet, and inscribe it in a book, that it may be for the time to come forever and ever. 9 For it is a rebellious people, lying children, children who will not hear Yahweh's law; 10 who tell the seers, "Don't see!" and the prophets, "Don't prophesy to us right things. Tell us pleasant things. Prophesy deceits. 11 Get out of the way. Turn away from the path. Cause the Holy One of Israel to cease from before us." 12 Therefore the Holy One of Israel says, "Because you despise this word, and trust in oppression and perverseness, and rely on it, 13 therefore this iniquity shall be to you like a breach ready to fall, swelling out in a high wall, whose breaking comes suddenly in an instant. 14 He will break it as a potter's vessel is broken, breaking it in pieces without sparing, so that there won't be found among the broken pieces a piece good enough to take fire from the hearth, or to dip up water out of the cistern." 15 For thus said the Lord Yahweh, the Holy One of Israel, "You will be saved in returning and rest. Your strength will be in quietness and in confidence." You refused, 16 but you said, "No, for we will flee on horses;" therefore you will flee; and, "We will ride on the swift;" therefore those who pursue you will be swift. 17 One thousand will flee at the threat of one. At the threat of five, you will flee until you are left like a beacon on the top of a mountain, and like a banner on a hill. 18 Therefore Yahweh will wait, that he may be gracious to you; and therefore he will be exalted, that he may have mercy on you, for Yahweh is a God of justice. Blessed are all those who wait for him. 19 For the people will dwell in Zion at Jerusalem. You will weep no more. He will surely be gracious to you at the voice of your cry. When he hears you, he will answer you. 20 Though the Lord may give you the bread of adversity and the water of affliction, yet your teachers won't be hidden any more, but your eyes will see your teachers; 21 and when you turn to the right hand, and when you turn to the left, your ears will hear a voice behind you, saying, "This is the way. Walk in it." 22 You shall defile the overlaying of your engraved images of silver, and the plating of your molten images of gold. You shall cast them away as an unclean thing. You shall tell it, "Go away!" 23 He will give the rain for your seed, with which you will sow the ground; and bread of the increase of the ground will be rich and plentiful. In that day, your livestock will feed in large pastures. 24 The oxen likewise and the young donkeys that till the ground will eat savory feed, which has been winnowed with the shovel and with the fork. 25 There will be brooks and streams of water on every lofty mountain and on every high hill in the day of the great slaughter, when the towers fall. 26 Moreover the light of the moon will be like the light of the sun, and the light of the sun will be seven times brighter, like the light of seven days, in the day that Yahweh binds up the fracture of his people, and heals the wound they were struck with. 27 Behold, Yahweh's name comes from far away, burning with his anger, and in thick rising smoke. His lips are full of indignation. His tongue is as a devouring fire. 28 His breath is as an overflowing stream that reaches even to the neck, to sift the nations with the sieve of destruction. A bridle that leads to ruin will be in the jaws of the peoples. 29 You will have a song, as in the night when a holy feast is kept, and gladness of heart, as when one goes with a flute to come to Yahweh's mountain, to Israel's Rock. 30 Yahweh will cause his glorious voice to be heard, and will show the descent of his arm, with the indignation of his anger and the flame of a devouring fire, with a blast, storm, and hailstones. 31 For through Yahweh's voice the Assyrian will be dismayed. He will strike him with his rod. 32 Every stroke of the rod of punishment, which Yahweh will lay on him, will be with the sound of tambourines and harps. He will fight with them in battles, brandishing weapons. 33 For his burning place has long been ready. Yes, it is prepared for the king. He has made its pyre deep and large with fire and much wood. Yahweh's breath, like a stream of sulfur, kindles it.

31

1 Woe to those who go down to Egypt for help, and rely on horses, and trust in chariots because they are many, and in horsemen because they are very strong, but they don't look to the Holy One of Israel, and they don't seek Yahweh! 2 Yet he also is wise, and will bring disaster, and will not call back his words, but will arise against the house of the evildoers, and against the help of those who work iniquity. 3 Now the Egyptians are men, and not God; and their horses flesh, and not spirit. When Yahweh stretches out his hand, both he who helps shall stumble, and he who is helped shall fall, and they all shall be consumed together. 4 For Yahweh says to me, "As the lion and the young lion growling over his prey, if a multitude of shepherds is called together against him, will not be dismayed at their voice, nor abase himself for their noise, so Yahweh of Armies will come down to fight on Mount Zion and on its heights. 5 As birds hovering, so Yahweh of Armies will protect Jerusalem. He will protect and deliver it. He will pass over and preserve it." 6 Return to him from whom you have deeply revolted, children of Israel. 7 For in that day everyone shall cast away his idols of silver and his idols of gold—sin which your own hands have made for you. 8"The Assyrian will fall by the sword, not of man; and the sword, not of mankind, shall devour him. He will flee from the sword, and his young men will become subject to forced labor. 9 His rock will pass away by reason of terror, and his princes will be afraid of the banner," says Yahweh, whose fire is in Zion, and his furnace in Jerusalem.

32

1 Behold, a king shall reign in righteousness, and princes shall rule in justice.

2 A man shall be as a hiding place from the wind, and a covert from the storm, as streams of water in a dry place, as the shade of a large rock in a weary land. 3 The eyes of those who see will not be dim, and the ears of those who hear will listen. 4 The heart of the rash will understand knowledge, and the tongue of the stammerers will be ready to speak plainly. 5 The fool will no longer be called noble, nor the scoundrel be highly respected. 6 For the fool will speak folly, and his heart will work iniquity, to practice profanity, and to utter error against Yahweh, to make empty the soul of the hungry, and to cause the drink of the thirsty to fail. 7 The ways of the scoundrel are evil. He devises wicked plans to destroy the humble with lying words, even when the needy speaks right. 8 But the noble devises noble things, and he will continue in noble things. 9 Rise up, you women who are at ease! Hear my voice! You careless daughters, give ear to my speech! 10 For days beyond a year you will be troubled, you careless women; for the vintage will fail. The harvest won't come. 11 Tremble, you women who are at ease! Be troubled, you careless ones! Strip yourselves, make yourselves naked, and put sackcloth on your waist. 12 Beat your breasts for the pleasant fields, for the fruitful vine. 13 Thorns and briers will come up on my people's land; yes, on all the houses of joy in the joyous city. 14 For the palace will be forsaken. The populous city will be deserted. The hill and the watchtower will be for dens forever, a delight for wild donkeys, a pasture of flocks, 15 until the Spirit is poured on us from on high, and the wilderness becomes a fruitful field, and the fruitful field is considered a forest. 16 Then justice will dwell in the wilderness; and righteousness will remain in the fruitful field. 17 The work of righteousness will be peace, and the effect of righteousness, quietness and confidence forever. 18 My people will live in a peaceful habitation, in safe dwellings, and in quiet resting places, 19 though hail flattens the forest, and the city is leveled completely. 20 Blessed are you who sow beside all waters, who send out the feet of the ox and the donkey.

33

1 Woe to you who destroy, but you weren't destroyed, and who betray, but nobody betrayed you! When you have finished destroying, you will be destroyed; and when you have finished betrayal, you will be betrayed. 2 Yahweh, be gracious to us. We have waited for you. Be our strength every morning, our salvation also in the time of trouble. 3 At the noise of the thunder, the peoples have fled. When you lift yourself up, the nations are scattered. 4 Your plunder will be gathered as the caterpillar gathers. Men will

leap on it as locusts leap. 5 Yahweh is exalted, for he dwells on high. He has filled Zion with justice and righteousness. 6 There will be stability in your times, abundance of salvation, wisdom, and knowledge. The fear of Yahweh is your treasure. 7 Behold, their valiant ones cry outside; the ambassadors of peace weep bitterly. 8 The highways are desolate. The traveling man ceases. The covenant is broken. He has despised the cities. He doesn't respect man. 9 The land mourns and languishes. Lebanon is confounded and withers away. Sharon is like a desert, and Bashan and Carmel are stripped bare. 10"Now I will arise," says Yahweh. "Now I will lift myself up. Now I will be exalted. 11 You will conceive chaff. You will give birth to stubble. Your breath is a fire that will devour you. 12 The peoples will be like the burning of lime, like thorns that are cut down and burned in the fire. 13 Hear, you who are far off, what I have done; and, you who are near, acknowledge my might." 14 The sinners in Zion are afraid. Trembling has seized the godless ones. Who among us can live with the devouring fire? Who among us can live with everlasting burning? 15 He who walks righteously and speaks blamelessly, he who despises the gain of oppressions, who gestures with his hands, refusing to take a bribe, who stops his ears from hearing of bloodshed, and shuts his eyes from looking at evil— 16 he will dwell on high. His place of defense will be the fortress of rocks. His bread will be supplied. His waters will be sure. 17 Your eyes will see the king in his beauty. They will see a distant land. 18 Your heart will meditate on the terror. Where is he who counted? Where is he who weighed? Where is he who counted the towers? 19 You will no longer see the fierce people, a people of a deep speech that you can't comprehend, with a strange language that you can't understand. 20 Look at Zion, the city of our appointed festivals. Your eyes will see Jerusalem, a quiet habitation, a tent that won't be removed. Its stakes will never be plucked up, nor will any of its cords be broken. 21 But there Yahweh will be with us in majesty, a place of wide rivers and streams, in which no galley with oars will go, neither will any gallant ship pass by there. 22 For Yahweh is our judge. Yahweh is our lawgiver. Yahweh is our king. He will save us. 23 Your rigging is untied. They couldn't strengthen the foot of their mast. They couldn't spread the sail. Then the prey of a great plunder was divided. The lame took the prey. 24 The inhabitant won't say, "I am sick." The people who dwell therein will be forgiven their iniquity.

34

1 Come near, you nations, to hear! Listen, you peoples. Let the earth and all

it contains hear, the world, and everything that comes from it. ² For Yahweh is enraged against all the nations, and angry with all their armies. He has utterly destroyed them. He has given them over for slaughter. ³ Their slain will also be cast out, and the stench of their dead bodies will come up. The mountains will melt in their blood. ⁴ All of the army of the sky will be dissolved. The sky will be rolled up like a scroll, and all its armies will fade away, as a leaf fades from off a vine or a fig tree. ⁵ For my sword has drunk its fill in the sky. Behold, it will come down on Edom, and on the people of my curse, for judgment. ⁶ Yahweh's sword is filled with blood. It is covered with fat, with the blood of lambs and goats, with the fat of the kidneys of rams; for Yahweh has a sacrifice in Bozrah, and a great slaughter in the land of Edom. ⁷ The wild oxen will come down with them, and the young bulls with the mighty bulls; and their land will be drunken with blood, and their dust made greasy with fat. ⁸ For Yahweh has a day of vengeance, a year of recompense for the cause of Zion. ⁹ Its streams will be turned into pitch, its dust into sulfur, and its land will become burning pitch. ¹⁰ It won't be quenched night or day. Its smoke will go up forever. From generation to generation, it will lie waste. No one will pass through it forever and ever. ¹¹ But the pelican and the porcupine will possess it. The owl and the raven will dwell in it. He will stretch the line of confusion over it, and the plumb line of emptiness. ¹² They shall call its nobles to the kingdom, but none shall be there; and all its princes shall be nothing. ¹³ Thorns will come up in its palaces, nettles and thistles in its fortresses; and it will be a habitation of jackals, a court for ostriches. ¹⁴ The wild animals of the desert will meet with the wolves, and the wild goat will cry to his fellow. Yes, the night creature shall settle there, and shall find herself a place of rest. ¹⁵ The arrow snake will make her nest there, and lay, hatch, and gather under her shade. Yes, the kites will be gathered there, every one with her mate. ¹⁶ Search in the book of Yahweh, and read: not one of these will be missing. None will lack her mate. For my mouth has commanded, and his Spirit has gathered them. ¹⁷ He has cast the lot for them, and his hand has divided it to them with a measuring line. They shall possess it forever. From generation to generation they will dwell in it.

35

¹ The wilderness and the dry land will be glad. The desert will rejoice and blossom like a rose. ² It will blossom abundantly, and rejoice even with joy and singing. Lebanon's glory will be given to it, the excellence of Carmel and

Sharon. They will see Yahweh's glory, the excellence of our God. 3 Strengthen the weak hands, and make the feeble knees firm. 4 Tell those who have a fearful heart, "Be strong! Don't be afraid! Behold, your God will come with vengeance, God's retribution. He will come and save you. 5 Then the eyes of the blind will be opened, and the ears of the deaf will be unstopped. 6 Then the lame man will leap like a deer, and the tongue of the mute will sing; for waters will break out in the wilderness, and streams in the desert. 7 The burning sand will become a pool, and the thirsty ground springs of water. Grass with reeds and rushes will be in the habitation of jackals, where they lay. 8 A highway will be there, a road, and it will be called "The Holy Way". The unclean shall not pass over it, but it will be for those who walk in the Way. Wicked fools shall not go there. 9 No lion will be there, nor will any ravenous animal go up on it. They will not be found there; but the redeemed will walk there. 10 Then Yahweh's ransomed ones will return, and come with singing to Zion; and everlasting joy will be on their heads. They will obtain gladness and joy, and sorrow and sighing will flee away."

36

1 Now in the fourteenth year of King Hezekiah, Sennacherib king of Assyria attacked all of the fortified cities of Judah and captured them. 2 The king of Assyria sent Rabshakeh from Lachish to Jerusalem to King Hezekiah with a large army. He stood by the aqueduct from the upper pool in the fuller's field highway. 3 Then Eliakim the son of Hilkiah, who was over the household, and Shebna the scribe, and Joah, the son of Asaph the recorder came out to him. 4 Rabshakeh said to them, "Now tell Hezekiah, 'The great king, the king of Assyria, says, "What confidence is this in which you trust? 5 I say that your counsel and strength for the war are only vain words. Now in whom do you trust, that you have rebelled against me? 6 Behold, you trust in the staff of this bruised reed, even in Egypt, which if a man leans on it, it will go into his hand and pierce it. So is Pharaoh king of Egypt to all who trust in him. 7 But if you tell me, 'We trust in Yahweh our God,' isn't that he whose high places and whose altars Hezekiah has taken away, and has said to Judah and to Jerusalem, 'You shall worship before this altar'?" 8 Now therefore, please make a pledge to my master the king of Assyria, and I will give you two thousand horses, if you are able on your part to set riders on them. 9 How then can you turn away the face of one captain of the least of my master's servants, and put your trust in Egypt for chariots and for horsemen? 10 Have I come up now without Yahweh against this land to destroy it? Yahweh said to

me, "Go up against this land, and destroy it."'" 11 Then Eliakim, Shebna and Joah said to Rabshakeh, "Please speak to your servants in Aramaic, for we understand it. Don't speak to us in the Jews' language in the hearing of the people who are on the wall." 12 But Rabshakeh said, "Has my master sent me only to your master and to you, to speak these words, and not to the men who sit on the wall, who will eat their own dung and drink their own urine with you?" 13 Then Rabshakeh stood, and called out with a loud voice in the Jews' language, and said, "Hear the words of the great king, the king of Assyria! 14 The king says, 'Don't let Hezekiah deceive you; for he will not be able to deliver you. 15 Don't let Hezekiah make you trust in Yahweh, saying, "Yahweh will surely deliver us. This city won't be given into the hand of the king of Assyria."' 16 Don't listen to Hezekiah, for the king of Assyria says, 'Make your peace with me, and come out to me; and each of you eat from his vine, and each one from his fig tree, and each one of you drink the waters of his own cistern; 17 until I come and take you away to a land like your own land, a land of grain and new wine, a land of bread and vineyards. 18 Beware lest Hezekiah persuade you, saying, "Yahweh will deliver us." Have any of the gods of the nations delivered their lands from the hand of the king of Assyria? 19 Where are the gods of Hamath and Arpad? Where are the gods of Sepharvaim? Have they delivered Samaria from my hand? 20 Who are they among all the gods of these countries that have delivered their country out of my hand, that Yahweh should deliver Jerusalem out of my hand?'" 21 But they remained silent, and said nothing in reply, for the king's commandment was, "Don't answer him." 22 Then Eliakim the son of Hilkiah, who was over the household, and Shebna the scribe, and Joah, the son of Asaph the recorder, came to Hezekiah with their clothes torn, and told him the words of Rabshakeh.

37

1 When King Hezekiah heard it, he tore his clothes, covered himself with sackcloth, and went into Yahweh's house. 2 He sent Eliakim, who was over the household, and Shebna the scribe, and the elders of the priests, covered with sackcloth, to Isaiah the prophet, the son of Amoz. 3 They said to him, "Hezekiah says, 'Today is a day of trouble, and of rebuke, and of rejection; for the children have come to the birth, and there is no strength to give birth. 4 It may be Yahweh your God will hear the words of Rabshakeh, whom the king of Assyria his master has sent to defy the living God, and will rebuke the words which Yahweh your God has heard. Therefore lift up your prayer

for the remnant that is left.'" 5 So the servants of King Hezekiah came to Isaiah. 6 Isaiah said to them, "Tell your master, 'Yahweh says, "Don't be afraid of the words that you have heard, with which the servants of the king of Assyria have blasphemed me. 7 Behold, I will put a spirit in him and he will hear news, and will return to his own land. I will cause him to fall by the sword in his own land."'" 8 So Rabshakeh returned, and found the king of Assyria warring against Libnah, for he heard that he had departed from Lachish. 9 He heard news concerning Tirhakah king of Ethiopia, "He has come out to fight against you." When he heard it, he sent messengers to Hezekiah, saying, 10"Thus you shall speak to Hezekiah king of Judah, saying, 'Don't let your God in whom you trust deceive you, saying, "Jerusalem won't be given into the hand of the king of Assyria." 11 Behold, you have heard what the kings of Assyria have done to all lands, by destroying them utterly. Shall you be delivered? 12 Have the gods of the nations delivered them, which my fathers have destroyed, Gozan, Haran, Rezeph, and the children of Eden who were in Telassar? 13 Where is the king of Hamath, and the king of Arpad, and the king of the city of Sepharvaim, of Hena, and Ivvah?'" 14 Hezekiah received the letter from the hand of the messengers and read it. Then Hezekiah went up to Yahweh's house, and spread it before Yahweh. 15 Hezekiah prayed to Yahweh, saying, 16"Yahweh of Armies, the God of Israel, who is enthroned among the cherubim, you are the God, even you alone, of all the kingdoms of the earth. You have made heaven and earth. 17 Turn your ear, Yahweh, and hear. Open your eyes, Yahweh, and behold. Hear all of the words of Sennacherib, who has sent to defy the living God. 18 Truly, Yahweh, the kings of Assyria have destroyed all the countries and their land, 19 and have cast their gods into the fire; for they were no gods, but the work of men's hands, wood and stone; therefore they have destroyed them. 20 Now therefore, Yahweh our God, save us from his hand, that all the kingdoms of the earth may know that you are Yahweh, even you only." 21 Then Isaiah the son of Amoz sent to Hezekiah, saying, "Yahweh, the God of Israel says, 'Because you have prayed to me against Sennacherib king of Assyria, 22 this is the word which Yahweh has spoken concerning him: The virgin daughter of Zion has despised you and ridiculed you. The daughter of Jerusalem has shaken her head at you. 23 Whom have you defied and blasphemed? Against whom have you exalted your voice and lifted up your eyes on high? Against the Holy One of Israel. 24 By your servants, you have defied the Lord, and have said, "With the multitude of my chariots I have come up to the height of the mountains, to the innermost parts of Lebanon. I will cut down its tall cedars and its choice cypress trees. I will enter into its farthest height, the forest of its fruitful field. 25 I have dug and drunk water, and with the sole of my feet I will dry up all the rivers of Egypt." 26 "Have you not heard how I have done it long ago, and formed it in ancient times? Now I have brought it to pass, that it should be yours to destroy fortified cities, turning them into ruinous heaps. 27 Therefore their inhabitants had little power. They were dismayed and confounded. They were like the grass of the field, and like the green herb, like the grass on the housetops, and like a field before its crop has grown. 28 But I know your sitting down, your going out, your coming in, and your raging against me. 29 Because of your raging against me, and because your arrogance has come up into my ears, therefore I will put my hook in your nose and my bridle in your lips, and I will turn you back by the way by which you came. 30 "This shall be the sign to you: You will eat this year that which grows of itself, and in the second year that which springs from it; and in the third year sow and reap and plant vineyards, and eat their fruit. 31 The remnant that is escaped of the house of Judah will again take root downward, and bear fruit upward. 32 For out of Jerusalem a remnant will go out, and survivors will escape from Mount Zion. The zeal of Yahweh of Armies will perform this.' 33 "Therefore Yahweh says concerning the king of Assyria, 'He will not come to this city, nor shoot an arrow there, neither will he come before it with shield, nor cast up a mound against it. 34 He will return the way that he came, and he won't come to this city,' says Yahweh. 35 'For I will defend this city to save it, for my own sake, and for my servant David's sake.'" 36 Then Yahweh's angel went out and struck one hundred and eighty-five thousand men in the camp of the Assyrians. When men arose early in the morning, behold, these were all dead bodies. 37 So Sennacherib king of Assyria departed, went away, returned to Nineveh, and stayed there. 38 As he was worshiping in the house of Nisroch his god, Adrammelech and Sharezer his sons struck him with the sword; and they escaped into the land of Ararat. Esar Haddon his son reigned in his place.

38

1 In those days Hezekiah was sick and near death. Isaiah the prophet, the son of Amoz, came to him, and said to him, "Yahweh says, 'Set your house in order, for you will die, and not live.'" 2 Then Hezekiah turned his face to the wall and prayed to Yahweh, 3 and said, "Remember now, Yahweh, I beg you, how I have walked before you in truth and with a perfect heart, and have

done that which is good in your sight." Then Hezekiah wept bitterly. 4 Then Yahweh's word came to Isaiah, saying, 5"Go, and tell Hezekiah, 'Yahweh, the God of David your father, says, "I have heard your prayer. I have seen your tears. Behold, I will add fifteen years to your life. 6 I will deliver you and this city out of the hand of the king of Assyria, and I will defend this city. 7 This shall be the sign to you from Yahweh, that Yahweh will do this thing that he has spoken. 8 Behold, I will cause the shadow on the sundial, which has gone down on the sundial of Ahaz with the sun, to return backward ten steps."'" So the sun returned ten steps on the sundial on which it had gone down. 9 The writing of Hezekiah king of Judah, when he had been sick, and had recovered of his sickness: 10 I said, "In the middle of my life I go into the gates of Sheol. I am deprived of the residue of my years." 11 I said, "I won't see Yah, Yah in the land of the living. I will see man no more with the inhabitants of the world. 12 My dwelling is removed, and is carried away from me like a shepherd's tent. I have rolled up my life like a weaver. He will cut me off from the loom. From day even to night you will make an end of me. 13 I waited patiently until morning. He breaks all my bones like a lion. From day even to night you will make an end of me. 14 I chattered like a swallow or a crane. I moaned like a dove. My eyes weaken looking upward. Lord, I am oppressed. Be my security." 15 What will I say? He has both spoken to me, and himself has done it. I will walk carefully all my years because of the anguish of my soul. 16 Lord, men live by these things; and my spirit finds life in all of them. You restore me, and cause me to live. 17 Behold, for peace I had great anguish, but you have in love for my soul delivered it from the pit of corruption; for you have cast all my sins behind your back. 18 For Sheol can't praise you. Death can't celebrate you. Those who go down into the pit can't hope for your truth. 19 The living, the living, he shall praise you, as I do today. The father shall make known your truth to the children. 20 Yahweh will save me. Therefore we will sing my songs with stringed instruments all the days of our life in Yahweh's house. 21 Now Isaiah had said, "Let them take a cake of figs, and lay it for a poultice on the boil, and he shall recover." 22 Hezekiah also had said, "What is the sign that I will go up to Yahweh's house?"

39

1 At that time, Merodach-baladan the son of Baladan, king of Babylon, sent letters and a present to Hezekiah, for he heard that he had been sick, and had recovered. 2 Hezekiah was pleased with them, and showed them the house of

his precious things, the silver, the gold, the spices, and the precious oil, and all the house of his armor, and all that was found in his treasures. There was nothing in his house, nor in all his dominion, that Hezekiah didn't show them. ³ Then Isaiah the prophet came to King Hezekiah, and asked him, "What did these men say? From where did they come to you?" Hezekiah said, "They have come from a country far from me, even from Babylon." ⁴ Then he asked, "What have they seen in your house?" Hezekiah answered, "They have seen all that is in my house. There is nothing among my treasures that I have not shown them." ⁵ Then Isaiah said to Hezekiah, "Hear the word of Yahweh of Armies: ⁶'Behold, the days are coming when all that is in your house, and that which your fathers have stored up until today, will be carried to Babylon. Nothing will be left,' says Yahweh. ⁷'They will take away your sons who will issue from you, whom you shall father, and they will be eunuchs in the king of Babylon's palace.'" ⁸ Then Hezekiah said to Isaiah, "Yahweh's word which you have spoken is good." He said moreover, "For there will be peace and truth in my days."

40

¹"Comfort, comfort my people," says your God. ²"Speak comfortably to Jerusalem, and call out to her that her warfare is accomplished, that her iniquity is pardoned, that she has received of Yahweh's hand double for all her sins." ³ The voice of one who calls out, "Prepare the way of Yahweh in the wilderness! Make a level highway in the desert for our God. ⁴ Every valley shall be exalted, and every mountain and hill shall be made low. The uneven shall be made level, and the rough places a plain. ⁵ Yahweh's glory shall be revealed, and all flesh shall see it together; for the mouth of Yahweh has spoken it." ⁶ The voice of one saying, "Cry out!" One said, "What shall I cry?" "All flesh is like grass, and all its glory is like the flower of the field. ⁷ The grass withers, the flower fades, because Yahweh's breath blows on it. Surely the people are like grass. ⁸ The grass withers, the flower fades; but the word of our God stands forever." ⁹ You who tell good news to Zion, go up on a high mountain. You who tell good news to Jerusalem, lift up your voice with strength! Lift it up! Don't be afraid! Say to the cities of Judah, "Behold, your God!" ¹⁰ Behold, the Lord Yahweh will come as a mighty one, and his arm will rule for him. Behold, his reward is with him, and his recompense before him. ¹¹ He will feed his flock like a shepherd. He will gather the lambs in his arm, and carry them in his bosom. He will gently lead those who have their young. ¹² Who has measured the waters in the hollow of his hand, and

marked off the sky with his span, and calculated the dust of the earth in a measuring basket, and weighed the mountains in scales, and the hills in a balance? 13 Who has directed Yahweh's Spirit, or has taught him as his counselor? 14 Who did he take counsel with, and who instructed him, and taught him in the path of justice, and taught him knowledge, and showed him the way of understanding? 15 Behold, the nations are like a drop in a bucket, and are regarded as a speck of dust on a balance. Behold, he lifts up the islands like a very little thing. 16 Lebanon is not sufficient to burn, nor its animals sufficient for a burnt offering. 17 All the nations are like nothing before him. They are regarded by him as less than nothing, and vanity. 18 To whom then will you liken God? Or what likeness will you compare to him? 19 A workman has cast an image, and the goldsmith overlays it with gold, and casts silver chains for it. 20 He who is too impoverished for such an offering chooses a tree that will not rot. He seeks a skillful workman to set up a carved image for him that will not be moved. 21 Haven't you known? Haven't you heard? Haven't you been told from the beginning? Haven't you understood from the foundations of the earth? 22 It is he who sits above the circle of the earth, and its inhabitants are like grasshoppers; who stretches out the heavens like a curtain, and spreads them out like a tent to dwell in, 23 who brings princes to nothing, who makes the judges of the earth meaningless. 24 They are planted scarcely. They are sown scarcely. Their stock has scarcely taken root in the ground. He merely blows on them, and they wither, and the whirlwind takes them away as stubble. 25"To whom then will you liken me? Who is my equal?" says the Holy One. 26 Lift up your eyes on high, and see who has created these, who brings out their army by number. He calls them all by name. By the greatness of his might, and because he is strong in power, not one is lacking. 27 Why do you say, Jacob, and speak, Israel, "My way is hidden from Yahweh, and the justice due me is disregarded by my God"? 28 Haven't you known? Haven't you heard? The everlasting God, Yahweh, the Creator of the ends of the earth, doesn't faint. He isn't weary. His understanding is unsearchable. 29 He gives power to the weak. He increases the strength of him who has no might. 30 Even the youths faint and get weary, and the young men utterly fall; 31 but those who wait for Yahweh will renew their strength. They will mount up with wings like eagles. They will run, and not be weary. They will walk, and not faint.

41

1"Keep silent before me, islands, and let the peoples renew their strength.

Let them come near, then let them speak. Let's meet together for judgment. 2 Who has raised up one from the east? Who called him to his feet in righteousness? He hands over nations to him and makes him rule over kings. He gives them like the dust to his sword, like the driven stubble to his bow. 3 He pursues them and passes by safely, even by a way that he had not gone with his feet. 4 Who has worked and done it, calling the generations from the beginning? I, Yahweh, the first, and with the last, I am he." 5 The islands have seen, and fear. The ends of the earth tremble. They approach, and come. 6 Everyone helps his neighbor. They say to their brothers, "Be strong!" 7 So the carpenter encourages the goldsmith. He who smooths with the hammer encourages him who strikes the anvil, saying of the soldering, "It is good;" and he fastens it with nails, that it might not totter. 8 "But you, Israel, my servant, Jacob whom I have chosen, the offspring of Abraham my friend, 9 you whom I have taken hold of from the ends of the earth, and called from its corners, and said to you, 'You are my servant. I have chosen you and have not cast you away.' 10 Don't you be afraid, for I am with you. Don't be dismayed, for I am your God. I will strengthen you. Yes, I will help you. Yes, I will uphold you with the right hand of my righteousness. 11 Behold, all those who are incensed against you will be disappointed and confounded. Those who strive with you will be like nothing, and shall perish. 12 You will seek them, and won't find them, even those who contend with you. Those who war against you will be as nothing, as a nonexistent thing. 13 For I, Yahweh your God, will hold your right hand, saying to you, 'Don't be afraid. I will help you.' 14 Don't be afraid, you worm Jacob, and you men of Israel. I will help you," says Yahweh. "Your Redeemer is the Holy One of Israel. 15 Behold, I have made you into a new sharp threshing instrument with teeth. You will thresh the mountains, and beat them small, and will make the hills like chaff. 16 You will winnow them, and the wind will carry them away, and the whirlwind will scatter them. You will rejoice in Yahweh. You will glory in the Holy One of Israel. 17 The poor and needy seek water, and there is none. Their tongue fails for thirst. I, Yahweh, will answer them. I, the God of Israel, will not forsake them. 18 I will open rivers on the bare heights, and springs in the middle of the valleys. I will make the wilderness a pool of water, and the dry land springs of water. 19 I will put cedar, acacia, myrtle, and oil trees in the wilderness. I will set cypress trees, pine, and box trees together in the desert; 20 that they may see, know, consider, and understand together, that Yahweh's hand has done this, and the Holy One of Israel has created it. 21 Produce your cause," says Yahweh. "Bring out your strong reasons!" says the King of Jacob. 22"Let them announce and declare to us what will happen! Declare the former things, what they are, that we may consider them, and know the latter end of them; or show us things to come. 23 Declare the things that are to come hereafter, that we may know that you are gods. Yes, do good, or do evil, that we may be dismayed, and see it together. 24 Behold, you are nothing, and your work is nothing. He who chooses you is an abomination. 25"I have raised up one from the north, and he has come, from the rising of the sun, one who calls on my name, and he shall come on rulers as on mortar, and as the potter treads clay. 26 Who has declared it from the beginning, that we may know? and before, that we may say, 'He is right'? Surely, there is no one who declares. Surely, there is no one who shows. Surely, there is no one who hears your words. 27 I am the first to say to Zion, 'Behold, look at them;' and I will give one who brings good news to Jerusalem. 28 When I look, there is no man, even among them there is no counselor who, when I ask, can answer a word. 29 Behold, all of their deeds are vanity and nothing. Their molten images are wind and confusion.

42

1"Behold, my servant, whom I uphold, my chosen, in whom my soul delights: I have put my Spirit on him. He will bring justice to the nations. 2 He will not shout, nor raise his voice, nor cause it to be heard in the street. 3 He won't break a bruised reed. He won't quench a dimly burning wick. He will faithfully bring justice. 4 He will not fail nor be discouraged, until he has set justice in the earth, and the islands wait for his law." 5 God Yahweh, he who created the heavens and stretched them out, he who spread out the earth and that which comes out of it, he who gives breath to its people and spirit to those who walk in it, says: 6"I, Yahweh, have called you in righteousness. I will hold your hand. I will keep you, and make you a covenant for the people, as a light for the nations, 7 to open the blind eyes, to bring the prisoners out of the dungeon, and those who sit in darkness out of the prison. 8"I am Yahweh. That is my name. I will not give my glory to another, nor my praise to engraved images. 9 Behold, the former things have happened and I declare new things. I tell you about them before they come up." 10 Sing to Yahweh a new song, and his praise from the end of the earth, you who go down to the sea, and all that is therein, the islands and their inhabitants. 11 Let the wilderness and its cities raise their voices, with the villages that Kedar inhabits. Let the inhabitants of Sela sing. Let them shout from the top of the mountains! 12 Let them give glory to Yahweh, and declare his praise in the islands. 13 Yahweh will go out like a mighty man. He will stir up zeal like a man of war. He will raise a war cry. Yes, he will shout aloud. He will triumph over his enemies. 14 "I have been silent a long time. I have been quiet and restrained myself. Now I will cry out like a travailing woman. I will both gasp and pant. 15 I will destroy mountains and hills, and dry up all their herbs. I will make the rivers islands, and will dry up the pools. 16 I will bring the blind by a way that they don't know. I will lead them in paths that they don't know. I will make darkness light before them, and crooked places straight. I will do these things, and I will not forsake them. 17 "Those who trust in engraved images, who tell molten images, 'You are our gods,' will be turned back. They will be utterly disappointed. 18 "Hear, you deaf, and look, you blind, that you may see. 19 Who is blind, but my servant? Or who is as deaf as my messenger whom I send? Who is as blind as he who is at peace, and as blind as Yahweh's servant? 20 You see many things, but don't observe. His ears are open, but he doesn't listen. 21 It pleased Yahweh, for his righteousness' sake, to magnify the law and make it honorable. 22 But this is a robbed and plundered people. All of them are snared in holes, and they are hidden in prisons. They have become captives, and no one delivers, and a plunder, and no one says, 'Restore them!' 23 Who is there among you who will give ear to this? Who will listen and hear for the time to come? 24 Who gave Jacob as plunder, and Israel to the robbers? Didn't Yahweh, he against whom we have sinned? For they would not walk in his ways, and they disobeyed his law. 25 Therefore he poured the fierceness of his anger on him, and the strength of battle. It set him on fire all around, but he didn't know. It burned him, but he didn't take it to heart."

43

1 But now Yahweh who created you, Jacob, and he who formed you, Israel, says: "Don't be afraid, for I have redeemed you. I have called you by your name. You are mine. 2 When you pass through the waters, I will be with you, and through the rivers, they will not overflow you. When you walk through the fire, you will not be burned, and flame will not scorch you. 3 For I am Yahweh your God, the Holy One of Israel, your Savior. I have given Egypt as your ransom, Ethiopia and Seba in your place. 4 Since you have been precious and honored in my sight, and I have loved you, therefore I will give people in your place, and nations instead of your life. 5 Don't be afraid, for I am with you. I will bring your offspring from the east, and gather you from the west. 6

I will tell the north, 'Give them up!' and tell the south, 'Don't hold them back! Bring my sons from far away, and my daughters from the ends of the earth— 7 everyone who is called by my name, and whom I have created for my glory, whom I have formed, yes, whom I have made.'" 8 Bring out the blind people who have eyes, and the deaf who have ears. 9 Let all the nations be gathered together, and let the peoples be assembled. Who among them can declare this, and show us former things? Let them bring their witnesses, that they may be justified, or let them hear, and say, "That is true." 10"You are my witnesses," says Yahweh, "With my servant whom I have chosen; that you may know and believe me, and understand that I am he. Before me there was no God formed, neither will there be after me. 11 I myself am Yahweh. Besides me, there is no savior. 12 I have declared, I have saved, and I have shown, and there was no strange god among you. Therefore you are my witnesses", says Yahweh, "and I am God. 13 Yes, since the day was, I am he. There is no one who can deliver out of my hand. I will work, and who can hinder it?" 14 Yahweh, your Redeemer, the Holy One of Israel says: "For your sake, I have sent to Babylon, and I will bring all of them down as fugitives, even the Chaldeans, in the ships of their rejoicing. 15 I am Yahweh, your Holy One, the Creator of Israel, your King." 16 Yahweh, who makes a way in the sea, and a path in the mighty waters, 17 who brings out the chariot and horse, the army and the mighty man (they lie down together, they shall not rise; they are extinct, they are quenched like a wick) says: 18"Don't remember the former things, and don't consider the things of old. 19 Behold, I will do a new thing. It springs out now. Don't you know it? I will even make a way in the wilderness, and rivers in the desert. 20 The animals of the field, the jackals and the ostriches, shall honor me, because I give water in the wilderness and rivers in the desert, to give drink to my people, my chosen, 21 the people which I formed for myself, that they might declare my praise. 22 Yet you have not called on me, Jacob; but you have been weary of me, Israel. 23 You have not brought me any of your sheep for burnt offerings, neither have you honored me with your sacrifices. I have not burdened you with offerings, nor wearied you with frankincense. 24 You have bought me no sweet cane with money, nor have you filled me with the fat of your sacrifices, but you have burdened me with your sins. You have wearied me with your iniquities. 25 I, even I, am he who blots out your transgressions for my own sake; and I will not remember your sins. 26 Put me in remembrance. Let us plead together. Declare your case, that you may be justified. 27 Your first father sinned, and your teachers have transgressed against me. 28 Therefore I will profane the princes of the sanctuary; and I will make Jacob a curse, and Israel an insult."

44

1 Yet listen now, Jacob my servant, and Israel, whom I have chosen. 2 This is what Yahweh who made you, and formed you from the womb, who will help you says: "Don't be afraid, Jacob my servant; and you, Jeshurun, whom I have chosen. 3 For I will pour water on him who is thirsty, and streams on the dry ground. I will pour my Spirit on your descendants, and my blessing on your offspring; 4 and they will spring up among the grass, as willows by the watercourses. 5 One will say, 'I am Yahweh's.' Another will be called by the name of Jacob; and another will write with his hand 'to Yahweh,' and honor the name of Israel." 6 This is what Yahweh, the King of Israel, and his Redeemer, Yahweh of Armies, says: "I am the first, and I am the last; and besides me there is no God. 7 Who is like me? Who will call, and will declare it, and set it in order for me, since I established the ancient people? Let them declare the things that are coming, and that will happen. 8 Don't fear, neither be afraid. Haven't I declared it to you long ago, and shown it? You are my witnesses. Is there a God besides me? Indeed, there is not. I don't know any other Rock." 9 Everyone who makes a carved image is vain. The things that they delight in will not profit. Their own witnesses don't see, nor know, that they may be disappointed. 10 Who has fashioned a god, or molds an image that is profitable for nothing? 11 Behold, all his fellows will be disappointed; and the workmen are mere men. Let them all be gathered together. Let them stand up. They will fear. They will be put to shame together. 12 The blacksmith takes an ax, works in the coals, fashions it with hammers, and works it with his strong arm. He is hungry, and his strength fails; he drinks no water, and is faint. 13 The carpenter stretches out a line. He marks it out with a pencil. He shapes it with planes. He marks it out with compasses, and shapes it like the figure of a man, with the beauty of a man, to reside in a house. 14 He cuts down cedars for himself, and takes the cypress and the oak, and strengthens for himself one among the trees of the forest. He plants a cypress tree, and the rain nourishes it. 15 Then it will be for a man to burn; and he takes some of it and warms himself. Yes, he burns it and bakes bread. Yes, he makes a god and worships it; he makes it a carved image, and falls down to it. 16 He burns part of it in the fire. With part of it, he eats meat. He roasts a roast and is satisfied. Yes, he warms himself and says, "Aha! I am warm. I have seen the fire." 17 The rest of it he makes into a god, even his engraved

image. He bows down to it and worships, and prays to it, and says, "Deliver me, for you are my god!" 18 They don't know, neither do they consider, for he has shut their eyes, that they can't see, and their hearts, that they can't understand. 19 No one thinks, neither is there knowledge nor understanding to say, "I have burned part of it in the fire. Yes, I have also baked bread on its coals. I have roasted meat and eaten it. Shall I make the rest of it into an abomination? Shall I bow down to a tree trunk?" 20 He feeds on ashes. A deceived heart has turned him aside; and he can't deliver his soul, nor say, "Isn't there a lie in my right hand?" 21 Remember these things, Jacob and Israel, for you are my servant. I have formed you. You are my servant. Israel, you will not be forgotten by me. 22 I have blotted out, as a thick cloud, your transgressions, and, as a cloud, your sins. Return to me, for I have redeemed you. 23 Sing, you heavens, for Yahweh has done it! Shout, you lower parts of the earth! Break out into singing, you mountains, O forest, all of your trees, for Yahweh has redeemed Jacob, and will glorify himself in Israel. 24 Yahweh, your Redeemer, and he who formed you from the womb says: "I am Yahweh, who makes all things; who alone stretches out the heavens; who spreads out the earth by myself; 25 who frustrates the signs of the liars, and makes diviners mad; who turns wise men backward, and makes their knowledge foolish; 26 who confirms the word of his servant, and performs the counsel of his messengers; who says of Jerusalem, 'She will be inhabited;' and of the cities of Judah, 'They will be built,' and 'I will raise up its waste places;' 27 who says to the deep, 'Be dry,' and 'I will dry up your rivers,' 28 who says of Cyrus, 'He is my shepherd, and shall perform all my pleasure,' even saying of Jerusalem, 'She will be built;' and of the temple, 'Your foundation will be laid.'"

45

1 Yahweh says to his anointed, to Cyrus, whose right hand I have held to subdue nations before him and strip kings of their armor, to open the doors before him, and the gates shall not be shut: 2 "I will go before you and make the rough places smooth. I will break the doors of bronze in pieces and cut apart the bars of iron. 3 I will give you the treasures of darkness and hidden riches of secret places, that you may know that it is I, Yahweh, who calls you by your name, even the God of Israel. 4 For Jacob my servant's sake, and Israel my chosen, I have called you by your name. I have given you a title, though you have not known me. 5 I am Yahweh, and there is no one else. Besides me, there is no God. I will strengthen you, though you have not

known me, 6 that they may know from the rising of the sun, and from the west, that there is no one besides me. I am Yahweh, and there is no one else. 7 I form the light and create darkness. I make peace and create calamity. I am Yahweh, who does all these things. 8 Rain, you heavens, from above, and let the skies pour down righteousness. Let the earth open, that it may produce salvation, and let it cause righteousness to spring up with it. I, Yahweh, have created it. 9 Woe to him who strives with his Maker— a clay pot among the clay pots of the earth! Shall the clay ask him who fashions it, 'What are you making?' or your work, 'He has no hands'? 10 Woe to him who says to a father, 'What have you become the father of?' or to a mother, 'What have you given birth to?'" 11 Yahweh, the Holy One of Israel and his Maker says: "You ask me about the things that are to come, concerning my sons, and you command me concerning the work of my hands! 12 I have made the earth, and created man on it. I, even my hands, have stretched out the heavens. I have commanded all their army. 13 I have raised him up in righteousness, and I will make all his ways straight. He shall build my city, and he shall let my exiles go free, not for price nor reward," says Yahweh of Armies. 14 Yahweh says: "The labor of Egypt, and the merchandise of Ethiopia, and the Sabeans, men of stature, will come over to you, and they will be yours. They will go after you. They shall come over in chains. They will bow down to you. They will make supplication to you: 'Surely God is in you; and there is no one else. There is no other god. 15 Most certainly you are a God who has hidden yourself, God of Israel, the Savior.'" 16 They will be disappointed, yes, confounded, all of them. Those who are makers of idols will go into confusion together. 17 Israel will be saved by Yahweh with an everlasting salvation. You will not be disappointed nor confounded to ages everlasting. 18 For Yahweh who created the heavens, the God who formed the earth and made it, who established it and didn't create it a waste, who formed it to be inhabited says: "I am Yahweh. There is no other. 19 I have not spoken in secret, in a place of the land of darkness. I didn't say to the offspring of Jacob, 'Seek me in vain.' I, Yahweh, speak righteousness. I declare things that are right. 20"Assemble yourselves and come. Draw near together, you who have escaped from the nations. Those have no knowledge who carry the wood of their engraved image, and pray to a god that can't save. 21 Declare and present it. Yes, let them take counsel together. Who has shown this from ancient time? Who has declared it of old? Haven't I, Yahweh? There is no other God besides me, a just God and a Savior. There is no one besides me.

²²"Look to me, and be saved, all the ends of the earth; for I am God, and there is no other. ²³ I have sworn by myself. The word has gone out of my mouth in righteousness, and will not be revoked, that to me every knee shall bow, every tongue shall take an oath. ²⁴ They will say of me, 'There is righteousness and strength only in Yahweh.'" Even to him will men come. All those who raged against him will be disappointed. ²⁵ All the offspring of Israel will be justified in Yahweh, and will rejoice!

46

¹ Bel bows down. Nebo stoops. Their idols are carried by animals, and on the livestock. The things that you carried around are heavy loads, a burden for the weary. ² They stoop and they bow down together. They could not deliver the burden, but they have gone into captivity. ³"Listen to me, house of Jacob, and all the remnant of the house of Israel, that have been carried from their birth, that have been carried from the womb. ⁴ Even to old age I am he, and even to gray hairs I will carry you. I have made, and I will bear. Yes, I will carry, and will deliver. ⁵"To whom will you compare me, and consider my equal, and compare me, as if we were the same? ⁶ Some pour out gold from the bag, and weigh silver in the balance. They hire a goldsmith, and he makes it a god. They fall down— yes, they worship. ⁷ They bear it on their shoulder. They carry it, and set it in its place, and it stands there. It cannot move from its place. Yes, one may cry to it, yet it can not answer. It cannot save him out of his trouble. ⁸"Remember this, and show yourselves men. Bring it to mind again, you transgressors. ⁹ Remember the former things of old; for I am God, and there is no other. I am God, and there is none like me. ¹⁰ I declare the end from the beginning, and from ancient times things that are not yet done. I say: My counsel will stand, and I will do all that I please. ¹¹ I call a ravenous bird from the east, the man of my counsel from a far country. Yes, I have spoken. I will also bring it to pass. I have planned. I will also do it. ¹² Listen to me, you stubborn-hearted, who are far from righteousness! ¹³ I bring my righteousness near. It is not far off, and my salvation will not wait. I will grant salvation to Zion, my glory to Israel.

47

¹"Come down and sit in the dust, virgin daughter of Babylon. Sit on the ground without a throne, daughter of the Chaldeans. For you will no longer be called tender and delicate. ² Take the millstones and grind flour. Remove your veil, lift up your skirt, uncover your legs, and wade through the rivers. ³

Your nakedness will be uncovered. Yes, your shame will be seen. I will take vengeance, and will spare no one." 4 Our Redeemer, Yahweh of Armies is his name, is the Holy One of Israel. 5"Sit in silence, and go into darkness, daughter of the Chaldeans. For you shall no longer be called the mistress of kingdoms. 6 I was angry with my people. I profaned my inheritance and gave them into your hand. You showed them no mercy. You laid a very heavy yoke on the aged. 7 You said, 'I will be a princess forever,' so that you didn't lay these things to your heart, nor did you remember the results. 8"Now therefore hear this, you who are given to pleasures, who sit securely, who say in your heart, 'I am, and there is no one else besides me. I won't sit as a widow, neither will I know the loss of children.' 9 But these two things will come to you in a moment in one day: the loss of children and widowhood. They will come on you in their full measure, in the multitude of your sorceries, and the great abundance of your enchantments. 10 For you have trusted in your wickedness. You have said, 'No one sees me.' Your wisdom and your knowledge has perverted you. You have said in your heart, 'I am, and there is no one else besides me.' 11 Therefore disaster will come on you. You won't know when it dawns. Mischief will fall on you. You won't be able to put it away. Desolation will come on you suddenly, which you don't understand. 12"Stand now with your enchantments and with the multitude of your sorceries, in which you have labored from your youth, as if you might profit, as if you might prevail. 13 You are wearied in the multitude of your counsels. Now let the astrologers, the stargazers, and the monthly prognosticators stand up and save you from the things that will happen to you. 14 Behold, they are like stubble. The fire will burn them. They won't deliver themselves from the power of the flame. It won't be a coal to warm at or a fire to sit by. 15 The things that you labored in will be like this: those who have trafficked with you from your youth will each wander in his own way. There will be no one to save you.

48

1"Hear this, house of Jacob, you who are called by the name of Israel, and have come out of the waters of Judah. You swear by Yahweh's name, and make mention of the God of Israel, but not in truth, nor in righteousness— 2 for they call themselves citizens of the holy city, and rely on the God of Israel; Yahweh of Armies is his name. 3 I have declared the former things from of old. Yes, they went out of my mouth, and I revealed them. I did them suddenly, and they happened. 4 Because I knew that you are obstinate, and your neck is an iron sinew, and your brow bronze; 5 therefore I have declared it to you from of old; before it came to pass I showed it to you; lest you should say, 'My idol has done them. My engraved image and my molten image has commanded them.' 6 You have heard it. Now see all this. And you, won't you declare it? "I have shown you new things from this time, even hidden things, which you have not known. 7 They are created now, and not from of old. Before today, you didn't hear them, lest you should say, 'Behold, I knew them.' 8 Yes, you didn't hear. Yes, you didn't know. Yes, from of old your ear was not opened, for I knew that you dealt very treacherously, and were called a transgressor from the womb. 9 For my name's sake, I will defer my anger, and for my praise, I hold it back for you so that I don't cut you off. 10 Behold, I have refined you, but not as silver. I have chosen you in the furnace of affliction. 11 For my own sake, for my own sake, I will do it; for how would my name be profaned? I will not give my glory to another. 12"Listen to me, O Jacob, and Israel my called: I am he. I am the first. I am also the last. 13 Yes, my hand has laid the foundation of the earth, and my right hand has spread out the heavens. when I call to them, they stand up together. 14"Assemble yourselves, all of you, and hear! Who among them has declared these things? He whom Yahweh loves will do what he likes to Babylon, and his arm will be against the Chaldeans. 15 I, even I, have spoken. Yes, I have called him. I have brought him and he shall make his way prosperous. 16"Come near to me and hear this: "From the beginning I have not spoken in secret; from the time that it happened, I was there." Now the Lord Yahweh has sent me with his Spirit. 17 Yahweh, your Redeemer, the Holy One of Israel, says: "I am Yahweh your God, who teaches you to profit, who leads you by the way that you should go. 18 Oh that you had listened to my commandments! Then your peace would have been like a river and your righteousness like the waves of the sea. 19 Your offspring also would have been as the sand and the descendants of your body like its grains. His name would not be cut off nor destroyed from before me." 20 Leave Babylon! Flee from the Chaldeans! With the sound of joyful shouting announce this, tell it even to the end of the earth; say, "Yahweh has redeemed his servant Jacob!" 21 They didn't thirst when he led them through the deserts. He caused the waters to flow out of the rock for them. He also split the rock and the waters gushed out. 22"There is no peace", says Yahweh, "for the wicked."

49

1 Listen, islands, to me. Listen, you peoples, from afar: Yahweh has called

me from the womb; from the inside of my mother, he has mentioned my name. ² He has made my mouth like a sharp sword. He has hidden me in the shadow of his hand. He has made me a polished shaft. He has kept me close in his quiver. ³ He said to me, "You are my servant, Israel, in whom I will be glorified." ⁴ But I said, "I have labored in vain. I have spent my strength in vain for nothing; yet surely the justice due to me is with Yahweh, and my reward with my God." ⁵ Now Yahweh, he who formed me from the womb to be his servant, says to bring Jacob again to him, and to gather Israel to him, for I am honorable in Yahweh's eyes, and my God has become my strength. ⁶ Indeed, he says, "It is too light a thing that you should be my servant to raise up the tribes of Jacob, and to restore the preserved of Israel. I will also give you as a light to the nations, that you may be my salvation to the end of the earth." ⁷ Yahweh, the Redeemer of Israel, and his Holy One, says to him whom man despises, to him whom the nation abhors, to a servant of rulers: "Kings shall see and rise up, princes, and they shall worship, because of Yahweh who is faithful, even the Holy One of Israel, who has chosen you." ⁸ Yahweh says, "I have answered you in an acceptable time. I have helped you in a day of salvation. I will preserve you and give you for a covenant of the people, to raise up the land, to make them inherit the desolate heritage, ⁹ saying to those who are bound, 'Come out!'; to those who are in darkness, 'Show yourselves!' "They shall feed along the paths, and their pasture shall be on all treeless heights. ¹⁰ They shall not hunger nor thirst; neither shall the heat nor sun strike them, for he who has mercy on them will lead them. He will guide them by springs of water. ¹¹ I will make all my mountains a road, and my highways shall be exalted. ¹² Behold, these shall come from afar, and behold, these from the north and from the west, and these from the land of Sinim." ¹³ Sing, heavens, and be joyful, earth! Break out into singing, mountains! For Yahweh has comforted his people, and will have compassion on his afflicted. ¹⁴ But Zion said, "Yahweh has forsaken me, and the Lord has forgotten me." ¹⁵"Can a woman forget her nursing child, that she should not have compassion on the son of her womb? Yes, these may forget, yet I will not forget you! ¹⁶ Behold, I have engraved you on the palms of my hands. Your walls are continually before me. ¹⁷ Your children hurry. Your destroyers and those who devastated you will leave you. ¹⁸ Lift up your eyes all around, and see: all these gather themselves together, and come to you. As I live," says Yahweh, "you shall surely clothe yourself with them all as with an ornament, and dress yourself with them, like a bride. ¹⁹"For, as for your waste and your desolate places, and your land that has been destroyed, surely now that land will be too small for the inhabitants, and those who swallowed you up will be far away. 20 The children of your bereavement will say in your ears, 'This place is too small for me. Give me a place to live in.' 21 Then you will say in your heart, 'Who has conceived these for me, since I have been bereaved of my children and am alone, an exile, and wandering back and forth? Who has brought these up? Behold, I was left alone. Where were these?'" 22 The Lord Yahweh says, "Behold, I will lift up my hand to the nations, and lift up my banner to the peoples. They shall bring your sons in their bosom, and your daughters shall be carried on their shoulders. 23 Kings shall be your foster fathers, and their queens your nursing mothers. They will bow down to you with their faces to the earth, and lick the dust of your feet. Then you will know that I am Yahweh; and those who wait for me won't be disappointed." 24 Shall the plunder be taken from the mighty, or the lawful captives be delivered? 25 But Yahweh says, "Even the captives of the mighty shall be taken away, and the plunder retrieved from the fierce, for I will contend with him who contends with you and I will save your children. 26 I will feed those who oppress you with their own flesh; and they will be drunk on their own blood, as with sweet wine. Then all flesh shall know that I, Yahweh, am your Savior and your Redeemer, the Mighty One of Jacob."

50

1 Yahweh says, "Where is the bill of your mother's divorce, with which I have put her away? Or to which of my creditors have I sold you? Behold, you were sold for your iniquities, and your mother was put away for your transgressions. 2 Why, when I came, was there no one? When I called, why was there no one to answer? Is my hand shortened at all, that it can't redeem? Or have I no power to deliver? Behold, at my rebuke I dry up the sea. I make the rivers a wilderness. Their fish stink because there is no water, and die of thirst. 3 I clothe the heavens with blackness. I make sackcloth their covering." 4 The Lord Yahweh has given me the tongue of those who are taught, that I may know how to sustain with words him who is weary. He awakens morning by morning, he awakens my ear to hear as those who are taught. 5 The Lord Yahweh has opened my ear. I was not rebellious. I have not turned back. 6 I gave my back to those who beat me, and my cheeks to those who plucked off the hair. I didn't hide my face from shame and spitting. 7 For the Lord Yahweh will help me. Therefore I have not been confounded. Therefore I have set my face like a flint, and I know that I won't be disappointed. 8 He

who justifies me is near. Who will bring charges against me? Let us stand up together. Who is my adversary? Let him come near to me. ⁹ Behold, the Lord Yahweh will help me! Who is he who will condemn me? Behold, they will all grow old like a garment. The moths will eat them up. ¹⁰ Who among you fears Yahweh and obeys the voice of his servant? He who walks in darkness and has no light, let him trust in Yahweh's name, and rely on his God. ¹¹ Behold, all you who kindle a fire, who adorn yourselves with torches around yourselves, walk in the flame of your fire, and among the torches that you have kindled. You will have this from my hand: you will lie down in sorrow.

51

¹"Listen to me, you who follow after righteousness, you who seek Yahweh. Look to the rock you were cut from, and to the quarry you were dug from. ² Look to Abraham your father, and to Sarah who bore you; for when he was but one I called him, I blessed him, and made him many. ³ For Yahweh has comforted Zion. He has comforted all her waste places, and has made her wilderness like Eden, and her desert like the garden of Yahweh. Joy and gladness will be found in them, thanksgiving, and the voice of melody. ⁴"Listen to me, my people; and hear me, my nation, for a law will go out from me, and I will establish my justice for a light to the peoples. ⁵ My righteousness is near. My salvation has gone out, and my arms will judge the peoples. The islands will wait for me, and they will trust my arm. ⁶ Lift up your eyes to the heavens, and look at the earth beneath; for the heavens will vanish away like smoke, and the earth will wear out like a garment. Its inhabitants will die in the same way, but my salvation will be forever, and my righteousness will not be abolished. ⁷"Listen to me, you who know righteousness, the people in whose heart is my law. Don't fear the reproach of men, and don't be dismayed at their insults. ⁸ For the moth will eat them up like a garment, and the worm will eat them like wool; but my righteousness will be forever, and my salvation to all generations." ⁹ Awake, awake, put on strength, arm of Yahweh! Awake, as in the days of old, the generations of ancient times. Isn't it you who cut Rahab in pieces, who pierced the monster? ¹⁰ Isn't it you who dried up the sea, the waters of the great deep; who made the depths of the sea a way for the redeemed to pass over? ¹¹ Those ransomed by Yahweh will return, and come with singing to Zion. Everlasting joy shall be on their heads. They will obtain gladness and joy. Sorrow and sighing shall flee away. ¹²"I, even I, am he who comforts you. Who are you, that you are afraid of man who shall die, and of the son of

man who will be made as grass? 13 Have you forgotten Yahweh your Maker, who stretched out the heavens, and laid the foundations of the earth? Do you live in fear continually all day because of the fury of the oppressor, when he prepares to destroy? Where is the fury of the oppressor? 14 The captive exile will speedily be freed. He will not die and go down into the pit. His bread won't fail. 15 For I am Yahweh your God, who stirs up the sea so that its waves roar. Yahweh of Armies is his name. 16 I have put my words in your mouth and have covered you in the shadow of my hand, that I may plant the heavens, and lay the foundations of the earth, and tell Zion, 'You are my people.'" 17 Awake, awake! Stand up, Jerusalem, you who have drunk from Yahweh's hand the cup of his wrath. You have drunken the bowl of the cup of staggering, and drained it. 18 There is no one to guide her among all the sons to whom she has given birth; and there is no one who takes her by the hand among all the sons whom she has brought up. 19 These two things have happened to you— who will grieve with you?— desolation and destruction, and famine and the sword. How can I comfort you? 20 Your sons have fainted. They lie at the head of all the streets, like an antelope in a net. They are full of Yahweh's wrath, the rebuke of your God. 21 Therefore now hear this, you afflicted, and drunken, but not with wine: 22 Your Lord Yahweh, your God who pleads the cause of his people, says, "Behold, I have taken out of your hand the cup of staggering, even the bowl of the cup of my wrath. You will not drink it any more. 23 I will put it into the hand of those who afflict you, who have said to your soul, 'Bow down, that we may walk over you;' and you have laid your back as the ground, like a street to those who walk over."

52

1 Awake, awake! Put on your strength, Zion. Put on your beautiful garments, Jerusalem, the holy city, for from now on the uncircumcised and the unclean will no more come into you. 2 Shake yourself from the dust! Arise, sit up, Jerusalem! Release yourself from the bonds of your neck, captive daughter of Zion! 3 For Yahweh says, "You were sold for nothing; and you will be redeemed without money." 4 For the Lord Yahweh says: "My people went down at the first into Egypt to live there; and the Assyrian has oppressed them without cause. 5 "Now therefore, what do I do here," says Yahweh, "seeing that my people are taken away for nothing? Those who rule over them mock," says Yahweh, "and my name is blasphemed continually all day long. 6 Therefore my people shall know my name. Therefore they shall know in that day that I am he who speaks. Behold, it is I." 7 How beautiful on the

mountains are the feet of him who brings good news, who publishes peace, who brings good news, who proclaims salvation, who says to Zion, "Your God reigns!" 8 Your watchmen lift up their voice. Together they sing; for they shall see eye to eye when Yahweh returns to Zion. 9 Break out into joy! Sing together, you waste places of Jerusalem; for Yahweh has comforted his people. He has redeemed Jerusalem. 10 Yahweh has made his holy arm bare in the eyes of all the nations. All the ends of the earth have seen the salvation of our God. 11 Depart! Depart! Go out from there! Touch no unclean thing! Go out from among her! Cleanse yourselves, you who carry Yahweh's vessels. 12 For you shall not go out in haste, neither shall you go by flight; for Yahweh will go before you, and the God of Israel will be your rear guard. 13 Behold, my servant will deal wisely. He will be exalted and lifted up, and will be very high. 14 Just as many were astonished at you— his appearance was marred more than any man, and his form more than the sons of men— 15 so he will cleanse many nations. Kings will shut their mouths at him; for they will see that which had not been told them, and they will understand that which they had not heard.

53

1 Who has believed our message? To whom has Yahweh's arm been revealed? 2 For he grew up before him as a tender plant, and as a root out of dry ground. He has no good looks or majesty. When we see him, there is no beauty that we should desire him. 3 He was despised and rejected by men, a man of suffering and acquainted with disease. He was despised as one from whom men hide their face; and we didn't respect him. 4 Surely he has borne our sickness and carried our suffering; yet we considered him plagued, struck by God, and afflicted. 5 But he was pierced for our transgressions. He was crushed for our iniquities. The punishment that brought our peace was on him; and by his wounds we are healed. 6 All we like sheep have gone astray. Everyone has turned to his own way; and Yahweh has laid on him the iniquity of us all. 7 He was oppressed, yet when he was afflicted he didn't open his mouth. As a lamb that is led to the slaughter, and as a sheep that before its shearers is silent, so he didn't open his mouth. 8 He was taken away by oppression and judgment. As for his generation, who considered that he was cut off out of the land of the living and stricken for the disobedience of my people? 9 They made his grave with the wicked, and with a rich man in his death, although he had done no violence, nor was any deceit in his mouth. 10 Yet it pleased Yahweh to bruise him. He has caused him to suffer. When

you make his soul an offering for sin, he will see his offspring. He will prolong his days and Yahweh's pleasure will prosper in his hand. ¹¹ After the suffering of his soul, he will see the light and be satisfied. My righteous servant will justify many by the knowledge of himself; and he will bear their iniquities. ¹² Therefore I will give him a portion with the great. He will divide the plunder with the strong, because he poured out his soul to death and was counted with the transgressors; yet he bore the sins of many and made intercession for the transgressors.

54

¹"Sing, barren, you who didn't give birth! Break out into singing, and cry aloud, you who didn't travail with child! For more are the children of the desolate than the children of the married wife," says Yahweh. ²"Enlarge the place of your tent, and let them stretch out the curtains of your habitations; don't spare; lengthen your cords, and strengthen your stakes. ³ For you will spread out on the right hand and on the left; and your offspring will possess the nations and settle in desolate cities. ⁴"Don't be afraid, for you will not be ashamed. Don't be confounded, for you will not be disappointed. For you will forget the shame of your youth. You will remember the reproach of your widowhood no more. ⁵ For your Maker is your husband; Yahweh of Armies is his name. The Holy One of Israel is your Redeemer. He will be called the God of the whole earth. ⁶ For Yahweh has called you as a wife forsaken and grieved in spirit, even a wife of youth, when she is cast off," says your God. ⁷"For a small moment I have forsaken you, but I will gather you with great mercies. ⁸ In overflowing wrath I hid my face from you for a moment, but with everlasting loving kindness I will have mercy on you," says Yahweh your Redeemer. ⁹"For this is like the waters of Noah to me; for as I have sworn that the waters of Noah will no more go over the earth, so I have sworn that I will not be angry with you, nor rebuke you. ¹⁰ For the mountains may depart, and the hills be removed, but my loving kindness will not depart from you, and my covenant of peace will not be removed," says Yahweh who has mercy on you. ¹¹"You afflicted, tossed with storms, and not comforted, behold, I will set your stones in beautiful colors, and lay your foundations with sapphires. ¹² I will make your pinnacles of rubies, your gates of sparkling jewels, and all your walls of precious stones. ¹³ All your children will be taught by Yahweh, and your children's peace will be great. ¹⁴ You will be established in righteousness. You will be far from oppression, for you will not be afraid, and far from terror, for it shall not come near you. ¹⁵

Behold, they may gather together, but not by me. Whoever gathers together against you will fall because of you. ¹⁶"Behold, I have created the blacksmith who fans the coals into flame, and forges a weapon for his work; and I have created the destroyer to destroy. ¹⁷ No weapon that is formed against you will prevail; and you will condemn every tongue that rises against you in judgment. This is the heritage of Yahweh's servants, and their righteousness is of me," says Yahweh.

55

¹"Hey! Come, everyone who thirsts, to the waters! Come, he who has no money, buy, and eat! Yes, come, buy wine and milk without money and without price. ² Why do you spend money for that which is not bread, and your labor for that which doesn't satisfy? Listen diligently to me, and eat that which is good, and let your soul delight itself in richness. ³ Turn your ear, and come to me. Hear, and your soul will live. I will make an everlasting covenant with you, even the sure mercies of David. ⁴ Behold, I have given him for a witness to the peoples, a leader and commander to the peoples. ⁵ Behold, you shall call a nation that you don't know; and a nation that didn't know you shall run to you, because of Yahweh your God, and for the Holy One of Israel; for he has glorified you." ⁶ Seek Yahweh while he may be found. Call on him while he is near. ⁷ Let the wicked forsake his way, and the unrighteous man his thoughts. Let him return to Yahweh, and he will have mercy on him, to our God, for he will freely pardon. ⁸"For my thoughts are not your thoughts, and your ways are not my ways," says Yahweh. ⁹"For as the heavens are higher than the earth, so are my ways higher than your ways, and my thoughts than your thoughts. ¹⁰ For as the rain comes down and the snow from the sky, and doesn't return there, but waters the earth, and makes it grow and bud, and gives seed to the sower and bread to the eater; ¹¹ so is my word that goes out of my mouth: it will not return to me void, but it will accomplish that which I please, and it will prosper in the thing I sent it to do. ¹² For you shall go out with joy, and be led out with peace. The mountains and the hills will break out before you into singing; and all the trees of the fields will clap their hands. ¹³ Instead of the thorn the cypress tree will come up; and instead of the brier the myrtle tree will come up. It will make a name for Yahweh, for an everlasting sign that will not be cut off."

56

¹ Yahweh says: "Maintain justice and do what is right, for my salvation is

near and my righteousness will soon be revealed. 2 Blessed is the man who does this, and the son of man who holds it fast; who keeps the Sabbath without profaning it and keeps his hand from doing any evil." 3 Let no foreigner who has joined himself to Yahweh speak, saying, "Yahweh will surely separate me from his people." Do not let the eunuch say, "Behold, I am a dry tree." 4 For Yahweh says, "To the eunuchs who keep my Sabbaths, choose the things that please me, and hold fast to my covenant, 5 I will give them in my house and within my walls a memorial and a name better than of sons and of daughters. I will give them an everlasting name that will not be cut off. 6 Also the foreigners who join themselves to Yahweh to serve him, and to love Yahweh's name, to be his servants, everyone who keeps the Sabbath from profaning it, and holds fast my covenant, 7 I will bring these to my holy mountain, and make them joyful in my house of prayer. Their burnt offerings and their sacrifices will be accepted on my altar; for my house will be called a house of prayer for all peoples." 8 The Lord Yahweh, who gathers the outcasts of Israel, says, "I will yet gather others to him, in addition to his own who are gathered." 9 All you animals of the field, come to devour, all you animals in the forest. 10 His watchmen are blind. They are all without knowledge. They are all mute dogs. They can't bark— dreaming, lying down, loving to slumber. 11 Yes, the dogs are greedy. They can never have enough. They are shepherds who can't understand. They have all turned to their own way, each one to his gain, from every quarter. 12 "Come," they say, "I will get wine, and we will fill ourselves with strong drink; and tomorrow will be as today, great beyond measure."

57

1 The righteous perish, and no one lays it to heart. Merciful men are taken away, and no one considers that the righteous is taken away from the evil. 2 He enters into peace. They rest in their beds, each one who walks in his uprightness. 3 "But draw near here, you sons of a sorceress, you offspring of adulterers and prostitutes. 4 Whom do you mock? Against whom do you make a wide mouth and stick out your tongue? Aren't you children of disobedience and offspring of falsehood, 5 you who inflame yourselves among the oaks, under every green tree; who kill the children in the valleys, under the clefts of the rocks? 6 Among the smooth stones of the valley is your portion. They, they are your lot. You have even poured a drink offering to them. You have offered an offering. Shall I be appeased for these things? 7 On a high and lofty mountain you have set your bed. You also went up there

to offer sacrifice. 8 You have set up your memorial behind the doors and the posts, for you have exposed yourself to someone besides me, and have gone up. You have enlarged your bed and made you a covenant with them. You loved what you saw on their bed. 9 You went to the king with oil, increased your perfumes, sent your ambassadors far off, and degraded yourself even to Sheol. 10 You were wearied with the length of your ways; yet you didn't say, 'It is in vain.' You found a reviving of your strength; therefore you weren't faint. 11"Whom have you dreaded and feared, so that you lie, and have not remembered me, nor laid it to your heart? Haven't I held my peace for a long time, and you don't fear me? 12 I will declare your righteousness; and as for your works, they will not benefit you. 13 When you cry, let those whom you have gathered deliver you, but the wind will take them. A breath will carry them all away, but he who takes refuge in me will possess the land, and will inherit my holy mountain." 14 He will say, "Build up, build up, prepare the way! Remove the stumbling-block out of the way of my people." 15 For the high and lofty One who inhabits eternity, whose name is Holy, says: "I dwell in the high and holy place, with him also who is of a contrite and humble spirit, to revive the spirit of the humble, and to revive the heart of the contrite. 16 For I will not contend forever, neither will I always be angry; for the spirit would faint before me, and the souls whom I have made. 17 I was angry because of the iniquity of his covetousness and struck him. I hid myself and was angry; and he went on backsliding in the way of his heart. 18 I have seen his ways, and will heal him. I will lead him also, and restore comforts to him and to his mourners. 19 I create the fruit of the lips: Peace, peace, to him who is far off and to him who is near," says Yahweh; "and I will heal them." 20 But the wicked are like the troubled sea; for it can't rest and its waters cast up mire and mud. 21"There is no peace", says my God, "for the wicked."

58

1"Cry aloud! Don't spare! Lift up your voice like a trumpet! Declare to my people their disobedience, and to the house of Jacob their sins. 2 Yet they seek me daily, and delight to know my ways. As a nation that did righteousness, and didn't forsake the ordinance of their God, they ask of me righteous judgments. They delight to draw near to God. 3'Why have we fasted,' they say, 'and you don't see? Why have we afflicted our soul, and you don't notice?' "Behold, in the day of your fast you find pleasure, and oppress all your laborers. 4 Behold, you fast for strife and contention, and to strike with the fist of wickedness. You don't fast today so as to make your voice to be heard on high. 5 Is this the fast that I have chosen? A day for a man to humble his soul? Is it to bow down his head like a reed, and to spread sackcloth and ashes under himself? Will you call this a fast, and an acceptable day to Yahweh? 6 "Isn't this the fast that I have chosen: to release the bonds of wickedness, to undo the straps of the yoke, to let the oppressed go free, and that you break every yoke? 7 Isn't it to distribute your bread to the hungry, and that you bring the poor who are cast out to your house? When you see the naked, that you cover him; and that you not hide yourself from your own flesh? 8 Then your light will break out as the morning, and your healing will appear quickly; then your righteousness shall go before you, and Yahweh's glory will be your rear guard. 9 Then you will call, and Yahweh will answer. You will cry for help, and he will say, 'Here I am.' "If you take away from among you the yoke, finger pointing, and speaking wickedly; 10 and if you pour out your soul to the hungry, and satisfy the afflicted soul, then your light will rise in darkness, and your obscurity will be as the noonday; 11 and Yahweh will guide you continually, satisfy your soul in dry places, and make your bones strong. You will be like a watered garden, and like a spring of water whose waters don't fail. 12 Those who will be of you will build the old waste places. You will raise up the foundations of many generations. You will be called Repairer of the Breach, Restorer of Paths with Dwellings. 13 "If you turn away your foot from the Sabbath, from doing your pleasure on my holy day, and call the Sabbath a delight, and the holy of Yahweh honorable, and honor it, not doing your own ways, nor finding your own pleasure, nor speaking your own words, 14 then you will delight yourself in Yahweh, and I will make you to ride on the high places of the earth, and I will feed you with the heritage of Jacob your father;" for Yahweh's mouth has spoken it.

59

1 Behold, Yahweh's hand is not shortened, that it can't save; nor his ear dull, that it can't hear. 2 But your iniquities have separated you and your God, and your sins have hidden his face from you, so that he will not hear. 3 For your hands are defiled with blood, and your fingers with iniquity. Your lips have spoken lies. Your tongue mutters wickedness. 4 No one sues in righteousness, and no one pleads in truth. They trust in vanity and speak lies. They conceive mischief and give birth to iniquity. 5 They hatch adders' eggs and weave the spider's web. He who eats of their eggs dies; and that which is crushed breaks out into a viper. 6 Their webs won't become garments. They won't cover

themselves with their works. Their works are works of iniquity, and acts of violence are in their hands. ⁷ Their feet run to evil, and they hurry to shed innocent blood. Their thoughts are thoughts of iniquity. Desolation and destruction are in their paths. ⁸ They don't know the way of peace; and there is no justice in their ways. They have made crooked paths for themselves; whoever goes in them doesn't know peace. ⁹ Therefore justice is far from us, and righteousness doesn't overtake us. We look for light, but see darkness; for brightness, but we walk in obscurity. ¹⁰ We grope for the wall like the blind. Yes, we grope as those who have no eyes. We stumble at noon as if it were twilight. Among those who are strong, we are like dead men. ¹¹ We all roar like bears and moan sadly like doves. We look for justice, but there is none, for salvation, but it is far off from us. ¹² For our transgressions are multiplied before you, and our sins testify against us; for our transgressions are with us, and as for our iniquities, we know them: ¹³ transgressing and denying Yahweh, and turning away from following our God, speaking oppression and revolt, conceiving and uttering from the heart words of falsehood. ¹⁴ Justice is turned away backward, and righteousness stands far away; for truth has fallen in the street, and uprightness can't enter. ¹⁵ Yes, truth is lacking; and he who departs from evil makes himself a prey. Yahweh saw it, and it displeased him that there was no justice. ¹⁶ He saw that there was no man, and wondered that there was no intercessor. Therefore his own arm brought salvation to him; and his righteousness sustained him. ¹⁷ He put on righteousness as a breastplate, and a helmet of salvation on his head. He put on garments of vengeance for clothing, and was clad with zeal as a mantle. ¹⁸ According to their deeds, he will repay as appropriate: wrath to his adversaries, recompense to his enemies. He will repay the islands their due. ¹⁹ So they will fear Yahweh's name from the west, and his glory from the rising of the sun; for he will come as a rushing stream, which Yahweh's breath drives. ²⁰"A Redeemer will come to Zion, and to those who turn from disobedience in Jacob," says Yahweh. ²¹"As for me, this is my covenant with them," says Yahweh. "My Spirit who is on you, and my words which I have put in your mouth shall not depart out of your mouth, nor out of the mouth of your offspring, nor out of the mouth of your offspring's offspring," says Yahweh, "from now on and forever."

60

¹"Arise, shine; for your light has come, and Yahweh's glory has risen on you! ² For behold, darkness will cover the earth, and thick darkness the

peoples; but Yahweh will arise on you, and his glory shall be seen on you. ³ Nations will come to your light, and kings to the brightness of your rising. ⁴"Lift up your eyes all around, and see: they all gather themselves together. They come to you. Your sons will come from far away, and your daughters will be carried in arms. ⁵ Then you shall see and be radiant, and your heart will thrill and be enlarged; because the abundance of the sea will be turned to you. The wealth of the nations will come to you. ⁶ A multitude of camels will cover you, the dromedaries of Midian and Ephah. All from Sheba will come. They will bring gold and frankincense, and will proclaim the praises of Yahweh. ⁷ All the flocks of Kedar will be gathered together to you. The rams of Nebaioth will serve you. They will be accepted as offerings on my altar; and I will beautify my glorious house. ⁸"Who are these who fly as a cloud, and as the doves to their windows? ⁹ Surely the islands will wait for me, and the ships of Tarshish first, to bring your sons from far away, their silver and their gold with them, for the name of Yahweh your God, and for the Holy One of Israel, because he has glorified you. ¹⁰"Foreigners will build up your walls, and their kings will serve you; for in my wrath I struck you, but in my favor I have had mercy on you. ¹¹ Your gates also shall be open continually; they shall not be shut day nor night, that men may bring to you the wealth of the nations, and their kings led captive. ¹² For that nation and kingdom that will not serve you shall perish; yes, those nations shall be utterly wasted. ¹³"The glory of Lebanon shall come to you, the cypress tree, the pine, and the box tree together, to beautify the place of my sanctuary; and I will make the place of my feet glorious. ¹⁴ The sons of those who afflicted you will come bowing to you; and all those who despised you will bow themselves down at the soles of your feet. They will call you Yahweh's City, the Zion of the Holy One of Israel. ¹⁵"Whereas you have been forsaken and hated, so that no one passed through you, I will make you an eternal excellency, a joy of many generations. ¹⁶ You will also drink the milk of the nations, and will nurse from royal breasts. Then you will know that I, Yahweh, am your Savior, your Redeemer, the Mighty One of Jacob. ¹⁷ For bronze I will bring gold; for iron I will bring silver; for wood, bronze, and for stones, iron. I will also make peace your governor, and righteousness your ruler. ¹⁸ Violence shall no more be heard in your land, nor desolation or destruction within your borders; but you will call your walls Salvation, and your gates Praise. ¹⁹ The sun will be no more your light by day, nor will the brightness of the moon give light to you, but Yahweh will be your everlasting light, and your God will be your glory. 20 Your sun will not go down any more, nor will your moon withdraw itself; for Yahweh will be your everlasting light, and the days of your mourning will end. 21 Then your people will all be righteous. They will inherit the land forever, the branch of my planting, the work of my hands, that I may be glorified. 22 The little one will become a thousand, and the small one a strong nation. I, Yahweh, will do this quickly in its time."

61

1 The Lord Yahweh's Spirit is on me, because Yahweh has anointed me to preach good news to the humble. He has sent me to bind up the broken hearted, to proclaim liberty to the captives and release to those who are bound, 2 to proclaim the year of Yahweh's favor and the day of vengeance of our God, to comfort all who mourn, 3 to provide for those who mourn in Zion, to give to them a garland for ashes, the oil of joy for mourning, the garment of praise for the spirit of heaviness, that they may be called trees of righteousness, the planting of Yahweh, that he may be glorified. 4 They will rebuild the old ruins. They will raise up the former devastated places. They will repair the ruined cities that have been devastated for many generations. 5 Strangers will stand and feed your flocks. Foreigners will work your fields and your vineyards. 6 But you will be called Yahweh's priests. Men will call you the servants of our God. You will eat the wealth of the nations. You will boast in their glory. 7 Instead of your shame you will have double. Instead of dishonor, they will rejoice in their portion. Therefore in their land they will possess double. Everlasting joy will be to them. 8 "For I, Yahweh, love justice. I hate robbery and iniquity. I will give them their reward in truth and I will make an everlasting covenant with them. 9 Their offspring will be known among the nations, and their offspring among the peoples. All who see them will acknowledge them, that they are the offspring which Yahweh has blessed." 10 I will greatly rejoice in Yahweh! My soul will be joyful in my God, for he has clothed me with the garments of salvation. He has covered me with the robe of righteousness, as a bridegroom decks himself with a garland and as a bride adorns herself with her jewels. 11 For as the earth produces its bud, and as the garden causes the things that are sown in it to spring up, so the Lord Yahweh will cause righteousness and praise to spring up before all the nations.

62

1 For Zion's sake I will not hold my peace, and for Jerusalem's sake I will

not rest, until her righteousness shines out like the dawn, and her salvation like a burning lamp. 2 The nations will see your righteousness, and all kings your glory. You will be called by a new name, which Yahweh's mouth will name. 3 You will also be a crown of beauty in Yahweh's hand, and a royal diadem in your God's hand. 4 You will not be called Forsaken any more, nor will your land be called Desolate any more; but you will be called Hephzibah, and your land Beulah; for Yahweh delights in you, and your land will be married. 5 For as a young man marries a virgin, so your sons will marry you. As a bridegroom rejoices over his bride, so your God will rejoice over you. 6 I have set watchmen on your walls, Jerusalem. They will never be silent day nor night. You who call on Yahweh, take no rest, 7 and give him no rest until he establishes, and until he makes Jerusalem a praise in the earth. 8 Yahweh has sworn by his right hand, and by the arm of his strength, "Surely I will no more give your grain to be food for your enemies, and foreigners will not drink your new wine, for which you have labored, 9 but those who have harvested it will eat it, and praise Yahweh. Those who have gathered it will drink it in the courts of my sanctuary." 10 Go through, go through the gates! Prepare the way of the people! Build up, build up the highway! Gather out the stones! Lift up a banner for the peoples. 11 Behold, Yahweh has proclaimed to the end of the earth: "Say to the daughter of Zion, 'Behold, your salvation comes! Behold, his reward is with him, and his recompense before him!'" 12 They will call them "The Holy People, Yahweh's Redeemed". You will be called "Sought Out, A City Not Forsaken".

63

1 Who is this who comes from Edom, with dyed garments from Bozrah? Who is this who is glorious in his clothing, marching in the greatness of his strength? "It is I who speak in righteousness, mighty to save." 2 Why is your clothing red, and your garments like him who treads in the wine vat? 3"I have trodden the wine press alone. Of the peoples, no one was with me. Yes, I trod them in my anger and trampled them in my wrath. Their lifeblood is sprinkled on my garments, and I have stained all my clothing. 4 For the day of vengeance was in my heart, and the year of my redeemed has come. 5 I looked, and there was no one to help; and I wondered that there was no one to uphold. Therefore my own arm brought salvation to me. My own wrath upheld me. 6 I trod down the peoples in my anger and made them drunk in my wrath. I poured their lifeblood out on the earth." 7 I will tell of the loving kindnesses of Yahweh and the praises of Yahweh, according to all that

Yahweh has given to us, and the great goodness toward the house of Israel, which he has given to them according to his mercies, and according to the multitude of his loving kindnesses. 8 For he said, "Surely, they are my people, children who will not deal falsely;" so he became their Savior. 9 In all their affliction he was afflicted, and the angel of his presence saved them. In his love and in his pity he redeemed them. He bore them, and carried them all the days of old. 10 But they rebelled and grieved his Holy Spirit. Therefore he turned and became their enemy, and he himself fought against them. 11 Then he remembered the days of old, Moses and his people, saying, "Where is he who brought them up out of the sea with the shepherds of his flock? Where is he who put his Holy Spirit among them?" 12 Who caused his glorious arm to be at Moses' right hand? Who divided the waters before them, to make himself an everlasting name? 13 Who led them through the depths, like a horse in the wilderness, so that they didn't stumble? 14 As the livestock that go down into the valley, Yahweh's Spirit caused them to rest. So you led your people to make yourself a glorious name. 15 Look down from heaven, and see from the habitation of your holiness and of your glory. Where are your zeal and your mighty acts? The yearning of your heart and your compassion is restrained toward me. 16 For you are our Father, though Abraham doesn't know us, and Israel does not acknowledge us. You, Yahweh, are our Father. Our Redeemer from everlasting is your name. 17 O Yahweh, why do you make us wander from your ways, and harden our heart from your fear? Return for your servants' sake, the tribes of your inheritance. 18 Your holy people possessed it but a little while. Our adversaries have trodden down your sanctuary. 19 We have become like those over whom you never ruled, like those who were not called by your name.

64

1 Oh that you would tear the heavens, that you would come down, that the mountains might quake at your presence— 2 as when fire kindles the brushwood, and the fire causes the water to boil. Make your name known to your adversaries, that the nations may tremble at your presence! 3 When you did awesome things which we didn't look for, you came down, and the mountains quaked at your presence. 4 For from of old men have not heard, nor perceived by the ear, nor has the eye seen a God besides you, who works for him who waits for him. 5 You meet him who rejoices and does righteousness, those who remember you in your ways. Behold, you were angry, and we sinned. We have been in sin for a long time. Shall we be

saved? 6 For we have all become like one who is unclean, and all our righteousness is like a polluted garment. We all fade like a leaf; and our iniquities, like the wind, take us away. 7 There is no one who calls on your name, who stirs himself up to take hold of you; for you have hidden your face from us, and have consumed us by means of our iniquities. 8 But now, Yahweh, you are our Father. We are the clay and you our potter. We all are the work of your hand. 9 Don't be furious, Yahweh. Don't remember iniquity forever. Look and see, we beg you, we are all your people. 10 Your holy cities have become a wilderness. Zion has become a wilderness, Jerusalem a desolation. 11 Our holy and our beautiful house where our fathers praised you is burned with fire. All our pleasant places are laid waste. 12 Will you hold yourself back for these things, Yahweh? Will you keep silent and punish us very severely?

65

1"I am inquired of by those who didn't ask. I am found by those who didn't seek me. I said, 'See me, see me,' to a nation that was not called by my name. 2 I have spread out my hands all day to a rebellious people, who walk in a way that is not good, after their own thoughts; 3 a people who provoke me to my face continually, sacrificing in gardens, and burning incense on bricks; 4 who sit among the graves, and spend nights in secret places; who eat pig's meat, and broth of abominable things is in their vessels; 5 who say, 'Stay by yourself, don't come near to me, for I am holier than you.' These are smoke in my nose, a fire that burns all day. 6"Behold, it is written before me: I will not keep silence, but will repay, yes, I will repay into their bosom 7 your own iniquities and the iniquities of your fathers together", says Yahweh, "who have burned incense on the mountains, and blasphemed me on the hills. Therefore I will first measure their work into their bosom." 8 Yahweh says, "As the new wine is found in the cluster, and one says, 'Don't destroy it, for a blessing is in it:' so I will do for my servants' sake, that I may not destroy them all. 9 I will bring offspring out of Jacob, and out of Judah an inheritor of my mountains. My chosen will inherit it, and my servants will dwell there. 10 Sharon will be a fold of flocks, and the valley of Achor a place for herds to lie down in, for my people who have sought me. 11"But you who forsake Yahweh, who forget my holy mountain, who prepare a table for Fortune, and who fill up mixed wine to Destiny; 12 I will destine you to the sword, and you will all bow down to the slaughter; because when I called, you didn't answer. When I spoke, you didn't listen; but you did that which was evil in my eyes, and chose that in which I didn't delight." 13 Therefore the Lord Yahweh says, "Behold, my servants will eat, but you will be hungry; behold, my servants will drink, but you will be thirsty. Behold, my servants will rejoice, but you will be disappointed. 14 Behold, my servants will sing for joy of heart, but you will cry for sorrow of heart, and will wail for anguish of spirit. 15 You will leave your name for a curse to my chosen, and the Lord Yahweh will kill you. He will call his servants by another name, 16 so that he who blesses himself in the earth will bless himself in the God of truth; and he who swears in the earth will swear by the God of truth; because the former troubles are forgotten, and because they are hidden from my eyes. 17 "For, behold, I create new heavens and a new earth; and the former things will not be remembered, nor come into mind. 18 But be glad and rejoice forever in that which I create; for, behold, I create Jerusalem to be a delight, and her people a joy. 19 I will rejoice in Jerusalem, and delight in my people; and the voice of weeping and the voice of crying will be heard in her no more. 20 "No more will there be an infant who only lives a few days, nor an old man who has not filled his days; for the child will die one hundred years old, and the sinner being one hundred years old will be accursed. 21 They will build houses and inhabit them. They will plant vineyards and eat their fruit. 22 They will not build and another inhabit. They will not plant and another eat; for the days of my people will be like the days of a tree, and my chosen will long enjoy the work of their hands. 23 They will not labor in vain nor give birth for calamity; for they are the offspring of Yahweh's blessed and their descendants with them. 24 It will happen that before they call, I will answer; and while they are yet speaking, I will hear. 25 The wolf and the lamb will feed together. The lion will eat straw like the ox. Dust will be the serpent's food. They will not hurt nor destroy in all my holy mountain," says Yahweh.

66

1 Yahweh says: "Heaven is my throne, and the earth is my footstool. What kind of house will you build to me? Where will I rest? 2 For my hand has made all these things, and so all these things came to be," says Yahweh: "but I will look to this man, even to he who is poor and of a contrite spirit, and who trembles at my word. 3 He who kills an ox is as he who kills a man; he who sacrifices a lamb, as he who breaks a dog's neck; he who offers an offering, as he who offers pig's blood; he who burns frankincense, as he who blesses an idol. Yes, they have chosen their own ways, and their soul delights in their abominations. 4 I also will choose their delusions, and will bring their

fears on them, because when I called, no one answered; when I spoke, they didn't listen, but they did that which was evil in my eyes, and chose that in which I didn't delight." 5 Hear Yahweh's word, you who tremble at his word: "Your brothers who hate you, who cast you out for my name's sake, have said, 'Let Yahweh be glorified, that we may see your joy;' but it is those who shall be disappointed. 6 A voice of tumult from the city, a voice from the temple, a voice of Yahweh that repays his enemies what they deserve. 7"Before she travailed, she gave birth. Before her pain came, she delivered a son. 8 Who has heard of such a thing? Who has seen such things? Shall a land be born in one day? Shall a nation be born at once? For as soon as Zion travailed, she gave birth to her children. 9 Shall I bring to the birth, and not cause to be delivered?" says Yahweh. "Shall I who cause to give birth shut the womb?" says your God. 10"Rejoice with Jerusalem, and be glad for her, all you who love her. Rejoice for joy with her, all you who mourn over her; 11 that you may nurse and be satisfied at the comforting breasts; that you may drink deeply, and be delighted with the abundance of her glory." 12 For Yahweh says, "Behold, I will extend peace to her like a river, and the glory of the nations like an overflowing stream, and you will nurse. You will be carried on her side, and will be dandled on her knees. 13 As one whom his mother comforts, so I will comfort you. You will be comforted in Jerusalem." 14 You will see it, and your heart shall rejoice, and your bones will flourish like the tender grass. Yahweh's hand will be known among his servants; and he will have indignation against his enemies. 15 For, behold, Yahweh will come with fire, and his chariots will be like the whirlwind; to render his anger with fierceness, and his rebuke with flames of fire. 16 For Yahweh will execute judgment by fire and by his sword on all flesh; and those slain by Yahweh will be many. 17"Those who sanctify themselves and purify themselves to go to the gardens, following one in the middle, eating pig's meat, abominable things, and the mouse, they shall come to an end together," says Yahweh. 18"For I know their works and their thoughts. The time comes that I will gather all nations and languages, and they will come, and will see my glory. 19"I will set a sign among them, and I will send those who escape of them to the nations, to Tarshish, Pul, and Lud, who draw the bow, to Tubal and Javan, to far-away islands, who have not heard my fame, nor have seen my glory; and they shall declare my glory among the nations. 20 They shall bring all your brothers out of all the nations for an offering to Yahweh, on horses, in chariots, in litters, on mules, and on camels, to my holy mountain

Jerusalem, says Yahweh, as the children of Israel bring their offering in a clean vessel into Yahweh's house. 21 Of them I will also select priests and Levites," says Yahweh. 22"For as the new heavens and the new earth, which I will make, shall remain before me," says Yahweh, "so your offspring and your name shall remain. 23 It shall happen that from one new moon to another, and from one Sabbath to another, all flesh will come to worship before me," says Yahweh. 24"They will go out, and look at the dead bodies of the men who have transgressed against me; for their worm will not die, nor will their fire be quenched, and they will be loathsome to all mankind."

The Book of Jeremiah

1

¹ The words of Jeremiah the son of Hilkiah, one of the priests who were in Anathoth in the land of Benjamin. ² Yahweh's word came to him in the days of Josiah the son of Amon, king of Judah, in the thirteenth year of his reign. ³ It came also in the days of Jehoiakim the son of Josiah, king of Judah, to the end of the eleventh year of Zedekiah, the son of Josiah, king of Judah, to the carrying away of Jerusalem captive in the fifth month. ⁴ Now Yahweh's word came to me, saying, ⁵"Before I formed you in the womb, I knew you. Before you were born, I sanctified you. I have appointed you a prophet to the nations." ⁶ Then I said, "Ah, Lord Yahweh! Behold, I don't know how to speak; for I am a child." ⁷ But Yahweh said to me, "Don't say, 'I am a child;' for you must go to whomever I send you, and you must say whatever I command you. ⁸ Don't be afraid because of them, for I am with you to rescue you," says Yahweh. ⁹ Then Yahweh stretched out his hand and touched my mouth. Then Yahweh said to me, "Behold, I have put my words in your mouth. ¹⁰ Behold, I have today set you over the nations and over the kingdoms, to uproot and to tear down, to destroy and to overthrow, to build and to plant." ¹¹ Moreover Yahweh's word came to me, saying, "Jeremiah, what do you see?" I said, "I see a branch of an almond tree." ¹² Then Yahweh said to me, "You have seen well; for I watch over my word to perform it." ¹³ Yahweh's word came to me the second time, saying, "What do you see?" I said, "I see a boiling cauldron; and it is tipping away from the north." ¹⁴ Then Yahweh said to me, "Out of the north, evil will break out on all the inhabitants of the land. ¹⁵ For behold, I will call all the families of the kingdoms of the north," says Yahweh. "They will come, and they will each set his throne at the entrance of the gates of Jerusalem, and against all its walls all around, and against all the cities of Judah. ¹⁶ I will utter my judgments against them concerning all their wickedness, in that they have forsaken me, and have burned incense to other gods, and worshiped the works of their own hands. ¹⁷"You therefore put your belt on your waist, arise, and say to them all that I command you. Don't be dismayed at them, lest I dismay you before them. ¹⁸ For behold, I have made you today a fortified city, an iron pillar, and bronze walls against the whole land—against the kings of Judah, against its princes, against its priests, and against the people of the land. ¹⁹ They will fight against you, but they will not prevail against

you; for I am with you", says Yahweh, "to rescue you."

2

1 Yahweh's word came to me, saying, 2"Go and proclaim in the ears of Jerusalem, saying, 'Yahweh says, "I remember for you the kindness of your youth, your love as a bride, how you went after me in the wilderness, in a land that was not sown. 3 Israel was holiness to Yahweh, the first fruits of his increase. All who devour him will be held guilty. Evil will come on them,"' says Yahweh." 4 Hear Yahweh's word, O house of Jacob, and all the families of the house of Israel! 5 Yahweh says, "What unrighteousness have your fathers found in me, that they have gone far from me, and have walked after worthless vanity, and have become worthless? 6 They didn't say, 'Where is Yahweh who brought us up out of the land of Egypt, who led us through the wilderness, through a land of deserts and of pits, through a land of drought and of the shadow of death, through a land that no one passed through, and where no man lived?' 7 I brought you into a plentiful land to eat its fruit and its goodness; but when you entered, you defiled my land, and made my heritage an abomination. 8 The priests didn't say, 'Where is Yahweh?' and those who handle the law didn't know me. The rulers also transgressed against me, and the prophets prophesied by Baal and followed things that do not profit. 9"Therefore I will yet contend with you," says Yahweh, "and I will contend with your children's children. 10 For pass over to the islands of Kittim, and see. Send to Kedar, and consider diligently, and see if there has been such a thing. 11 Has a nation changed its gods, which really are no gods? But my people have changed their glory for that which doesn't profit. 12"Be astonished, you heavens, at this and be horribly afraid. Be very desolate," says Yahweh. 13"For my people have committed two evils: they have forsaken me, the spring of living waters, and cut out cisterns for themselves: broken cisterns that can't hold water. 14 Is Israel a slave? Is he born into slavery? Why has he become a captive? 15 The young lions have roared at him and raised their voices. They have made his land waste. His cities are burned up, without inhabitant. 16 The children also of Memphis and Tahpanhes have broken the crown of your head. 17"Haven't you brought this on yourself, in that you have forsaken Yahweh your God, when he led you by the way? 18 Now what do you gain by going to Egypt, to drink the waters of the Shihor? Or why do you go on the way to Assyria, to drink the waters of the River? 19"Your own wickedness will correct you, and your backsliding will rebuke you. Know therefore and see that it is an evil and bitter thing, that

you have forsaken Yahweh your God, and that my fear is not in you," says the Lord, Yahweh of Armies. 20"For long ago I broke off your yoke, and burst your bonds. You said, 'I will not serve;' for on every high hill and under every green tree you bowed yourself, playing the prostitute. 21 Yet I had planted you a noble vine, a pure and faithful seed. How then have you turned into the degenerate branches of a foreign vine to me? 22 For though you wash yourself with lye, and use much soap, yet your iniquity is marked before me," says the Lord Yahweh. 23"How can you say, 'I am not defiled. I have not gone after the Baals'? See your way in the valley. Know what you have done. You are a swift dromedary traversing her ways, 24 a wild donkey used to the wilderness, that sniffs the wind in her craving. When she is in heat, who can turn her away? All those who seek her will not weary themselves. In her month, they will find her. 25"Keep your feet from being bare, and your throat from thirst. But you said, 'It is in vain. No, for I have loved strangers, and I will go after them.' 26 As the thief is ashamed when he is found, so the house of Israel is ashamed— they, their kings, their princes, their priests, and their prophets, 27 who tell wood, 'You are my father,' and a stone, 'You have given birth to me,' for they have turned their back to me, and not their face, but in the time of their trouble they will say, 'Arise, and save us!' 28"But where are your gods that you have made for yourselves? Let them arise, if they can save you in the time of your trouble, for you have as many gods as you have towns, O Judah. 29"Why will you contend with me? You all have transgressed against me," says Yahweh. 30"I have struck your children in vain. They received no correction. Your own sword has devoured your prophets, like a destroying lion. 31 Generation, consider Yahweh's word. Have I been a wilderness to Israel? Or a land of thick darkness? Why do my people say, 'We have broken loose. We will come to you no more'? 32"Can a virgin forget her ornaments, or a bride her attire? Yet my people have forgotten me for days without number. 33 How well you prepare your way to seek love! Therefore you have even taught the wicked women your ways. 34 Also the blood of the souls of the innocent poor is found in your skirts. You didn't find them breaking in, but it is because of all these things. 35"Yet you said, 'I am innocent. Surely his anger has turned away from me.' "Behold, I will judge you, because you say, 'I have not sinned.' 36 Why do you go about so much to change your ways? You will be ashamed of Egypt also, as you were ashamed of Assyria. 37 You will also leave that place with your hands on your head; for Yahweh has rejected those in whom you trust, and you won't prosper with them.

3

¹"They say, 'If a man puts away his wife, and she goes from him, and becomes another man's, should he return to her again?' Wouldn't that land be greatly polluted? But you have played the prostitute with many lovers; yet return again to me," says Yahweh. ²"Lift up your eyes to the bare heights, and see! Where have you not been lain with? You have sat waiting for them by the road, as an Arabian in the wilderness. You have polluted the land with your prostitution and with your wickedness. ³ Therefore the showers have been withheld and there has been no latter rain; yet you have had a prostitute's forehead and you refused to be ashamed. ⁴ Will you not from this time cry to me, 'My Father, you are the guide of my youth!'? ⁵"Will he retain his anger forever? Will he keep it to the end?' Behold, you have spoken and have done evil things, and have had your way." ⁶ Moreover, Yahweh said to me in the days of Josiah the king, "Have you seen that which backsliding Israel has done? She has gone up on every high mountain and under every green tree, and has played the prostitute there. ⁷ I said after she had done all these things, 'She will return to me;' but she didn't return, and her treacherous sister Judah saw it. ⁸ I saw when, for this very cause, that backsliding Israel had committed adultery, I had put her away and given her a certificate of divorce, yet treacherous Judah, her sister, had no fear, but she also went and played the prostitute. ⁹ Because she took her prostitution lightly, the land was polluted, and she committed adultery with stones and with wood. ¹⁰ Yet for all this her treacherous sister, Judah, has not returned to me with her whole heart, but only in pretense," says Yahweh. ¹¹ Yahweh said to me, "Backsliding Israel has shown herself more righteous than treacherous Judah. ¹² Go, and proclaim these words toward the north, and say, 'Return, you backsliding Israel,' says Yahweh; 'I will not look in anger on you, for I am merciful,' says Yahweh. 'I will not keep anger forever. ¹³ Only acknowledge your iniquity, that you have transgressed against Yahweh your God, and have scattered your ways to the strangers under every green tree, and you have not obeyed my voice,'" says Yahweh. ¹⁴"Return, backsliding children," says Yahweh, "for I am a husband to you. I will take one of you from a city, and two from a family, and I will bring you to Zion. ¹⁵ I will give you shepherds according to my heart, who will feed you with knowledge and understanding. ¹⁶ It will come to pass, when you are multiplied and increased in the land in those days," says Yahweh, "they will no longer say, 'the ark of

Yahweh's covenant!' It will not come to mind. They won't remember it. They won't miss it, nor will another be made. 17 At that time they will call Jerusalem 'Yahweh's Throne;' and all the nations will be gathered to it, to Yahweh's name, to Jerusalem. They will no longer walk after the stubbornness of their evil heart. 18 In those days the house of Judah will walk with the house of Israel, and they will come together out of the land of the north to the land that I gave for an inheritance to your fathers. 19"But I said, 'How I desire to put you among the children, and give you a pleasant land, a goodly heritage of the armies of the nations!' and I said, 'You shall call me "My Father", and shall not turn away from following me.' 20"Surely as a wife treacherously departs from her husband, so you have dealt treacherously with me, house of Israel," says Yahweh. 21 A voice is heard on the bare heights, the weeping and the petitions of the children of Israel; because they have perverted their way, they have forgotten Yahweh their God. 22 Return, you backsliding children, and I will heal your backsliding. "Behold, we have come to you; for you are Yahweh our God. 23 Truly help from the hills, the tumult on the mountains, is in vain. Truly the salvation of Israel is in Yahweh our God. 24 But the shameful thing has devoured the labor of our fathers from our youth, their flocks and their herds, their sons and their daughters. 25 Let us lie down in our shame, and let our confusion cover us; for we have sinned against Yahweh our God, we and our fathers, from our youth even to this day. We have not obeyed Yahweh our God's voice."

4

1"If you will return, Israel," says Yahweh, "if you will return to me, and if you will put away your abominations out of my sight; then you will not be removed; 2 and you will swear, 'As Yahweh lives,' in truth, in justice, and in righteousness. The nations will bless themselves in him, and they will glory in him." 3 For Yahweh says to the men of Judah and to Jerusalem, "Break up your fallow ground, and don't sow among thorns. 4 Circumcise yourselves to Yahweh, and take away the foreskins of your heart, you men of Judah and inhabitants of Jerusalem; lest my wrath go out like fire, and burn so that no one can quench it, because of the evil of your doings. 5 Declare in Judah, and publish in Jerusalem; and say, 'Blow the trumpet in the land!' Cry aloud and say, 'Assemble yourselves! Let's go into the fortified cities!' 6 Set up a standard toward Zion. Flee for safety! Don't wait; for I will bring evil from the north, and a great destruction." 7 A lion has gone up from his thicket, and a destroyer of nations. He is on his way. He has gone out from his place, to make your land desolate, that your cities be laid waste, without inhabitant. 8 For this, clothe yourself with sackcloth, lament and wail; for the fierce anger of Yahweh hasn't turned back from us. 9"It will happen at that day," says Yahweh, "that the heart of the king will perish, along with the heart of the princes. The priests will be astonished, and the prophets will wonder." 10 Then I said, "Ah, Lord Yahweh! Surely you have greatly deceived this people and Jerusalem, saying, 'You will have peace;' whereas the sword reaches to the heart." 11 At that time it will be said to this people and to Jerusalem, "A hot wind blows from the bare heights in the wilderness toward the daughter of my people, not to winnow, nor to cleanse. 12 A full wind from these will come for me. Now I will also utter judgments against them." 13 Behold, he will come up as clouds, and his chariots will be as the whirlwind. His horses are swifter than eagles. Woe to us! For we are ruined. 14 Jerusalem, wash your heart from wickedness, that you may be saved. How long will your evil thoughts lodge within you? 15 For a voice declares from Dan, and publishes evil from the hills of Ephraim: 16"Tell the nations, behold, publish against Jerusalem, 'Watchers come from a far country, and raise their voice against the cities of Judah. 17 As keepers of a field, they are against her all around, because she has been rebellious against me,'" says Yahweh. 18"Your way and your doings have brought these things to you. This is your wickedness, for it is bitter, for it reaches to your heart." 19 My anguish, my anguish! I am pained at my very heart! My heart trembles within me. I can't hold my peace, because you have heard, O my soul, the sound of the trumpet, the alarm of war. 20 Destruction on destruction is decreed, for the whole land is laid waste. Suddenly my tents are destroyed, and my curtains gone in a moment. 21 How long will I see the standard and hear the sound of the trumpet? 22"For my people are foolish. They don't know me. They are foolish children, and they have no understanding. They are skillful in doing evil, but they don't know how to do good." 23 I saw the earth and, behold, it was waste and void, and the heavens, and they had no light. 24 I saw the mountains, and behold, they trembled, and all the hills moved back and forth. 25 I saw, and behold, there was no man, and all the birds of the sky had fled. 26 I saw, and behold, the fruitful field was a wilderness, and all its cities were broken down at the presence of Yahweh, before his fierce anger. 27 For Yahweh says, "The whole land will be a desolation; yet I will not make a full end. 28 For this the earth will mourn, and the heavens above be black, because I have spoken it. I have planned it, and I have not repented, neither will I turn back from it." 29

Every city flees for the noise of the horsemen and archers. They go into the thickets and climb up on the rocks. Every city is forsaken, and not a man dwells therein. 30 You, when you are made desolate, what will you do? Though you clothe yourself with scarlet, though you deck yourself with ornaments of gold, though you enlarge your eyes with makeup, you make yourself beautiful in vain. Your lovers despise you. They seek your life. 31 For I have heard a voice as of a woman in travail, the anguish as of her who gives birth to her first child, the voice of the daughter of Zion, who gasps for breath, who spreads her hands, saying, "Woe is me now! For my soul faints before the murderers."

5

1"Run back and forth through the streets of Jerusalem, and see now, and know, and seek in its wide places, if you can find a man, if there is anyone who does justly, who seeks truth, then I will pardon her. 2 Though they say, 'As Yahweh lives,' surely they swear falsely." 3 O Yahweh, don't your eyes look on truth? You have stricken them, but they were not grieved. You have consumed them, but they have refused to receive correction. They have made their faces harder than a rock. They have refused to return. 4 Then I said, "Surely these are poor. They are foolish; for they don't know Yahweh's way, nor the law of their God. 5 I will go to the great men and will speak to them, for they know the way of Yahweh, and the law of their God." But these with one accord have broken the yoke, and burst the bonds. 6 Therefore a lion out of the forest will kill them. A wolf of the evenings will destroy them. A leopard will watch against their cities. Everyone who goes out there will be torn in pieces, because their transgressions are many and their backsliding has increased. 7"How can I pardon you? Your children have forsaken me, and sworn by what are no gods. When I had fed them to the full, they committed adultery, and assembled themselves in troops at the prostitutes' houses. 8 They were as fed horses roaming at large. Everyone neighed after his neighbor's wife. 9 Shouldn't I punish them for these things?" says Yahweh. "Shouldn't my soul be avenged on such a nation as this? 10"Go up on her walls, and destroy, but don't make a full end. Take away her branches, for they are not Yahweh's. 11 For the house of Israel and the house of Judah have dealt very treacherously against me," says Yahweh. 12 They have denied Yahweh, and said, "It is not he. Evil won't come on us. We won't see sword or famine. 13 The prophets will become wind, and the word is not in them. Thus it will be done to them." 14 Therefore Yahweh, the God of Armies says,

"Because you speak this word, behold, I will make my words in your mouth fire, and this people wood, and it will devour them. 15 Behold, I will bring a nation on you from far away, house of Israel," says Yahweh. "It is a mighty nation. It is an ancient nation, a nation whose language you don't know and don't understand what they say. 16 Their quiver is an open tomb. They are all mighty men. 17 They will eat up your harvest and your bread, which your sons and your daughters should eat. They will eat up your flocks and your herds. They will eat up your vines and your fig trees. They will beat down your fortified cities in which you trust with the sword. 18"But even in those days," says Yahweh, "I will not make a full end of you. 19 It will happen when you say, 'Why has Yahweh our God done all these things to us?' Then you shall say to them, 'Just as you have forsaken me and served foreign gods in your land, so you will serve strangers in a land that is not yours.' 20"Declare this in the house of Jacob, and publish it in Judah, saying, 21'Hear this now, foolish people without understanding, who have eyes, and don't see, who have ears, and don't hear: 22 Don't you fear me?' says Yahweh; 'Won't you tremble at my presence, who have placed the sand for the bound of the sea by a perpetual decree, that it can't pass it? Though its waves toss themselves, yet they can't prevail. Though they roar, they still can't pass over it.' 23"But this people has a revolting and a rebellious heart. They have revolted and gone. 24 They don't say in their heart, 'Let's now fear Yahweh our God, who gives rain, both the former and the latter, in its season, who preserves to us the appointed weeks of the harvest.' 25"Your iniquities have turned away these things, and your sins have withheld good from you. 26 For wicked men are found among my people. They watch, as fowlers lie in wait. They set a trap. They catch men. 27 As a cage is full of birds, so are their houses full of deceit. Therefore they have become great, and grew rich. 28 They have grown fat. They shine; yes, they excel in deeds of wickedness. They don't plead the cause, the cause of the fatherless, that they may prosper; and they don't defend the rights of the needy. 29"Shouldn't I punish for these things?" says Yahweh. "Shouldn't my soul be avenged on such a nation as this? 30"An astonishing and horrible thing has happened in the land. 31 The prophets prophesy falsely, and the priests rule by their own authority; and my people love to have it so. What will you do in the end of it?

6

1"Flee for safety, you children of Benjamin, out of the middle of Jerusalem! Blow the trumpet in Tekoa and raise up a signal on Beth Haccherem, for evil looks out from the north with a great destruction. 2 I will cut off the beautiful and delicate one, the daughter of Zion. 3 Shepherds with their flocks will come to her. They will pitch their tents against her all around. They will feed everyone in his place." 4"Prepare war against her! Arise! Let's go up at noon. Woe to us! For the day declines, for the shadows of the evening are stretched out. 5 Arise! Let's go up by night, and let's destroy her palaces." 6 For Yahweh of Armies said, "Cut down trees, and cast up a mound against Jerusalem. This is the city to be visited. She is filled with oppression within herself. 7 As a well produces its waters, so she produces her wickedness. Violence and destruction is heard in her. Sickness and wounds are continually before me. 8 Be instructed, Jerusalem, lest my soul be alienated from you, lest I make you a desolation, an uninhabited land." 9 Yahweh of Armies says, "They will thoroughly glean the remnant of Israel like a vine. Turn again your hand as a grape gatherer into the baskets." 10 To whom should I speak and testify, that they may hear? Behold, their ear is uncircumcised, and they can't listen. Behold, Yahweh's word has become a reproach to them. They have no delight in it. 11 Therefore I am full of Yahweh's wrath. I am weary with holding it in. "Pour it out on the children in the street, and on the assembly of young men together; for even the husband with the wife will be taken, the aged with him who is full of days. 12 Their houses will be turned to others, their fields and their wives together; for I will stretch out my hand on the inhabitants of the land, says Yahweh." 13"For from their least even to their greatest, everyone is given to covetousness. From the prophet even to the priest, everyone deals falsely. 14 They have healed also the hurt of my people superficially, saying, 'Peace, peace!' when there is no peace. 15 Were they ashamed when they had committed abomination? No, they were not at all ashamed, neither could they blush. Therefore they will fall among those who fall. When I visit them, they will be cast down," says Yahweh. 16 Yahweh says, "Stand in the ways and see, and ask for the old paths, 'Where is the good way?' and walk in it, and you will find rest for your souls. But they said, 'We will not walk in it.' 17 I set watchmen over you, saying, 'Listen to the sound of the trumpet!' But they said, 'We will not listen!' 18 Therefore hear, you nations, and know, congregation, what is among them. 19 Hear, earth! Behold, I will bring evil on this people, even the fruit of their thoughts, because they have not listened to my words; and as for my law, they have rejected it. 20 To what purpose does frankincense from Sheba come to me, and the sweet cane from a far country? Your burnt offerings are not acceptable, and your sacrifices are not pleasing to me." 21 Therefore Yahweh says, "Behold, I will lay stumbling blocks before this people. The fathers and the sons together will stumble against them. The neighbor and his friend will perish." 22 Yahweh says, "Behold, a people comes from the north country. A great nation will be stirred up from the uttermost parts of the earth. 23 They take hold of bow and spear. They are cruel, and have no mercy. Their voice roars like the sea, and they ride on horses, everyone set in array, as a man to the battle, against you, daughter of Zion." 24 We have heard its report. Our hands become feeble. Anguish has taken hold of us, and pains as of a woman in labor. 25 Don't go out into the field or walk by the way; for the sword of the enemy and terror are on every side. 26 Daughter of my people, clothe yourself with sackcloth, and wallow in ashes! Mourn, as for an only son, most bitter lamentation, for the destroyer will suddenly come on us. 27 "I have made you a tester of metals and a fortress among my people, that you may know and try their way. 28 They are all grievous rebels, going around to slander. They are bronze and iron. All of them deal corruptly. 29 The bellows blow fiercely. The lead is consumed in the fire. In vain they go on refining, for the wicked are not plucked away. 30 Men will call them rejected silver, because Yahweh has rejected them."

7

1 The word that came to Jeremiah from Yahweh, saying, 2 "Stand in the gate of Yahweh's house, and proclaim this word there, and say, 'Hear Yahweh's word, all you of Judah, who enter in at these gates to worship Yahweh.'" 3 Yahweh of Armies, the God of Israel says, "Amend your ways and your doings, and I will cause you to dwell in this place. 4 Don't trust in lying words, saying, 'Yahweh's temple, Yahweh's temple, Yahweh's temple, are these.' 5 For if you thoroughly amend your ways and your doings, if you thoroughly execute justice between a man and his neighbor; 6 if you don't oppress the foreigner, the fatherless, and the widow, and don't shed innocent blood in this place, and don't walk after other gods to your own hurt, 7 then I will cause you to dwell in this place, in the land that I gave to your fathers, from of old even forever more. 8 Behold, you trust in lying words that can't profit. 9 Will you steal, murder, commit adultery, swear falsely, burn incense to Baal, and walk after other gods that you have not known, 10 then come and stand before me in this house, which is called by my name, and say, 'We are delivered,' that you may do all these abominations? 11 Has this house, which is called by my name, become a den of robbers in your eyes? Behold, I

myself have seen it," says Yahweh. 12"But go now to my place which was in Shiloh, where I caused my name to dwell at the first, and see what I did to it for the wickedness of my people Israel. 13 Now, because you have done all these works," says Yahweh, "and I spoke to you, rising up early and speaking, but you didn't hear; and I called you, but you didn't answer; 14 therefore I will do to the house which is called by my name, in which you trust, and to the place which I gave to you and to your fathers, as I did to Shiloh. 15 I will cast you out of my sight, as I have cast out all your brothers, even the whole offspring of Ephraim. 16"Therefore don't pray for this people. Don't lift up a cry or prayer for them or make intercession to me; for I will not hear you. 17 Don't you see what they do in the cities of Judah and in the streets of Jerusalem? 18 The children gather wood, and the fathers kindle the fire, and the women knead the dough, to make cakes to the queen of the sky, and to pour out drink offerings to other gods, that they may provoke me to anger. 19 Do they provoke me to anger?" says Yahweh. "Don't they provoke themselves, to the confusion of their own faces?" 20 Therefore the Lord Yahweh says: "Behold, my anger and my wrath will be poured out on this place, on man, on animal, on the trees of the field, and on the fruit of the ground; and it will burn and will not be quenched." 21 Yahweh of Armies, the God of Israel says: "Add your burnt offerings to your sacrifices and eat meat. 22 For I didn't speak to your fathers or command them in the day that I brought them out of the land of Egypt concerning burnt offerings or sacrifices; 23 but this thing I commanded them, saying, 'Listen to my voice, and I will be your God, and you shall be my people. Walk in all the way that I command you, that it may be well with you.' 24 But they didn't listen or turn their ear, but walked in their own counsels and in the stubbornness of their evil heart, and went backward, and not forward. 25 Since the day that your fathers came out of the land of Egypt to this day, I have sent to you all my servants the prophets, daily rising up early and sending them. 26 Yet they didn't listen to me or incline their ear, but made their neck stiff. They did worse than their fathers. 27"You shall speak all these words to them, but they will not listen to you. You shall also call to them, but they will not answer you. 28 You shall tell them, 'This is the nation that has not listened to Yahweh their God's voice, nor received instruction. Truth has perished, and is cut off from their mouth.' 29 Cut off your hair, and throw it away, and take up a lamentation on the bare heights; for Yahweh has rejected and forsaken the generation of his wrath. 30"For the children of Judah have done that which is evil in my sight," says Yahweh. "They have set their abominations in the house which is called by my name, to defile it. 31 They have built the high places of Topheth, which is in the valley of the son of Hinnom, to burn their sons and their daughters in the fire, which I didn't command, nor did it come into my mind. 32 Therefore behold, the days come", says Yahweh, "that it will no more be called 'Topheth' or 'The valley of the son of Hinnom', but 'The valley of Slaughter'; for they will bury in Topheth until there is no place to bury. 33 The dead bodies of this people will be food for the birds of the sky, and for the animals of the earth. No one will frighten them away. 34 Then I will cause to cease from the cities of Judah and from the streets of Jerusalem the voice of mirth and the voice of gladness, the voice of the bridegroom and the voice of the bride; for the land will become a waste."

8

1"At that time," says Yahweh, "they will bring the bones of the kings of Judah, the bones of his princes, the bones of the priests, the bones of the prophets, and the bones of the inhabitants of Jerusalem, out of their graves. 2 They will spread them before the sun, the moon, and all the army of the sky, which they have loved, which they have served, after which they have walked, which they have sought, and which they have worshiped. They will not be gathered or be buried. They will be like dung on the surface of the earth. 3 Death will be chosen rather than life by all the residue that remain of this evil family, that remain in all the places where I have driven them," says Yahweh of Armies. 4"Moreover you shall tell them, 'Yahweh says: "'Do men fall, and not rise up again? Does one turn away, and not return? 5 Why then have the people of Jerusalem fallen back by a perpetual backsliding? They cling to deceit. They refuse to return. 6 I listened and heard, but they didn't say what is right. No one repents of his wickedness, saying, "What have I done?" Everyone turns to his course, as a horse that rushes headlong in the battle. 7 Yes, the stork in the sky knows her appointed times. The turtledove, the swallow, and the crane observe the time of their coming; but my people don't know Yahweh's law. 8"'How do you say, "We are wise, and Yahweh's law is with us"? But, behold, the false pen of the scribes has made that a lie. 9 The wise men are disappointed. They are dismayed and trapped. Behold, they have rejected Yahweh's word. What kind of wisdom is in them? 10 Therefore I will give their wives to others and their fields to those who will possess them. For everyone from the least even to the greatest is given to covetousness; from the prophet even to the priest everyone deals falsely. 11

They have healed the hurt of the daughter of my people slightly, saying, "Peace, peace," when there is no peace. 12 Were they ashamed when they had committed abomination? No, they were not at all ashamed. They couldn't blush. Therefore they will fall among those who fall. In the time of their visitation they will be cast down, says Yahweh. 13"'I will utterly consume them, says Yahweh. No grapes will be on the vine, no figs on the fig tree, and the leaf will fade. The things that I have given them will pass away from them.'" 14"Why do we sit still? Assemble yourselves! Let's enter into the fortified cities, and let's be silent there; for Yahweh our God has put us to silence, and given us poisoned water to drink, because we have sinned against Yahweh. 15 We looked for peace, but no good came; and for a time of healing, and behold, dismay! 16 The snorting of his horses is heard from Dan. The whole land trembles at the sound of the neighing of his strong ones; for they have come, and have devoured the land and all that is in it, the city and those who dwell therein." 17"For, behold, I will send serpents, adders among you, which will not be charmed; and they will bite you," says Yahweh. 18 Oh that I could comfort myself against sorrow! My heart is faint within me. 19 Behold, the voice of the cry of the daughter of my people from a land that is very far off: "Isn't Yahweh in Zion? Isn't her King in her?" "Why have they provoked me to anger with their engraved images, and with foreign idols?" 20"The harvest is past. The summer has ended, and we are not saved." 21 For the hurt of the daughter of my people, I am hurt. I mourn. Dismay has taken hold of me. 22 Is there no balm in Gilead? Is there no physician there? Why then isn't the health of the daughter of my people recovered?

9

1 Oh that my head were waters, and my eyes a spring of tears, that I might weep day and night for the slain of the daughter of my people! 2 Oh that I had in the wilderness a lodging place of wayfaring men, that I might leave my people and go from them! For they are all adulterers, an assembly of treacherous men. 3"They bend their tongue, as their bow, for falsehood. They have grown strong in the land, but not for truth; for they proceed from evil to evil, and they don't know me," says Yahweh. 4"Everyone beware of his neighbor, and don't trust in any brother; for every brother will utterly supplant, and every neighbor will go around like a slanderer. 5 Friends deceive each other, and will not speak the truth. They have taught their tongue to speak lies. They weary themselves committing iniquity. 6 Your habitation is in the middle of deceit. Through deceit, they refuse to know

me," says Yahweh. 7 Therefore Yahweh of Armies says, "Behold, I will melt them and test them; for how should I deal with the daughter of my people? 8 Their tongue is a deadly arrow. It speaks deceit. One speaks peaceably to his neighbor with his mouth, but in his heart, he waits to ambush him. 9 Shouldn't I punish them for these things?" says Yahweh. "Shouldn't my soul be avenged on a nation such as this? 10 I will weep and wail for the mountains, and lament for the pastures of the wilderness, because they are burned up, so that no one passes through; Men can't hear the voice of the livestock. Both the birds of the sky and the animals have fled. They are gone. 11 "I will make Jerusalem heaps, a dwelling place of jackals. I will make the cities of Judah a desolation, without inhabitant." 12 Who is wise enough to understand this? Who is he to whom the mouth of Yahweh has spoken, that he may declare it? Why has the land perished and burned up like a wilderness, so that no one passes through? 13 Yahweh says, "Because they have forsaken my law which I set before them, and have not obeyed my voice or walked in my ways, 14 but have walked after the stubbornness of their own heart and after the Baals, which their fathers taught them." 15 Therefore Yahweh of Armies, the God of Israel, says, "Behold, I will feed them, even this people, with wormwood and give them poisoned water to drink. 16 I will scatter them also among the nations, whom neither they nor their fathers have known. I will send the sword after them, until I have consumed them." 17 Yahweh of Armies says, "Consider, and call for the mourning women, that they may come. Send for the skillful women, that they may come. 18 Let them make haste and take up a wailing for us, that our eyes may run down with tears and our eyelids gush out with waters. 19 For a voice of wailing is heard out of Zion, 'How we are ruined! We are greatly confounded because we have forsaken the land, because they have cast down our dwellings.'" 20 Yet hear Yahweh's word, you women. Let your ear receive the word of his mouth. Teach your daughters wailing. Everyone teach her neighbor a lamentation. 21 For death has come up into our windows. It has entered into our palaces to cut off the children from outside, and the young men from the streets. 22 Speak, "Yahweh says, "'The dead bodies of men will fall as dung on the open field, and as the handful after the harvester. No one will gather them.'" 23 Yahweh says, "Don't let the wise man glory in his wisdom. Don't let the mighty man glory in his might. Don't let the rich man glory in his riches. 24 But let him who glories glory in this, that he has understanding, and knows me, that I am Yahweh who exercises loving kindness, justice, and righteousness in the earth, for I delight in these things," says Yahweh. ²⁵"Behold, the days come," says Yahweh, "that I will punish all those who are circumcised only in their flesh: ²⁶ Egypt, Judah, Edom, the children of Ammon, Moab, and all who have the corners of their hair cut off, who dwell in the wilderness, for all the nations are uncircumcised, and all the house of Israel are uncircumcised in heart."

10

¹ Hear the word which Yahweh speaks to you, house of Israel! ² Yahweh says, "Don't learn the way of the nations, and don't be dismayed at the signs of the sky; for the nations are dismayed at them. ³ For the customs of the peoples are vanity; for one cuts a tree out of the forest, the work of the hands of the workman with the ax. ⁴ They deck it with silver and with gold. They fasten it with nails and with hammers, so that it can't move. ⁵ They are like a palm tree, of turned work, and don't speak. They must be carried, because they can't move. Don't be afraid of them; for they can't do evil, neither is it in them to do good." ⁶ There is no one like you, Yahweh. You are great, and your name is great in might. ⁷ Who shouldn't fear you, King of the nations? For it belongs to you. Because among all the wise men of the nations, and in all their royal estate, there is no one like you. ⁸ But they are together brutish and foolish, instructed by idols! It is just wood. ⁹ There is silver beaten into plates, which is brought from Tarshish, and gold from Uphaz, the work of the engraver and of the hands of the goldsmith. Their clothing is blue and purple. They are all the work of skillful men. ¹⁰ But Yahweh is the true God. He is the living God, and an everlasting King. At his wrath, the earth trembles. The nations aren't able to withstand his indignation. ¹¹"You shall say this to them: 'The gods that have not made the heavens and the earth will perish from the earth, and from under the heavens.'" ¹² God has made the earth by his power. He has established the world by his wisdom, and by his understanding has he stretched out the heavens. ¹³ When he utters his voice, the waters in the heavens roar, and he causes the vapors to ascend from the ends of the earth. He makes lightnings for the rain, and brings the wind out of his treasuries. ¹⁴ Every man has become brutish and without knowledge. Every goldsmith is disappointed by his engraved image; for his molten image is falsehood, and there is no breath in them. ¹⁵ They are vanity, a work of delusion. In the time of their visitation they will perish. ¹⁶ The portion of Jacob is not like these; for he is the maker of all things; and Israel is the tribe of his inheritance. Yahweh of Armies is his name. ¹⁷ Gather up your wares out of the land, you who live

under siege. 18 For Yahweh says, "Behold, I will sling out the inhabitants of the land at this time, and will distress them, that they may feel it." 19 Woe is me because of my injury! My wound is serious; but I said, "Truly this is my grief, and I must bear it." 20 My tent has been destroyed, and all my cords are broken. My children have gone away from me, and they are no more. There is no one to spread my tent any more, to set up my curtains. 21 For the shepherds have become brutish, and have not inquired of Yahweh. Therefore they have not prospered, and all their flocks have scattered. 22 The voice of news, behold, it comes, and a great commotion out of the north country, to make the cities of Judah a desolation, a dwelling place of jackals. 23 Yahweh, I know that the way of man is not in himself. It is not in man who walks to direct his steps. 24 Yahweh, correct me, but gently; not in your anger, lest you reduce me to nothing. 25 Pour out your wrath on the nations that don't know you, and on the families that don't call on your name; for they have devoured Jacob. Yes, they have devoured him, consumed him, and have laid waste his habitation.

11

1 The word that came to Jeremiah from Yahweh, saying, 2"Hear the words of this covenant, and speak to the men of Judah, and to the inhabitants of Jerusalem; 3 and say to them, Yahweh, the God of Israel says: 'Cursed is the man who doesn't hear the words of this covenant, 4 which I commanded your fathers in the day that I brought them out of the land of Egypt, out of the iron furnace,' saying, 'Obey my voice and do them, according to all which I command you; so you shall be my people, and I will be your God; 5 that I may establish the oath which I swore to your fathers, to give them a land flowing with milk and honey,' as it is today." Then I answered, and said, "Amen, Yahweh." 6 Yahweh said to me, "Proclaim all these words in the cities of Judah, and in the streets of Jerusalem, saying, 'Hear the words of this covenant, and do them. 7 For I earnestly protested to your fathers in the day that I brought them up out of the land of Egypt, even to this day, rising early and protesting, saying, "Obey my voice." 8 Yet they didn't obey, nor turn their ear, but everyone walked in the stubbornness of their evil heart. Therefore I brought on them all the words of this covenant, which I commanded them to do, but they didn't do them.'" 9 Yahweh said to me, "A conspiracy is found among the men of Judah, and among the inhabitants of Jerusalem. 10 They have turned back to the iniquities of their forefathers, who refused to hear my words. They have gone after other gods to serve them.

The house of Israel and the house of Judah have broken my covenant which I made with their fathers. 11 Therefore Yahweh says, 'Behold, I will bring evil on them which they will not be able to escape; and they will cry to me, but I will not listen to them. 12 Then the cities of Judah and the inhabitants of Jerusalem will go and cry to the gods to which they offer incense, but they will not save them at all in the time of their trouble. 13 For according to the number of your cities are your gods, Judah; and according to the number of the streets of Jerusalem you have set up altars to the shameful thing, even altars to burn incense to Baal.' 14"Therefore don't pray for this people. Don't lift up cry or prayer for them; for I will not hear them in the time that they cry to me because of their trouble. 15 What has my beloved to do in my house, since she has behaved lewdly with many, and the holy flesh has passed from you? When you do evil, then you rejoice." 16 Yahweh called your name, "A green olive tree, beautiful with goodly fruit." With the noise of a great roar he has kindled fire on it, and its branches are broken. 17 For Yahweh of Armies, who planted you, has pronounced evil against you, because of the evil of the house of Israel and of the house of Judah, which they have done to themselves in provoking me to anger by offering incense to Baal. 18 Yahweh gave me knowledge of it, and I knew it. Then you showed me their doings. 19 But I was like a gentle lamb that is led to the slaughter. I didn't know that they had devised plans against me, saying, "Let's destroy the tree with its fruit, and let's cut him off from the land of the living, that his name may be no more remembered." 20 But, Yahweh of Armies, who judges righteously, who tests the heart and the mind, I will see your vengeance on them; for to you I have revealed my cause. 21"Therefore Yahweh says concerning the men of Anathoth, who seek your life, saying, 'You shall not prophesy in Yahweh's name, that you not die by our hand'— 22 therefore Yahweh of Armies says, 'Behold, I will punish them. The young men will die by the sword. Their sons and their daughters will die by famine. 23 There will be no remnant to them, for I will bring evil on the men of Anathoth, even the year of their visitation.'"

12

1 You are righteous, Yahweh, when I contend with you; yet I would like to plead a case with you. Why does the way of the wicked prosper? Why are they all at ease who deal very treacherously? 2 You have planted them. Yes, they have taken root. They grow. Yes, they produce fruit. You are near in their mouth, and far from their heart. 3 But you, Yahweh, know me. You see

me, and test my heart toward you. Pull them out like sheep for the slaughter, and prepare them for the day of slaughter. 4 How long will the land mourn, and the herbs of the whole country wither? Because of the wickedness of those who dwell therein, the animals and birds are consumed; because they said, "He won't see our latter end." 5"If you have run with the footmen, and they have wearied you, then how can you contend with horses? Though in a land of peace you are secure, yet how will you do in the pride of the Jordan? 6 For even your brothers, and the house of your father, even they have dealt treacherously with you! Even they have cried aloud after you! Don't believe them, though they speak beautiful words to you. 7"I have forsaken my house. I have cast off my heritage. I have given the dearly beloved of my soul into the hand of her enemies. 8 My heritage has become to me as a lion in the forest. She has uttered her voice against me. Therefore I have hated her. 9 Is my heritage to me as a speckled bird of prey? Are the birds of prey against her all around? Go, assemble all the animals of the field. Bring them to devour. 10 Many shepherds have destroyed my vineyard. They have trodden my portion under foot. They have made my pleasant portion a desolate wilderness. 11 They have made it a desolation. It mourns to me, being desolate. The whole land is made desolate, because no one cares. 12 Destroyers have come on all the bare heights in the wilderness; for the sword of Yahweh devours from the one end of the land even to the other end of the land. No flesh has peace. 13 They have sown wheat, and have reaped thorns. They have exhausted themselves, and profit nothing. You will be ashamed of your fruits, because of Yahweh's fierce anger." 14 Yahweh says, "Concerning all my evil neighbors, who touch the inheritance which I have caused my people Israel to inherit: Behold, I will pluck them up from off their land, and will pluck up the house of Judah from among them. 15 It will happen that after I have plucked them up, I will return and have compassion on them. I will bring them again, every man to his heritage, and every man to his land. 16 It will happen, if they will diligently learn the ways of my people, to swear by my name, 'As Yahweh lives;' even as they taught my people to swear by Baal, then they will be built up in the middle of my people. 17 But if they will not hear, then I will pluck up that nation, plucking up and destroying it," says Yahweh.

13

1 Yahweh said to me, "Go, and buy yourself a linen belt, and put it on your waist, and don't put it in water." 2 So I bought a belt according to Yahweh's

word, and put it on my waist. 3 Yahweh's word came to me the second time, saying, 4"Take the belt that you have bought, which is on your waist, and arise, go to the Euphrates, and hide it there in a cleft of the rock." 5 So I went and hid it by the Euphrates, as Yahweh commanded me. 6 After many days, Yahweh said to me, "Arise, go to the Euphrates, and take the belt from there, which I commanded you to hide there." 7 Then I went to the Euphrates, and dug, and took the belt from the place where I had hidden it; and behold, the belt was ruined. It was profitable for nothing. 8 Then Yahweh's word came to me, saying, 9"Yahweh says, 'In this way I will ruin the pride of Judah, and the great pride of Jerusalem. 10 This evil people, who refuse to hear my words, who walk in the stubbornness of their heart, and have gone after other gods to serve them and to worship them, will even be as this belt, which is profitable for nothing. 11 For as the belt clings to the waist of a man, so I have caused the whole house of Israel and the whole house of Judah to cling to me,' says Yahweh; 'that they may be to me for a people, for a name, for praise, and for glory; but they would not hear.' 12"Therefore you shall speak to them this word: 'Yahweh, the God of Israel says, "Every container should be filled with wine."' They will tell you, 'Do we not certainly know that every container should be filled with wine?' 13 Then tell them, 'Yahweh says, "Behold, I will fill all the inhabitants of this land, even the kings who sit on David's throne, the priests, the prophets, and all the inhabitants of Jerusalem, with drunkenness. 14 I will dash them one against another, even the fathers and the sons together," says Yahweh: "I will not pity, spare, or have compassion, that I should not destroy them."'" 15 Hear, and give ear. Don't be proud, for Yahweh has spoken. 16 Give glory to Yahweh your God, before he causes darkness, and before your feet stumble on the dark mountains, and while you look for light, he turns it into the shadow of death, and makes it deep darkness. 17 But if you will not hear it, my soul will weep in secret for your pride. My eye will weep bitterly, and run down with tears, because Yahweh's flock has been taken captive. 18 Say to the king and to the queen mother, "Humble yourselves. Sit down, for your crowns have come down, even the crown of your glory. 19 The cities of the South are shut up, and there is no one to open them. Judah is carried away captive: all of them. They are wholly carried away captive. 20 Lift up your eyes, and see those who come from the north. Where is the flock that was given to you, your beautiful flock? 21 What will you say when he sets over you as head those whom you have yourself taught to be friends to you? Won't sorrows take hold of you, as of a woman in travail? 22 If you say in your heart, "Why have these things come on me?" Your skirts are uncovered because of the greatness of your iniquity, and your heels suffer violence. 23 Can the Ethiopian change his skin, or the leopard his spots? Then may you also do good, who are accustomed to do evil. 24"Therefore I will scatter them as the stubble that passes away by the wind of the wilderness. 25 This is your lot, the portion measured to you from me," says Yahweh, "because you have forgotten me, and trusted in falsehood." 26 Therefore I will also uncover your skirts on your face, and your shame will appear. 27 I have seen your abominations, even your adulteries and your neighing, the lewdness of your prostitution, on the hills in the field. Woe to you, Jerusalem! You will not be made clean. How long will it yet be?"

14

1 This is Yahweh's word that came to Jeremiah concerning the drought: 2"Judah mourns, and its gates languish. They sit in black on the ground. The cry of Jerusalem goes up. 3 Their nobles send their little ones to the waters. They come to the cisterns, and find no water. They return with their vessels empty. They are disappointed and confounded, and cover their heads. 4 Because of the ground which is cracked, because no rain has been in the land, the plowmen are disappointed. They cover their heads. 5 Yes, the doe in the field also calves and forsakes her young, because there is no grass. 6 The wild donkeys stand on the bare heights. They pant for air like jackals. Their eyes fail, because there is no vegetation. 7 Though our iniquities testify against us, work for your name's sake, Yahweh; for our rebellions are many. We have sinned against you. 8 You hope of Israel, its Savior in the time of trouble, why should you be as a foreigner in the land, and as a wayfaring man who turns aside to stay for a night? 9 Why should you be like a scared man, as a mighty man who can't save? Yet you, Yahweh, are in the middle of us, and we are called by your name. Don't leave us. 10 Yahweh says to this people: "Even so they have loved to wander. They have not restrained their feet. Therefore Yahweh does not accept them. Now he will remember their iniquity, and punish them for their sins." 11 Yahweh said to me, "Don't pray for this people for their good. 12 When they fast, I will not hear their cry; and when they offer burnt offering and meal offering, I will not accept them; but I will consume them by the sword, by famine, and by pestilence." 13 Then I said, "Ah, Lord Yahweh! Behold, the prophets tell them, 'You will not see the sword, neither will you have famine; but I will give you assured peace in this place.'" 14 Then Yahweh said to me, "The prophets prophesy lies in my name. I didn't

send them. I didn't command them. I didn't speak to them. They prophesy to you a lying vision, divination, and a thing of nothing, and the deceit of their own heart. 15 Therefore Yahweh says concerning the prophets who prophesy in my name, but I didn't send them, yet they say, 'Sword and famine will not be in this land.' Those prophets will be consumed by sword and famine. 16 The people to whom they prophesy will be cast out in the streets of Jerusalem because of the famine and the sword. They will have no one to bury them—them, their wives, their sons, or their daughters, for I will pour their wickedness on them. 17 "You shall say this word to them: "'Let my eyes run down with tears night and day, and let them not cease; for the virgin daughter of my people is broken with a great breach, with a very grievous wound. 18 If I go out into the field, then behold, the slain with the sword! If I enter into the city, then behold, those who are sick with famine! For both the prophet and the priest go about in the land, and have no knowledge.'" 19 Have you utterly rejected Judah? Has your soul loathed Zion? Why have you struck us, and there is no healing for us? We looked for peace, but no good came; and for a time of healing, and behold, dismay! 20 We acknowledge, Yahweh, our wickedness, and the iniquity of our fathers; for we have sinned against you. 21 Do not abhor us, for your name's sake. Do not disgrace the throne of your glory. Remember, and don't break your covenant with us. 22 Are there any among the vanities of the nations that can cause rain? Or can the sky give showers? Aren't you he, Yahweh our God? Therefore we will wait for you; for you have made all these things.

15

1 Then Yahweh said to me, "Though Moses and Samuel stood before me, yet my mind would not turn toward this people. Cast them out of my sight, and let them go out! 2 It will happen when they ask you, 'Where shall we go out?' then you shall tell them, 'Yahweh says: "Such as are for death, to death; such as are for the sword, to the sword; such as are for the famine, to the famine; and such as are for captivity, to captivity."' 3 "I will appoint over them four kinds," says Yahweh: "the sword to kill, the dogs to tear, the birds of the sky, and the animals of the earth, to devour and to destroy. 4 I will cause them to be tossed back and forth among all the kingdoms of the earth, because of Manasseh, the son of Hezekiah, king of Judah, for that which he did in Jerusalem. 5 For who will have pity on you, Jerusalem? Who will mourn you? Who will come to ask of your welfare? 6 You have rejected me," says Yahweh. "You have gone backward. Therefore I have stretched out my hand

against you and destroyed you. I am weary of showing compassion. 7 I have winnowed them with a fan in the gates of the land. I have bereaved them of children. I have destroyed my people. They didn't return from their ways. 8 Their widows are increased more than the sand of the seas. I have brought on them against the mother of the young men a destroyer at noonday. I have caused anguish and terrors to fall on her suddenly. 9 She who has borne seven languishes. She has given up the spirit. Her sun has gone down while it was yet day. She has been disappointed and confounded. I will deliver their residue to the sword before their enemies," says Yahweh. 10 Woe is me, my mother, that you have borne me, a man of strife, and a man of contention to the whole earth! I have not lent, neither have men lent to me; yet every one of them curses me. 11 Yahweh said, "Most certainly I will strengthen you for good. Most certainly I will cause the enemy to make supplication to you in the time of evil and in the time of affliction. 12 Can one break iron, even iron from the north, and bronze? 13 I will give your substance and your treasures for a plunder without price, and that for all your sins, even in all your borders. 14 I will make them to pass with your enemies into a land which you don't know; for a fire is kindled in my anger, which will burn on you." 15 Yahweh, you know. Remember me, visit me, and avenge me of my persecutors. You are patient, so don't take me away. Know that for your sake I have suffered reproach. 16 Your words were found, and I ate them. Your words were to me a joy and the rejoicing of my heart, for I am called by your name, Yahweh, God of Armies. 17 I didn't sit in the assembly of those who make merry and rejoice. I sat alone because of your hand, for you have filled me with indignation. 18 Why is my pain perpetual, and my wound incurable, which refuses to be healed? Will you indeed be to me as a deceitful brook, like waters that fail? 19 Therefore Yahweh says, "If you return, then I will bring you again, that you may stand before me; and if you take out the precious from the vile, you will be as my mouth. They will return to you, but you will not return to them. 20 I will make you to this people a fortified bronze wall. They will fight against you, but they will not prevail against you; for I am with you to save you and to deliver you," says Yahweh. 21 " I will deliver you out of the hand of the wicked, and I will redeem you out of the hand of the terrible."

16

1 Then Yahweh's word came to me, saying, 2"You shall not take a wife, neither shall you have sons or daughters, in this place." 3 For Yahweh says

concerning the sons and concerning the daughters who are born in this place, and concerning their mothers who bore them, and concerning their fathers who became their father in this land: 4"They will die grievous deaths. They will not be lamented, neither will they be buried. They will be as dung on the surface of the ground. They will be consumed by the sword and by famine. Their dead bodies will be food for the birds of the sky and for the animals of the earth." 5 For Yahweh says, "Don't enter into the house of mourning. Don't go to lament. Don't bemoan them, for I have taken away my peace from this people," says Yahweh, "even loving kindness and tender mercies. 6 Both great and small will die in this land. They will not be buried. Men won't lament for them, cut themselves, or make themselves bald for them. 7 Men won't break bread for them in mourning, to comfort them for the dead. Men won't give them the cup of consolation to drink for their father or for their mother. 8"You shall not go into the house of feasting to sit with them, to eat and to drink." 9 For Yahweh of Armies, the God of Israel says: "Behold, I will cause to cease out of this place, before your eyes and in your days, the voice of mirth and the voice of gladness, the voice of the bridegroom and the voice of the bride. 10 It will happen, when you tell this people all these words, and they ask you, 'Why has Yahweh pronounced all this great evil against us?' or 'What is our iniquity?' or 'What is our sin that we have committed against Yahweh our God?' 11 then you shall tell them, 'Because your fathers have forsaken me,' says Yahweh, 'and have walked after other gods, have served them, have worshiped them, have forsaken me, and have not kept my law. 12 You have done evil more than your fathers, for behold, you each walk after the stubbornness of his evil heart, so that you don't listen to me. 13 Therefore I will cast you out of this land into the land that you have not known, neither you nor your fathers. There you will serve other gods day and night, for I will show you no favor.' 14"Therefore behold, the days come," says Yahweh, "that it will no more be said, 'As Yahweh lives, who brought up the children of Israel out of the land of Egypt;' 15 but, 'As Yahweh lives, who brought up the children of Israel from the land of the north, and from all the countries where he had driven them.' I will bring them again into their land that I gave to their fathers. 16"Behold, I will send for many fishermen," says Yahweh, "and they will fish them up. Afterward I will send for many hunters, and they will hunt them from every mountain, from every hill, and out of the clefts of the rocks. 17 For my eyes are on all their ways. They are not hidden from my face. Their iniquity isn't concealed from my eyes. 18 First

I will recompense their iniquity and their sin double, because they have polluted my land with the carcasses of their detestable things, and have filled my inheritance with their abominations." 19 Yahweh, my strength, my stronghold, and my refuge in the day of affliction, the nations will come to you from the ends of the earth, and will say, "Our fathers have inherited nothing but lies, vanity and things in which there is no profit. 20 Should a man make to himself gods which yet are no gods?" 21 "Therefore behold, I will cause them to know, this once I will cause them to know my hand and my might. Then they will know that my name is Yahweh."

17

1 "The sin of Judah is written with a pen of iron, and with the point of a diamond. It is engraved on the tablet of their heart, and on the horns of your altars. 2 Even their children remember their altars and their Asherah poles by the green trees on the high hills. 3 My mountain in the field, I will give your substance and all your treasures for a plunder, and your high places, because of sin, throughout all your borders. 4 You, even of yourself, will discontinue from your heritage that I gave you. I will cause you to serve your enemies in the land which you don't know, for you have kindled a fire in my anger which will burn forever." 5 Yahweh says: "Cursed is the man who trusts in man, relies on strength of flesh, and whose heart departs from Yahweh. 6 For he will be like a bush in the desert, and will not see when good comes, but will inhabit the parched places in the wilderness, an uninhabited salt land. 7 "Blessed is the man who trusts in Yahweh, and whose confidence is in Yahweh. 8 For he will be as a tree planted by the waters, who spreads out its roots by the river, and will not fear when heat comes, but its leaf will be green, and will not be concerned in the year of drought. It won't cease from yielding fruit. 9 The heart is deceitful above all things and it is exceedingly corrupt. Who can know it? 10 "I, Yahweh, search the mind. I try the heart, even to give every man according to his ways, according to the fruit of his doings." 11 As the partridge that sits on eggs which she has not laid, so is he who gets riches, and not by right. In the middle of his days, they will leave him. At his end, he will be a fool. 12 A glorious throne, set on high from the beginning, is the place of our sanctuary. 13 Yahweh, the hope of Israel, all who forsake you will be disappointed. Those who depart from me will be written in the earth, because they have forsaken Yahweh, the spring of living waters. 14 Heal me, O Yahweh, and I will be healed. Save me, and I will be saved; for you are my praise. 15 Behold, they ask me, "Where is Yahweh's

word? Let it be fulfilled now." 16 As for me, I have not hurried from being a shepherd after you. I haven't desired the woeful day. You know. That which came out of my lips was before your face. 17 Don't be a terror to me. You are my refuge in the day of evil. 18 Let them be disappointed who persecute me, but don't let me be disappointed. Let them be dismayed, but don't let me be dismayed. Bring on them the day of evil, and destroy them with double destruction. 19 Yahweh said this to me: "Go and stand in the gate of the children of the people, through which the kings of Judah come in and by which they go out, and in all the gates of Jerusalem. 20 Tell them, 'Hear Yahweh's word, you kings of Judah, all Judah, and all the inhabitants of Jerusalem, that enter in by these gates: 21 Yahweh says, "Be careful, and bear no burden on the Sabbath day, nor bring it in by the gates of Jerusalem. 22 Don't carry a burden out of your houses on the Sabbath day. Don't do any work, but make the Sabbath day holy, as I commanded your fathers. 23 But they didn't listen. They didn't turn their ear, but made their neck stiff, that they might not hear, and might not receive instruction. 24 It will happen, if you diligently listen to me," says Yahweh, "to bring in no burden through the gates of this city on the Sabbath day, but to make the Sabbath day holy, to do no work therein; 25 then there will enter in by the gates of this city kings and princes sitting on David's throne, riding in chariots and on horses, they and their princes, the men of Judah and the inhabitants of Jerusalem; and this city will remain forever. 26 They will come from the cities of Judah, and from the places around Jerusalem, from the land of Benjamin, from the lowland, from the hill country, and from the South, bringing burnt offerings, sacrifices, meal offerings, and frankincense, and bringing sacrifices of thanksgiving to Yahweh's house. 27 But if you will not listen to me to make the Sabbath day holy, and not to bear a burden and enter in at the gates of Jerusalem on the Sabbath day, then I will kindle a fire in its gates, and it will devour the palaces of Jerusalem. It will not be quenched."'"

18

1 The word which came to Jeremiah from Yahweh, saying, 2 "Arise, and go down to the potter's house, and there I will cause you to hear my words."

3 Then I went down to the potter's house, and behold, he was making something on the wheels. 4 When the vessel that he made of the clay was marred in the hand of the potter, he made it again another vessel, as seemed good to the potter to make it. 5 Then Yahweh's word came to me, saying, 6 "House of Israel, can't I do with you as this potter?" says Yahweh. "Behold,

as the clay in the potter's hand, so are you in my hand, house of Israel. 7 At the instant I speak concerning a nation, and concerning a kingdom, to pluck up and to break down and to destroy it, 8 if that nation, concerning which I have spoken, turns from their evil, I will repent of the evil that I thought to do to them. 9 At the instant I speak concerning a nation, and concerning a kingdom, to build and to plant it, 10 if they do that which is evil in my sight, that they not obey my voice, then I will repent of the good with which I said I would benefit them. 11"Now therefore, speak to the men of Judah, and to the inhabitants of Jerusalem, saying, 'Yahweh says: "Behold, I frame evil against you, and devise a plan against you. Everyone return from his evil way now, and amend your ways and your doings."' 12 But they say, 'It is in vain; for we will walk after our own plans, and we will each follow the stubbornness of his evil heart.'" 13 Therefore Yahweh says: "Ask now among the nations, 'Who has heard such things?' The virgin of Israel has done a very horrible thing. 14 Will the snow of Lebanon fail from the rock of the field? Will the cold waters that flow down from afar be dried up? 15 For my people have forgotten me. They have burned incense to false gods. They have been made to stumble in their ways in the ancient paths, to walk in byways, in a way not built up, 16 to make their land an astonishment, and a perpetual hissing. Everyone who passes by it will be astonished, and shake his head. 17 I will scatter them as with an east wind before the enemy. I will show them the back, and not the face, in the day of their calamity. 18 Then they said, "Come! Let's devise plans against Jeremiah; for the law won't perish from the priest, nor counsel from the wise, nor the word from the prophet. Come, and let's strike him with the tongue, and let's not give heed to any of his words." 19 Give heed to me, Yahweh, and listen to the voice of those who contend with me. 20 Should evil be recompensed for good? For they have dug a pit for my soul. Remember how I stood before you to speak good for them, to turn away your wrath from them. 21 Therefore deliver up their children to the famine, and give them over to the power of the sword. Let their wives become childless and widows. Let their men be killed and their young men struck by the sword in battle. 22 Let a cry be heard from their houses when you bring a troop suddenly on them; for they have dug a pit to take me and hidden snares for my feet. 23 Yet, Yahweh, you know all their counsel against me to kill me. Don't forgive their iniquity. Don't blot out their sin from your sight, Let them be overthrown before you. Deal with them in the time of your anger.

19

1 Thus said Yahweh, "Go, and buy a potter's earthen container, and take some of the elders of the people and of the elders of the priests; 2 and go out to the valley of the son of Hinnom, which is by the entry of the gate Harsith, and proclaim there the words that I will tell you. 3 Say, 'Hear Yahweh's word, kings of Judah and inhabitants of Jerusalem: Yahweh of Armies, the God of Israel says, "Behold, I will bring evil on this place, which whoever hears, his ears will tingle. 4 Because they have forsaken me, and have defiled this place, and have burned incense in it to other gods that they didn't know —they, their fathers, and the kings of Judah—and have filled this place with the blood of innocents, 5 and have built the high places of Baal to burn their children in the fire for burnt offerings to Baal, which I didn't command, nor speak, which didn't even enter into my mind. 6 Therefore, behold, the days come," says Yahweh, "that this place will no more be called 'Topheth', nor 'The Valley of the son of Hinnom', but 'The valley of Slaughter'. 7 "'I will make the counsel of Judah and Jerusalem void in this place. I will cause them to fall by the sword before their enemies, and by the hand of those who seek their life. I will give their dead bodies to be food for the birds of the sky and for the animals of the earth. 8 I will make this city an astonishment and a hissing. Everyone who passes by it will be astonished and hiss because of all its plagues. 9 I will cause them to eat the flesh of their sons and the flesh of their daughters. They will each eat the flesh of his friend in the siege and in the distress with which their enemies, and those who seek their life, will distress them.'" 10 "Then you shall break the container in the sight of the men who go with you, 11 and shall tell them, 'Yahweh of Armies says: "Even so I will break this people and this city as one breaks a potter's vessel, that can't be made whole again. They will bury in Topheth until there is no place to bury. 12 This is what I will do to this place," says Yahweh, "and to its inhabitants, even making this city as Topheth. 13 The houses of Jerusalem and the houses of the kings of Judah, which are defiled, will be as the place of Topheth, even all the houses on whose roofs they have burned incense to all the army of the sky and have poured out drink offerings to other gods."'" 14 Then Jeremiah came from Topheth, where Yahweh had sent him to prophesy, and he stood in the court of Yahweh's house, and said to all the people: 15 " Yahweh of Armies, the God of Israel says, 'Behold, I will bring on this city and on all its towns all the evil that I have pronounced against it, because they have made their neck stiff, that they may not hear my words.'"

20

1 Now Pashhur, the son of Immer the priest, who was chief officer in Yahweh's house, heard Jeremiah prophesying these things. 2 Then Pashhur struck Jeremiah the prophet and put him in the stocks that were in the upper gate of Benjamin, which was in Yahweh's house. 3 On the next day, Pashhur released Jeremiah out of the stocks. Then Jeremiah said to him, "Yahweh has not called your name Pashhur, but Magormissabib. 4 For Yahweh says, 'Behold, I will make you a terror to yourself and to all your friends. They will fall by the sword of their enemies, and your eyes will see it. I will give all Judah into the hand of the king of Babylon, and he will carry them captive to Babylon, and will kill them with the sword. 5 Moreover I will give all the riches of this city, and all its gains, and all its precious things, yes, I will give all the treasures of the kings of Judah into the hand of their enemies. They will make them captives, take them, and carry them to Babylon. 6 You, Pashhur, and all who dwell in your house will go into captivity. You will come to Babylon, and there you will die, and there you will be buried, you, and all your friends, to whom you have prophesied falsely.'" 7 Yahweh, you have persuaded me, and I was persuaded. You are stronger than I, and have prevailed. I have become a laughingstock all day. Everyone mocks me. 8 For as often as I speak, I cry out; I cry, "Violence and destruction!" because Yahweh's word has been made a reproach to me, and a derision, all day. 9 If I say that I will not make mention of him, or speak any more in his name, then there is in my heart as it were a burning fire shut up in my bones. I am weary with holding it in. I can't. 10 For I have heard the defaming of many: "Terror on every side! Denounce, and we will denounce him!" say all my familiar friends, those who watch for my fall. "Perhaps he will be persuaded, and we will prevail against him, and we will take our revenge on him." 11 But Yahweh is with me as an awesome mighty one. Therefore my persecutors will stumble, and they won't prevail. They will be utterly disappointed because they have not dealt wisely, even with an everlasting dishonor which will never be forgotten. 12 But Yahweh of Armies, who tests the righteous, who sees the heart and the mind, let me see your vengeance on them, for I have revealed my cause to you. 13 Sing to Yahweh! Praise Yahweh, for he has delivered the soul of the needy from the hand of evildoers. 14 Cursed is the day in which I was born. Don't let the day in which my mother bore me be blessed. 15 Cursed is the man who brought news to my father, saying, "A boy is born to you," making him very glad. 16 Let that man be as the cities which Yahweh overthrew, and didn't repent. Let him hear a cry in the morning, and

shouting at noontime, 17 because he didn't kill me from the womb. So my mother would have been my grave, and her womb always great. 18 Why did I come out of the womb to see labor and sorrow, that my days should be consumed with shame?

21

1 The word which came to Jeremiah from Yahweh, when King Zedekiah sent to him Pashhur the son of Malchijah, and Zephaniah the son of Maaseiah, the priest, saying, 2"Please inquire of Yahweh for us; for Nebuchadnezzar king of Babylon makes war against us. Perhaps Yahweh will deal with us according to all his wondrous works, that he may withdraw from us." 3 Then Jeremiah said to them, "Tell Zedekiah: 4'Yahweh, the God of Israel says, "Behold, I will turn back the weapons of war that are in your hands, with which you fight against the king of Babylon, and against the Chaldeans who besiege you outside the walls; and I will gather them into the middle of this city. 5 I myself will fight against you with an outstretched hand and with a strong arm, even in anger, in wrath, and in great indignation. 6 I will strike the inhabitants of this city, both man and animal. They will die of a great pestilence. 7 Afterward," says Yahweh, "I will deliver Zedekiah king of Judah, his servants, and the people, even those who are left in this city from the pestilence, from the sword, and from the famine, into the hand of Nebuchadnezzar king of Babylon, and into the hand of their enemies, and into the hand of those who seek their life. He will strike them with the edge of the sword. He will not spare them, have pity, or have mercy."' 8"You shall say to this people, 'Yahweh says: "Behold, I set before you the way of life and the way of death. 9 He who remains in this city will die by the sword, by the famine, and by the pestilence, but he who goes out and passes over to the Chaldeans who besiege you, he will live, and he will escape with his life. 10 For I have set my face on this city for evil, and not for good," says Yahweh. "It will be given into the hand of the king of Babylon, and he will burn it with fire."' 11"Concerning the house of the king of Judah, hear Yahweh's word: 12 House of David, Yahweh says, 'Execute justice in the morning, and deliver him who is robbed out of the hand of the oppressor, lest my wrath go out like fire, and burn so that no one can quench it, because of the evil of your doings. 13 Behold, I am against you, O inhabitant of the valley, and of the rock of the plain,' says Yahweh. 'You that say, "Who would come down against us?" or, "Who would enter into our homes?" 14 I will punish you according to the fruit of your doings,' says Yahweh; 'and I will kindle a fire in her forest, and it

will devour all that is around her.'"

22

1 Yahweh said, "Go down to the house of the king of Judah, and speak this word there: 2'Hear Yahweh's word, king of Judah, who sits on David's throne—you, your servants, and your people who enter in by these gates. 3 Yahweh says: "Execute justice and righteousness, and deliver him who is robbed out of the hand of the oppressor. Do no wrong. Do no violence to the foreigner, the fatherless, or the widow. Don't shed innocent blood in this place. 4 For if you do this thing indeed, then kings sitting on David's throne will enter in by the gates of this house, riding in chariots and on horses—they, their servants, and their people. 5 But if you will not hear these words, I swear by myself," says Yahweh, "that this house will become a desolation."'" 6 For Yahweh says concerning the house of the king of Judah: "You are Gilead to me, the head of Lebanon. Yet surely I will make you a wilderness, cities which are not inhabited. 7 I will prepare destroyers against you, everyone with his weapons, and they will cut down your choice cedars, and cast them into the fire. 8"Many nations will pass by this city, and they will each ask his neighbor, 'Why has Yahweh done this to this great city?' 9 Then they will answer, 'Because they abandoned the covenant of Yahweh their God, worshiped other gods, and served them.'" 10 Don't weep for the dead. Don't bemoan him; but weep bitterly for him who goes away, for he will return no more, and not see his native country. 11 For Yahweh says touching Shallum the son of Josiah, king of Judah, who reigned instead of Josiah his father, and who went out of this place: "He won't return there any more. 12 But he will die in the place where they have led him captive. He will see this land no more." 13"Woe to him who builds his house by unrighteousness, and his rooms by injustice; who uses his neighbor's service without wages, and doesn't give him his hire; 14 who says, 'I will build myself a wide house and spacious rooms,' and cuts out windows for himself, with a cedar ceiling, and painted with red. 15"Should you reign because you strive to excel in cedar? Didn't your father eat and drink, and do justice and righteousness? Then it was well with him. 16 He judged the cause of the poor and needy; so then it was well. Wasn't this to know me?" says Yahweh. 17 But your eyes and your heart are only for your covetousness, for shedding innocent blood, for oppression, and for doing violence." 18 Therefore Yahweh says concerning Jehoiakim the son of Josiah, king of Judah: "They won't lament for him, saying, 'Ah my brother!' or, 'Ah sister!' They won't lament

for him, saying 'Ah lord!' or, 'Ah his glory!' 19 He will be buried with the burial of a donkey, drawn and cast out beyond the gates of Jerusalem." 20"Go up to Lebanon, and cry out. Lift up your voice in Bashan, and cry from Abarim; for all your lovers have been destroyed. 21 I spoke to you in your prosperity, but you said, 'I will not listen.' This has been your way from your youth, that you didn't obey my voice. 22 The wind will feed all your shepherds, and your lovers will go into captivity. Surely then you will be ashamed and confounded for all your wickedness. 23 Inhabitant of Lebanon, who makes your nest in the cedars, how greatly to be pitied you will be when pangs come on you, the pain as of a woman in travail! 24"As I live," says Yahweh, "though Coniah the son of Jehoiakim king of Judah were the signet on my right hand, I would still pluck you from there. 25 I would give you into the hand of those who seek your life, and into the hand of them of whom you are afraid, even into the hand of Nebuchadnezzar king of Babylon, and into the hand of the Chaldeans. 26 I will cast you out with your mother who bore you into another country, where you were not born; and there you will die. 27 But to the land to which their soul longs to return, there they will not return." 28 Is this man Coniah a despised broken vessel? Is he a vessel in which no one delights? Why are they cast out, he and his offspring, and cast into a land which they don't know? 29 O earth, earth, earth, hear Yahweh's word! 30 Yahweh says, "Record this man as childless, a man who will not prosper in his days; for no more will a man of his offspring prosper, sitting on David's throne and ruling in Judah."

23

1"Woe to the shepherds who destroy and scatter the sheep of my pasture!" says Yahweh. 2 Therefore Yahweh, the God of Israel, says against the shepherds who feed my people: "You have scattered my flock, driven them away, and have not visited them. Behold, I will visit on you the evil of your doings," says Yahweh. 3"I will gather the remnant of my flock out of all the countries where I have driven them, and will bring them again to their folds; and they will be fruitful and multiply. 4 I will set up shepherds over them who will feed them. They will no longer be afraid or dismayed, neither will any be lacking," says Yahweh. 5"Behold, the days come," says Yahweh, "that I will raise to David a righteous Branch; and he will reign as king and deal wisely, and will execute justice and righteousness in the land. 6 In his days Judah will be saved, and Israel will dwell safely. This is his name by which he will be called: Yahweh our righteousness. 7"Therefore, behold, the days come," says

Yahweh, "that they will no more say, 'As Yahweh lives, who brought up the children of Israel out of the land of Egypt;' 8 but, 'As Yahweh lives, who brought up and who led the offspring of the house of Israel out of the north country, and from all the countries where I had driven them.' Then they will dwell in their own land." 9 Concerning the prophets: My heart within me is broken. All my bones shake. I am like a drunken man, and like a man whom wine has overcome, because of Yahweh, and because of his holy words. 10"For the land is full of adulterers; for because of the curse the land mourns. The pastures of the wilderness have dried up. Their course is evil, and their might is not right; 11 for both prophet and priest are profane. Yes, in my house I have found their wickedness," says Yahweh. 12 Therefore their way will be to them as slippery places in the darkness. They will be driven on, and fall therein; for I will bring evil on them, even the year of their visitation," says Yahweh. 13"I have seen folly in the prophets of Samaria. They prophesied by Baal, and caused my people Israel to err. 14 In the prophets of Jerusalem I have also seen a horrible thing: they commit adultery and walk in lies. They strengthen the hands of evildoers, so that no one returns from his wickedness. They have all become to me as Sodom, and its inhabitants as Gomorrah." 15 Therefore Yahweh of Armies says concerning the prophets: "Behold, I will feed them with wormwood, and make them drink poisoned water; for from the prophets of Jerusalem ungodliness has gone out into all the land." 16 Yahweh of Armies says, "Don't listen to the words of the prophets who prophesy to you. They teach you vanity. They speak a vision of their own heart, and not out of the mouth of Yahweh. 17 They say continually to those who despise me, 'Yahweh has said, "You will have peace;"' and to everyone who walks in the stubbornness of his own heart they say, 'No evil will come on you.' 18 For who has stood in the council of Yahweh, that he should perceive and hear his word? Who has listened to my word, and heard it? 19 Behold, Yahweh's storm, his wrath, has gone out. Yes, a whirling storm! It will burst on the head of the wicked. 20 Yahweh's anger will not return until he has executed and performed the intents of his heart. In the latter days, you will understand it perfectly. 21 I didn't send these prophets, yet they ran. I didn't speak to them, yet they prophesied. 22 But if they had stood in my council, then they would have caused my people to hear my words, and would have turned them from their evil way, and from the evil of their doings. 23"Am I a God at hand," says Yahweh, "and not a God afar off? 24 Can anyone hide himself in secret places so that I can't see him?" says

Yahweh. "Don't I fill heaven and earth?" says Yahweh. 25"I have heard what the prophets have said, who prophesy lies in my name, saying, 'I had a dream! I had a dream!' 26 How long will this be in the heart of the prophets who prophesy lies, even the prophets of the deceit of their own heart? 27 They intend to cause my people to forget my name by their dreams which they each tell his neighbor, as their fathers forgot my name because of Baal. 28 The prophet who has a dream, let him tell a dream; and he who has my word, let him speak my word faithfully. What is the straw to the wheat?" says Yahweh. 29"Isn't my word like fire?" says Yahweh; "and like a hammer that breaks the rock in pieces? 30"Therefore behold, I am against the prophets," says Yahweh, "who each steal my words from his neighbor. 31 Behold, I am against the prophets," says Yahweh, "who use their tongues, and say, 'He says.' 32 Behold, I am against those who prophesy lying dreams," says Yahweh, "who tell them, and cause my people to err by their lies, and by their vain boasting; yet I didn't send them or command them. They don't profit this people at all," says Yahweh. 33"When this people, or the prophet, or a priest, asks you, saying, 'What is the message from Yahweh?' Then you shall tell them, '"What message? I will cast you off," says Yahweh.' 34 As for the prophet, the priest, and the people, who say, 'The message from Yahweh,' I will even punish that man and his household. 35 You will say everyone to his neighbor, and everyone to his brother, 'What has Yahweh answered?' and, 'What has Yahweh said?' 36 You will mention the message from Yahweh no more, for every man's own word has become his message; for you have perverted the words of the living God, of Yahweh of Armies, our God. 37 You will say to the prophet, 'What has Yahweh answered you?' and, 'What has Yahweh spoken?' 38 Although you say, 'The message from Yahweh,' therefore Yahweh says: 'Because you say this word, "The message from Yahweh," and I have sent to you, telling you not to say, "The message from Yahweh," 39 therefore behold, I will utterly forget you, and I will cast you off with the city that I gave to you and to your fathers, away from my presence. 40 I will bring an everlasting reproach on you, and a perpetual shame, which will not be forgotten.'"

24

1 Yahweh showed me, and behold, two baskets of figs were set before Yahweh's temple, after Nebuchadnezzar king of Babylon had carried away captive Jeconiah the son of Jehoiakim, king of Judah, and the princes of Judah, with the craftsmen and smiths, from Jerusalem, and had brought them

to Babylon. 2 One basket had very good figs, like the figs that are first-ripe; and the other basket had very bad figs, which could not be eaten, they were so bad. 3 Then Yahweh asked me, "What do you see, Jeremiah?" I said, "Figs. The good figs are very good, and the bad are very bad, so bad that they can't be eaten." 4 Yahweh's word came to me, saying, 5"Yahweh, the God of Israel says: 'Like these good figs, so I will regard the captives of Judah, whom I have sent out of this place into the land of the Chaldeans, as good. 6 For I will set my eyes on them for good, and I will bring them again to this land. I will build them, and not pull them down. I will plant them, and not pluck them up. 7 I will give them a heart to know me, that I am Yahweh. They will be my people, and I will be their God; for they will return to me with their whole heart. 8"'As the bad figs, which can't be eaten, they are so bad,' surely Yahweh says, 'So I will give up Zedekiah the king of Judah, and his princes, and the remnant of Jerusalem who remain in this land, and those who dwell in the land of Egypt. 9 I will even give them up to be tossed back and forth among all the kingdoms of the earth for evil, to be a reproach and a proverb, a taunt and a curse, in all places where I will drive them. 10 I will send the sword, the famine, and the pestilence among them, until they are consumed from off the land that I gave to them and to their fathers.'"

25

1 The word that came to Jeremiah concerning all the people of Judah, in the fourth year of Jehoiakim the son of Josiah, king of Judah (this was the first year of Nebuchadnezzar king of Babylon), 2 which Jeremiah the prophet spoke to all the people of Judah, and to all the inhabitants of Jerusalem: 3 From the thirteenth year of Josiah the son of Amon, king of Judah, even to this day, these twenty-three years, Yahweh's word has come to me, and I have spoken to you, rising up early and speaking; but you have not listened. 4 Yahweh has sent to you all his servants the prophets, rising up early and sending them (but you have not listened or inclined your ear to hear), 5 saying, "Return now everyone from his evil way, and from the evil of your doings, and dwell in the land that Yahweh has given to you and to your fathers, from of old and even forever more. 6 Don't go after other gods to serve them or worship them, and don't provoke me to anger with the work of your hands; then I will do you no harm." 7"Yet you have not listened to me," says Yahweh, "that you may provoke me to anger with the work of your hands to your own hurt." 8 Therefore Yahweh of Armies says: "Because you have not heard my words, 9 behold, I will send and take all the families of the

north," says Yahweh, "and I will send to Nebuchadnezzar the king of Babylon, my servant, and will bring them against this land, and against its inhabitants, and against all these nations around. I will utterly destroy them, and make them an astonishment, and a hissing, and perpetual desolations. 10 Moreover I will take from them the voice of mirth and the voice of gladness, the voice of the bridegroom and the voice of the bride, the sound of the millstones, and the light of the lamp. 11 This whole land will be a desolation, and an astonishment; and these nations will serve the king of Babylon seventy years. 12 "It will happen, when seventy years are accomplished, that I will punish the king of Babylon and that nation," says Yahweh, "for their iniquity. I will make the land of the Chaldeans desolate forever. 13 I will bring on that land all my words which I have pronounced against it, even all that is written in this book, which Jeremiah has prophesied against all the nations. 14 For many nations and great kings will make bondservants of them, even of them. I will recompense them according to their deeds, and according to the work of their hands." 15 For Yahweh, the God of Israel, says to me: "Take this cup of the wine of wrath from my hand, and cause all the nations to whom I send you to drink it. 16 They will drink, and reel back and forth, and be insane, because of the sword that I will send among them." 17 Then I took the cup at Yahweh's hand, and made all the nations to drink, to whom Yahweh had sent me: 18 Jerusalem, and the cities of Judah, with its kings and its princes, to make them a desolation, an astonishment, a hissing, and a curse, as it is today; 19 Pharaoh king of Egypt, with his servants, his princes, and all his people; 20 and all the mixed people, and all the kings of the land of Uz, all the kings of the Philistines, Ashkelon, Gaza, Ekron, and the remnant of Ashdod; 21 Edom, Moab, and the children of Ammon; 22 and all the kings of Tyre, all the kings of Sidon, and the kings of the isle which is beyond the sea; 23 Dedan, Tema, Buz, and all who have the corners of their beard cut off; 24 and all the kings of Arabia, all the kings of the mixed people who dwell in the wilderness; 25 and all the kings of Zimri, all the kings of Elam, and all the kings of the Medes; 26 and all the kings of the north, far and near, one with another; and all the kingdoms of the world, which are on the surface of the earth. The king of Sheshach will drink after them. 27 "You shall tell them, 'Yahweh of Armies, the God of Israel says: "Drink, and be drunk, vomit, fall, and rise no more, because of the sword which I will send among you."' 28 It shall be, if they refuse to take the cup at your hand to drink, then you shall tell them, 'Yahweh of Armies says: "You shall surely drink. 29 For, behold, I begin to work evil at the city which is called by my name; and should you be utterly unpunished? You will not be unpunished; for I will call for a sword on all the inhabitants of the earth, says Yahweh of Armies."' 30"Therefore prophesy against them all these words, and tell them, "'Yahweh will roar from on high, and utter his voice from his holy habitation. He will mightily roar against his fold. He will give a shout, as those who tread grapes, against all the inhabitants of the earth. 31 A noise will come even to the end of the earth; for Yahweh has a controversy with the nations. He will enter into judgment with all flesh. As for the wicked, he will give them to the sword,'" says Yahweh." 32 Yahweh of Armies says, "Behold, evil will go out from nation to nation, and a great storm will be raised up from the uttermost parts of the earth." 33 The slain of Yahweh will be at that day from one end of the earth even to the other end of the earth. They won't be lamented. They won't be gathered or buried. They will be dung on the surface of the ground. 34 Wail, you shepherds, and cry. Wallow in dust, you leader of the flock; for the days of your slaughter and of your dispersions have fully come, and you will fall like fine pottery. 35 The shepherds will have no way to flee. The leader of the flock will have no escape. 36 A voice of the cry of the shepherds, and the wailing of the leader of the flock, for Yahweh destroys their pasture. 37 The peaceful folds are brought to silence because of the fierce anger of Yahweh. 38 He has left his covert, as the lion; for their land has become an astonishment because of the fierceness of the oppression, and because of his fierce anger.

26

1 In the beginning of the reign of Jehoiakim the son of Josiah, king of Judah, this word came from Yahweh: 2"Yahweh says: 'Stand in the court of Yahweh's house, and speak to all the cities of Judah which come to worship in Yahweh's house, all the words that I command you to speak to them. Don't omit a word. 3 It may be they will listen, and every man turn from his evil way, that I may relent from the evil which I intend to do to them because of the evil of their doings.'" 4 You shall tell them, "Yahweh says: 'If you will not listen to me, to walk in my law which I have set before you, 5 to listen to the words of my servants the prophets whom I send to you, even rising up early and sending them—but you have not listened— 6 then I will make this house like Shiloh, and will make this city a curse to all the nations of the earth.'" 7 The priests and the prophets and all the people heard Jeremiah speaking these words in Yahweh's house. 8 When Jeremiah had finished

speaking all that Yahweh had commanded him to speak to all the people, the priests and the prophets and all the people seized him, saying, "You shall surely die! 9 Why have you prophesied in Yahweh's name, saying, 'This house will be like Shiloh, and this city will be desolate, without inhabitant'?" All the people were crowded around Jeremiah in Yahweh's house. 10 When the princes of Judah heard these things, they came up from the king's house to Yahweh's house; and they sat in the entry of the new gate of Yahweh's house. 11 Then the priests and the prophets spoke to the princes and to all the people, saying, "This man is worthy of death, for he has prophesied against this city, as you have heard with your ears." 12 Then Jeremiah spoke to all the princes and to all the people, saying, "Yahweh sent me to prophesy against this house and against this city all the words that you have heard. 13 Now therefore amend your ways and your doings, and obey Yahweh your God's voice; then Yahweh will relent from the evil that he has pronounced against you. 14 But as for me, behold, I am in your hand. Do with me what is good and right in your eyes. 15 Only know for certain that if you put me to death, you will bring innocent blood on yourselves, on this city, and on its inhabitants; for in truth Yahweh has sent me to you to speak all these words in your ears." 16 Then the princes and all the people said to the priests and to the prophets: "This man is not worthy of death; for he has spoken to us in the name of Yahweh our God." 17 Then certain of the elders of the land rose up, and spoke to all the assembly of the people, saying, 18"Micah the Morashtite prophesied in the days of Hezekiah king of Judah; and he spoke to all the people of Judah, saying, 'Yahweh of Armies says: "'Zion will be plowed as a field, and Jerusalem will become heaps, and the mountain of the house as the high places of a forest.' 19 Did Hezekiah king of Judah and all Judah put him to death? Didn't he fear Yahweh, and entreat the favor of Yahweh, and Yahweh relented of the disaster which he had pronounced against them? We would commit great evil against our own souls that way!" 20 There was also a man who prophesied in Yahweh's name, Uriah the son of Shemaiah of Kiriath Jearim; and he prophesied against this city and against this land according to all the words of Jeremiah. 21 When Jehoiakim the king, with all his mighty men and all the princes heard his words, the king sought to put him to death; but when Uriah heard it, he was afraid, and fled, and went into Egypt. 22 Then Jehoiakim the king sent Elnathan the son of Achbor and certain men with him into Egypt. 23 They fetched Uriah out of Egypt and brought him to Jehoiakim the king, who killed him with the sword and cast his dead body into the graves of the common people. 24 But the hand of Ahikam the son of Shaphan was with Jeremiah, so that they didn't give him into the hand of the people to put him to death.

27

1 In the beginning of the reign of Jehoiakim the son of Josiah, king of Judah, this word came to Jeremiah from Yahweh, saying, 2 Yahweh says to me: "Make bonds and bars, and put them on your neck. 3 Then send them to the king of Edom, to the king of Moab, to the king of the children of Ammon, to the king of Tyre, and to the king of Sidon, by the hand of the messengers who come to Jerusalem to Zedekiah king of Judah. 4 Give them a command to their masters, saying, 'Yahweh of Armies, the God of Israel says, "You shall tell your masters: 5'I have made the earth, the men, and the animals that are on the surface of the earth by my great power and by my outstretched arm. I give it to whom it seems right to me. 6 Now I have given all these lands into the hand of Nebuchadnezzar the king of Babylon, my servant. I have also given the animals of the field to him to serve him. 7 All the nations will serve him, his son, and his son's son, until the time of his own land comes. Then many nations and great kings will make him their bondservant. 8""It will happen that I will punish the nation and the kingdom which will not serve the same Nebuchadnezzar king of Babylon, and that will not put their neck under the yoke of the king of Babylon,' says Yahweh, 'with the sword, with famine, and with pestilence, until I have consumed them by his hand. 9 But as for you, don't listen to your prophets, to your diviners, to your dreams, to your soothsayers, or to your sorcerers, who speak to you, saying, "You shall not serve the king of Babylon;" 10 for they prophesy a lie to you, to remove you far from your land, so that I would drive you out, and you would perish. 11 But the nation that brings their neck under the yoke of the king of Babylon and serves him, that nation I will let remain in their own land,' says Yahweh; 'and they will till it and dwell in it.'"" 12 I spoke to Zedekiah king of Judah according to all these words, saying, "Bring your necks under the yoke of the king of Babylon, and serve him and his people, and live. 13 Why will you die, you and your people, by the sword, by the famine, and by the pestilence, as Yahweh has spoken concerning the nation that will not serve the king of Babylon? 14 Don't listen to the words of the prophets who speak to you, saying, 'You shall not serve the king of Babylon;' for they prophesy a lie to you. 15 For I have not sent them," says Yahweh, "but they prophesy falsely in my name; that I may drive you out, and that you may perish, you, and the

prophets who prophesy to you." 16 Also I spoke to the priests and to all this people, saying, Yahweh says, "Don't listen to the words of your prophets who prophesy to you, saying, 'Behold, the vessels of Yahweh's house will now shortly be brought again from Babylon;' for they prophesy a lie to you. 17 Don't listen to them. Serve the king of Babylon, and live. Why should this city become a desolation? 18 But if they are prophets, and if Yahweh's word is with them, let them now make intercession to Yahweh of Armies, that the vessels which are left in Yahweh's house, in the house of the king of Judah, and at Jerusalem, don't go to Babylon. 19 For Yahweh of Armies says concerning the pillars, concerning the sea, concerning the bases, and concerning the rest of the vessels that are left in this city, 20 which Nebuchadnezzar king of Babylon didn't take when he carried away captive Jeconiah the son of Jehoiakim, king of Judah, from Jerusalem to Babylon, and all the nobles of Judah and Jerusalem— 21 yes, Yahweh of Armies, the God of Israel, says concerning the vessels that are left in Yahweh's house, and in the house of the king of Judah, and at Jerusalem: 22 'They will be carried to Babylon, and there they will be, until the day that I visit them,' says Yahweh; 'then I will bring them up, and restore them to this place.'"

28

1 That same year, in the beginning of the reign of Zedekiah king of Judah, in the fourth year, in the fifth month, Hananiah the son of Azzur, the prophet, who was of Gibeon, spoke to me in Yahweh's house, in the presence of the priests and of all the people, saying, 2"Yahweh of Armies, the God of Israel, says, 'I have broken the yoke of the king of Babylon. 3 Within two full years I will bring again into this place all the vessels of Yahweh's house that Nebuchadnezzar king of Babylon took away from this place and carried to Babylon. 4 I will bring again to this place Jeconiah the son of Jehoiakim, king of Judah, with all the captives of Judah, who went to Babylon,' says Yahweh; 'for I will break the yoke of the king of Babylon.'" 5 Then the prophet Jeremiah said to the prophet Hananiah in the presence of the priests, and in the presence of all the people who stood in Yahweh's house, 6 even the prophet Jeremiah said, "Amen! May Yahweh do so. May Yahweh perform your words which you have prophesied, to bring again the vessels of Yahweh's house, and all those who are captives, from Babylon to this place. 7 Nevertheless listen now to this word that I speak in your ears, and in the ears of all the people: 8 The prophets who have been before me and before you of old prophesied against many countries, and against great kingdoms, of war,

of evil, and of pestilence. 9 As for the prophet who prophesies of peace, when the word of the prophet happens, then the prophet will be known, that Yahweh has truly sent him." 10 Then Hananiah the prophet took the bar from off the prophet Jeremiah's neck, and broke it. 11 Hananiah spoke in the presence of all the people, saying, "Yahweh says: 'Even so I will break the yoke of Nebuchadnezzar king of Babylon from off the neck of all the nations within two full years.'" Then the prophet Jeremiah went his way. 12 Then Yahweh's word came to Jeremiah, after Hananiah the prophet had broken the bar from off the neck of the prophet Jeremiah, saying, 13"Go, and tell Hananiah, saying, 'Yahweh says, "You have broken the bars of wood, but you have made in their place bars of iron." 14 For Yahweh of Armies, the God of Israel says, "I have put a yoke of iron on the neck of all these nations, that they may serve Nebuchadnezzar king of Babylon; and they will serve him. I have also given him the animals of the field."'" 15 Then the prophet Jeremiah said to Hananiah the prophet, "Listen, Hananiah! Yahweh has not sent you, but you make this people trust in a lie. 16 Therefore Yahweh says, 'Behold, I will send you away from off the surface of the earth. This year you will die, because you have spoken rebellion against Yahweh.'" 17 So Hananiah the prophet died the same year in the seventh month. **29** 1 Now these are the words of the letter that Jeremiah the prophet sent from Jerusalem to the residue of the elders of the captivity, and to the priests, to the prophets, and to all the people whom Nebuchadnezzar had carried away captive from Jerusalem to Babylon, 2(after Jeconiah the king, the queen mother, the eunuchs, the princes of Judah and Jerusalem, the craftsmen, and the smiths had departed from Jerusalem), 3 by the hand of Elasah the son of Shaphan and Gemariah the son of Hilkiah, (whom Zedekiah king of Judah sent to Babylon to Nebuchadnezzar king of Babylon). It said: 4 Yahweh of Armies, the God of Israel, says to all the captives whom I have caused to be carried away captive from Jerusalem to Babylon: 5"Build houses and dwell in them. Plant gardens and eat their fruit. 6 Take wives and father sons and daughters. Take wives for your sons, and give your daughters to husbands, that they may bear sons and daughters. Multiply there, and don't be diminished. 7 Seek the peace of the city where I have caused you to be carried away captive, and pray to Yahweh for it; for in its peace you will have peace." 8 For Yahweh of Armies, the God of Israel says: "Don't let your prophets who are among you and your diviners deceive you. Don't listen to your dreams which you cause to be dreamed. 9

For they prophesy falsely to you in my name. I have not sent them," says Yahweh. 10 For Yahweh says, "After seventy years are accomplished for Babylon, I will visit you and perform my good word toward you, in causing you to return to this place. 11 For I know the thoughts that I think toward you," says Yahweh, "thoughts of peace, and not of evil, to give you hope and a future. 12 You shall call on me, and you shall go and pray to me, and I will listen to you. 13 You shall seek me and find me, when you search for me with all your heart. 14 I will be found by you," says Yahweh, "and I will turn again your captivity, and I will gather you from all the nations, and from all the places where I have driven you, says Yahweh. I will bring you again to the place from where I caused you to be carried away captive." 15 Because you have said, "Yahweh has raised us up prophets in Babylon," 16 Yahweh says concerning the king who sits on David's throne, and concerning all the people who dwell in this city, your brothers who haven't gone with you into captivity, 17 Yahweh of Armies says: "Behold, I will send on them the sword, the famine, and the pestilence, and will make them like rotten figs that can't be eaten, they are so bad. 18 I will pursue after them with the sword, with the famine, and with the pestilence, and will deliver them to be tossed back and forth among all the kingdoms of the earth, to be an object of horror, an astonishment, a hissing, and a reproach among all the nations where I have driven them, 19 because they have not listened to my words," says Yahweh, "with which I sent to them my servants the prophets, rising up early and sending them; but you would not hear," says Yahweh. 20 Hear therefore Yahweh's word, all you captives whom I have sent away from Jerusalem to Babylon. 21 Yahweh of Armies, the God of Israel, says concerning Ahab the son of Kolaiah, and concerning Zedekiah the son of Maaseiah, who prophesy a lie to you in my name: "Behold, I will deliver them into the hand of Nebuchadnezzar king of Babylon; and he will kill them before your eyes. 22 A curse will be taken up about them by all the captives of Judah who are in Babylon, saying, 'Yahweh make you like Zedekiah and like Ahab, whom the king of Babylon roasted in the fire;' 23 because they have done foolish things in Israel, and have committed adultery with their neighbors' wives, and have spoken words in my name falsely, which I didn't command them. I am he who knows, and am witness," says Yahweh. 24 Concerning Shemaiah the Nehelamite you shall speak, saying, 25"Yahweh of Armies, the God of Israel, says, 'Because you have sent letters in your own name to all the people who are at Jerusalem, and to Zephaniah the son of Maaseiah, the priest, and to all the priests, saying, 26"Yahweh has made you priest in the place of Jehoiada the priest, that there may be officers in Yahweh's house, for every man who is crazy and makes himself a prophet, that you should put him in the stocks and in shackles. 27 Now therefore, why have you not rebuked Jeremiah of Anathoth, who makes himself a prophet to you, 28 because he has sent to us in Babylon, saying, The captivity is long. Build houses, and dwell in them. Plant gardens, and eat their fruit?"'" 29 Zephaniah the priest read this letter in the hearing of Jeremiah the prophet. 30 Then Yahweh's word came to Jeremiah, saying, 31"Send to all of the captives, saying, 'Yahweh says concerning Shemaiah the Nehelamite: "Because Shemaiah has prophesied to you, and I didn't send him, and he has caused you to trust in a lie," 32 therefore Yahweh says, "Behold, I will punish Shemaiah the Nehelamite and his offspring. He will not have a man to dwell among this people. He won't see the good that I will do to my people," says Yahweh, "because he has spoken rebellion against Yahweh."'"

30

1 The word that came to Jeremiah from Yahweh, saying, 2"Yahweh, the God of Israel, says, 'Write all the words that I have spoken to you in a book. 3 For, behold, the days come,' says Yahweh, 'that I will reverse the captivity of my people Israel and Judah,' says Yahweh. 'I will cause them to return to the land that I gave to their fathers, and they will possess it.'" 4 These are the words that Yahweh spoke concerning Israel and concerning Judah. 5 For Yahweh says: "We have heard a voice of trembling; a voice of fear, and not of peace. 6 Ask now, and see whether a man travails with child. Why do I see every man with his hands on his waist, as a woman in travail, and all faces are turned pale? 7 Alas, for that day is great, so that none is like it! It is even the time of Jacob's trouble; but he will be saved out of it. 8 It will come to pass in that day, says Yahweh of Armies, that I will break his yoke from off your neck, and will burst your bonds. Strangers will no more make them their bondservants; 9 but they will serve Yahweh their God, and David their king, whom I will raise up to them. 10 Therefore don't be afraid, O Jacob my servant, says Yahweh. Don't be dismayed, Israel. For, behold, I will save you from afar, and save your offspring from the land of their captivity. Jacob will return, and will be quiet and at ease. No one will make him afraid. 11 For I am with you, says Yahweh, to save you; for I will make a full end of all the nations where I have scattered you, but I will not make a full end of you; but I will correct you in measure, and will in no way leave you unpunished." 12

For Yahweh says, "Your hurt is incurable. Your wound is grievous. 13 There is no one to plead your cause, that you may be bound up. You have no healing medicines. 14 All your lovers have forgotten you. They don't seek you. For I have wounded you with the wound of an enemy, with the chastisement of a cruel one, for the greatness of your iniquity, because your sins were increased. 15 Why do you cry over your injury? Your pain is incurable. For the greatness of your iniquity, because your sins have increased, I have done these things to you. 16 Therefore all those who devour you will be devoured. All your adversaries, everyone of them, will go into captivity. Those who plunder you will be plunder. I will make all who prey on you become prey. 17 For I will restore health to you, and I will heal you of your wounds," says Yahweh, "because they have called you an outcast, saying, 'It is Zion, whom no man seeks after.'" 18 Yahweh says: "Behold, I will reverse the captivity of Jacob's tents, and have compassion on his dwelling places. The city will be built on its own hill, and the palace will be inhabited in its own place. 19 Thanksgiving will proceed out of them with the voice of those who make merry. I will multiply them, and they will not be few; I will also glorify them, and they will not be small. 20 Their children also will be as before, and their congregation will be established before me. I will punish all who oppress them. 21 Their prince will be one of them, and their ruler will proceed from among them. I will cause him to draw near, and he will approach me; for who is he who has had boldness to approach me?" says Yahweh. 22 "You shall be my people, and I will be your God. 23 Behold, Yahweh's storm, his wrath, has gone out, a sweeping storm; it will burst on the head of the wicked. 24 The fierce anger of Yahweh will not return until he has accomplished, and until he has performed the intentions of his heart. In the latter days you will understand it."

31

1 "At that time," says Yahweh, "I will be the God of all the families of Israel, and they will be my people." 2 Yahweh says, "The people who survive the sword found favor in the wilderness; even Israel, when I went to cause him to rest." 3 Yahweh appeared of old to me, saying, "Yes, I have loved you with an everlasting love. Therefore I have drawn you with loving kindness. 4 I will build you again, and you will be built, O virgin of Israel. You will again be adorned with your tambourines, and will go out in the dances of those who make merry. 5 Again you will plant vineyards on the mountains of Samaria. The planters will plant, and will enjoy its fruit. 6 For there will be a day that

the watchmen on the hills of Ephraim cry, 'Arise! Let's go up to Zion to Yahweh our God.'" 7 For Yahweh says, "Sing with gladness for Jacob, and shout for the chief of the nations. Publish, praise, and say, 'Yahweh, save your people, the remnant of Israel!' 8 Behold, I will bring them from the north country, and gather them from the uttermost parts of the earth, along with the blind and the lame, the woman with child and her who travails with child together. They will return as a great company. 9 They will come with weeping. I will lead them with petitions. I will cause them to walk by rivers of waters, in a straight way in which they won't stumble; for I am a father to Israel. Ephraim is my firstborn. 10 "Hear Yahweh's word, you nations, and declare it in the distant islands. Say, 'He who scattered Israel will gather him, and keep him, as a shepherd does his flock.' 11 For Yahweh has ransomed Jacob, and redeemed him from the hand of him who was stronger than he. 12 They will come and sing in the height of Zion, and will flow to the goodness of Yahweh, to the grain, to the new wine, to the oil, and to the young of the flock and of the herd. Their soul will be as a watered garden. They will not sorrow any more at all. 13 Then the virgin will rejoice in the dance, the young men and the old together; for I will turn their mourning into joy, and will comfort them, and make them rejoice from their sorrow. 14 I will satiate the soul of the priests with fatness, and my people will be satisfied with my goodness," says Yahweh. 15 Yahweh says: "A voice is heard in Ramah, lamentation and bitter weeping, Rachel weeping for her children. She refuses to be comforted for her children, because they are no more." 16 Yahweh says: "Refrain your voice from weeping, and your eyes from tears, for your work will be rewarded," says Yahweh. "They will come again from the land of the enemy. 17 There is hope for your latter end," says Yahweh. "Your children will come again to their own territory. 18 "I have surely heard Ephraim grieving thus, 'You have chastised me, and I was chastised, as an untrained calf. Turn me, and I will be turned, for you are Yahweh my God. 19 Surely after that I was turned. I repented. After that I was instructed. I struck my thigh. I was ashamed, yes, even confounded, because I bore the reproach of my youth.' 20 Is Ephraim my dear son? Is he a darling child? For as often as I speak against him, I still earnestly remember him. Therefore my heart yearns for him. I will surely have mercy on him," says Yahweh. 21 "Set up road signs. Make guideposts. Set your heart toward the highway, even the way by which you went. Turn again, virgin of Israel. Turn again to these your cities. 22 How long will you go here and there, you backsliding daughter? For Yahweh has created a new thing in the earth: a woman will encompass a man." 23 Yahweh of Armies, the God of Israel, says: "Yet again they will use this speech in the land of Judah and in its cities, when I reverse their captivity: 'Yahweh bless you, habitation of righteousness, mountain of holiness.' 24 Judah and all its cities will dwell therein together, the farmers, and those who go about with flocks. 25 For I have satiated the weary soul, and I have replenished every sorrowful soul." 26 On this I awakened, and saw; and my sleep was sweet to me. 27"Behold, the days come," says Yahweh, "that I will sow the house of Israel and the house of Judah with the seed of man and with the seed of animal. 28 It will happen that, like as I have watched over them to pluck up and to break down and to overthrow and to destroy and to afflict, so I will watch over them to build and to plant," says Yahweh. 29"In those days they will say no more, "'The fathers have eaten sour grapes, and the children's teeth are set on edge.' 30 But everyone will die for his own iniquity. Every man who eats the sour grapes, his teeth will be set on edge. 31"Behold, the days come," says Yahweh, "that I will make a new covenant with the house of Israel, and with the house of Judah, 32 not according to the covenant that I made with their fathers in the day that I took them by the hand to bring them out of the land of Egypt, which covenant of mine they broke, although I was a husband to them," says Yahweh. 33"But this is the covenant that I will make with the house of Israel after those days," says Yahweh: "I will put my law in their inward parts, and I will write it in their heart. I will be their God, and they shall be my people. 34 They will no longer each teach his neighbor, and every man teach his brother, saying, 'Know Yahweh;' for they will all know me, from their least to their greatest," says Yahweh, "for I will forgive their iniquity, and I will remember their sin no more." 35 Yahweh, who gives the sun for a light by day, and the ordinances of the moon and of the stars for a light by night, who stirs up the sea, so that its waves roar— Yahweh of Armies is his name, says: 36"If these ordinances depart from before me," says Yahweh, "then the offspring of Israel also will cease from being a nation before me forever." 37 Yahweh says: "If heaven above can be measured, and the foundations of the earth searched out beneath, then I will also cast off all the offspring of Israel for all that they have done," says Yahweh. 38"Behold, the days come," says Yahweh, "that the city will be built to Yahweh from the tower of Hananel to the gate of the corner. 39 The measuring line will go out further straight onward to the hill Gareb, and will turn toward Goah. 40 The whole valley of the dead bodies and of the ashes, and all the fields to the brook Kidron, to the corner of the horse gate toward the east, will be holy to Yahweh. It will not be plucked up or thrown down any more forever."

32

1 This is the word that came to Jeremiah from Yahweh in the tenth year of Zedekiah king of Judah, which was the eighteenth year of Nebuchadnezzar. 2 Now at that time the king of Babylon's army was besieging Jerusalem. Jeremiah the prophet was shut up in the court of the guard, which was in the king of Judah's house. 3 For Zedekiah king of Judah had shut him up, saying, "Why do you prophesy, and say, 'Yahweh says, "Behold, I will give this city into the hand of the king of Babylon, and he will take it; 4 and Zedekiah king of Judah won't escape out of the hand of the Chaldeans, but will surely be delivered into the hand of the king of Babylon, and will speak with him mouth to mouth, and his eyes will see his eyes; 5 and he will bring Zedekiah to Babylon, and he will be there until I visit him," says Yahweh, "though you fight with the Chaldeans, you will not prosper"'?" 6 Jeremiah said, "Yahweh's word came to me, saying, 7'Behold, Hanamel the son of Shallum your uncle will come to you, saying, "Buy my field that is in Anathoth; for the right of redemption is yours to buy it."'" 8"So Hanamel my uncle's son came to me in the court of the guard according to Yahweh's word, and said to me, 'Please buy my field that is in Anathoth, which is in the land of Benjamin; for the right of inheritance is yours, and the redemption is yours. Buy it for yourself.' "Then I knew that this was Yahweh's word. 9 I bought the field that was in Anathoth of Hanamel my uncle's son, and weighed him the money, even seventeen shekels of silver. 10 I signed the deed, sealed it, called witnesses, and weighed the money in the balances to him. 11 So I took the deed of the purchase, both that which was sealed, containing the terms and conditions, and that which was open; 12 and I delivered the deed of the purchase to Baruch the son of Neriah, the son of Mahseiah, in the presence of Hanamel my uncle's son, and in the presence of the witnesses who signed the deed of the purchase, before all the Jews who sat in the court of the guard. 13"I commanded Baruch before them, saying, 14 Yahweh of Armies, the God of Israel, says: 'Take these deeds, this deed of the purchase which is sealed, and this deed which is open, and put them in an earthen vessel, that they may last many days.' 15 For Yahweh of Armies, the God of Israel says: 'Houses and fields and vineyards will yet again be bought in this land.' 16 Now after I had delivered the deed of the purchase to Baruch the son of Neriah, I prayed to Yahweh, saying, 17"Ah Lord Yahweh! Behold, you have made the heavens

and the earth by your great power and by your outstretched arm. There is nothing too hard for you. 18 You show loving kindness to thousands, and repay the iniquity of the fathers into the bosom of their children after them. The great, the mighty God, Yahweh of Armies is your name: 19 great in counsel, and mighty in work; whose eyes are open to all the ways of the children of men, to give everyone according to his ways, and according to the fruit of his doings; 20 who performed signs and wonders in the land of Egypt, even to this day, both in Israel and among other men; and made yourself a name, as it is today; 21 and brought your people Israel out of the land of Egypt with signs, with wonders, with a strong hand, with an outstretched arm, and with great terror; 22 and gave them this land, which you swore to their fathers to give them, a land flowing with milk and honey. 23 They came in and possessed it, but they didn't obey your voice and didn't walk in your law. They have done nothing of all that you commanded them to do. Therefore you have caused all this evil to come upon them. 24"Behold, siege ramps have been built against the city to take it. The city is given into the hand of the Chaldeans who fight against it, because of the sword, of the famine, and of the pestilence. What you have spoken has happened. Behold, you see it. 25 You have said to me, Lord Yahweh, 'Buy the field for money, and call witnesses;' whereas the city is given into the hand of the Chaldeans." 26 Then Yahweh's word came to Jeremiah, saying, 27"Behold, I am Yahweh, the God of all flesh. Is there anything too hard for me? 28 Therefore Yahweh says: Behold, I will give this city into the hand of the Chaldeans, and into the hand of Nebuchadnezzar king of Babylon, and he will take it. 29 The Chaldeans, who fight against this city, will come and set this city on fire, and burn it with the houses on whose roofs they have offered incense to Baal, and poured out drink offerings to other gods, to provoke me to anger. 30"For the children of Israel and the children of Judah have done only that which was evil in my sight from their youth; for the children of Israel have only provoked me to anger with the work of their hands, says Yahweh. 31 For this city has been to me a provocation of my anger and of my wrath from the day that they built it even to this day, so that I should remove it from before my face, 32 because of all the evil of the children of Israel and of the children of Judah, which they have done to provoke me to anger—they, their kings, their princes, their priests, their prophets, the men of Judah, and the inhabitants of Jerusalem. 33 They have turned their backs to me, and not their faces. Although I taught them, rising up early and teaching them, yet they have not listened to receive instruction. 34 But they set their abominations in the house which is called by my name, to defile it. 35 They built the high places of Baal, which are in the valley of the son of Hinnom, to cause their sons and their daughters to pass through fire to Molech, which I didn't command them. It didn't even come into my mind, that they should do this abomination, to cause Judah to sin." 36 Now therefore Yahweh, the God of Israel, says concerning this city, about which you say, "It is given into the hand of the king of Babylon by the sword, by the famine, and by the pestilence:" 37"Behold, I will gather them out of all the countries where I have driven them in my anger, and in my wrath, and in great indignation; and I will bring them again to this place. I will cause them to dwell safely. 38 Then they will be my people, and I will be their God. 39 I will give them one heart and one way, that they may fear me forever, for their good and the good of their children after them. 40 I will make an everlasting covenant with them, that I will not turn away from following them, to do them good. I will put my fear in their hearts, that they may not depart from me. 41 Yes, I will rejoice over them to do them good, and I will plant them in this land assuredly with my whole heart and with my whole soul." 42 For Yahweh says: "Just as I have brought all this great evil on this people, so I will bring on them all the good that I have promised them. 43 Fields will be bought in this land, about which you say, 'It is desolate, without man or animal. It is given into the hand of the Chaldeans.' 44 Men will buy fields for money, sign the deeds, seal them, and call witnesses, in the land of Benjamin, and in the places around Jerusalem, in the cities of Judah, in the cities of the hill country, in the cities of the lowland, and in the cities of the South; for I will cause their captivity to be reversed," says Yahweh.

33

1 Moreover Yahweh's word came to Jeremiah the second time, while he was still locked up in the court of the guard, saying, 2"Yahweh who does it, Yahweh who forms it to establish it—Yahweh is his name, says: 3'Call to me, and I will answer you, and will show you great and difficult things, which you don't know.' 4 For Yahweh, the God of Israel, says concerning the houses of this city and concerning the houses of the kings of Judah, which are broken down to make a defense against the mounds and against the sword: 5'While men come to fight with the Chaldeans, and to fill them with the dead bodies of men, whom I have killed in my anger and in my wrath, and for all whose wickedness I have hidden my face from this city, 6 behold, I will bring it health and healing, and I will cure them; and I will reveal to them

abundance of peace and truth. 7 I will restore the fortunes of Judah and Israel, and will build them as at the first. 8 I will cleanse them from all their iniquity by which they have sinned against me. I will pardon all their iniquities by which they have sinned against me and by which they have transgressed against me. 9 This city will be to me for a name of joy, for praise, and for glory, before all the nations of the earth, which will hear all the good that I do to them, and will fear and tremble for all the good and for all the peace that I provide to it.'" 10 Yahweh says: "Yet again there will be heard in this place, about which you say, 'It is waste, without man and without animal, even in the cities of Judah, and in the streets of Jerusalem, that are desolate, without man and without inhabitant and without animal,' 11 the voice of joy and the voice of gladness, the voice of the bridegroom and the voice of the bride, the voice of those who say, 'Give thanks to Yahweh of Armies, for Yahweh is good, for his loving kindness endures forever;' who bring thanksgiving into Yahweh's house. For I will cause the captivity of the land to be reversed as at the first," says Yahweh. 12 Yahweh of Armies says: "Yet again there will be in this place, which is waste, without man and without animal, and in all its cities, a habitation of shepherds causing their flocks to lie down. 13 In the cities of the hill country, in the cities of the lowland, in the cities of the South, in the land of Benjamin, in the places around Jerusalem, and in the cities of Judah, the flocks will again pass under the hands of him who counts them," says Yahweh. 14"Behold, the days come," says Yahweh, "that I will perform that good word which I have spoken concerning the house of Israel and concerning the house of Judah. 15"In those days and at that time, I will cause a Branch of righteousness to grow up to David. He will execute justice and righteousness in the land. 16 In those days Judah will be saved, and Jerusalem will dwell safely. This is the name by which she will be called: Yahweh our righteousness." 17 For Yahweh says: "David will never lack a man to sit on the throne of the house of Israel. 18 The Levitical priests won't lack a man before me to offer burnt offerings, to burn meal offerings, and to do sacrifice continually." 19 Yahweh's word came to Jeremiah, saying, 20"Yahweh says: 'If you can break my covenant of the day and my covenant of the night, so that there will not be day and night in their time, 21 then my covenant could also be broken with David my servant, that he won't have a son to reign on his throne; and with the Levitical priests, my ministers. 22 As the army of the sky can't be counted, and the sand of the sea can't be measured, so I will multiply the offspring of David my servant and the Levites who minister to me.'" 23 Yahweh's word came to Jeremiah, saying, 24"Don't consider what this people has spoken, saying, 'Has Yahweh cast off the two families which he chose?' Thus they despise my people, that they should be no more a nation before them." 25 Yahweh says: "If my covenant of day and night fails, if I have not appointed the ordinances of heaven and earth, 26 then I will also cast away the offspring of Jacob, and of David my servant, so that I will not take of his offspring to be rulers over the offspring of Abraham, Isaac, and Jacob; for I will cause their captivity to be reversed and will have mercy on them."

34

1 The word which came to Jeremiah from Yahweh, when Nebuchadnezzar king of Babylon, with all his army, all the kingdoms of the earth that were under his dominion, and all the peoples, were fighting against Jerusalem and against all its cities, saying: 2"Yahweh, the God of Israel, says, 'Go, and speak to Zedekiah king of Judah, and tell him, Yahweh says, "Behold, I will give this city into the hand of the king of Babylon and he will burn it with fire. 3 You won't escape out of his hand, but will surely be taken and delivered into his hand. Your eyes will see the eyes of the king of Babylon, and he will speak with you mouth to mouth. You will go to Babylon."' 4"Yet hear Yahweh's word, O Zedekiah king of Judah. Yahweh says concerning you, 'You won't die by the sword. 5 You will die in peace; and with the burnings of your fathers, the former kings who were before you, so they will make a burning for you. They will lament you, saying, "Ah Lord!" for I have spoken the word,' says Yahweh." 6 Then Jeremiah the prophet spoke all these words to Zedekiah king of Judah in Jerusalem, 7 when the king of Babylon's army was fighting against Jerusalem and against all the cities of Judah that were left, against Lachish and against Azekah; for these alone remained of the cities of Judah as fortified cities. 8 The word came to Jeremiah from Yahweh, after King Zedekiah had made a covenant with all the people who were at Jerusalem, to proclaim liberty to them, 9 that every man should let his male servant, and every man his female servant, who is a Hebrew or a Hebrewess, go free, that no one should make bondservants of them, of a Jew his brother. 10 All the princes and all the people obeyed who had entered into the covenant, that everyone should let his male servant and everyone his female servant go free, that no one should make bondservants of them any more. They obeyed and let them go, 11 but afterwards they turned, and caused the servants and the handmaids whom they had let go free to return, and brought them into subjection for servants and for handmaids. 12 Therefore

Yahweh's word came to Jeremiah from Yahweh, saying, 13"Yahweh, the God of Israel, says: 'I made a covenant with your fathers in the day that I brought them out of the land of Egypt, out of the house of bondage, saying: 14 At the end of seven years, every man of you shall release his brother who is a Hebrew, who has been sold to you, and has served you six years. You shall let him go free from you. But your fathers didn't listen to me, and didn't incline their ear. 15 You had now turned, and had done that which is right in my eyes, in every man proclaiming liberty to his neighbor. You had made a covenant before me in the house which is called by my name; 16 but you turned and profaned my name, and every man caused his servant and every man his handmaid, whom you had let go free at their pleasure, to return. You brought them into subjection, to be to you for servants and for handmaids.'"

17 Therefore Yahweh says: "You have not listened to me, to proclaim liberty, every man to his brother, and every man to his neighbor. Behold, I proclaim to you a liberty," says Yahweh, "to the sword, to the pestilence, and to the famine. I will make you be tossed back and forth among all the kingdoms of the earth. 18 I will give the men who have transgressed my covenant, who have not performed the words of the covenant which they made before me when they cut the calf in two and passed between its parts: 19 the princes of Judah, the princes of Jerusalem, the eunuchs, the priests, and all the people of the land, who passed between the parts of the calf. 20 I will even give them into the hand of their enemies and into the hand of those who seek their life. Their dead bodies will be food for the birds of the sky and for the animals of the earth. 21"I will give Zedekiah king of Judah and his princes into the hands of their enemies, into the hands of those who seek their life and into the hands of the king of Babylon's army, who has gone away from you. 22 Behold, I will command," says Yahweh, "and cause them to return to this city. They will fight against it, take it, and burn it with fire. I will make the cities of Judah a desolation, without inhabitant."

35

1 The word which came to Jeremiah from Yahweh in the days of Jehoiakim the son of Josiah, king of Judah, saying, 2"Go to the house of the Rechabites, and speak to them, and bring them into Yahweh's house, into one of the rooms, and give them wine to drink." 3 Then I took Jaazaniah the son of Jeremiah, the son of Habazziniah, with his brothers, all his sons, and the whole house of the Rechabites; 4 and I brought them into Yahweh's house, into the room of the sons of Hanan the son of Igdaliah, the man of God,

which was by the room of the princes, which was above the room of Maaseiah the son of Shallum, the keeper of the threshold. 5 I set before the sons of the house of the Rechabites bowls full of wine, and cups; and I said to them, "Drink wine!" 6 But they said, "We will drink no wine; for Jonadab the son of Rechab, our father, commanded us, saying, 'You shall drink no wine, neither you nor your children, forever. 7 You shall not build a house, sow seed, plant a vineyard, or have any; but all your days you shall dwell in tents, that you may live many days in the land in which you live as nomads.' 8 We have obeyed the voice of Jonadab the son of Rechab, our father, in all that he commanded us, to drink no wine all our days, we, our wives, our sons, or our daughters; 9 and not to build houses for ourselves to dwell in. We have no vineyard, field, or seed; 10 but we have lived in tents, and have obeyed, and done according to all that Jonadab our father commanded us. 11 But when Nebuchadnezzar king of Babylon came up into the land, we said, 'Come! Let's go to Jerusalem for fear of the army of the Chaldeans, and for fear of the army of the Syrians; so we will dwell at Jerusalem.'" 12 Then Yahweh's word came to Jeremiah, saying, 13"Yahweh of Armies, the God of Israel, says: 'Go and tell the men of Judah and the inhabitants of Jerusalem, "Will you not receive instruction to listen to my words?" says Yahweh. 14"The words of Jonadab the son of Rechab that he commanded his sons, not to drink wine, are performed; and to this day they drink none, for they obey their father's commandment; but I have spoken to you, rising up early and speaking, and you have not listened to me. 15 I have sent also to you all my servants the prophets, rising up early and sending them, saying, 'Every one of you must return now from his evil way, amend your doings, and don't go after other gods to serve them. Then you will dwell in the land which I have given to you and to your fathers;' but you have not inclined your ear, nor listened to me. 16 The sons of Jonadab the son of Rechab have performed the commandment of their father which he commanded them, but this people has not listened to me."' 17"Therefore Yahweh, the God of Armies, the God of Israel, says: 'Behold, I will bring on Judah and on all the inhabitants of Jerusalem all the evil that I have pronounced against them, because I have spoken to them, but they have not heard; and I have called to them, but they have not answered.'" 18 Jeremiah said to the house of the Rechabites, "Yahweh of Armies, the God of Israel, says: 'Because you have obeyed the commandment of Jonadab your father, and kept all his precepts, and done according to all that he commanded you,' 19 therefore Yahweh of Armies, the

God of Israel, says: 'Jonadab the son of Rechab will not lack a man to stand before me forever.'"

36

1 In the fourth year of Jehoiakim the son of Josiah, king of Judah, this word came to Jeremiah from Yahweh, saying, 2"Take a scroll of a book, and write in it all the words that I have spoken to you against Israel, against Judah, and against all the nations, from the day I spoke to you, from the days of Josiah even to this day. 3 It may be that the house of Judah will hear all the evil which I intend to do to them, that they may each return from his evil way; that I may forgive their iniquity and their sin." 4 Then Jeremiah called Baruch the son of Neriah; and Baruch wrote from the mouth of Jeremiah all Yahweh's words, which he had spoken to him, on a scroll of a book. 5 Jeremiah commanded Baruch, saying, "I am restricted. I can't go into Yahweh's house. 6 Therefore you go, and read from the scroll which you have written from my mouth, Yahweh's words, in the ears of the people in Yahweh's house on the fast day. Also you shall read them in the ears of all Judah who come out of their cities. 7 It may be they will present their supplication before Yahweh, and will each return from his evil way; for Yahweh has pronounced great anger and wrath against this people." 8 Baruch the son of Neriah did according to all that Jeremiah the prophet commanded him, reading in the book Yahweh's words in Yahweh's house. 9 Now in the fifth year of Jehoiakim the son of Josiah, king of Judah, in the ninth month, all the people in Jerusalem and all the people who came from the cities of Judah to Jerusalem, proclaimed a fast before Yahweh. 10 Then Baruch read the words of Jeremiah from the book in Yahweh's house, in the room of Gemariah the son of Shaphan the scribe, in the upper court, at the entry of the new gate of Yahweh's house, in the ears of all the people. 11 When Micaiah the son of Gemariah, the son of Shaphan, had heard out of the book all Yahweh's words, 12 he went down into the king's house, into the scribe's room; and behold, all the princes were sitting there, Elishama the scribe, Delaiah the son of Shemaiah, Elnathan the son of Achbor, Gemariah the son of Shaphan, Zedekiah the son of Hananiah, and all the princes. 13 Then Micaiah declared to them all the words that he had heard, when Baruch read the book in the ears of the people. 14 Therefore all the princes sent Jehudi the son of Nethaniah, the son of Shelemiah, the son of Cushi, to Baruch, saying, "Take in your hand the scroll in which you have read in the ears of the people, and come." So Baruch the son of Neriah took the scroll in his hand,

and came to them. 15 They said to him, "Sit down now, and read it in our hearing." So Baruch read it in their hearing. 16 Now when they had heard all the words, they turned in fear one toward another, and said to Baruch, "We will surely tell the king of all these words." 17 They asked Baruch, saying, "Tell us now, how did you write all these words at his mouth?" 18 Then Baruch answered them, "He dictated all these words to me with his mouth, and I wrote them with ink in the book." 19 Then the princes said to Baruch, "You and Jeremiah go hide. Don't let anyone know where you are." 20 They went in to the king into the court, but they had laid up the scroll in the room of Elishama the scribe. Then they told all the words in the hearing of the king. 21 So the king sent Jehudi to get the scroll, and he took it out of the room of Elishama the scribe. Jehudi read it in the hearing of the king, and in the hearing of all the princes who stood beside the king. 22 Now the king was sitting in the winter house in the ninth month, and there was a fire in the brazier burning before him. 23 When Jehudi had read three or four columns, the king cut it with the penknife, and cast it into the fire that was in the brazier, until all the scroll was consumed in the fire that was in the brazier. 24 The king and his servants who heard all these words were not afraid, and didn't tear their garments. 25 Moreover Elnathan and Delaiah and Gemariah had made intercession to the king that he would not burn the scroll; but he would not listen to them. 26 The king commanded Jerahmeel the king's son, and Seraiah the son of Azriel, and Shelemiah the son of Abdeel, to arrest Baruch the scribe and Jeremiah the prophet; but Yahweh hid them. 27 Then Yahweh's word came to Jeremiah, after the king had burned the scroll, and the words which Baruch wrote at the mouth of Jeremiah, saying, 28"Take again another scroll, and write in it all the former words that were in the first scroll, which Jehoiakim the king of Judah has burned. 29 Concerning Jehoiakim king of Judah you shall say, 'Yahweh says: "You have burned this scroll, saying, 'Why have you written therein, saying, "The king of Babylon will certainly come and destroy this land, and will cause to cease from there man and animal"?'" 30 Therefore Yahweh says concerning Jehoiakim king of Judah: "He will have no one to sit on David's throne. His dead body will be cast out in the day to the heat, and in the night to the frost. 31 I will punish him, his offspring, and his servants for their iniquity. I will bring on them, on the inhabitants of Jerusalem, and on the men of Judah, all the evil that I have pronounced against them, but they didn't listen."'" 32 Then Jeremiah took another scroll, and gave it to Baruch the scribe, the son of Neriah, who wrote therein from the mouth of Jeremiah all the words of the book which Jehoiakim king of Judah had burned in the fire; and many similar words were added to them.

37

1 Zedekiah the son of Josiah reigned as king instead of Coniah the son of Jehoiakim, whom Nebuchadnezzar king of Babylon made king in the land of Judah. 2 But neither he, nor his servants, nor the people of the land, listened to Yahweh's words, which he spoke by the prophet Jeremiah. 3 Zedekiah the king sent Jehucal the son of Shelemiah and Zephaniah the son of Maaseiah, the priest, to the prophet Jeremiah, saying, "Pray now to Yahweh our God for us." 4 Now Jeremiah came in and went out among the people, for they had not put him into prison. 5 Pharaoh's army had come out of Egypt; and when the Chaldeans who were besieging Jerusalem heard news of them, they withdrew from Jerusalem. 6 Then Yahweh's word came to the prophet Jeremiah, saying, 7"Yahweh, the God of Israel, says, 'You shall tell the king of Judah, who sent you to me to inquire of me: "Behold, Pharaoh's army, which has come out to help you, will return to Egypt into their own land. 8 The Chaldeans will come again, and fight against this city. They will take it and burn it with fire."' 9"Yahweh says, 'Don't deceive yourselves, saying, "The Chaldeans will surely depart from us;" for they will not depart. 10 For though you had struck the whole army of the Chaldeans who fight against you, and only wounded men remained among them, they would each rise up in his tent and burn this city with fire.'" 11 When the army of the Chaldeans had withdrawn from Jerusalem for fear of Pharaoh's army, 12 then Jeremiah went out of Jerusalem to go into the land of Benjamin, to receive his portion there, in the middle of the people. 13 When he was in Benjamin's gate, a captain of the guard was there, whose name was Irijah, the son of Shelemiah, the son of Hananiah; and he seized Jeremiah the prophet, saying, "You are defecting to the Chaldeans!" 14 Then Jeremiah said, "That is false! I am not defecting to the Chaldeans." But he didn't listen to him; so Irijah seized Jeremiah, and brought him to the princes. 15 The princes were angry with Jeremiah, and struck him, and put him in prison in the house of Jonathan the scribe; for they had made that the prison. 16 When Jeremiah had come into the dungeon house and into the cells, and Jeremiah had remained there many days, 17 then Zedekiah the king sent and had him brought out. The king asked him secretly in his house, "Is there any word from Yahweh?" Jeremiah said, "There is." He also said, "You will be delivered into the hand of the king of Babylon." 18

Moreover Jeremiah said to King Zedekiah, "How have I sinned against you, against your servants, or against this people, that you have put me in prison? 19 Now where are your prophets who prophesied to you, saying, 'The king of Babylon will not come against you, nor against this land'? 20 Now please hear, my lord the king: please let my supplication be presented before you, that you not cause me to return to the house of Jonathan the scribe, lest I die there." 21 Then Zedekiah the king commanded, and they committed Jeremiah into the court of the guard. They gave him daily a loaf of bread out of the bakers' street, until all the bread in the city was gone. Thus Jeremiah remained in the court of the guard.

38

1 Shephatiah the son of Mattan, Gedaliah the son of Pashhur, Jucal the son of Shelemiah, and Pashhur the son of Malchijah heard the words that Jeremiah spoke to all the people, saying, 2"Yahweh says, 'He who remains in this city will die by the sword, by the famine, and by the pestilence, but he who goes out to the Chaldeans will live. He will escape with his life and he will live.' 3 Yahweh says, 'This city will surely be given into the hand of the army of the king of Babylon, and he will take it.'" 4 Then the princes said to the king, "Please let this man be put to death, because he weakens the hands of the men of war who remain in this city, and the hands of all the people, in speaking such words to them; for this man doesn't seek the welfare of this people, but harm." 5 Zedekiah the king said, "Behold, he is in your hand; for the king can't do anything to oppose you." 6 Then they took Jeremiah and threw him into the dungeon of Malchijah the king's son, that was in the court of the guard. They let down Jeremiah with cords. In the dungeon there was no water, but mire; and Jeremiah sank in the mire. 7 Now when Ebedmelech the Ethiopian, a eunuch, who was in the king's house, heard that they had put Jeremiah in the dungeon (the king was then sitting in Benjamin's gate), 8 Ebedmelech went out of the king's house, and spoke to the king, saying, 9"My lord the king, these men have done evil in all that they have done to Jeremiah the prophet, whom they have cast into the dungeon. He is likely to die in the place where he is, because of the famine; for there is no more bread in the city." 10 Then the king commanded Ebedmelech the Ethiopian, saying, "Take from here thirty men with you, and take up Jeremiah the prophet out of the dungeon, before he dies." 11 So Ebedmelech took the men with him, and went into the house of the king under the treasury, and took from there rags and worn-out garments, and let them down by cords into the dungeon to

Jeremiah. 12 Ebedmelech the Ethiopian said to Jeremiah, "Now put these rags and worn-out garments under your armpits under the cords." Jeremiah did so. 13 So they lifted Jeremiah up with the cords, and took him up out of the dungeon; and Jeremiah remained in the court of the guard. 14 Then Zedekiah the king sent and took Jeremiah the prophet to himself into the third entry that is in Yahweh's house. Then the king said to Jeremiah, "I will ask you something. Hide nothing from me." 15 Then Jeremiah said to Zedekiah, "If I declare it to you, will you not surely put me to death? If I give you counsel, you will not listen to me." 16 So Zedekiah the king swore secretly to Jeremiah, saying, "As Yahweh lives, who made our souls, I will not put you to death, neither will I give you into the hand of these men who seek your life." 17 Then Jeremiah said to Zedekiah, "Yahweh, the God of Armies, the God of Israel, says: 'If you will go out to the king of Babylon's princes, then your soul will live, and this city will not be burned with fire. You will live, along with your house. 18 But if you will not go out to the king of Babylon's princes, then this city will be given into the hand of the Chaldeans, and they will burn it with fire, and you won't escape out of their hand.'" 19 Zedekiah the king said to Jeremiah, "I am afraid of the Jews who have defected to the Chaldeans, lest they deliver me into their hand, and they mock me." 20 But Jeremiah said, "They won't deliver you. Obey, I beg you, Yahweh's voice, in that which I speak to you; so it will be well with you, and your soul will live. 21 But if you refuse to go out, this is the word that Yahweh has shown me: 22 'Behold, all the women who are left in the king of Judah's house will be brought out to the king of Babylon's princes, and those women will say, "Your familiar friends have turned on you, and have prevailed over you. Your feet are sunk in the mire, they have turned away from you." 23 They will bring out all your wives and your children to the Chaldeans. You won't escape out of their hand, but will be taken by the hand of the king of Babylon. You will cause this city to be burned with fire.'" 24 Then Zedekiah said to Jeremiah, "Let no man know of these words, and you won't die. 25 But if the princes hear that I have talked with you, and they come to you, and tell you, 'Declare to us now what you have said to the king; don't hide it from us, and we will not put you to death; also tell us what the king said to you;' 26 then you shall tell them, 'I presented my supplication before the king, that he would not cause me to return to Jonathan's house, to die there.'" 27 Then all the princes came to Jeremiah, and asked him; and he told them according to all these words that the king had commanded. So they stopped speaking with him, for the matter was not perceived. 28 So Jeremiah stayed in the court of the guard until the day that Jerusalem was taken.

39

1 In the ninth year of Zedekiah king of Judah, in the tenth month, Nebuchadnezzar king of Babylon and all his army came against Jerusalem, and besieged it. 2 In the eleventh year of Zedekiah, in the fourth month, the ninth day of the month, a breach was made in the city. 3 All the princes of the king of Babylon came in, and sat in the middle gate: Nergal Sharezer, Samgarnebo, Sarsechim the Rabsaris, Nergal Sharezer the Rabmag, with all the rest of the princes of the king of Babylon. 4 When Zedekiah the king of Judah and all the men of war saw them, then they fled and went out of the city by night, by the way of the king's garden, through the gate between the two walls; and he went out toward the Arabah. 5 But the army of the Chaldeans pursued them, and overtook Zedekiah in the plains of Jericho. When they had taken him, they brought him up to Nebuchadnezzar king of Babylon to Riblah in the land of Hamath; and he pronounced judgment on him. 6 Then the king of Babylon killed Zedekiah's sons in Riblah before his eyes. The king of Babylon also killed all the nobles of Judah. 7 Moreover he put out Zedekiah's eyes and bound him in fetters, to carry him to Babylon. 8 The Chaldeans burned the king's house and the people's houses with fire and broke down the walls of Jerusalem. 9 Then Nebuzaradan the captain of the guard carried away captive into Babylon the rest of the people who remained in the city, the deserters also who fell away to him, and the rest of the people who remained. 10 But Nebuzaradan the captain of the guard left of the poor of the people, who had nothing, in the land of Judah, and gave them vineyards and fields at the same time. 11 Now Nebuchadnezzar king of Babylon commanded Nebuzaradan the captain of the guard concerning Jeremiah, saying, 12"Take him and take care of him. Do him no harm; but do to him even as he tells you." 13 So Nebuzaradan the captain of the guard, Nebushazban, Rabsaris, and Nergal Sharezer, Rabmag, and all the chief officers of the king of Babylon 14 sent and took Jeremiah out of the court of the guard, and committed him to Gedaliah the son of Ahikam, the son of Shaphan, that he should bring him home. So he lived among the people. 15 Now Yahweh's word came to Jeremiah while he was shut up in the court of the guard, saying, 16"Go, and speak to Ebedmelech the Ethiopian, saying, 'Yahweh of Armies, the God of Israel, says: "Behold, I will bring my words on this city for evil, and not for good; and they will be accomplished before

you in that day. 17 But I will deliver you in that day," says Yahweh; "and you will not be given into the hand of the men of whom you are afraid. 18 For I will surely save you. You won't fall by the sword, but you will escape with your life, because you have put your trust in me," says Yahweh.'"

40

1 The word which came to Jeremiah from Yahweh, after Nebuzaradan the captain of the guard had let him go from Ramah, when he had taken him being bound in chains among all the captives of Jerusalem and Judah who were carried away captive to Babylon. 2 The captain of the guard took Jeremiah and said to him, "Yahweh your God pronounced this evil on this place; 3 and Yahweh has brought it, and done according as he spoke. Because you have sinned against Yahweh, and have not obeyed his voice, therefore this thing has come on you. 4 Now, behold, I release you today from the chains which are on your hand. If it seems good to you to come with me into Babylon, come, and I will take care of you; but if it seems bad to you to come with me into Babylon, don't. Behold, all the land is before you. Where it seems good and right to you to go, go there." 5 Now while he had not yet gone back, "Go back then," he said, "to Gedaliah the son of Ahikam, the son of Shaphan, whom the king of Babylon has made governor over the cities of Judah, and dwell with him among the people; or go wherever it seems right to you to go." So the captain of the guard gave him food and a present, and let him go. 6 Then Jeremiah went to Gedaliah the son of Ahikam to Mizpah, and lived with him among the people who were left in the land. 7 Now when all the captains of the forces who were in the fields, even they and their men, heard that the king of Babylon had made Gedaliah the son of Ahikam governor in the land, and had committed to him men, women, children, and of the poorest of the land, of those who were not carried away captive to Babylon, 8 then Ishmael the son of Nethaniah, and Johanan and Jonathan the sons of Kareah, and Seraiah the son of Tanhumeth, and the sons of Ephai the Netophathite, and Jezaniah the son of the Maacathite, they and their men came to Gedaliah to Mizpah. 9 Gedaliah the son of Ahikam the son of Shaphan swore to them and to their men, saying, "Don't be afraid to serve the Chaldeans. Dwell in the land, and serve the king of Babylon, and it will be well with you. 10 As for me, behold, I will dwell at Mizpah, to stand before the Chaldeans who will come to us; but you, gather wine and summer fruits and oil, and put them in your vessels, and dwell in your cities that you have taken." 11 Likewise when all the Jews who were in Moab, and among the

children of Ammon, and in Edom, and who were in all the countries, heard that the king of Babylon had left a remnant of Judah, and that he had set over them Gedaliah the son of Ahikam, the son of Shaphan, 12 then all the Jews returned out of all places where they were driven, and came to the land of Judah, to Gedaliah, to Mizpah, and gathered very much wine and summer fruits. 13 Moreover Johanan the son of Kareah, and all the captains of the forces who were in the fields, came to Gedaliah to Mizpah, 14 and said to him, "Do you know that Baalis the king of the children of Ammon has sent Ishmael the son of Nethaniah to take your life?" But Gedaliah the son of Ahikam didn't believe them. 15 Then Johanan the son of Kareah spoke to Gedaliah in Mizpah secretly, saying, "Please let me go, and I will kill Ishmael the son of Nethaniah, and no man will know it. Why should he take your life, that all the Jews who are gathered to you should be scattered, and the remnant of Judah perish?" 16 But Gedaliah the son of Ahikam said to Johanan the son of Kareah, "You shall not do this thing, for you speak falsely of Ishmael."

41

1 Now in the seventh month, Ishmael the son of Nethaniah, the son of Elishama, of the royal offspring and one of the chief officers of the king, and ten men with him, came to Gedaliah the son of Ahikam to Mizpah; and there they ate bread together in Mizpah. 2 Then Ishmael the son of Nethaniah arose, and the ten men who were with him, and struck Gedaliah the son of Ahikam the son of Shaphan with the sword and killed him, whom the king of Babylon had made governor over the land. 3 Ishmael also killed all the Jews who were with Gedaliah at Mizpah, and the Chaldean men of war who were found there. 4 The second day after he had killed Gedaliah, and no man knew it, 5 men came from Shechem, from Shiloh, and from Samaria, even eighty men, having their beards shaved and their clothes torn, and having cut themselves, with meal offerings and frankincense in their hand, to bring them to Yahweh's house. 6 Ishmael the son of Nethaniah went out from Mizpah to meet them, weeping all along as he went, and as he met them, he said to them, "Come to Gedaliah the son of Ahikam." 7 It was so, when they came into the middle of the city, that Ishmael the son of Nethaniah killed them, and cast them into the middle of the pit, he, and the men who were with him. 8 But ten men were found among those who said to Ishmael, "Don't kill us; for we have stores hidden in the field, of wheat, and of barley, and of oil, and of honey." So he stopped, and didn't kill them among their brothers. 9 Now the pit in which Ishmael cast all the dead bodies of the men whom he had killed,

by the side of Gedaliah (this was that which Asa the king had made for fear of Baasha king of Israel), Ishmael the son of Nethaniah filled it with those who were killed. 10 Then Ishmael carried away captive all of the people who were left in Mizpah, even the king's daughters, and all the people who remained in Mizpah, whom Nebuzaradan the captain of the guard had committed to Gedaliah the son of Ahikam. Ishmael the son of Nethaniah carried them away captive, and departed to go over to the children of Ammon. 11 But when Johanan the son of Kareah, and all the captains of the forces who were with him, heard of all the evil that Ishmael the son of Nethaniah had done, 12 then they took all the men, and went to fight with Ishmael the son of Nethaniah, and found him by the great waters that are in Gibeon. 13 Now when all the people who were with Ishmael saw Johanan the son of Kareah, and all the captains of the forces who were with him, then they were glad. 14 So all the people who Ishmael had carried away captive from Mizpah turned about and came back, and went to Johanan the son of Kareah. 15 But Ishmael the son of Nethaniah escaped from Johanan with eight men, and went to the children of Ammon. 16 Then Johanan the son of Kareah and all the captains of the forces who were with him took all the remnant of the people whom he had recovered from Ishmael the son of Nethaniah, from Mizpah, after he had killed Gedaliah the son of Ahikam—the men of war, with the women, the children, and the eunuchs, whom he had brought back from Gibeon. 17 They departed and lived in Geruth Chimham, which is by Bethlehem, to go to enter into Egypt 18 because of the Chaldeans; for they were afraid of them, because Ishmael the son of Nethaniah had killed Gedaliah the son of Ahikam, whom the king of Babylon made governor over the land.

42

1 Then all the captains of the forces, and Johanan the son of Kareah, and Jezaniah the son of Hoshaiah, and all the people from the least even to the greatest, came near, 2 and said to Jeremiah the prophet, "Please let our supplication be presented before you, and pray for us to Yahweh your God, even for all this remnant, for we are left but a few of many, as your eyes see us, 3 that Yahweh your God may show us the way in which we should walk, and the things that we should do." 4 Then Jeremiah the prophet said to them, "I have heard you. Behold, I will pray to Yahweh your God according to your words; and it will happen that whatever thing Yahweh answers you, I will declare it to you. I will keep nothing back from you." 5 Then they said to

Jeremiah, "May Yahweh be a true and faithful witness among us, if we don't do according to all the word with which Yahweh your God sends you to tell us. 6 Whether it is good, or whether it is bad, we will obey the voice of Yahweh our God, to whom we send you; that it may be well with us, when we obey the voice of Yahweh our God." 7 After ten days, Yahweh's word came to Jeremiah. 8 Then he called Johanan the son of Kareah, and all the captains of the forces who were with him, and all the people from the least even to the greatest, 9 and said to them, "Yahweh, the God of Israel, to whom you sent me to present your supplication before him, says: 10'If you will still live in this land, then I will build you, and not pull you down, and I will plant you, and not pluck you up; for I grieve over the distress that I have brought on you. 11 Don't be afraid of the king of Babylon, of whom you are afraid. Don't be afraid of him,' says Yahweh, 'for I am with you to save you, and to deliver you from his hand. 12 I will grant you mercy, that he may have mercy on you, and cause you to return to your own land. 13"'But if you say, "We will not dwell in this land," so that you don't obey Yahweh your God's voice, 14 saying, "No, but we will go into the land of Egypt, where we will see no war, nor hear the sound of the trumpet, nor have hunger of bread; and there we will dwell;"' 15 now therefore hear Yahweh's word, O remnant of Judah! Yahweh of Armies, the God of Israel, says, 'If you indeed set your faces to enter into Egypt, and go to live there, 16 then it will happen that the sword, which you fear, will overtake you there in the land of Egypt; and the famine, about which you are afraid, will follow close behind you there in Egypt; and you will die there. 17 So will it be with all the men who set their faces to go into Egypt to live there. They will die by the sword, by the famine, and by the pestilence. None of them will remain or escape from the evil that I will bring on them.' 18 For Yahweh of Armies, the God of Israel, says: 'As my anger and my wrath has been poured out on the inhabitants of Jerusalem, so my wrath will be poured out on you, when you enter into Egypt; and you will be an object of horror, an astonishment, a curse, and a reproach; and you will see this place no more.' 19"Yahweh has spoken concerning you, remnant of Judah, 'Don't go into Egypt!' Know certainly that I have testified to you today. 20 For you have dealt deceitfully against your own souls; for you sent me to Yahweh your God, saying, 'Pray for us to Yahweh our God; and according to all that Yahweh our God says, so declare to us, and we will do it.' 21 I have declared it to you today; but you have not obeyed Yahweh your God's voice in anything for which he has sent me to you. 22 Now therefore know certainly that you will die by the sword, by the famine, and by the pestilence in the place where you desire to go to live."

43

1 When Jeremiah had finished speaking to all the people all the words of Yahweh their God, with which Yahweh their God had sent him to them, even all these words, 2 then Azariah the son of Hoshaiah, Johanan the son of Kareah, and all the proud men spoke, saying to Jeremiah, "You speak falsely. Yahweh our God has not sent you to say, 'You shall not go into Egypt to live there;' 3 but Baruch the son of Neriah has turned you against us, to deliver us into the hand of the Chaldeans, that they may put us to death or carry us away captive to Babylon." 4 So Johanan the son of Kareah, and all the captains of the forces, and all the people, didn't obey Yahweh's voice, to dwell in the land of Judah. 5 But Johanan the son of Kareah and all the captains of the forces took all the remnant of Judah, who had returned from all the nations where they had been driven, to live in the land of Judah— 6 the men, the women, the children, the king's daughters, and every person who Nebuzaradan the captain of the guard had left with Gedaliah the son of Ahikam, the son of Shaphan; and Jeremiah the prophet, and Baruch the son of Neriah. 7 They came into the land of Egypt, for they didn't obey Yahweh's voice; and they came to Tahpanhes. 8 Then Yahweh's word came to Jeremiah in Tahpanhes, saying, 9"Take great stones in your hand and hide them in mortar in the brick work which is at the entry of Pharaoh's house in Tahpanhes, in the sight of the men of Judah. 10 Tell them, Yahweh of Armies, the God of Israel, says: 'Behold, I will send and take Nebuchadnezzar the king of Babylon, my servant, and will set his throne on these stones that I have hidden; and he will spread his royal pavilion over them. 11 He will come, and will strike the land of Egypt; such as are for death will be put to death, and such as are for captivity to captivity, and such as are for the sword to the sword. 12 I will kindle a fire in the houses of the gods of Egypt. He will burn them, and carry them away captive. He will array himself with the land of Egypt, as a shepherd puts on his garment; and he will go out from there in peace. 13 He will also break the pillars of Beth Shemesh that is in the land of Egypt; and he will burn the houses of the gods of Egypt with fire.'"

44

1 The word that came to Jeremiah concerning all the Jews who lived in the land of Egypt, who lived at Migdol, and at Tahpanhes, and at Memphis, and

in the country of Pathros, saying, 2"Yahweh of Armies, the God of Israel, says: 'You have seen all the evil that I have brought on Jerusalem, and on all the cities of Judah. Behold, today they are a desolation, and no man dwells in them, 3 because of their wickedness which they have committed to provoke me to anger, in that they went to burn incense, to serve other gods that they didn't know, neither they, nor you, nor your fathers. 4 However I sent to you all my servants the prophets, rising up early and sending them, saying, "Oh, don't do this abominable thing that I hate." 5 But they didn't listen and didn't incline their ear. They didn't turn from their wickedness, to stop burning incense to other gods. 6 Therefore my wrath and my anger was poured out, and was kindled in the cities of Judah and in the streets of Jerusalem; and they are wasted and desolate, as it is today.' 7"Therefore now Yahweh, the God of Armies, the God of Israel, says: 'Why do you commit great evil against your own souls, to cut off from yourselves man and woman, infant and nursing child out of the middle of Judah, to leave yourselves no one remaining, 8 in that you provoke me to anger with the works of your hands, burning incense to other gods in the land of Egypt where you have gone to live, that you may be cut off, and that you may be a curse and a reproach among all the nations of the earth? 9 Have you forgotten the wickedness of your fathers, the wickedness of the kings of Judah, the wickedness of their wives, your own wickedness, and the wickedness of your wives which they committed in the land of Judah and in the streets of Jerusalem? 10 They are not humbled even to this day, neither have they feared, nor walked in my law, nor in my statutes, that I set before you and before your fathers.' 11"Therefore Yahweh of Armies, the God of Israel, says: 'Behold, I will set my face against you for evil, even to cut off all Judah. 12 I will take the remnant of Judah that have set their faces to go into the land of Egypt to live there, and they will all be consumed. They will fall in the land of Egypt. They will be consumed by the sword and by the famine. They will die, from the least even to the greatest, by the sword and by the famine. They will be an object of horror, an astonishment, a curse, and a reproach. 13 For I will punish those who dwell in the land of Egypt, as I have punished Jerusalem, by the sword, by the famine, and by the pestilence; 14 so that none of the remnant of Judah, who have gone into the land of Egypt to live there, will escape or be left to return into the land of Judah, to which they have a desire to return to dwell there; for no one will return except those who will escape.'" 15 Then all the men who knew that their wives burned incense to other gods, and all the women who stood by, a great assembly, even all the people who lived in the land of Egypt, in Pathros, answered Jeremiah, saying, 16"As for the word that you have spoken to us in Yahweh's name, we will not listen to you. 17 But we will certainly perform every word that has gone out of our mouth, to burn incense to the queen of the sky and to pour out drink offerings to her, as we have done, we and our fathers, our kings and our princes, in the cities of Judah and in the streets of Jerusalem; for then we had plenty of food, and were well, and saw no evil. 18 But since we stopped burning incense to the queen of the sky, and pouring out drink offerings to her, we have lacked all things, and have been consumed by the sword and by the famine." 19 The women said, "When we burned incense to the queen of the sky and poured out drink offerings to her, did we make her cakes to worship her, and pour out drink offerings to her, without our husbands?" 20 Then Jeremiah said to all the people—to the men and to the women, even to all the people who had given him an answer, saying, 21"The incense that you burned in the cities of Judah, and in the streets of Jerusalem, you and your fathers, your kings and your princes, and the people of the land, didn't Yahweh remember them, and didn't it come into his mind? 22 Thus Yahweh could no longer bear it, because of the evil of your doings and because of the abominations which you have committed. Therefore your land has become a desolation, an astonishment, and a curse, without inhabitant, as it is today. 23 Because you have burned incense and because you have sinned against Yahweh, and have not obeyed Yahweh's voice, nor walked in his law, nor in his statutes, nor in his testimonies; therefore this evil has happened to you, as it is today." 24 Moreover Jeremiah said to all the people, including all the women, "Hear Yahweh's word, all Judah who are in the land of Egypt! 25 Yahweh of Armies, the God of Israel, says, 'You and your wives have both spoken with your mouths, and with your hands have fulfilled it, saying, "We will surely perform our vows that we have vowed, to burn incense to the queen of the sky, and to pour out drink offerings to her." "'Establish then your vows, and perform your vows.' 26"Therefore hear Yahweh's word, all Judah who dwell in the land of Egypt: 'Behold, I have sworn by my great name,' says Yahweh, 'that my name will no more be named in the mouth of any man of Judah in all the land of Egypt, saying, "As the Lord Yahweh lives." 27 Behold, I watch over them for evil, and not for good; and all the men of Judah who are in the land of Egypt will be consumed by the sword and by the famine, until they are all gone. 28 Those who escape the sword will return out of the land of

Egypt into the land of Judah few in number. All the remnant of Judah, who have gone into the land of Egypt to live there, will know whose word will stand, mine or theirs. 29"'This will be the sign to you,' says Yahweh, 'that I will punish you in this place, that you may know that my words will surely stand against you for evil.' 30 Yahweh says, 'Behold, I will give Pharaoh Hophra king of Egypt into the hand of his enemies and into the hand of those who seek his life, just as I gave Zedekiah king of Judah into the hand of Nebuchadnezzar king of Babylon, who was his enemy and sought his life.'"

45

1 The message that Jeremiah the prophet spoke to Baruch the son of Neriah, when he wrote these words in a book at the mouth of Jeremiah, in the fourth year of Jehoiakim the son of Josiah, king of Judah, saying, 2"Yahweh, the God of Israel, says to you, Baruch: 3'You said, "Woe is me now! For Yahweh has added sorrow to my pain! I am weary with my groaning, and I find no rest."' 4"You shall tell him, Yahweh says: 'Behold, that which I have built, I will break down, and that which I have planted I will pluck up; and this in the whole land. 5 Do you seek great things for yourself? Don't seek them; for, behold, I will bring evil on all flesh,' says Yahweh, 'but I will let you escape with your life wherever you go.'"

46

1 Yahweh's word which came to Jeremiah the prophet concerning the nations. 2 Of Egypt: concerning the army of Pharaoh Necoh king of Egypt, which was by the river Euphrates in Carchemish, which Nebuchadnezzar king of Babylon struck in the fourth year of Jehoiakim the son of Josiah, king of Judah. 3"Prepare the buckler and shield, and draw near to battle! 4 Harness the horses, and get up, you horsemen, and stand up with your helmets. Polish the spears, put on the coats of mail. 5 Why have I seen it? They are dismayed and are turned backward. Their mighty ones are beaten down, have fled in haste, and don't look back. Terror is on every side," says Yahweh. 6"Don't let the swift flee away, nor the mighty man escape. In the north by the river Euphrates they have stumbled and fallen. 7"Who is this who rises up like the Nile, like rivers whose waters surge? 8 Egypt rises up like the Nile, like rivers whose waters surge. He says, 'I will rise up. I will cover the earth. I will destroy cities and its inhabitants.' 9 Go up, you horses! Rage, you chariots! Let the mighty men go out: Cush and Put, who handle the shield; and the Ludim, who handle and bend the bow. 10 For that day is of the Lord, Yahweh

of Armies, a day of vengeance, that he may avenge himself of his adversaries. The sword will devour and be satiated, and will drink its fill of their blood; for the Lord, Yahweh of Armies, has a sacrifice in the north country by the river Euphrates. 11 Go up into Gilead, and take balm, virgin daughter of Egypt. You use many medicines in vain. There is no healing for you. 12 The nations have heard of your shame, and the earth is full of your cry; for the mighty man has stumbled against the mighty, they both fall together." 13 The word that Yahweh spoke to Jeremiah the prophet, how that Nebuchadnezzar king of Babylon should come and strike the land of Egypt: 14"Declare in Egypt, publish in Migdol, and publish in Memphis and in Tahpanhes; say, 'Stand up, and prepare, for the sword has devoured around you.' 15 Why are your strong ones swept away? They didn't stand, because Yahweh pushed them. 16 He made many to stumble. Yes, they fell on one another. They said, 'Arise! Let's go again to our own people, and to the land of our birth, from the oppressing sword.' 17 They cried there, 'Pharaoh king of Egypt is but a noise; he has let the appointed time pass by.' 18"As I live," says the King, whose name is Yahweh of Armies, "surely like Tabor among the mountains, and like Carmel by the sea, so he will come. 19 You daughter who dwells in Egypt, furnish yourself to go into captivity; for Memphis will become a desolation, and will be burned up, without inhabitant. 20"Egypt is a very beautiful heifer; but destruction out of the north has come. It has come. 21 Also her hired men in the middle of her are like calves of the stall, for they also are turned back. They have fled away together. They didn't stand, for the day of their calamity has come on them, the time of their visitation. 22 Its sound will go like the serpent, for they will march with an army, and come against her with axes, as wood cutters. 23 They will cut down her forest," says Yahweh, "though it can't be searched; because they are more than the locusts, and are innumerable. 24 The daughter of Egypt will be disappointed; she will be delivered into the hand of the people of the north." 25 Yahweh of Armies, the God of Israel, says: "Behold, I will punish Amon of No, and Pharaoh, and Egypt, with her gods and her kings, even Pharaoh, and those who trust in him. 26 I will deliver them into the hand of those who seek their lives, and into the hand of Nebuchadnezzar king of Babylon, and into the hand of his servants. Afterwards it will be inhabited, as in the days of old," says Yahweh. 27"But don't you be afraid, Jacob my servant. Don't be dismayed, Israel; for, behold, I will save you from afar, and your offspring from the land of their captivity. Jacob will return, and will be quiet and at ease. No one will make him afraid. 28 Don't be afraid, O Jacob my servant," says Yahweh, "for I am with you; for I will make a full end of all the nations where I have driven you, but I will not make a full end of you, but I will correct you in measure, and will in no way leave you unpunished."

47

1 Yahweh's word that came to Jeremiah the prophet concerning the Philistines, before Pharaoh struck Gaza. 2 Yahweh says: "Behold, waters rise up out of the north, and will become an overflowing stream, and will overflow the land and all that is therein, the city and those who dwell therein. The men will cry, and all the inhabitants of the land will wail. 3 At the noise of the stamping of the hoofs of his strong ones, at the rushing of his chariots, at the rumbling of his wheels, the fathers don't look back for their children because their hands are so feeble, 4 because of the day that comes to destroy all the Philistines, to cut off from Tyre and Sidon every helper who remains; for Yahweh will destroy the Philistines, the remnant of the isle of Caphtor. 5 Baldness has come on Gaza; Ashkelon is brought to nothing. You remnant of their valley, how long will you cut yourself? 6 "You sword of Yahweh, how long will it be before you are quiet? Put yourself back into your scabbard; rest, and be still.' 7 "How can you be quiet, since Yahweh has given you a command? Against Ashkelon, and against the seashore, there he has appointed it."

48

1 Of Moab. Yahweh of Armies, the God of Israel, says: "Woe to Nebo! For it is laid waste. Kiriathaim is disappointed. It is taken. Misgab is put to shame and broken down. 2 The praise of Moab is no more. In Heshbon they have devised evil against her: 'Come! Let's cut her off from being a nation.' You also, Madmen, will be brought to silence. The sword will pursue you. 3 The sound of a cry from Horonaim, desolation and great destruction! 4 Moab is destroyed. Her little ones have caused a cry to be heard. 5 For they will go up by the ascent of Luhith with continual weeping. For at the descent of Horonaim they have heard the distress of the cry of destruction. 6 Flee! Save your lives! Be like the juniper bush in the wilderness. 7 For, because you have trusted in your works and in your treasures, you also will be taken. Chemosh will go out into captivity, his priests and his princes together. 8 The destroyer will come on every city, and no city will escape; the valley also will perish, and the plain will be destroyed, as Yahweh has spoken. 9 Give wings to

Moab, that she may fly and get herself away: and her cities will become a desolation, without anyone to dwell in them. 10"Cursed is he who does the work of Yahweh negligently; and cursed is he who keeps back his sword from blood. 11"Moab has been at ease from his youth, and he has settled on his dregs, and has not been emptied from vessel to vessel, neither has he gone into captivity; therefore his taste remains in him, and his scent is not changed. 12 Therefore behold, the days come," says Yahweh, "that I will send to him those who pour off, and they will pour him off; and they will empty his vessels, and break their containers in pieces. 13 Moab will be ashamed of Chemosh, as the house of Israel was ashamed of Bethel, their confidence. 14"How do you say, 'We are mighty men, and valiant men for the war'? 15 Moab is laid waste, and they have gone up into his cities, and his chosen young men have gone down to the slaughter," says the King, whose name is Yahweh of Armies. 16"The calamity of Moab is near to come, and his affliction hurries fast. 17 All you who are around him, bemoan him; and all you who know his name, say, 'How the strong staff is broken, the beautiful rod!' 18"You daughter who dwells in Dibon, come down from your glory, and sit in thirst; for the destroyer of Moab has come up against you. He has destroyed your strongholds. 19 Inhabitant of Aroer, stand by the way and watch. Ask him who flees, and her who escapes; say, 'What has been done?' 20 Moab is disappointed; for it is broken down. Wail and cry! Tell it by the Arnon, that Moab is laid waste. 21 Judgment has come on the plain country— on Holon, on Jahzah, on Mephaath, 22 on Dibon, on Nebo, on Beth Diblathaim, 23 on Kiriathaim, on Beth Gamul, on Beth Meon, 24 on Kerioth, on Bozrah, and on all the cities of the land of Moab, far or near. 25 The horn of Moab is cut off, and his arm is broken," says Yahweh. 26"Make him drunk, for he magnified himself against Yahweh. Moab will wallow in his vomit, and he also will be in derision. 27 For wasn't Israel a derision to you? Was he found among thieves? For as often as you speak of him, you shake your head. 28 You inhabitants of Moab, leave the cities, and dwell in the rock. Be like the dove that makes her nest over the mouth of the abyss. 29"We have heard of the pride of Moab. He is very proud in his loftiness, his pride, his arrogance, and the arrogance of his heart. 30 I know his wrath," says Yahweh, "that it is nothing; his boastings have done nothing. 31 Therefore I will wail for Moab. Yes, I will cry out for all Moab. They will mourn for the men of Kir Heres. 32 With more than the weeping of Jazer I will weep for you, vine of Sibmah. Your branches passed over the sea. They reached even to the sea of Jazer.

The destroyer has fallen on your summer fruits and on your vintage. 33 Gladness and joy is taken away from the fruitful field and from the land of Moab. I have caused wine to cease from the wine presses. No one will tread with shouting. The shouting will be no shouting. 34 From the cry of Heshbon even to Elealeh, even to Jahaz they have uttered their voice, from Zoar even to Horonaim, to Eglath Shelishiyah; for the waters of Nimrim will also become desolate. 35 Moreover I will cause to cease in Moab," says Yahweh, "him who offers in the high place, and him who burns incense to his gods. 36 Therefore my heart sounds for Moab like flutes, and my heart sounds like flutes for the men of Kir Heres. Therefore the abundance that he has gotten has perished. 37 For every head is bald, and every beard clipped. There are cuttings on all the hands, and sackcloth on the waist. 38 On all the housetops of Moab, and in its streets, there is lamentation everywhere; for I have broken Moab like a vessel in which no one delights," says Yahweh. 39"How it is broken down! How they wail! How Moab has turned the back with shame! So will Moab become a derision and a terror to all who are around him." 40 For Yahweh says: "Behold, he will fly as an eagle, and will spread out his wings against Moab. 41 Kerioth is taken, and the strongholds are seized. The heart of the mighty men of Moab at that day will be as the heart of a woman in her pangs. 42 Moab will be destroyed from being a people, because he has magnified himself against Yahweh. 43 Terror, the pit, and the snare are on you, inhabitant of Moab," says Yahweh. 44"He who flees from the terror will fall into the pit; and he who gets up out of the pit will be taken in the snare, for I will bring on him, even on Moab, the year of their visitation," says Yahweh. 45"Those who fled stand without strength under the shadow of Heshbon; for a fire has gone out of Heshbon, and a flame from the middle of Sihon, and has devoured the corner of Moab, and the crown of the head of the tumultuous ones. 46 Woe to you, O Moab! The people of Chemosh are undone; for your sons are taken away captive, and your daughters into captivity. 47" Yet I will reverse the captivity of Moab in the latter days," says Yahweh. Thus far is the judgment of Moab.

49

1 Of the children of Ammon. Yahweh says: "Has Israel no sons? Has he no heir? Why then does Malcam possess Gad, and his people dwell in its cities? 2 Therefore behold, the days come," says Yahweh, "that I will cause an alarm of war to be heard against Rabbah of the children of Ammon, and it will become a desolate heap, and her daughters will be burned with fire; then

Israel will possess those who possessed him," says Yahweh. ³"Wail, Heshbon, for Ai is laid waste! Cry, you daughters of Rabbah! Clothe yourself in sackcloth. Lament, and run back and forth among the fences; for Malcam will go into captivity, his priests and his princes together. ⁴ Why do you boast in the valleys, your flowing valley, backsliding daughter? You trusted in her treasures, saying, 'Who will come to me?' ⁵ Behold, I will bring a terror on you," says the Lord, Yahweh of Armies, "from all who are around you. All of you will be driven completely out, and there will be no one to gather together the fugitives. ⁶"But afterward I will reverse the captivity of the children of Ammon," says Yahweh. ⁷ Of Edom, Yahweh of Armies says: "Is wisdom no more in Teman? Has counsel perished from the prudent? Has their wisdom vanished? ⁸ Flee! Turn back! Dwell in the depths, inhabitants of Dedan; for I will bring the calamity of Esau on him when I visit him. ⁹ If grape gatherers came to you, would they not leave some gleaning grapes? If thieves came by night, wouldn't they steal until they had enough? ¹⁰ But I have made Esau bare, I have uncovered his secret places, and he will not be able to hide himself. His offspring is destroyed, with his brothers and his neighbors; and he is no more. ¹¹ Leave your fatherless children. I will preserve them alive. Let your widows trust in me." ¹² For Yahweh says: "Behold, they to whom it didn't pertain to drink of the cup will certainly drink; and are you he who will altogether go unpunished? You won't go unpunished, but you will surely drink. ¹³ For I have sworn by myself," says Yahweh, "that Bozrah will become an astonishment, a reproach, a waste, and a curse. All its cities will be perpetual wastes." ¹⁴ I have heard news from Yahweh, and an ambassador is sent among the nations, saying, "Gather yourselves together! Come against her! Rise up to the battle!" ¹⁵"For, behold, I have made you small among the nations, and despised among men. ¹⁶ As for your terror, the pride of your heart has deceived you, O you who dwell in the clefts of the rock, who hold the height of the hill, though you should make your nest as high as the eagle, I will bring you down from there," says Yahweh. ¹⁷"Edom will become an astonishment. Everyone who passes by it will be astonished, and will hiss at all its plagues. ¹⁸ As in the overthrow of Sodom and Gomorrah and its neighbor cities," says Yahweh, "no man will dwell there, neither will any son of man live therein. ¹⁹"Behold, he will come up like a lion from the pride of the Jordan against the strong habitation; for I will suddenly make them run away from it, and whoever is chosen, I will appoint him over it. For who is like me? Who will appoint me a time? Who is the shepherd who will stand before me?" 20 Therefore hear the counsel of Yahweh, that he has taken against Edom, and his purposes that he has purposed against the inhabitants of Teman: Surely they will drag them away, the little ones of the flock. Surely he will make their habitation desolate over them. 21 The earth trembles at the noise of their fall; there is a cry, the noise which is heard in the Red Sea. 22 Behold, he will come up and fly as the eagle, and spread out his wings against Bozrah. The heart of the mighty men of Edom at that day will be as the heart of a woman in her pangs. 23 Of Damascus: "Hamath and Arpad are confounded, for they have heard evil news. They have melted away. There is sorrow on the sea. It can't be quiet. 24 Damascus has grown feeble, she turns herself to flee, and trembling has seized her. Anguish and sorrows have taken hold of her, as of a woman in travail. 25 How is the city of praise not forsaken, the city of my joy? 26 Therefore her young men will fall in her streets, and all the men of war will be brought to silence in that day," says Yahweh of Armies. 27 "I will kindle a fire in the wall of Damascus, and it will devour the palaces of Ben Hadad." 28 Of Kedar, and of the kingdoms of Hazor, which Nebuchadnezzar king of Babylon struck, Yahweh says: "Arise, go up to Kedar, and destroy the children of the east. 29 They will take their tents and their flocks. they will carry away for themselves their curtains, all their vessels, and their camels; and they will cry to them, 'Terror on every side!' 30 Flee! Wander far off! Dwell in the depths, you inhabitants of Hazor," says Yahweh; "for Nebuchadnezzar king of Babylon has taken counsel against you, and has conceived a purpose against you. 31 Arise! Go up to a nation that is at ease, that dwells without care," says Yahweh; "that has neither gates nor bars, that dwells alone. 32 Their camels will be a booty, and the multitude of their livestock a plunder. I will scatter to all winds those who have the corners of their beards cut off; and I will bring their calamity from every side of them," says Yahweh. 33 Hazor will be a dwelling place of jackals, a desolation forever. No man will dwell there, neither will any son of man live therein." 34 Yahweh's word that came to Jeremiah the prophet concerning Elam, in the beginning of the reign of Zedekiah king of Judah, saying, 35 "Yahweh of Armies says: 'Behold, I will break the bow of Elam, the chief of their might. 36 I will bring on Elam the four winds from the four quarters of the sky, and will scatter them toward all those winds. There will be no nation where the outcasts of Elam will not come. 37 I will cause Elam to be dismayed before their enemies, and before those who seek their life. I will bring evil on them, even my fierce anger,' says Yahweh; 'and I will send the sword after them, until I have consumed them. 38 I will set my throne in Elam, and will destroy from there king and princes,' says Yahweh. 39 'But it will happen in the latter days that I will reverse the captivity of Elam,' says Yahweh."

50

1 The word that Yahweh spoke concerning Babylon, concerning the land of the Chaldeans, by Jeremiah the prophet. 2 "Declare among the nations and publish, and set up a standard; publish, and don't conceal; say, 'Babylon has been taken, Bel is disappointed, Merodach is dismayed! Her images are disappointed. Her idols are dismayed.' 3 For a nation comes up out of the north against her, which will make her land desolate, and no one will dwell in it. They have fled. They are gone, both man and animal. 4 "In those days, and in that time," says Yahweh, "the children of Israel will come, they and the children of Judah together; they will go on their way weeping, and will seek Yahweh their God. 5 They will inquire concerning Zion with their faces turned toward it, saying, 'Come, and join yourselves to Yahweh in an everlasting covenant that will not be forgotten.' 6 My people have been lost sheep. Their shepherds have caused them to go astray. They have turned them away on the mountains. They have gone from mountain to hill. They have forgotten their resting place. 7 All who found them have devoured them. Their adversaries said, 'We are not guilty, because they have sinned against Yahweh, the habitation of righteousness, even Yahweh, the hope of their fathers.' 8 "Flee out of the middle of Babylon! Go out of the land of the Chaldeans, and be as the male goats before the flocks. 9 For, behold, I will stir up and cause to come up against Babylon a company of great nations from the north country; and they will set themselves in array against her. She will be taken from there. Their arrows will be as of an expert mighty man. None of them will return in vain. 10 Chaldea will be a prey. All who prey on her will be satisfied," says Yahweh. 11 "Because you are glad, because you rejoice, O you who plunder my heritage, because you are wanton as a heifer that treads out the grain, and neigh as strong horses, 12 your mother will be utterly disappointed. She who bore you will be confounded. Behold, she will be the least of the nations, a wilderness, a dry land, and a desert. 13 Because of Yahweh's wrath she won't be inhabited, but she will be wholly desolate. Everyone who goes by Babylon will be astonished, and hiss at all her plagues. 14 Set yourselves in array against Babylon all around, all you who bend the bow; shoot at her. Spare no arrows, for she has sinned against Yahweh. 15 Shout against her all around. She has submitted herself. Her

bulwarks have fallen. Her walls have been thrown down, for it is the vengeance of Yahweh. Take vengeance on her. As she has done, do to her. 16 Cut off the sower from Babylon, and him who handles the sickle in the time of harvest. For fear of the oppressing sword, they will each return to their own people, and they will each flee to their own land. 17"Israel is a hunted sheep. The lions have driven him away. First, the king of Assyria devoured him, and now at last Nebuchadnezzar king of Babylon has broken his bones." 18 Therefore Yahweh of Armies, the God of Israel, says: "Behold, I will punish the king of Babylon and his land, as I have punished the king of Assyria. 19 I will bring Israel again to his pasture, and he will feed on Carmel and Bashan. His soul will be satisfied on the hills of Ephraim and in Gilead. 20 In those days, and in that time," says Yahweh, "the iniquity of Israel will be sought for, and there will be none, also the sins of Judah, and they won't be found; for I will pardon them whom I leave as a remnant. 21"Go up against the land of Merathaim, even against it, and against the inhabitants of Pekod. Kill and utterly destroy after them," says Yahweh, "and do according to all that I have commanded you. 22 A sound of battle is in the land, and of great destruction. 23 How the hammer of the whole earth is cut apart and broken! How Babylon has become a desolation among the nations! 24 I have laid a snare for you, and you are also taken, Babylon, and you weren't aware. You are found, and also caught, because you have fought against Yahweh. 25 Yahweh has opened his armory, and has brought out the weapons of his indignation; for the Lord, Yahweh of Armies, has a work to do in the land of the Chaldeans. 26 Come against her from the farthest border. Open her storehouses. Cast her up as heaps. Destroy her utterly. Let nothing of her be left. 27 Kill all her bulls. Let them go down to the slaughter. Woe to them! For their day has come, the time of their visitation. 28 Listen to those who flee and escape out of the land of Babylon, to declare in Zion the vengeance of Yahweh our God, the vengeance of his temple. 29"Call together the archers against Babylon, all those who bend the bow. Encamp against her all around. Let none of it escape. Pay her back according to her work. According to all that she has done, do to her; for she has been proud against Yahweh, against the Holy One of Israel. 30 Therefore her young men will fall in her streets. All her men of war will be brought to silence in that day," says Yahweh. 31"Behold, I am against you, you proud one," says the Lord, Yahweh of Armies; "for your day has come, the time that I will visit you. 32 The proud one will stumble and fall, and no one will raise him up. I will kindle a fire in his cities, and it will devour all who are around him." ³³ Yahweh of Armies says: "The children of Israel and the children of Judah are oppressed together. All who took them captive hold them fast. They refuse to let them go. ³⁴ Their Redeemer is strong. Yahweh of Armies is his name. He will thoroughly plead their cause, that he may give rest to the earth, and disquiet the inhabitants of Babylon. ³⁵"A sword is on the Chaldeans," says Yahweh, "and on the inhabitants of Babylon, on her princes, and on her wise men. ³⁶ A sword is on the boasters, and they will become fools. A sword is on her mighty men, and they will be dismayed. ³⁷ A sword is on their horses, on their chariots, and on all the mixed people who are in the middle of her; and they will become as women. A sword is on her treasures, and they will be robbed. ³⁸ A drought is on her waters, and they will be dried up; for it is a land of engraved images, and they are mad over idols. ³⁹ Therefore the wild animals of the desert with the wolves will dwell there. The ostriches will dwell therein. It will be inhabited no more forever, neither will it be lived in from generation to generation. ⁴⁰ As when God overthrew Sodom and Gomorrah and its neighbor cities," says Yahweh, "so no man will dwell there, neither will any son of man live therein. ⁴¹"Behold, a people comes from the north. A great nation and many kings will be stirred up from the uttermost parts of the earth. ⁴² They take up bow and spear. They are cruel, and have no mercy. Their voice roars like the sea. They ride on horses, everyone set in array, as a man to the battle, against you, daughter of Babylon. ⁴³ The king of Babylon has heard the news of them, and his hands become feeble. Anguish has taken hold of him, pains as of a woman in labor. ⁴⁴ Behold, the enemy will come up like a lion from the thickets of the Jordan against the strong habitation; for I will suddenly make them run away from it. Whoever is chosen, I will appoint him over it, for who is like me? Who will appoint me a time? Who is the shepherd who can stand before me?" ⁴⁵ Therefore hear the counsel of Yahweh that he has taken against Babylon; and his purposes that he has purposed against the land of the Chaldeans: Surely they will drag them away, even the little ones of the flock. Surely he will make their habitation desolate over them. ⁴⁶ The earth trembles at the noise of the taking of Babylon. The cry is heard among the nations.

51

¹ Yahweh says: "Behold, I will raise up against Babylon, and against those who dwell in Lebkamai, a destroying wind. ² I will send to Babylon strangers, who will winnow her. They will empty her land; for in the day of trouble they

will be against her all around. ³ Against him who bends, let the archer bend his bow, also against him who lifts himself up in his coat of mail. Don't spare her young men! Utterly destroy all her army! ⁴ They will fall down slain in the land of the Chaldeans, and thrust through in her streets. ⁵ For Israel is not forsaken, nor Judah, by his God, by Yahweh of Armies; though their land is full of guilt against the Holy One of Israel. ⁶"Flee out of the middle of Babylon! Everyone save his own life! Don't be cut off in her iniquity, for it is the time of Yahweh's vengeance. He will render to her a recompense. ⁷ Babylon has been a golden cup in Yahweh's hand, who made all the earth drunk. The nations have drunk of her wine; therefore the nations have gone mad. ⁸ Babylon has suddenly fallen and been destroyed! Wail for her! Take balm for her pain. Perhaps she may be healed. ⁹"We would have healed Babylon, but she is not healed. Forsake her, and let's each go into his own country; for her judgment reaches to heaven, and is lifted up even to the skies. ¹⁰'Yahweh has produced our righteousness. Come, and let's declare in Zion the work of Yahweh our God.' ¹¹"Make the arrows sharp! Hold the shields firmly! Yahweh has stirred up the spirit of the kings of the Medes, because his purpose is against Babylon, to destroy it; for it is the vengeance of Yahweh, the vengeance of his temple. ¹² Set up a standard against the walls of Babylon! Make the watch strong! Set the watchmen, and prepare the ambushes; for Yahweh has both purposed and done that which he spoke concerning the inhabitants of Babylon. ¹³ You who dwell on many waters, abundant in treasures, your end has come, the measure of your covetousness. ¹⁴ Yahweh of Armies has sworn by himself, saying, 'Surely I will fill you with men, as with locusts, and they will lift up a shout against you.' ¹⁵"He has made the earth by his power. He has established the world by his wisdom. By his understanding he has stretched out the heavens. ¹⁶ When he utters his voice, there is a roar of waters in the heavens, and he causes the vapors to ascend from the ends of the earth. He makes lightning for the rain, and brings the wind out of his treasuries. ¹⁷"Every man has become stupid and without knowledge. Every goldsmith is disappointed by his image, for his molten images are falsehood, and there is no breath in them. ¹⁸ They are vanity, a work of delusion. In the time of their visitation, they will perish. ¹⁹ The portion of Jacob is not like these, for he formed all things, including the tribe of his inheritance. Yahweh of Armies is his name. ²⁰"You are my battle ax and weapons of war. With you I will break the nations into pieces. With you I will destroy kingdoms. ²¹ With you I will break in pieces the horse and his rider. 22 With you I will break in pieces the chariot and him who rides therein. With you I will break in pieces man and woman. With you I will break in pieces the old man and the youth. With you I will break in pieces the young man and the virgin. 23 With you I will break in pieces the shepherd and his flock. With you I will break in pieces the farmer and his yoke. With you I will break in pieces governors and deputies. 24"I will render to Babylon and to all the inhabitants of Chaldea all their evil that they have done in Zion in your sight," says Yahweh. 25"Behold, I am against you, destroying mountain," says Yahweh, "which destroys all the earth. I will stretch out my hand on you, roll you down from the rocks, and will make you a burned mountain. 26 They won't take a cornerstone from you, nor a stone for foundations; but you will be desolate forever," says Yahweh. 27"Set up a standard in the land! Blow the trumpet among the nations! Prepare the nations against her! Call together against her the kingdoms of Ararat, Minni, and Ashkenaz! Appoint a marshal against her! Cause the horses to come up as the swarming locusts! 28 Prepare against her the nations, the kings of the Medes, its governors, and all its deputies, and all the land of their dominion! 29 The land trembles and is in pain; for the purposes of Yahweh against Babylon stand, to make the land of Babylon a desolation, without inhabitant. 30 The mighty men of Babylon have stopped fighting, they remain in their strongholds. Their might has failed. They have become as women. Her dwelling places are set on fire. Her bars are broken. 31 One runner will run to meet another, and one messenger to meet another, to show the king of Babylon that his city is taken on every quarter. 32 So the passages are seized. They have burned the reeds with fire. The men of war are frightened." 33 For Yahweh of Armies, the God of Israel says: "The daughter of Babylon is like a threshing floor at the time when it is trodden. Yet a little while, and the time of harvest comes for her." 34"Nebuchadnezzar the king of Babylon has devoured me. He has crushed me. He has made me an empty vessel. He has, like a monster, swallowed me up. He has filled his mouth with my delicacies. He has cast me out. 35 May the violence done to me and to my flesh be on Babylon!" the inhabitant of Zion will say; and, "May my blood be on the inhabitants of Chaldea!" will Jerusalem say. 36 Therefore Yahweh says: "Behold, I will plead your cause, and take vengeance for you. I will dry up her sea, and make her fountain dry. 37 Babylon will become heaps, a dwelling place for jackals, an astonishment, and a hissing, without inhabitant. 38 They will roar together like young lions. They will growl as lions' cubs. 39 When they are inflamed, I will make their feast, and I will make them drunk, that they may rejoice, and sleep a perpetual sleep, and not wake up," says Yahweh. 40"I will bring them down like lambs to the slaughter, like rams with male goats. 41"How Sheshach is taken! How the praise of the whole earth is seized! How Babylon has become a desolation among the nations! 42 The sea has come up on Babylon. She is covered with the multitude of its waves. 43 Her cities have become a desolation, a dry land, and a desert, a land in which no man dwells. No son of man passes by it. 44 I will execute judgment on Bel in Babylon, and I will bring out of his mouth that which he has swallowed up. The nations will not flow any more to him. Yes, the wall of Babylon will fall. 45"My people, go away from the middle of her, and each of you save yourselves from Yahweh's fierce anger. 46 Don't let your heart faint. Don't fear for the news that will be heard in the land. For news will come one year, and after that in another year news will come, and violence in the land, ruler against ruler. 47 Therefore behold, the days come that I will execute judgment on the engraved images of Babylon; and her whole land will be confounded. All her slain will fall in the middle of her. 48 Then the heavens and the earth, and all that is therein, will sing for joy over Babylon; for the destroyers will come to her from the north," says Yahweh. 49"As Babylon has caused the slain of Israel to fall, so the slain of all the land will fall at Babylon. 50 You who have escaped the sword, go! Don't stand still! Remember Yahweh from afar, and let Jerusalem come into your mind." 51"We are confounded because we have heard reproach. Confusion has covered our faces, for strangers have come into the sanctuaries of Yahweh's house." 52"Therefore behold, the days come," says Yahweh, "that I will execute judgment on her engraved images; and through all her land the wounded will groan. 53 Though Babylon should mount up to the sky, and though she should fortify the height of her strength, yet destroyers will come to her from me," says Yahweh. 54"The sound of a cry comes from Babylon, and of great destruction from the land of the Chaldeans! 55 For Yahweh lays Babylon waste, and destroys out of her the great voice! Their waves roar like many waters. The noise of their voice is uttered. 56 For the destroyer has come on her, even on Babylon. Her mighty men are taken. Their bows are broken in pieces, for Yahweh is a God of retribution. He will surely repay. 57 I will make her princes, her wise men, her governors, her deputies, and her mighty men drunk. They will sleep a perpetual sleep, and not wake up," says the King, whose name is Yahweh of Armies. 58 Yahweh of Armies says: "The wide walls of Babylon will be utterly overthrown. Her high gates will be burned with fire. The peoples will labor for vanity, and the nations for the fire; and they will be weary." 59 The word which Jeremiah the prophet commanded Seraiah the son of Neriah, the son of Mahseiah, when he went with Zedekiah the king of Judah to Babylon in the fourth year of his reign. Now Seraiah was chief quartermaster. 60 Jeremiah wrote in a book all the evil that should come on Babylon, even all these words that are written concerning Babylon. 61 Jeremiah said to Seraiah, "When you come to Babylon, then see that you read all these words, 62 and say, 'Yahweh, you have spoken concerning this place, to cut it off, that no one will dwell in it, neither man nor animal, but that it will be desolate forever.' 63 It will be, when you have finished reading this book, that you shall bind a stone to it, and cast it into the middle of the Euphrates. 64 Then you shall say, 'Thus will Babylon sink, and will not rise again because of the evil that I will bring on her; and they will be weary.'" Thus far are the words of Jeremiah.

52

1 Zedekiah was twenty-one years old when he began to reign. He reigned eleven years in Jerusalem. His mother's name was Hamutal the daughter of Jeremiah of Libnah. 2 He did that which was evil in Yahweh's sight, according to all that Jehoiakim had done. 3 For through Yahweh's anger this happened in Jerusalem and Judah, until he had cast them out from his presence. Zedekiah rebelled against the king of Babylon. 4 In the ninth year of his reign, in the tenth month, in the tenth day of the month, Nebuchadnezzar king of Babylon came, he and all his army, against Jerusalem, and encamped against it; and they built forts against it round about. 5 So the city was besieged to the eleventh year of King Zedekiah. 6 In the fourth month, in the ninth day of the month, the famine was severe in the city, so that there was no bread for the people of the land. 7 Then a breach was made in the city, and all the men of war fled, and went out of the city by night by the way of the gate between the two walls, which was by the king's garden. Now the Chaldeans were against the city all around. The men of war went toward the Arabah, 8 but the army of the Chaldeans pursued the king, and overtook Zedekiah in the plains of Jericho; and all his army was scattered from him. 9 Then they took the king, and carried him up to the king of Babylon to Riblah in the land of Hamath; and he pronounced judgment on him. 10 The king of Babylon killed the sons of Zedekiah before his eyes. He also killed all the princes of Judah in Riblah. 11 He put out the eyes of Zedekiah; and the king of Babylon bound

him in fetters, and carried him to Babylon, and put him in prison until the day of his death. 12 Now in the fifth month, in the tenth day of the month, which was the nineteenth year of King Nebuchadnezzar, king of Babylon, Nebuzaradan the captain of the guard, who stood before the king of Babylon, came into Jerusalem. 13 He burned Yahweh's house, and the king's house; and all the houses of Jerusalem, even every great house, he burned with fire. 14 All the army of the Chaldeans, who were with the captain of the guard, broke down all the walls of Jerusalem all around. 15 Then Nebuzaradan the captain of the guard carried away captive of the poorest of the people, and the rest of the people who were left in the city, and those who fell away, who defected to the king of Babylon, and the rest of the multitude. 16 But Nebuzaradan the captain of the guard left of the poorest of the land to be vineyard keepers and farmers. 17 The Chaldeans broke the pillars of bronze that were in Yahweh's house and the bases and the bronze sea that were in Yahweh's house in pieces, and carried all of their bronze to Babylon. 18 They also took away the pots, the shovels, the snuffers, the basins, the spoons, and all the vessels of bronze with which they ministered. 19 The captain of the guard took away the cups, the fire pans, the basins, the pots, the lamp stands, the spoons, and the bowls; that which was of gold, as gold, and that which was of silver, as silver. 20 They took the two pillars, the one sea, and the twelve bronze bulls that were under the bases, which King Solomon had made for Yahweh's house. The bronze of all these vessels was without weight. 21 As for the pillars, the height of the one pillar was eighteen cubits; and a line of twelve cubits encircled it; and its thickness was four fingers. It was hollow. 22 A capital of bronze was on it; and the height of the one capital was five cubits, with network and pomegranates on the capital all around, all of bronze. The second pillar also had the same, with pomegranates. 23 There were ninety-six pomegranates on the sides; all the pomegranates were one hundred on the network all around. 24 The captain of the guard took Seraiah the chief priest, and Zephaniah the second priest, and the three keepers of the threshold, 25 and out of the city he took an officer who was set over the men of war; and seven men of those who saw the king's face, who were found in the city; and the scribe of the captain of the army, who mustered the people of the land; and sixty men of the people of the land, who were found in the middle of the city. 26 Nebuzaradan the captain of the guard took them, and brought them to the king of Babylon to Riblah. 27 The king of Babylon struck them, and put them to death at Riblah in the land of Hamath. So Judah was carried away captive out of his land. 28 This is the number of the people whom Nebuchadnezzar carried away captive: in the seventh year, three thousand twenty-three Jews; 29 in the eighteenth year of Nebuchadnezzar, he carried away captive from Jerusalem eight hundred thirty-two persons; 30 in the twenty-third year of Nebuchadnezzar, Nebuzaradan the captain of the guard carried away captive of the Jews seven hundred forty-five people. All the people numbered four thousand six hundred. 31 In the thirty-seventh year of the captivity of Jehoiachin king of Judah, in the twelfth month, in the twenty-fifth day of the month, Evilmerodach king of Babylon, in the first year of his reign, lifted up the head of Jehoiachin king of Judah, and released him from prison. 32 He spoke kindly to him, and set his throne above the throne of the kings who were with him in Babylon, 33 and changed his prison garments. Jehoiachin ate bread before him continually all the days of his life. 34 For his allowance, there was a continual allowance given him by the king of Babylon, every day a portion until the day of his death, all the days of his life.

The Lamentations of Jeremiah

1

1 How the city sits solitary, that was full of people! She has become as a widow, who was great among the nations! She who was a princess among the provinces has become a slave! 2 She weeps bitterly in the night. Her tears are on her cheeks. Among all her lovers she has no one to comfort her. All her friends have dealt treacherously with her. They have become her enemies. 3 Judah has gone into captivity because of affliction and because of great servitude. She dwells among the nations. She finds no rest. All her persecutors overtook her in her distress. 4 The roads to Zion mourn, because no one comes to the solemn assembly. All her gates are desolate. Her priests sigh. Her virgins are afflicted, and she herself is in bitterness. 5 Her adversaries have become the head. Her enemies prosper; for Yahweh has afflicted her for the multitude of her transgressions. Her young children have gone into captivity before the adversary. 6 All majesty has departed from the daughter of Zion. Her princes have become like deer that find no pasture. They have gone without strength before the pursuer. 7 Jerusalem remembers in the days of her affliction and of her miseries all her pleasant things that were from the days of old; when her people fell into the hand of the adversary, and no one helped her. The adversaries saw her. They mocked at her desolations. 8 Jerusalem has grievously sinned. Therefore she has become unclean. All who honored her despise her, because they have seen her nakedness. Yes, she sighs and turns backward. 9 Her filthiness was in her skirts. She didn't remember her latter end. Therefore she has come down astoundingly. She has no comforter. "See, Yahweh, my affliction; for the enemy has magnified himself." 10 The adversary has spread out his hand on all her pleasant things; for she has seen that the nations have entered into her sanctuary, concerning whom you commanded that they should not enter into your assembly. 11 All her people sigh. They seek bread. They have given their pleasant things for food to refresh their soul. "Look, Yahweh, and see, for I have become despised." 12"Is it nothing to you, all you who pass by? Look, and see if there is any sorrow like my sorrow, which is brought on me, with which Yahweh has afflicted me in the day of his fierce anger. 13"From on high has he sent fire into my bones, and it prevails against them. He has spread a net for my feet. He has turned me back. He has made me desolate and I faint all day long. 14"The yoke of my transgressions is bound by his

hand. They are knit together. They have come up on my neck. He made my strength fail. The Lord has delivered me into their hands, against whom I am not able to stand. ¹⁵"The Lord has set at nothing all my mighty men within me. He has called a solemn assembly against me to crush my young men. The Lord has trodden the virgin daughter of Judah as in a wine press. ¹⁶"For these things I weep. My eye, my eye runs down with water, because the comforter who should refresh my soul is far from me. My children are desolate, because the enemy has prevailed." ¹⁷ Zion spreads out her hands. There is no one to comfort her. Yahweh has commanded concerning Jacob, that those who are around him should be his adversaries. Jerusalem is among them as an unclean thing. ¹⁸"Yahweh is righteous, for I have rebelled against his commandment. Please hear all you peoples, and see my sorrow. My virgins and my young men have gone into captivity. ¹⁹"I called for my lovers, but they deceived me. My priests and my elders gave up the spirit in the city, while they sought food for themselves to refresh their souls. ²⁰"Look, Yahweh; for I am in distress. My heart is troubled. My heart turns over within me, for I have grievously rebelled. Abroad, the sword bereaves. At home, it is like death. ²¹"They have heard that I sigh. There is no one to comfort me. All my enemies have heard of my trouble. They are glad that you have done it. You will bring the day that you have proclaimed, and they will be like me. ²²"Let all their wickedness come before you. Do to them as you have done to me for all my transgressions. For my sighs are many, and my heart is faint.

2

¹ How has the Lord covered the daughter of Zion with a cloud in his anger! He has cast the beauty of Israel down from heaven to the earth, and hasn't remembered his footstool in the day of his anger. ² The Lord has swallowed up all the dwellings of Jacob without pity. He has thrown down in his wrath the strongholds of the daughter of Judah. He has brought them down to the ground. He has profaned the kingdom and its princes. ³ He has cut off all the horn of Israel in fierce anger. He has drawn back his right hand from before the enemy. He has burned up Jacob like a flaming fire, which devours all around. ⁴ He has bent his bow like an enemy. He has stood with his right hand as an adversary. He has killed all that were pleasant to the eye. In the tent of the daughter of Zion, he has poured out his wrath like fire. ⁵ The Lord has become as an enemy. He has swallowed up Israel. He has swallowed up all her palaces. He has destroyed his strongholds. He has multiplied mourning

and lamentation in the daughter of Judah. 6 He has violently taken away his tabernacle, as if it were a garden. He has destroyed his place of assembly. Yahweh has caused solemn assembly and Sabbath to be forgotten in Zion. In the indignation of his anger, he has despised the king and the priest. 7 The Lord has cast off his altar. He has abhorred his sanctuary. He has given the walls of her palaces into the hand of the enemy. They have made a noise in Yahweh's house, as in the day of a solemn assembly. 8 Yahweh has purposed to destroy the wall of the daughter of Zion. He has stretched out the line. He has not withdrawn his hand from destroying; He has made the rampart and wall lament. They languish together. 9 Her gates have sunk into the ground. He has destroyed and broken her bars. Her king and her princes are among the nations where the law is not. Yes, her prophets find no vision from Yahweh. 10 The elders of the daughter of Zion sit on the ground. They keep silence. They have cast up dust on their heads. They have clothed themselves with sackcloth. The virgins of Jerusalem hang down their heads to the ground. 11 My eyes fail with tears. My heart is troubled. My bile is poured on the earth, because of the destruction of the daughter of my people, because the young children and the infants swoon in the streets of the city. 12 They ask their mothers, "Where is grain and wine?" when they swoon as the wounded in the streets of the city, when their soul is poured out into their mothers' bosom. 13 What shall I testify to you? What shall I liken to you, daughter of Jerusalem? What shall I compare to you, that I may comfort you, virgin daughter of Zion? For your breach is as big as the sea. Who can heal you? 14 Your prophets have seen false and foolish visions for you. They have not uncovered your iniquity, to reverse your captivity, but have seen for you false revelations and causes of banishment. 15 All that pass by clap their hands at you. They hiss and wag their head at the daughter of Jerusalem, saying, "Is this the city that men called 'The perfection of beauty, the joy of the whole earth'?" 16 All your enemies have opened their mouth wide against you. They hiss and gnash their teeth. They say, "We have swallowed her up. Certainly this is the day that we looked for. We have found it. We have seen it." 17 Yahweh has done that which he planned. He has fulfilled his word that he commanded in the days of old. He has thrown down, and has not pitied. He has caused the enemy to rejoice over you. He has exalted the horn of your adversaries. 18 Their heart cried to the Lord. O wall of the daughter of Zion, let tears run down like a river day and night. Give yourself no relief. Don't let your eyes rest. 19 Arise, cry out in the night, at the beginning of the watches!

Pour out your heart like water before the face of the Lord. Lift up your hands toward him for the life of your young children, who faint for hunger at the head of every street. 20"Look, Yahweh, and see to whom you have done thus! Should the women eat their offspring, the children that they held and bounced on their knees? Should the priest and the prophet be killed in the sanctuary of the Lord? 21"The youth and the old man lie on the ground in the streets. My virgins and my young men have fallen by the sword. You have killed them in the day of your anger. You have slaughtered, and not pitied. 22"You have called, as in the day of a solemn assembly, my terrors on every side. There was no one that escaped or remained in the day of Yahweh's anger. My enemy has consumed those whom I have cared for and brought up.

3

1 I am the man who has seen affliction by the rod of his wrath. 2 He has led me and caused me to walk in darkness, and not in light. 3 Surely he turns his hand against me again and again all day long. 4 He has made my flesh and my skin old. He has broken my bones. 5 He has built against me, and surrounded me with bitterness and hardship. 6 He has made me dwell in dark places, as those who have been long dead. 7 He has walled me about, so that I can't go out. He has made my chain heavy. 8 Yes, when I cry, and call for help, he shuts out my prayer. 9 He has walled up my ways with cut stone. He has made my paths crooked. 10 He is to me as a bear lying in wait, as a lion in hiding. 11 He has turned away my path, and pulled me in pieces. He has made me desolate. 12 He has bent his bow, and set me as a mark for the arrow. 13 He has caused the shafts of his quiver to enter into my kidneys. 14 I have become a derision to all my people, and their song all day long. 15 He has filled me with bitterness. He has stuffed me with wormwood. 16 He has also broken my teeth with gravel. He has covered me with ashes. 17 You have removed my soul far away from peace. I forgot prosperity. 18 I said, "My strength has perished, along with my expectation from Yahweh." 19 Remember my affliction and my misery, the wormwood and the bitterness. 20 My soul still remembers them, and is bowed down within me. 21 This I recall to my mind; therefore I have hope. 22 It is because of Yahweh's loving kindnesses that we are not consumed, because his mercies don't fail. 23 They are new every morning. Great is your faithfulness. 24"Yahweh is my portion," says my soul. "Therefore I will hope in him." 25 Yahweh is good to those who wait for him, to the soul who seeks him. 26 It is good that a man should hope and quietly wait for the salvation of Yahweh. 27 It is good for a man that he bear the yoke

in his youth. 28 Let him sit alone and keep silence, because he has laid it on him. 29 Let him put his mouth in the dust, if it is so that there may be hope. 30 Let him give his cheek to him who strikes him. Let him be filled full of reproach. 31 For the Lord will not cast off forever. 32 For though he causes grief, yet he will have compassion according to the multitude of his loving kindnesses. 33 For he does not afflict willingly, nor grieve the children of men. 34 To crush under foot all the prisoners of the earth, 35 to turn away the right of a man before the face of the Most High, 36 to subvert a man in his cause, the Lord doesn't approve. 37 Who is he who says, and it comes to pass, when the Lord doesn't command it? 38 Doesn't evil and good come out of the mouth of the Most High? 39 Why should a living man complain, a man for the punishment of his sins? 40 Let us search and try our ways, and turn again to Yahweh. 41 Let's lift up our heart with our hands to God in the heavens. 42 "We have transgressed and have rebelled. You have not pardoned. 43 "You have covered us with anger and pursued us. You have killed. You have not pitied. 44 You have covered yourself with a cloud, so that no prayer can pass through. 45 You have made us an off-scouring and refuse in the middle of the peoples. 46 "All our enemies have opened their mouth wide against us. 47 Terror and the pit have come on us, devastation and destruction." 48 My eye runs down with streams of water, for the destruction of the daughter of my people. 49 My eye pours down and doesn't cease, without any intermission, 50 until Yahweh looks down, and sees from heaven. 51 My eye affects my soul, because of all the daughters of my city. 52 They have chased me relentlessly like a bird, those who are my enemies without cause. 53 They have cut off my life in the dungeon, and have cast a stone on me. 54 Waters flowed over my head. I said, "I am cut off." 55 I called on your name, Yahweh, out of the lowest dungeon. 56 You heard my voice: "Don't hide your ear from my sighing, and my cry." 57 You came near in the day that I called on you. You said, "Don't be afraid." 58 Lord, you have pleaded the causes of my soul. You have redeemed my life. 59 Yahweh, you have seen my wrong. Judge my cause. 60 You have seen all their vengeance and all their plans against me. 61 You have heard their reproach, Yahweh, and all their plans against me, 62 the lips of those that rose up against me, and their plots against me all day long. 63 You see their sitting down and their rising up. I am their song. 64 You will pay them back, Yahweh, according to the work of their hands. 65 You will give them hardness of heart, your curse to them. 66 You will pursue them in anger, and destroy them from under the heavens of Yahweh.

4

1 How the gold has become dim! The most pure gold has changed! The stones of the sanctuary are poured out at the head of every street. 2 The precious sons of Zion, comparable to fine gold, how they are esteemed as earthen pitchers, the work of the hands of the potter! 3 Even the jackals offer their breast. They nurse their young ones. But the daughter of my people has become cruel, like the ostriches in the wilderness. 4 The tongue of the nursing child clings to the roof of his mouth for thirst. The young children ask for bread, and no one breaks it for them. 5 Those who ate delicacies are desolate in the streets. Those who were brought up in purple embrace dunghills. 6 For the iniquity of the daughter of my people is greater than the sin of Sodom, which was overthrown as in a moment. No hands were laid on her. 7 Her nobles were purer than snow. They were whiter than milk. They were more ruddy in body than rubies. Their polishing was like sapphire. 8 Their appearance is blacker than a coal. They are not known in the streets. Their skin clings to their bones. It is withered. It has become like wood. 9 Those who are killed with the sword are better than those who are killed with hunger; for these pine away, stricken through, for lack of the fruits of the field. 10 The hands of the pitiful women have boiled their own children. They were their food in the destruction of the daughter of my people. 11 Yahweh has accomplished his wrath. He has poured out his fierce anger. He has kindled a fire in Zion, which has devoured its foundations. 12 The kings of the earth didn't believe, neither did all the inhabitants of the world, that the adversary and the enemy would enter into the gates of Jerusalem. 13 It is because of the sins of her prophets and the iniquities of her priests, that have shed the blood of the just in the middle of her. 14 They wander as blind men in the streets. They are polluted with blood, So that men can't touch their garments. 15 "Go away!" they cried to them. "Unclean! Go away! Go away! Don't touch! When they fled away and wandered, men said among the nations, "They can't live here any more." 16 Yahweh's anger has scattered them. He will not pay attention to them any more. They didn't respect the persons of the priests. They didn't favor the elders. 17 Our eyes still fail, looking in vain for our help. In our watching we have watched for a nation that could not save. 18 They hunt our steps, so that we can't go in our streets. Our end is near. Our days are fulfilled, for our end has come. 19 Our pursuers were swifter than the eagles of the sky. They chased us on the mountains. They set an ambush for us in the wilderness. 20 The breath of our nostrils, the

anointed of Yahweh, was taken in their pits; of whom we said, under his shadow we will live among the nations. 21 Rejoice and be glad, daughter of Edom, who dwells in the land of Uz. The cup will pass through to you also. You will be drunken, and will make yourself naked. 22 The punishment of your iniquity is accomplished, daughter of Zion. He will no more carry you away into captivity. He will visit your iniquity, daughter of Edom. He will uncover your sins.

5

1 Remember, Yahweh, what has come on us. Look, and see our reproach. 2 Our inheritance has been turned over to strangers, our houses to aliens. 3 We are orphans and fatherless. Our mothers are as widows. 4 We must pay for water to drink. Our wood is sold to us. 5 Our pursuers are on our necks. We are weary, and have no rest. 6 We have given our hands to the Egyptians, and to the Assyrians, to be satisfied with bread. 7 Our fathers sinned, and are no more. We have borne their iniquities. 8 Servants rule over us. There is no one to deliver us out of their hand. 9 We get our bread at the peril of our lives, because of the sword in the wilderness. 10 Our skin is black like an oven, because of the burning heat of famine. 11 They ravished the women in Zion, the virgins in the cities of Judah. 12 Princes were hanged up by their hands. The faces of elders were not honored. 13 The young men carry millstones. The children stumbled under loads of wood. 14 The elders have ceased from the gate, and the young men from their music. 15 The joy of our heart has ceased. Our dance is turned into mourning. 16 The crown has fallen from our head. Woe to us, for we have sinned! 17 For this our heart is faint. For these things our eyes are dim: 18 for the mountain of Zion, which is desolate. The foxes walk on it. 19 You, Yahweh, remain forever. Your throne is from generation to generation. 20 Why do you forget us forever, and forsake us for so long a time? 21 Turn us to yourself, Yahweh, and we will be turned. Renew our days as of old. 22 But you have utterly rejected us. You are very angry against us.

The Book of Baruch

The book of *Baruch* is recognized as Deuterocanonical Scripture by the Roman Catholic, Greek Orthodox, and Russian Orthodox Churches. In some Bibles, Baruch chapter **6** is listed as a separate book called *The Letter of Jeremiah*, reflecting its separation from Baruch in some copies of the Greek Septuagint.

1

1 These are the words of the book which Baruch the son of Nerias, the son of Maaseas, the son of Sedekias, the son of Asadias, the son of Helkias, wrote in Babylon, 2 in the fifth year, in the seventh day of the month, at the time when the Chaldeans took Jerusalem and burned it with fire. 3 Baruch read the words of this book in the hearing of Jechonias the son of Joakim king of Judah, and in the hearing of all the people who came to hear the book, 4 and in the hearing of the mighty men, and of the kings' sons, and in the hearing of the elders, and in the hearing of all the people, from the least to the greatest, even of all those who lived at Babylon by the river Sud. 5 Then they wept, fasted, and prayed before the Lord. 6 They also made a collection of money according to every man's ability; 7 and they sent it to Jerusalem to Joakim the high priest, the son of Helkias, the son of Salom, and to the priests and to all the people who were found with him at Jerusalem, 8 at the same time when he took the vessels of the house of the Lord, that had been carried out of the temple, to return them into the land of Judah, the tenth day of Sivan—silver vessels which Sedekias the son of Josias king of Judah had made, 9 after Nabuchodonosor king of Babylon had carried away Jechonias, the princes, the captives, the mighty men, and the people of the land from Jerusalem, and brought them to Babylon. 10 And they said: Behold, we have sent you money; therefore buy with the money burnt offerings, sin offerings, and incense, and prepare an oblation, and offer upon the altar of the Lord our God; 11 and pray for the life of Nabuchodonosor king of Babylon, and for the life of Baltasar his son, that their days may be as the days of heaven above the earth. 12 The Lord will give us strength and light to our eyes. We will live under the shadow of Nabuchodonosor king of Babylon and under the shadow of Baltasar his son, and we shall serve them many days, and find favor in their sight. 13 Pray for us also to the Lord our God, for we have sinned against the Lord our God. To this day the wrath of the Lord and his indignation is not turned from us. 14 You shall read this book which we have sent to you, to

160

make confession in the house of the Lord upon the day of the feast and on the days of the solemn assembly. 15 You shall say: To the Lord our God belongs righteousness, but to us confusion of face, as at this day—to the men of Judah, to the inhabitants of Jerusalem, 16 to our kings, to our princes, to our priests, to our prophets, and to our fathers, 17 because we have sinned before the Lord. 18 We have disobeyed him and have not listened to the voice of the Lord our God, to walk in the commandments of the Lord that he has set before us. 19 Since the day that the Lord brought our fathers out of the land of Egypt to this present day, we have been disobedient to the Lord our God, and we have been negligent in not listening to his voice. 20 Therefore the plagues have clung to us, along with the curse which the Lord declared through Moses his servant in the day that he brought our fathers out of the land of Egypt to give us a land that flows with milk and honey, as at this day. 21 Nevertheless we didn't listen to the voice of the Lord our God, according to all the words of the prophets whom he sent to us, 22 but we each walked in the imagination of his own wicked heart, to serve strange gods and to do what is evil in the sight of the Lord our God.

2

1 Therefore the Lord has made good his word which he pronounced against us, and against our judges who judged Israel, and against our kings, and against our princes, and against the men of Israel and Judah, 2 to bring upon us great plagues such as never happened before under the whole heaven, as it came to pass in Jerusalem, according to the things that are written in the law of Moses, 3 that we should each eat the flesh of our own son, and each eat the flesh of our own daughter. 4 Moreover he has given them to be in subjection to all the kingdoms that are around us, to be a reproach and a desolation among all the people around us, where the Lord has scattered them. 5 Thus they were cast down and not exalted, because we sinned against the Lord our God in not listening to his voice. 6 To the Lord our God belongs righteousness, but to us and to our fathers confusion of face, as at this day. 7 All these plagues have come upon us which the Lord has pronounced against us. 8 Yet have we not entreated the favor of the Lord by everyone turning from the thoughts of his wicked heart. 9 Therefore the Lord has kept watch over the plagues. The Lord has brought them upon us, for the Lord is righteous in all his works which he has commanded us. 10 Yet we have not listened to his voice, to walk in the commandments of the Lord that he has set before us. 11 And now, O Lord, you God of Israel who have brought your

people out of the land of Egypt with a mighty hand, with signs, with wonders, with great power, and with a high arm, and have gotten yourself a name, as at this day: 12 O Lord our God, we have sinned. We have been ungodly. We have done wrong in all your ordinances. 13 Let your wrath turn from us, for we are but a few left among the heathen where you have scattered us. 14 Hear our prayer, O Lord, and our petition, and deliver us for your own sake. Give us favor in the sight of those who have led us away captive, 15 that all the earth may know that you are the Lord our God, because Israel and his posterity is called by your name. 16 O Lord, look down from your holy house and consider us. Incline your ear, O Lord, and hear. 17 Open your eyes, and see; for the dead that are in Hades, whose breath is taken from their bodies, will give to the Lord neither glory nor righteousness; 18 but the soul who is greatly vexed, who goes stooping and feeble, and the eyes that fail, and the hungry soul, will declare your glory and righteousness, O Lord. 19 For we do not present our supplication before you, O Lord our God, for the righteousness of our fathers and of our kings. 20 For you have sent your wrath and your indignation upon us, as you have spoken by your servants the prophets, saying, 21"The Lord says, 'Bow your shoulders to serve the king of Babylon, and remain in the land that I gave to your fathers. 22 But if you won't hear the voice of the Lord to serve the king of Babylon, 23 I will cause to cease out of the cities of Judah and from the region near Jerusalem the voice of mirth, the voice of gladness, voice of the bridegroom, and the voice of the bride. The whole land will be desolate without inhabitant.'" 24 But we wouldn't listen to your voice, to serve the king of Babylon. Therefore you have made good your words that you spoke by your servants the prophets, that the bones of our kings and the bones of our fathers would be taken out of their places. 25 Behold, they are cast out to the heat by day and to the frost by night. They died in great miseries by famine, by sword, and by pestilence. 26 You have made the house that is called by your name as it is today because of the wickedness of the house of Israel and the house of Judah. 27 Yet, O Lord our God, you have dealt with us after all your kindness and according to all your great mercy, 28 as you spoke by your servant Moses in the day when you commanded him to write your law in the presence of the children of Israel, saying, 29"If you won't hear my voice, surely this very great multitude will be turned into a small number among the nations where I will scatter them. 30 For I know that they will not hear me, because they are a stiff-necked people; but in the land of their captivity they will take it to heart, 31 and will know that I am the Lord their God. I will give them a heart and ears to hear. ³² Then they will praise me in the land of their captivity, and think about my name, ³³ and will return from their stiff neck and from their wicked deeds; for they will remember the way of their fathers who sinned before the Lord. ³⁴ I will bring them again into the land which I promised to their fathers, to Abraham, to Isaac, and to Jacob, and they will rule over it. I will increase them, and they won't be diminished. ³⁵ And I will make an everlasting covenant with them to be their God, and they will be my people. I will no more remove my people Israel out of the land that I have given them."

3

¹ O Lord Almighty, you God of Israel, the soul in anguish and the troubled spirit cries to you. ² Hear, O Lord, and have mercy; for you are a merciful God. Yes, have mercy upon us, because we have sinned before you. ³ For you are enthroned forever, and we keep perishing. ⁴ O Lord Almighty, you God of Israel, hear now the prayer of the dead Israelites, and of the children of those who were sinners before you, who didn't listen to the voice of you their God; because of this, these plagues cling to us. ⁵ Don't remember the iniquities of our fathers, but remember your power and your name at this time. ⁶ For you are the Lord our God, and we will praise you, O Lord. ⁷ For this cause, you have put your fear in our hearts, to the intent that we should call upon your name. We will praise you in our captivity, for we have called to mind all the iniquity of our fathers who sinned before you. ⁸ Behold, we are yet this day in our captivity where you have scattered us, for a reproach and a curse, and to be subject to penalty according to all the iniquities of our fathers who departed from the Lord our God. ⁹ Hear, O Israel, the commandments of life! Give ear to understand wisdom! ¹⁰ How is it, O Israel, that you are in your enemies' land, that you have become old in a strange country, that you are defiled with the dead, ¹¹ that you are counted with those who are in Hades? ¹² You have forsaken the fountain of wisdom. ¹³ If you had walked in the way of God, you would have dwelled in peace forever. ¹⁴ Learn where there is wisdom, where there is strength, and where there is understanding, that you may also know where there is length of days and life, where there is the light of the eyes and peace. ¹⁵ Who has found out her place? Who has come into her treasuries? ¹⁶ Where are the princes of the heathen, and those who ruled the beasts that are on the earth, ¹⁷ those who had their pastime with the fowls of the air, and those who hoarded up silver and gold, in which people trust, and of their getting there is no end? ¹⁸ For those who diligently sought silver,

and were so anxious, and whose works are past finding out, 19 they have vanished and gone down to Hades, and others have come up in their place. 20 Younger men have seen the light and lived upon the earth, but they haven't known the way of knowledge, 21 nor understood its paths. Their children haven't embraced it. They are far off from their way. 22 It has not been heard of in Canaan, neither has it been seen in Teman. 23 The sons also of Agar who seek understanding, which are in the land, the merchants of Merran and Teman, and the authors of fables, and the searchers out of understanding— none of these have known the way of wisdom or remembered her paths. 24 O Israel, how great is the house of God! How large is the place of his possession! 25 It is great and has no end. It is high and unmeasurable. 26 Giants were born that were famous of old, great of stature, and expert in war. 27 God didn't choose these, nor did he give the way of knowledge to them, 28 so they perished, because they had no wisdom. They perished through their own foolishness. 29 Who has gone up into heaven, taken her, and brought her down from the clouds? 30 Who has gone over the sea, found her, and will bring her for choice gold? 31 There is no one who knows her way, nor any who comprehend her path. 32 But he that knows all things knows her, he found her out with his understanding. He who prepared the earth for all time has filled it with four-footed beasts. 33 It is he who sends forth the light, and it goes. He called it, and it obeyed him with fear. 34 The stars shone in their watches, and were glad. When he called them, they said, "Here we are." They shone with gladness to him who made them. 35 This is our God. No other can be compared to him. 36 He has found out all the way of knowledge, and has given it to Jacob his servant and to Israel who is loved by him. 37 Afterward she appeared upon earth, and lived with men.

4

1 This is the book of God's commandments and the law that endures forever. All those who hold it fast will live, but those who leave it will die. 2 Turn, O Jacob, and take hold of it. Walk toward the shining of its light. 3 Don't give your glory to another, nor the things that are to your advantage to a foreign nation. 4 O Israel, we are happy; for the things that are pleasing to God are made known to us. 5 Be of good cheer, my people, the memorial of Israel. 6 You were not sold to the nations for destruction, but because you moved God to wrath, you were delivered to your adversaries. 7 For you provoked him who made you by sacrificing to demons and not to God. 8 You forgot the everlasting God who brought you up. You also grieved Jerusalem, who

nursed you. 9 For she saw the wrath that came upon you from God, and said, "Listen, you who dwell near Zion; for God has brought upon me great mourning. 10 For I have seen the captivity of my sons and daughters, which the Everlasting has brought upon them. 11 For with joy I nourished them, but sent them away with weeping and mourning. 12 Let no man rejoice over me, a widow and forsaken by many. For the sins of my children, I am left desolate, because they turned away from the law of God 13 and had no regard for his statutes. They didn't walk in the ways of God's commandments or tread in the paths of discipline in his righteousness. 14 Let those who dwell near Zion come and remember the captivity of my sons and daughters, which the Everlasting has brought upon them. 15 For he has brought a nation upon them from afar, a shameless nation with a strange language, who didn't respect old men or pity children. 16 They have carried away the dear beloved sons of the widow, and left her who was alone desolate of her daughters." 17 But I—how can I help you? 18 For he who brought these calamities upon you will deliver you from the hand of your enemies. 19 Go your way, O my children. Go your way, for I am left desolate. 20 I have put off the garment of peace, and put on the sackcloth of my petition. I will cry to the Everlasting as long as I live. 21 Take courage, my children. Cry to God, and he will deliver you from the power and hand of the enemies. 22 For I have trusted in the Everlasting, that he will save you; and joy has come to me from the Holy One, because of the mercy that will soon come to you from your Everlasting Savior. 23 For I sent you out with mourning and weeping, but God will give you to me again with joy and gladness forever. 24 For as now those who dwell near Zion have seen your captivity, so they will shortly see your salvation from our God which will come upon you with great glory and brightness of the Everlasting. 25 My children, suffer patiently the wrath that has come upon you from God, for your enemy has persecuted you; but shortly you will see his destruction and will tread upon their necks. 26 My delicate ones have traveled rough roads. They were taken away like a flock carried off by enemies. 27 Take courage, my children, and cry to God; for you will be remembered by him who has brought this upon you. 28 For as it was your decision to go astray from God, return and seek him ten times more. 29 For he who brought these calamities upon you will bring you everlasting joy again with your salvation. 30 Take courage, O Jerusalem, for he who called you by name will comfort you. 31 Miserable are those who afflicted you and rejoiced at your fall. 32 Miserable are the cities which your children served. Miserable is she who received your sons. 33 For as she rejoiced at your fall and was glad of your ruin, so she will be grieved at her own desolation. 34 And I will take away her pride in her great multitude and her boasting will be turned into mourning. 35 For fire will come upon her from the Everlasting for many days; and she will be inhabited by demons for a long time. 36 O Jerusalem, look around you toward the east, and behold the joy that comes to you from God. 37 Behold, your sons come, whom you sent away. They come gathered together from the east to the west at the word of the Holy One, rejoicing in the glory of God.

5

1 Take off the garment of your mourning and affliction, O Jerusalem, and put on forever the beauty of the glory from God. 2 Put on the robe of the righteousness from God. Set on your head a diadem of the glory of the Everlasting. 3 For God will show your splendor everywhere under heaven. 4 For your name will be called by God forever "Righteous Peace, Godly Glory". 5 Arise, O Jerusalem, and stand upon the height. Look around you toward the east and see your children gathered from the going down of the sun to its rising at the word of the Holy One, rejoicing that God has remembered them. 6 For they went from you on foot, being led away by their enemies, but God brings them in to you carried on high with glory, on a royal throne. 7 For God has appointed that every high mountain and the everlasting hills should be made low, and the valleys filled up to make the ground level, that Israel may go safely in the glory of God. 8 Moreover the woods and every sweet smelling tree have shaded Israel by the commandment of God. 9 For God will lead Israel with joy in the light of his glory with the mercy and righteousness that come from him.

The Letter of Jeremiah

6

1 A copy of a letter that Jeremy sent to those who were to be led captives into Babylon by the king of the Babylonians, to give them the message that God commanded him. 2 Because of the sins which you have committed before God, you will be led away captives to Babylon by Nabuchodonosor king of the Babylonians. 3 So when you come to Babylon, you will remain there many years, and for a long season, even for seven generations. After that, I will bring you out peacefully from there. 4 But now you will see in Babylon gods of silver, gold, wood carried on shoulders, which cause the nations to fear. 5 Beware therefore that you in no way become like these foreigners. Don't let fear take hold of you because of them when you see the multitude before them and behind them, worshiping them. 6 But say in your hearts, "O Lord, we must worship you." 7 For my angel is with you, and I myself care for your souls. 8 For their tongue is polished by the workman, and they themselves are overlaid with gold and with silver; yet they are only fake, and can't speak. 9 And taking gold, as if it were for a virgin who loves to be happy, they make crowns for the heads of their gods. 10 Sometimes also the priests take gold and silver from their gods, and spend it on themselves. 11 They will even give some of it to the common prostitutes. They dress them like men with garments, even the gods of silver, gods of gold, and gods of wood. 12 Yet these gods can't save themselves from rust and moths, even though they are covered with purple garments. 13 They wipe their faces because of the dust of the temple, which is thick upon them. 14 And he who can't put to death one who offends against him holds a sceptre, as though he were judge of a country. 15 He has also a dagger in his right hand, and an axe, but can't deliver himself from war and robbers. 16 By this they are known not to be gods. Therefore don't fear them. 17 For like a vessel that a man uses is worth nothing when it is broken, even so it is with their gods. When they are set up in the temples, their eyes are full of dust through the feet of those who come in. 18 As the courts are secured on every side upon him who offends the king, as being committed to suffer death, even so the priests secure their temples with doors, with locks, and bars, lest they be carried off by robbers. 19 They light candles for them, yes, more than for themselves, even though they can't see one. 20 They are like one of the beams of the temple. Men say their hearts are eaten out when things creeping out of the earth devour both them

and their clothing. They don't feel it ²¹ when their faces are blackened through the smoke that comes out of the temple. ²² Bats, swallows, and birds land on their bodies and heads. So do the cats. ²³ By this you may know that they are no gods. Therefore don't fear them. ²⁴ Notwithstanding the gold with which they are covered to make them beautiful, unless someone wipes off the tarnish, they won't shine; for they didn't even feel it when they were molten. ²⁵ Things in which there is no breath are bought at any cost. ²⁶ Having no feet, they are carried upon shoulders. By this, they declare to men that they are worth nothing. ²⁷ Those who serve them are also ashamed, for if they fall to the ground at any time, they can't rise up again by themselves. If they are bowed down, they can't make themselves straight; but the offerings are set before them, as if they were dead men. ²⁸ And the things that are sacrificed to them, their priests sell and spend. In like manner, their wives also lay up part of it in salt; but to the poor and to the impotent they give none of it. ²⁹ The menstruous woman and the woman in childbed touch their sacrifices, knowing therefore by these things that they are no gods. Don't fear them. ³⁰ For how can they be called gods? Because women set food before the gods of silver, gold, and wood. ³¹ And in their temples the priests sit on seats, having their clothes torn and their heads and beards shaven, and nothing on their heads. ³² They roar and cry before their gods, as men do at the feast when one is dead. ³³ The priests also take off garments from them and clothe their wives and children with them. ³⁴ Whether it is evil or good what one does to them, they are not able to repay it. They can't set up a king or put him down. ³⁵ In like manner, they can neither give riches nor money. Though a man make a vow to them and doesn't keep it, they will never exact it. ³⁶ They can save no man from death. They can't deliver the weak from the mighty. ³⁷ They can't restore a blind man to his sight, or deliver anyone who is in distress. ³⁸ They can show no mercy to the widow, or do good to the fatherless. ³⁹ They are like the stones that are cut out of the mountain, these gods of wood that are overlaid with gold and with silver. Those who minister to them will be confounded. ⁴⁰ How could a man then think or say that they are gods, when even the Chaldeans themselves dishonor them? ⁴¹ If they shall see one mute who can't speak, they bring him and ask him to call upon Bel, as though he were able to understand. ⁴² Yet they can't perceive this themselves, and forsake them; for they have no understanding. ⁴³ The women also with cords around them sit in the ways, burning bran for incense; but if any of them, drawn by someone who passes by, lies with him, she reproaches her fellow, that she was not thought as worthy as herself and her cord wasn't broken. 44 Whatever is done among them is false. How could a man then think or say that they are gods? 45 They are fashioned by carpenters and goldsmiths. They can be nothing else than what the workmen make them to be. 46 And they themselves who fashioned them can never continue long. How then should the things that are fashioned by them? 47 For they have left lies and reproaches to those who come after. 48 For when there comes any war or plague upon them, the priests consult with themselves, where they may be hidden with them. 49 How then can't men understand that they are no gods, which can't save themselves from war or from plague? 50 For seeing they are only wood and overlaid with gold and silver, it will be known hereafter that they are false. 51 It will be manifest to all nations and kings that they are no gods, but the works of men's hands, and that there is no work of God in them. 52 Who then may not know that they are not gods? 53 For they can't set up a king in a land or give rain to men. 54 They can't judge their own cause, or redress a wrong, being unable; for they are like crows between heaven and earth. 55 For even when fire falls upon the house of gods of wood overlaid with gold or with silver, their priests will flee away, and escape, but they themselves will be burned apart like beams. 56 Moreover they can't withstand any king or enemies. How could a man then admit or think that they are gods? 57 Those gods of wood overlaid with silver or with gold aren't able to escape from thieves or robbers. 58 The gold, silver, and garments with which they are clothed—those who are strong will take from them, and go away with them. They won't be able to help themselves. 59 Therefore it is better to be a king who shows his manhood, or else a vessel in a house profitable for whatever the owner needs, than such false gods—or even a door in a house, to keep the things safe that are in it, than such false gods; or better to be a pillar of wood in a palace than such false gods. 60 For sun, moon, and stars, being bright and sent to do their jobs, are obedient. 61 Likewise also the lightning when it flashes is beautiful to see. In the same way, the wind also blows in every country. 62 And when God commands the clouds to go over the whole world, they do as they are told. 63 And the fire sent from above to consume mountains and woods does as it is commanded; but these are to be compared to them neither in show nor power. 64 Therefore a man shouldn't think or say that they are gods, seeing they aren't able to judge causes or to do good to men. 65 Knowing therefore that they are no gods, don't fear them. 66 For they can neither curse nor bless kings. 67 They can't show signs in the heavens among the nations, or shine as the sun, or give light as the moon. 68 The beasts are better than they; for they can get under a covert, and help themselves. 69 In no way then is it manifest to us that they are gods. Therefore don't fear them. 70 For as a scarecrow in a garden of cucumbers that keeps nothing, so are their gods of wood overlaid with gold and silver. 71 Likewise also their gods of wood overlaid with gold and with silver, are like a white thorn in an orchard that every bird sits upon. They are also like a dead body that is thrown out into the dark. 72 You will know them to be no gods by the bright purple that rots upon them. They themselves will be consumed afterwards, and will be a reproach in the country. 73 Better therefore is the just man who has no idols; for he will be far from reproach.

4 Baruch, or Paralipomena of Jeremiah

1

1 It came to pass, when the children of Israel were taken captive by the king of the Chaldeans, that God spoke to Jeremiah saying: Jeremiah, my chosen [one] *[servant]*, arise and depart from this city, you and Baruch, since I am going to destroy it because of the multitude of the sins of those who dwell in it. 2 For your prayers are like a solid pillar in its midst, and like an indestructible wall surrounding it. 3 Now, then, arise and depart before the host of the Chaldeans surrounds it. 4 And Jeremiah answered, saying: I beseech you, Lord, permit me, your servant, to speak in your presence. 5 And the Lord said to him: Speak, my chosen [one] *[servant]* Jeremiah. 6 And Jeremiah spoke, saying: Lord Almighty, would you deliver the chosen city into the hands of the Chaldeans, so that the king with the multitude of his people might boast and say: "I have prevailed over the holy city of God"? 7 No, my Lord, but if it is your will, let it be destroyed by your hands. 8 And the Lord said to Jeremiah: Since you are my chosen one, arise and depart form this city, you and Baruch, for I am going to destroy it because of the multitude of the sins of those who dwell in it. 9 For neither the king nor his host will be able to enter it unless I first open its gates. 10 Arise, then, and go to Baruch, and tell him these words. 11 And when you have arisen at the sixth hour of the night, go out on the city walls and I will show you that unless I first destroy the city, they cannot enter it. 12 When the Lord had said this, he departed from Jeremiah.

2

1 And Jeremiah ran and told these things to Baruch; and as they went into the temple of God, Jeremiah tore his garments and put dust on his head and entered the holy place of God. 2 And when Baruch saw him with dust sprinkled on his head and his garments torn, he cried out in a loud voice, saying: Father Jeremiah, what are you doing? What sin has the people committed? 3 (For whenever the people sinned, Jeremiah would sprinkle dust on his head and would pray for the people until their sin was forgiven.) 4 So Baruch asked him, saying: Father, what is this? 5 And Jeremiah said to him: Refrain from rending your garments — rather, let us rend our hearts! And let us not draw water for the trough, but let us weep and fill them with tears! For the Lord will not have mercy on this people. 6 And Baruch said: Father Jeremiah, what has happened? 7 And Jeremiah said: God is delivering the city

into the hands of the king of the Chaldeans, to take the people captive into Babylon. 8 And when Baruch heard these things, he also tore his garments and said: Father Jeremiah, who has made this known to you? 9 And Jeremiah said to him: Stay with me awhile, until the sixth hour of the night, so that you may know that this word is true. 10 Therefore they both remained in the altar-area weeping, and their garments were torn.

3

1 And when the hour of the night arrived, as the Lord had told Jeremiah they came up together on the walls of the city, Jeremiah and Baruch. 2 And behold, there came a sound of trumpets; and angels emerged from heaven holding torches in their hands, and they set them on the walls of the city. 3 And when Jeremiah and Baruch saw them, they wept, saying: Now we know that the word is true! 4 And Jeremiah besought the angels, saying: I beseech you, do not destroy the city yet, until I say something to the Lord. 5 And the Lord spoke to the angels, saying: Do not destroy the city until I speak to my chosen one, Jeremiah. 6 Then Jeremiah spoke, saying: I beg you, Lord, bid me to speak in your presence. 7 And the Lord said: Speak, my chosen [one] [servant] Jeremiah. 8 And Jeremiah said: Behold, Lord, now we know that you are delivering the city into the hands of its enemies, and they will take the people away to Babylon. What do you want me to do with the holy vessels of the temple service? 10 And the Lord said to him: Take them and consign them to the earth, saying: Hear, Earth, the voice of your creator who formed you in the abundance of waters, who sealed you with seven seals for seven epochs, and after this you will receive your ornaments (?) — 11 Guard the vessels of the temple service until the gathering of the beloved. 12 And Jeremiah spoke, saying: I beseech you, Lord, show me what I should do for Abimelech the Ethiopian, for he has done many kindnesses to your servant Jeremiah. 13 For he pulled me out of the miry pit; and I do not wish that he should see the destruction and desolation of this city, but that you should be merciful to him and that he should not be grieved. 14 And the Lord said to Jeremiah: Send him to the vineyard of Agrippa, and I will hide him in the shadow of the mountain until I cause the people to return to the city. 15 And you, Jeremiah, go with your people into Babylon and stay with them, preaching to them, until I cause them to return to the city. 16 But leave Baruch here until I speak with him. 17 When he had said these things, the Lord ascended from Jeremiah into heaven. 18 But Jeremiah and Baruch entered the holy place, and taking the vessels of the temple service, they consigned them

to the earth as the Lord had told them. ¹⁹ And immediately the earth swallowed them. ²⁰ And they both sat down and wept. ²¹ And when morning came, Jeremiah sent Abimelech, saying: Take a basket and go to the estate of Agrippa by the mountain road, and bring back some figs to give to the sick among the people; for the favor of the Lord is on you and his glory is on your head. ²² And when he had said this, Jeremiah sent him away; and Abimelech went as he told him.

4

¹ And when morning came, behold the host of the Chaldeans surrounded the city. ² And the great angel trumpeted, saying: Enter the city, host of the Chaldeans; for behold, the gate is opened for you. ³ Therefore let the king enter, with his multitudes, and let him take all the people captive. ⁴ But taking the keys of the temple, Jeremiah went outside the city and threw them away in the presence of the sun, saying: I say to you, Sun, take the keys of the temple of God and guard them until the day in which the Lord asks you for them. ⁵ For we have not been found worthy to keep them, for we have become unfaithful guardians. ⁶ While Jeremiah was still weeping for the people, they brought him out with the people and dragged them into Babylon. ⁷ But Baruch put dust on his head and sat and wailed this lamentation, saying: Why has Jerusalem been devastated? Because of the sins of the beloved people she was delivered into the hands of enemies — because of our sins and those of the people. ⁸ But let not the lawless ones boast and say: "We were strong enough to take the city of God by our might;" but it was delivered to you because of our sins. ⁹ And God will pity us and cause us to return to our city, but you will not survive! ¹⁰ Blessed are our fathers, Abraham, Isaac and Jacob, for they departed from this world and did not see the destruction of this city. ¹¹ When he had said this, Baruch departed from the city, weeping and saying: Grieving because of you, Jerusalem, I went out from you. ¹² And he remained sitting in a tomb, while the angels came to him and explained to him everything that the Lord revealed to him through them.

5

¹ But Abimelech took the figs in the burning heat; and coming upon a tree, he sat under its shade to rest a bit. ² And leaning his head on the basket of figs, he fell asleep and slept for 66 years; and he was not awakened from his slumber. ³ And afterward, when he awoke from his sleep, he said: I slept sweetly for a little while, but my head is heavy because I did not get enough

sleep. 4 Then he uncovered the basket of figs and found them dripping milk. 5 And he said: I would like to sleep a little longer, because my head is heavy. But I am afraid that I might fall asleep and be late in awakening and my father Jeremiah would think badly of me; for if he were not in a hurry, he would not have sent me today at daybreak. 6 So I will get up, and proceed in the burning heat; for isn't there heat, isn't there toil every day? 7 So he got up and took the basket of figs and placed it on his shoulders, and he entered into Jerusalem and did not recognize it — neither his own house, nor the place — nor did he find his own family or any of his acquaintances. 8 And he said: The Lord be blessed, for a great trance has come over me today! 9 This is not the city Jerusalem — and I have lost my way because I came by the mountain road when I arose from my sleep; and since my head was heavy because I did not get enough sleep, I lost my way. 10 It will seem incredible to Jeremiah that I lost my way! 11 And he departed from the city; and as he searched he saw the landmarks of the city, and he said: Indeed, this is the city; I lost my way. 12 And again he returned to the city and searched, and found no one of his own people; and he said: The Lord be blessed, for a great trance has come over me! 13 And again he departed from the city, and he stayed there grieving, not knowing where he should go. 14 And he put down the basket, saying: I will sit here until the Lord takes this trance from me. 15 And as he sat, he saw an old man coming from the field; and Abimelech said to him: I say to you, old man, what city is this? 16 And he said to him: It is Jerusalem. 17 And Abimelech said to him: Where is Jeremiah the priest, and Baruch the secretary, and all the people of this city, for I could not find them? 18 And the old man said to him: Are you not from this city, seeing that you remember Jeremiah today, because you are asking about him after such a long time? 19 For Jeremiah is in Babylon with the people; for they were taken captive by king Nebuchadnezzar, and Jeremiah is with them to preach the good news to them and to teach them the word. 20 As soon as Abimelech heard this from the old man, he said: If you were not an old man, and if it were not for the fact that it is not lawful for a man to upbraid one older than himself, I would laugh at you and say that you are out of your mind — since you say that the people have been taken captive into Babylon. 21 Even if the heavenly torrents had descended on them, there has not yet been time for them to go into Babylon! 22 For how much time has passed since my father Jeremiah sent me to the estate of Agrippa to bring a few figs, so that I might give them to the sick among the people? 23 And I went and got them, and when I came to a certain tree in the burning heat, I sat to rest a little; and I leaned my head on the basket and fell asleep. 24 And when I awoke I uncovered the basket of figs, supposing that I was late; and I found the figs dripping milk, just as I had collected them. 25 But you claim that the people have been taken captive into Babylon. 26 But that you might know, take the figs and see! 27 And he uncovered the basket of figs for the old man, and he saw them dripping milk. 28 And when the old man saw them, he said: O my son, you are a righteous man, and God did not want you to see the desolation of the city, so he brought this trance upon you. 29 For behold it is 66 years today since the people were taken captive into Babylon. 30 But that you might learn, my son, that what I tell you is true — look into the field and see that the ripening of the crops has not appeared. 31 And notice that the figs are not in season, and be enlightened. 32 Then Abimelech cried out in a loud voice, saying: I bless you, God of heaven and earth, the Rest of the souls of the righteous in every place! 33 Then he said to the old man: What month is this? 34 And he said: Nisan (which is Abib). 35 And taking some of figs, he gave them to the old man and said to him: May God illumine your way to the city above, Jerusalem.

6

1 After this, Abimelech went out of the city and prayed to the Lord. 2 And behold, an angel of the Lord came and took him by the right hand and brought him back to where Baruch was sitting, and he found him in a tomb. 3 And when they saw each other, they both wept and kissed each other. 4 But when Baruch looked up he saw with his own eyes the figs that were covered in Abimelech's basket. 5 And lifting his eyes to heaven, he prayed, saying: 6 You are the God who gives a reward to those who love you. Prepare yourself, my heart, and rejoice and be glad while you are in your tabernacle, saying to your fleshly house, "your grief has been changed to joy;" for the Sufficient One is coming and will deliver you in your tabernacle — for there is no sin in you. 7 Revive in your tabernacle, in your virginal faith, and believe that you will live! 8 Look at this basket of figs — for behold, they are 66 years old and have not become shrivelled or rotten, but they are dripping milk. 9 So it will be with you, my flesh, if you do what is commanded you by the angel of righteousness. 10 He who preserved the basket of figs, the same will again preserve you by his power. 11 When Baruch had said this, he said to Abimelech: Stand up and let us pray that the Lord may make known to us how we shall be able to send to Jeremiah in Babylon the report about the

shelter provided for you on the way. 12 And Baruch prayed, saying: Lord God, our strength is the elect light which comes forth from your mouth. 13 We beseech and beg of your goodness — you whose great name no one is able to know — hear the voice of your servants and let knowledge come into our hearts. 14 What shall we do, and how shall we send this report to Jeremiah in Babylon? 15 And while Baruch was still praying, behold an angel of the Lord came and said all these words to Baruch: Agent of the light, do not be anxious about how you will send to Jeremiah; for an eagle is coming to you at the hour of light tomorrow, and you will direct him to Jeremiah. 16 Therefore, write in a letter: Say to the children of Israel: Let the stranger who comes among you be set apart and let 15 days go by; and after this I will lead you into your city, says the Lord. 17 He who is not separated from Babylon will not enter into the city; and I will punish them by keeping them from being received back by the Babylonians, says the Lord. 18 And when the angel had said this, he departed from Baruch. 19 And Baruch sent to the market of the gentiles and got papyrus and ink and wrote a letter as follows: Baruch, the servant of God, writes to Jeremiah in the captivity of Babylon: 20 Greetings! Rejoice, for God has not allowed us to depart from this body grieving for the city which was laid waste and outraged. 21 Wherefore the Lord has had compassion on our tears, and has remembered the covenant which he established with our fathers Abraham, Isaac and Jacob. 22 And he sent his angel to me, and he told me these words which I send to you. 23 These, then, are the words which the Lord, the God of Israel, spoke, who led us out of Egypt, out of the great furnace: Because you did not keep my ordinances, but your heart was lifted up, and you were haughty before me, in anger and wrath I delivered you to the furnace in Babylon. 24 If, therefore, says the Lord, you listen to my voice, from the mouth of Jeremiah my servant, I will bring the one who listens up from Babylon; but the one who does not listen will become a stranger to Jerusalem and to Babylon. 25 And you will test them by means of the water of the Jordan; whoever does not listen will be exposed — this is the sign of the great seal.

7

1 And Baruch got up and departed from the tomb and found the eagle sitting outside the tomb. 2 And the eagle said to him in a human voice: Hail, Baruch, steward of the faith. 3 And Baruch said to him: You who speak are chosen from among all the birds of heaven, for this is clear from the gleam of your eyes; tell me, then, what are you doing here? 4 And the eagle said to him: I

was sent here so that you might through me send whatever message you want. 5 And Baruch said to him: Can you carry this message to Jeremiah in Babylon? 6 And the eagle said to him: Indeed, it was for this reason I was sent. 7 And Baruch took the letter, and 15 figs from Abimelech's basket, and tied them to the eagle's neck and said to him: I say to you, king of the birds, go in peace with good health and carry the message for me. 8 Do not be like the raven which Noah sent out and which never came back to him in the ark; but be like the dove which, the third time, brought a report to the righteous one. 9 So you also, take this good message to Jeremiah and to those in bondage with him, that it may be well with you-take this papyrus to the people and to the chosen one of God. 10 Even if all the birds of heaven surround you and want to fight with you, struggle — the Lord will give you strength. 11 And do not turn aside to the right or to the left, but straight as a speeding arrow, go in the power of God, and the glory of the Lord will be with you the entire way. 12 Then the eagle took flight and went away to Babylon, having the letter tied to his neck; and when he arrived he rested on a post outside the city in a desert place. 13 And he kept silent until Jeremiah came along, for he and some of the people were coming out to bury a corpse outside the city. 14 (For Jeremiah had petitioned king Nebuchadnezzar, saying: "Give me a place where I may bury those of my people who have died;" and the king gave it to him.) 15 And as they were coming out with the body, and weeping, they came to where the eagle was. 16 And the eagle cried out in a loud voice, saying: I say to you, Jeremiah the chosen [one] *[servant]* of God, go and gather together the people and come here so that they may hear a letter which I have brought to you from Baruch and Abimelech. 17 And when Jeremiah heard this, he glorified God; and he went and gathered together the people along with their wives and children, and he came to where the eagle was. 18 And the eagle came down on the corpse, and it revived. 19 (Now this took place so that they might believe.) 20 And all the people were astounded at what had happened, and said: This is the God who appeared to our fathers in the wilderness through Moses, and now he has appeared to us through the eagle. 21 And the eagle said: I say to you, Jeremiah, come, untie this letter and read it to the people — So he untied the letter and read it to the people. 22 And when the people heard it, they wept and put dust on their heads, and they said to Jeremiah: Deliver us and tell us what to do that we may once again enter our city. 23 And Jeremiah answered and said to them: Do whatever you heard from the letter, and the Lord will lead us into our city. 24 And Jeremiah wrote a letter to Baruch, saying thus: My beloved son, do not be negligent in your prayers, beseeching God on our behalf, that he might direct our way until we come out of the jurisdiction of this lawless king. 25 For you have been found righteous before God, and he did not let you come here, lest you see the affliction which has come upon the people at the hands of the Babylonians. 26 For it is like a father with an only son, who is given over for punishment; and those who see his father and console him cover his face, lest he see how his son is being punished, and be even more ravaged by grief. 27 For thus God took pity on you and did not let you enter Babylon lest you see the affliction of the people. 28 For since we came here, grief has not left us, for 66 years today. 29 For many times when I went out I found some of the people hung up by king Nebuchadnezzar, crying and saying: "Have mercy on us, God-ZAR!" 30 When I heard this, I grieved and cried with two-fold mourning, not only because they were hung up, but because they were calling on a foreign God, saying "Have mercy on us." 31 But I remembered days of festivity which we celebrated in Jerusalem before our captivity; and when I remembered, I groaned, and returned to my house wailing and weeping. 32 Now, then, pray in the place where you are — you and Abimelech — for this people, that they may listen to my voice and to the decrees of my mouth, so that we may depart from here. 33 For I tell you that the entire time that we have spent here they have kept us in subjection, saying: Recite for us a song from the songs of Zion — the song of your God. *Psalm 3-4* 34 And we reply to them: How shall we sing for you since we are in a foreign land? 35 And after this, Jeremiah tied the letter to the eagle's neck, saying: Go in peace, and may the Lord watch over both of us. 36 And the eagle took flight and came to Jerusalem and gave the letter to Baruch; and when he had untied it he read it and kissed it and wept when he heard about the distresses and afflictions of the people. 37 But Jeremiah took the figs and distributed them to the sick among the people, and he kept teaching them to abstain from the pollutions of the gentiles of Babylon.

8

1 And the day came in which the Lord brought the people out of Babylon. 2 And the Lord said to Jeremiah: Rise up — you and the people — and come to the Jordan and say to the people: Let anyone who desires the Lord forsake the works of Babylon. 3 As for the men who took wives from them and the women who took husbands from them — those who listen to you shall cross over, and you take them into Jerusalem; but those who do not listen to you,

do not lead them there. 4 And Jeremiah spoke these words to the people, and they arose and came to the Jordan to cross over. 5 As he told them the words that the Lord had spoken to him, half of those who had taken spouses from them did not wish to listen to Jeremiah, but said to him: We will never forsake our wives, but we will bring them back with us into our city. 6 So they crossed the Jordan and came to Jerusalem. 7 And Jeremiah and Baruch and Abimelech stood up and said: No man joined with Babylonians shall enter this city! 8 And they said to one another: Let us arise and return to Babylon to our place — And they departed. 9 But while they were coming to Babylon, the Babylonians came out to meet them, saying: You shall not enter our city, for you hated us and you left us secretly; therefore you cannot come in with us. 10 For we have taken a solemn oath together in the name of our god to receive neither you nor your children, since you left us secretly. 11 And when they heard this, they returned and came to a desert place some distance from Jerusalem and built a city for themselves and named it 'SAMARIA.' 12 And Jeremiah sent to them, saying: Repent, for the angel of righteousness is coming and will lead you to your exalted place.

9

1 Now those who were with Jeremiah were rejoicing and offering sacrifices on behalf of the people for nine days. 2 But on the tenth, Jeremiah alone offered sacrifice. 3 And he prayed a prayer, saying: Holy, holy, holy, fragrant aroma of the living trees, true light that enlightens me until I ascend to you; 4 For your mercy, I beg you — for the sweet voice of the two seraphim, I beg — for another fragrant aroma. 5 And may Michael, archangel of righteousness, who opens the gates to the righteous, be my guardian (?) until he causes the righteous to enter. 6 I beg you, almighty Lord of all creation, unbegotten and incomprehensible, in whom all judgment was hidden before these things came into existence. 7 When Jeremiah had said this, and while he was standing in the altar-area with Baruch and Abimelech, he became as one whose soul had departed. 8 And Baruch and Abimelech were weeping and crying out in a loud voice: Woe to us! For our father Jeremiah has left us — the priest of God has departed! 9 And all the people heard their weeping and they all ran to them and saw Jeremiah lying on the ground as if dead. 10 And they tore their garments and put dust on their heads and wept bitterly. 11 And after this they prepared to bury him. 12 And behold, there came a voice saying: Do not bury the one who yet lives, for his soul is returning to his body! 13 And when they heard the voice they did not bury him, but stayed

around his tabernacle for three days saying, "when will he arise?" 14 And after three days his soul came back into his body and he raised his voice in the midst of them all and said: Glorify God with one voice! All of you glorify God and the son of God who awakens us — messiah Jesus — the light of all the ages, the inextinguishable lamp, the life of faith. 15 But after these times there shall be 477 years more and he comes to earth. 16 And the tree of life planted in the midst of paradise will cause all the unfruitful trees to bear fruit, and will grow and sprout forth. 17 And the trees that had sprouted and became haughty and said: "We have supplied our power (?) to the air," he will cause them to wither, with the grandeur of their branches, and he will cause them to be judged — that firmly rooted tree! 18 And what is crimson will become white as wool — the snow will be blackened — the sweet waters will become salty, and the salty sweet, in the intense light of the joy of God. 19 And he will bless the isles so that they become fruitful by the word of the mouth of his messiah. 20 For he shall come, and he will go out and choose for himself twelve apostles to proclaim the news among the nations– he whom I have seen adorned by his father and coming into the world on the Mount of Olives — and he shall fill the hungry souls. 21 When Jeremiah was saying this concerning the son of God — that he is coming into the world — the people became very angry and said: This is a repetition of the words spoken by Isaiah son of Amos, when he said: I saw God and the son of God. 22 Come, then, and let us not kill him by the same sort of death with which we killed Isaiah, but let us stone him with stones. 23 And Baruch and Abimelech were greatly grieved because they wanted to hear in full the mysteries that he had seen. 24 But Jeremiah said to them: Be silent and weep not, for they cannot kill me until I describe for you everything I saw. 25 And he said to them: Bring a stone here to me. 26 And he set it up and said: Light of the ages, make this stone to become like me in appearance, until I have described to Baruch and Abimelech everything I saw. 27 Then the stone, by God's command, took on the appearance of Jeremiah. 28 And they were stoning the stone, supposing that it was Jeremiah! 29 But Jeremiah delivered to Baruch and to Abimelech all the mysteries he had seen, and forthwith he stood in the midst of the people desiring to complete his ministry. 30 Then the stone cried out, saying: O foolish children of Israel, why do you stone me, supposing that I am Jeremiah? Behold, Jeremiah is standing in your midst! 31 And when they saw him, immediately they rushed upon him with many stones, and his ministry was fulfilled. 32 And when Baruch and Abimelech came, they buried him, and taking the stone they placed it on his tomb and inscribed it thus: This is the stone that was the ally of Jeremiah.

The Book of Ezekiel

1

1 Now in the thirtieth year, in the fourth month, in the fifth day of the month, as I was among the captives by the river Chebar, the heavens were opened, and I saw visions of God. 2 In the fifth of the month, which was the fifth year of King Jehoiachin's captivity, 3 Yahweh's word came to Ezekiel the priest, the son of Buzi, in the land of the Chaldeans by the river Chebar; and Yahweh's hand was there on him. 4 I looked, and behold, a stormy wind came out of the north: a great cloud, with flashing lightning, and a brightness around it, and out of the middle of it as it were glowing metal, out of the middle of the fire. 5 Out of its center came the likeness of four living creatures. This was their appearance: They had the likeness of a man. 6 Everyone had four faces, and each one of them had four wings. 7 Their feet were straight feet. The sole of their feet was like the sole of a calf's foot; and they sparkled like burnished bronze. 8 They had the hands of a man under their wings on their four sides. The four of them had their faces and their wings like this: 9 Their wings were joined to one another. They didn't turn when they went. Each one went straight forward. 10 As for the likeness of their faces, they had the face of a man. The four of them had the face of a lion on the right side. The four of them had the face of an ox on the left side. The four of them also had the face of an eagle. 11 Such were their faces. Their wings were spread out above. Two wings of each one touched another, and two covered their bodies. 12 Each one went straight forward. Where the spirit was to go, they went. They didn't turn when they went. 13 As for the likeness of the living creatures, their appearance was like burning coals of fire, like the appearance of torches. The fire went up and down among the living creatures. The fire was bright, and lightning went out of the fire. 14 The living creatures ran and returned as the appearance of a flash of lightning. 15 Now as I saw the living creatures, behold, there was one wheel on the earth beside the living creatures, for each of the four faces of it. 16 The appearance of the wheels and their work was like a beryl. The four of them had one likeness. Their appearance and their work was as it were a wheel within a wheel. 17 When they went, they went in their four directions. They didn't turn when they went. 18 As for their rims, they were high and dreadful; and the four of them had their rims full of eyes all around. 19 When the living creatures went, the wheels went beside them. When the living creatures were lifted up from

the earth, the wheels were lifted up. ²⁰ Wherever the spirit was to go, they went. The spirit was to go there. The wheels were lifted up beside them; for the spirit of the living creature was in the wheels. ²¹ When those went, these went. When those stood, these stood. When those were lifted up from the earth, the wheels were lifted up beside them; for the spirit of the living creature was in the wheels. ²² Over the head of the living creature there was the likeness of an expanse, like an awesome crystal to look at, stretched out over their heads above. ²³ Under the expanse, their wings were straight, one toward the other. Each one had two which covered on this side, and each one had two which covered their bodies on that side. ²⁴ When they went, I heard the noise of their wings like the noise of great waters, like the voice of the Almighty, a noise of tumult like the noise of an army. When they stood, they let down their wings. ²⁵ There was a voice above the expanse that was over their heads. When they stood, they let down their wings. ²⁶ Above the expanse that was over their heads was the likeness of a throne, as the appearance of a sapphire stone. On the likeness of the throne was a likeness as the appearance of a man on it above. ²⁷ I saw as it were glowing metal, as the appearance of fire within it all around, from the appearance of his waist and upward; and from the appearance of his waist and downward I saw as it were the appearance of fire, and there was brightness around him. ²⁸ As the appearance of the rainbow that is in the cloud in the day of rain, so was the appearance of the brightness all around. This was the appearance of the likeness of Yahweh's glory. When I saw it, I fell on my face, and I heard a voice of one that spoke.

2

¹ He said to me, "Son of man, stand on your feet, and I will speak with you." ² The Spirit entered into me when he spoke to me, and set me on my feet; and I heard him who spoke to me. ³ He said to me, "Son of man, I send you to the children of Israel, to a nation of rebels who have rebelled against me. They and their fathers have transgressed against me even to this very day. ⁴ The children are impudent and stiff-hearted. I am sending you to them, and you shall tell them, 'This is what the Lord Yahweh says.' ⁵ They, whether they will hear, or whether they will refuse—for they are a rebellious house—yet they will know that there has been a prophet among them. ⁶ You, son of man, don't be afraid of them, neither be afraid of their words, though briers and thorns are with you, and you dwell among scorpions. Don't be afraid of their words, nor be dismayed at their looks, though they are a rebellious house. ⁷

You shall speak my words to them, whether they will hear or whether they will refuse; for they are most rebellious. 8 But you, son of man, hear what I tell you. Don't be rebellious like that rebellious house. Open your mouth, and eat that which I give you." 9 When I looked, behold, a hand was stretched out to me; and behold, a scroll of a book was in it. 10 He spread it before me. It was written within and without; and lamentations, mourning, and woe were written in it.

3

1 He said to me, "Son of man, eat what you find. Eat this scroll, and go, speak to the house of Israel." 2 So I opened my mouth, and he caused me to eat the scroll. 3 He said to me, "Son of man, eat this scroll that I give you and fill your belly and your bowels with it." Then I ate it. It was as sweet as honey in my mouth. 4 He said to me, "Son of man, go to the house of Israel, and speak my words to them. 5 For you are not sent to a people of a strange speech and of a hard language, but to the house of Israel— 6 not to many peoples of a strange speech and of a hard language, whose words you can't understand. Surely, if I sent you to them, they would listen to you. 7 But the house of Israel will not listen to you, for they will not listen to me; for all the house of Israel are obstinate and hard-hearted. 8 Behold, I have made your face hard against their faces, and your forehead hard against their foreheads. 9 I have made your forehead as a diamond, harder than flint. Don't be afraid of them, neither be dismayed at their looks, though they are a rebellious house." 10 Moreover he said to me, "Son of man, receive in your heart and hear with your ears all my words that I speak to you. 11 Go to them of the captivity, to the children of your people, and speak to them, and tell them, 'This is what the Lord Yahweh says,' whether they will hear, or whether they will refuse." 12 Then the Spirit lifted me up, and I heard behind me the voice of a great rushing, saying, "Blessed be Yahweh's glory from his place." 13 I heard the noise of the wings of the living creatures as they touched one another, and the noise of the wheels beside them, even the noise of a great rushing. 14 So the Spirit lifted me up, and took me away; and I went in bitterness, in the heat of my spirit; and Yahweh's hand was strong on me. 15 Then I came to them of the captivity at Tel Aviv who lived by the river Chebar, and to where they lived; and I sat there overwhelmed among them seven days. 16 At the end of seven days, Yahweh's word came to me, saying, 17"Son of man, I have made you a watchman to the house of Israel. Therefore hear the word from my mouth, and warn them from me. 18 When I tell the wicked, 'You will surely

die;' and you give him no warning, nor speak to warn the wicked from his wicked way, to save his life, that wicked man will die in his iniquity; but I will require his blood at your hand. 19 Yet if you warn the wicked, and he doesn't turn from his wickedness, nor from his wicked way, he will die in his iniquity; but you have delivered your soul." 20"Again, when a righteous man turns from his righteousness and commits iniquity, and I lay a stumbling block before him, he will die. Because you have not given him warning, he will die in his sin, and his righteous deeds which he has done will not be remembered; but I will require his blood at your hand. 21 Nevertheless if you warn the righteous man, that the righteous not sin, and he does not sin, he will surely live, because he took warning; and you have delivered your soul." 22 Yahweh's hand was there on me; and he said to me, "Arise, go out into the plain, and I will talk with you there." 23 Then I arose, and went out into the plain, and behold, Yahweh's glory stood there, like the glory which I saw by the river Chebar. Then I fell on my face. 24 Then the Spirit entered into me and set me on my feet. He spoke with me, and said to me, "Go, shut yourself inside your house. 25 But you, son of man, behold, they will put ropes on you, and will bind you with them, and you will not go out among them. 26 I will make your tongue stick to the roof of your mouth so that you will be mute and will not be able to correct them, for they are a rebellious house. 27 But when I speak with you, I will open your mouth, and you shall tell them, 'This is what the Lord Yahweh says.' He who hears, let him hear; and he who refuses, let him refuse; for they are a rebellious house."

4

1"You also, son of man, take a tile, and lay it before yourself, and portray on it a city, even Jerusalem. 2 Lay siege against it, build forts against it, and cast up a mound against it. Also set camps against it and plant battering rams against it all around. 3 Take for yourself an iron pan and set it for a wall of iron between you and the city. Then set your face toward it. It will be besieged, and you shall lay siege against it. This shall be a sign to the house of Israel. 4"Moreover lie on your left side, and lay the iniquity of the house of Israel on it. According to the number of the days that you shall lie on it, you shall bear their iniquity. 5 For I have appointed the years of their iniquity to be to you a number of days, even three hundred ninety days. So you shall bear the iniquity of the house of Israel. 6"Again, when you have accomplished these, you shall lie on your right side, and shall bear the iniquity of the house of Judah. I have appointed forty days, each day for a year, to you. 7 You shall set your face toward the siege of Jerusalem, with your arm uncovered; and you shall prophesy against it. 8 Behold, I put ropes on you, and you shall not turn yourself from one side to the other, until you have accomplished the days of your siege. 9 "Take for yourself also wheat, barley, beans, lentils, millet, and spelt, and put them in one vessel. Make bread of it. According to the number of the days that you will lie on your side, even three hundred ninety days, you shall eat of it. 10 Your food which you shall eat shall be by weight, twenty shekels a day. From time to time you shall eat it. 11 You shall drink water by measure, the sixth part of a hin. From time to time you shall drink. 12 You shall eat it as barley cakes, and you shall bake it in their sight with dung that comes out of man." 13 Yahweh said, "Even thus will the children of Israel eat their bread unclean, among the nations where I will drive them." 14 Then I said, "Ah Lord Yahweh! Behold, my soul has not been polluted; for from my youth up even until now I have not eaten of that which dies of itself, or is torn of animals. No abominable meat has come into my mouth!" 15 Then he said to me, "Behold, I have given you cow's dung for man's dung, and you shall prepare your bread on it." 16 Moreover he said to me, "Son of man, behold, I will break the staff of bread in Jerusalem. They will eat bread by weight, and with fearfulness. They will drink water by measure, and in dismay; 17 that they may lack bread and water, be dismayed one with another, and pine away in their iniquity.

5

1 "You, son of man, take a sharp sword. You shall take it as a barber's razor to yourself, and shall cause it to pass over your head and over your beard. Then take balances to weigh and divide the hair. 2 A third part you shall burn in the fire in the middle of the city, when the days of the siege are fulfilled. You shall take a third part, and strike with the sword around it. A third part you shall scatter to the wind, and I will draw out a sword after them. 3 You shall take a small number of these and bind them in the folds of your robe. 4 Of these again you shall take, and cast them into the middle of the fire, and burn them in the fire. From it a fire will come out into all the house of Israel. 5 "The Lord Yahweh says: 'This is Jerusalem. I have set her in the middle of the nations, and countries are around her. 6 She has rebelled against my ordinances in doing wickedness more than the nations, and against my statutes more than the countries that are around her; for they have rejected my ordinances, and as for my statutes, they have not walked in them.' 7 "Therefore the Lord Yahweh says: 'Because you are more turbulent than the

nations that are around you, and have not walked in my statutes, neither have kept my ordinances, neither have followed the ordinances of the nations that are around you; 8 therefore the Lord Yahweh says: 'Behold, I, even I, am against you; and I will execute judgments among you in the sight of the nations. 9 I will do in you that which I have not done, and which I will not do anything like it any more, because of all your abominations. 10 Therefore the fathers will eat the sons within you, and the sons will eat their fathers. I will execute judgments on you; and I will scatter the whole remnant of you to all the winds. 11 Therefore as I live,' says the Lord Yahweh, 'surely, because you have defiled my sanctuary with all your detestable things, and with all your abominations, therefore I will also diminish you. My eye won't spare, and I will have no pity. 12 A third part of you will die with the pestilence, and they will be consumed with famine within you. A third part will fall by the sword around you. A third part I will scatter to all the winds, and will draw out a sword after them. 13"'Thus my anger will be accomplished, and I will cause my wrath toward them to rest, and I will be comforted. They will know that I, Yahweh, have spoken in my zeal, when I have accomplished my wrath on them. 14"'Moreover I will make you a desolation and a reproach among the nations that are around you, in the sight of all that pass by. 15 So it will be a reproach and a taunt, an instruction and an astonishment, to the nations that are around you, when I execute judgments on you in anger and in wrath, and in wrathful rebukes—I, Yahweh, have spoken it— 16 when I send on them the evil arrows of famine that are for destruction, which I will send to destroy you. I will increase the famine on you and will break your staff of bread. 17 I will send on you famine and evil animals, and they will bereave you. Pestilence and blood will pass through you. I will bring the sword on you. I, Yahweh, have spoken it.'"

6

1 Yahweh's word came to me, saying, 2"Son of man, set your face toward the mountains of Israel, and prophesy to them, 3 and say, 'You mountains of Israel, hear the word of the Lord Yahweh! The Lord Yahweh says to the mountains and to the hills, to the watercourses and to the valleys: "Behold, I, even I, will bring a sword on you, and I will destroy your high places. 4 Your altars will become desolate, and your incense altars will be broken. I will cast down your slain men before your idols. 5 I will lay the dead bodies of the children of Israel before their idols. I will scatter your bones around your altars. 6 In all your dwelling places, the cities will be laid waste and the high

places will be desolate, so that your altars may be laid waste and made desolate, and your idols may be broken and cease, and your incense altars may be cut down, and your works may be abolished. 7 The slain will fall among you, and you will know that I am Yahweh. 8““Yet I will leave a remnant, in that you will have some that escape the sword among the nations, when you are scattered through the countries. 9 Those of you that escape will remember me among the nations where they are carried captive, how I have been broken with their lewd heart, which has departed from me, and with their eyes, which play the prostitute after their idols. Then they will loathe themselves in their own sight for the evils which they have committed in all their abominations. 10 They will know that I am Yahweh. I have not said in vain that I would do this evil to them.”’ 11“The Lord Yahweh says: ‘Strike with your hand, and stamp with your foot, and say, “Alas!”, because of all the evil abominations of the house of Israel; for they will fall by the sword, by the famine, and by the pestilence. 12 He who is far off will die of the pestilence. He who is near will fall by the sword. He who remains and is besieged will die by the famine. Thus I will accomplish my wrath on them. 13 You will know that I am Yahweh when their slain men are among their idols around their altars, on every high hill, on all the tops of the mountains, under every green tree, and under every thick oak—the places where they offered pleasant aroma to all their idols. 14 I will stretch out my hand on them and make the land desolate and waste, from the wilderness toward Diblah, throughout all their habitations. Then they will know that I am Yahweh.’”

7

1 Moreover Yahweh’s word came to me, saying, 2“You, son of man, the Lord Yahweh says to the land of Israel, ‘An end! The end has come on the four corners of the land. 3 Now the end is on you, and I will send my anger on you, and will judge you according to your ways. I will bring on you all your abominations. 4 My eye will not spare you, neither will I have pity; but I will bring your ways on you, and your abominations will be among you. Then you will know that I am Yahweh.’ 5“The Lord Yahweh says: ‘A disaster! A unique disaster! Behold, it comes. 6 An end has come. The end has come! It awakes against you. Behold, it comes. 7 Your doom has come to you, inhabitant of the land! The time has come! The day is near, a day of tumult, and not of joyful shouting, on the mountains. 8 Now I will shortly pour out my wrath on you, and accomplish my anger against you, and will judge you according to your ways. I will bring on you all your abominations. 9 My eye

won't spare, neither will I have pity. I will punish you according to your ways. Your abominations will be among you. Then you will know that I, Yahweh, strike. 10 "Behold, the day! Behold, it comes! Your doom has gone out. The rod has blossomed. Pride has budded. 11 Violence has risen up into a rod of wickedness. None of them will remain, nor of their multitude, nor of their wealth. There will be nothing of value among them. 12 The time has come! The day draws near. Don't let the buyer rejoice, nor the seller mourn; for wrath is on all its multitude. 13 For the seller won't return to that which is sold, although they are still alive; for the vision concerns the whole multitude of it. None will return. None will strengthen himself in the iniquity of his life. 14 They have blown the trumpet, and have made all ready; but no one goes to the battle, for my wrath is on all its multitude. 15 "The sword is outside, and the pestilence and the famine within. He who is in the field will die by the sword. He who is in the city will be devoured by famine and pestilence. 16 But of those who escape, they will escape and will be on the mountains like doves of the valleys, all of them moaning, everyone in his iniquity. 17 All hands will be feeble, and all knees will be weak as water. 18 They will also clothe themselves with sackcloth, and horror will cover them. Shame will be on all faces, and baldness on all their heads. 19 They will cast their silver in the streets, and their gold will be as an unclean thing. Their silver and their gold won't be able to deliver them in the day of Yahweh's wrath. They won't satisfy their souls or fill their bellies; because it has been the stumbling block of their iniquity. 20 As for the beauty of his ornament, he set it in majesty; but they made the images of their abominations and their detestable things therein. Therefore I have made it to them as an unclean thing. 21 I will give it into the hands of the strangers for a prey, and to the wicked of the earth for a plunder; and they will profane it. 22 I will also turn my face from them, and they will profane my secret place. Robbers will enter into it, and profane it. 23 "Make chains, for the land is full of bloody crimes, and the city is full of violence. 24 Therefore I will bring the worst of the nations, and they will possess their houses. I will also make the pride of the strong to cease. Their holy places will be profaned. 25 Destruction comes! They will seek peace, and there will be none. 26 Mischief will come on mischief, and rumor will be on rumor. They will seek a vision of the prophet; but the law will perish from the priest, and counsel from the elders. 27 The king will mourn, and the prince will be clothed with desolation. The hands of the people of the land will be troubled. I will do to them after their way, and according to their own judgments I will judge them. Then they will know that I am Yahweh.'"

8

1 In the sixth year, in the sixth month, in the fifth day of the month, as I sat in my house, and the elders of Judah sat before me, the Lord Yahweh's hand fell on me there. 2 Then I saw, and behold, a likeness as the appearance of fire —from the appearance of his waist and downward, fire, and from his waist and upward, as the appearance of brightness, as it were glowing metal. 3 He stretched out the form of a hand, and took me by a lock of my head; and the Spirit lifted me up between earth and the sky, and brought me in the visions of God to Jerusalem, to the door of the gate of the inner court that looks toward the north, where there was the seat of the image of jealousy, which provokes to jealousy. 4 Behold, the glory of the God of Israel was there, according to the appearance that I saw in the plain. 5 Then he said to me, "Son of man, lift up your eyes now the way toward the north." So I lifted up my eyes the way toward the north, and saw, northward of the gate of the altar this image of jealousy in the entry. 6 He said to me, "Son of man, do you see what they do? Even the great abominations that the house of Israel commit here, that I should go far off from my sanctuary? But you will again see yet other great abominations." 7 He brought me to the door of the court; and when I looked, behold, a hole in the wall. 8 Then he said to me, "Son of man, dig now in the wall." When I had dug in the wall, I saw a door. 9 He said to me, "Go in, and see the wicked abominations that they do here." 10 So I went in and looked, and saw every form of creeping things, abominable animals, and all the idols of the house of Israel, portrayed around on the wall. 11 Seventy men of the elders of the house of Israel stood before them. In the middle of them Jaazaniah the son of Shaphan stood, every man with his censer in his hand; and the smell of the cloud of incense went up. 12 Then he said to me, "Son of man, have you seen what the elders of the house of Israel do in the dark, every man in his rooms of imagery? For they say, 'Yahweh doesn't see us. Yahweh has forsaken the land.'" 13 He said also to me, "You will again see more of the great abominations which they do." 14 Then he brought me to the door of the gate of Yahweh's house which was toward the north; and I saw the women sit there weeping for Tammuz. 15 Then he said to me, "Have you seen this, son of man? You will again see yet greater abominations than these." 16 He brought me into the inner court of Yahweh's house; and I saw at the door of Yahweh's temple, between the porch and the altar, there were about twenty-five men with their backs toward Yahweh's

temple and their faces toward the east. They were worshiping the sun toward the east. 17 Then he said to me, "Have you seen this, son of man? Is it a light thing to the house of Judah that they commit the abominations which they commit here? For they have filled the land with violence, and have turned again to provoke me to anger. Behold, they put the branch to their nose. 18 Therefore I will also deal in wrath. My eye won't spare, neither will I have pity. Though they cry in my ears with a loud voice, yet I will not hear them."

9

1 Then he cried in my ears with a loud voice, saying, "Cause those who are in charge of the city to draw near, each man with his destroying weapon in his hand." 2 Behold, six men came from the way of the upper gate, which lies toward the north, every man with his slaughter weapon in his hand. One man in the middle of them was clothed in linen, with a writer's inkhorn by his side. They went in, and stood beside the bronze altar. 3 The glory of the God of Israel went up from the cherub, whereupon it was, to the threshold of the house; and he called to the man clothed in linen, who had the writer's inkhorn by his side. 4 Yahweh said to him, "Go through the middle of the city, through the middle of Jerusalem, and set a mark on the foreheads of the men that sigh and that cry over all the abominations that are done within it." 5 To the others he said in my hearing, "Go through the city after him, and strike. Don't let your eye spare, neither have pity. 6 Kill utterly the old man, the young man, the virgin, little children and women; but don't come near any man on whom is the mark. Begin at my sanctuary." Then they began at the old men who were before the house. 7 He said to them, "Defile the house, and fill the courts with the slain. Go out!" They went out, and struck in the city. 8 While they were killing, and I was left, I fell on my face, and cried, and said, "Ah Lord Yahweh! Will you destroy all the residue of Israel in your pouring out of your wrath on Jerusalem?" 9 Then he said to me, "The iniquity of the house of Israel and Judah is exceedingly great, and the land is full of blood, and the city full of perversion; for they say, 'Yahweh has forsaken the land, and Yahweh doesn't see.' 10 As for me also, my eye won't spare, neither will I have pity, but I will bring their way on their head." 11 Behold, the man clothed in linen, who had the inkhorn by his side, reported the matter, saying, "I have done as you have commanded me."

10

1 Then I looked, and see, in the expanse that was over the head of the

cherubim there appeared above them as it were a sapphire stone, as the appearance of the likeness of a throne. 2 He spoke to the man clothed in linen, and said, "Go in between the whirling wheels, even under the cherub, and fill both your hands with coals of fire from between the cherubim, and scatter them over the city." He went in as I watched. 3 Now the cherubim stood on the right side of the house when the man went in; and the cloud filled the inner court. 4 Yahweh's glory mounted up from the cherub, and stood over the threshold of the house; and the house was filled with the cloud, and the court was full of the brightness of Yahweh's glory. 5 The sound of the wings of the cherubim was heard even to the outer court, as the voice of God Almighty when he speaks. 6 It came to pass, when he commanded the man clothed in linen, saying, "Take fire from between the whirling wheels, from between the cherubim," that he went in and stood beside a wheel. 7 The cherub stretched out his hand from between the cherubim to the fire that was between the cherubim, and took some of it, and put it into the hands of him who was clothed in linen, who took it and went out. 8 The form of a man's hand appeared here in the cherubim under their wings. 9 I looked, and behold, there were four wheels beside the cherubim, one wheel beside one cherub, and another wheel beside another cherub. The appearance of the wheels was like a beryl stone. 10 As for their appearance, the four of them had one likeness, like a wheel within a wheel. 11 When they went, they went in their four directions. They didn't turn as they went, but to the place where the head looked they followed it. They didn't turn as they went. 12 Their whole body, including their backs, their hands, their wings, and the wheels, were full of eyes all around, even the wheels that the four of them had. 13 As for the wheels, they were called in my hearing, "the whirling wheels". 14 Every one of them had four faces. The first face was the face of the cherub. The second face was the face of a man. The third face was the face of a lion. The fourth was the face of an eagle. 15 The cherubim mounted up. This is the living creature that I saw by the river Chebar. 16 When the cherubim went, the wheels went beside them; and when the cherubim lifted up their wings to mount up from the earth, the wheels also didn't turn from beside them. 17 When they stood, these stood. When they mounted up, these mounted up with them; for the spirit of the living creature was in them. 18 Yahweh's glory went out from over the threshold of the house and stood over the cherubim. 19 The cherubim lifted up their wings and mounted up from the earth in my sight when they went out, with the wheels beside them. Then they stood at the door of the east gate of Yahweh's house; and the glory of the God of Israel was over them above. 20 This is the living creature that I saw under the God of Israel by the river Chebar; and I knew that they were cherubim. 21 Every one had four faces, and every one four wings. The likeness of the hands of a man was under their wings. 22 As for the likeness of their faces, they were the faces which I saw by the river Chebar, their appearances and themselves. They each went straight forward.

11

1 Moreover the Spirit lifted me up and brought me to the east gate of Yahweh's house, which looks eastward. Behold, twenty-five men were at the door of the gate; and I saw among them Jaazaniah the son of Azzur, and Pelatiah the son of Benaiah, princes of the people. 2 He said to me, "Son of man, these are the men who devise iniquity, and who give wicked counsel in this city; 3 who say, 'The time is not near to build houses. This is the cauldron, and we are the meat.' 4 Therefore prophesy against them. Prophesy, son of man." 5 Yahweh's Spirit fell on me, and he said to me, "Speak, 'Yahweh says: "Thus you have said, house of Israel; for I know the things that come into your mind. 6 You have multiplied your slain in this city, and you have filled its streets with the slain." 7"'Therefore the Lord Yahweh says: "Your slain whom you have laid in the middle of it, they are the meat, and this is the cauldron; but you will be brought out of the middle of it. 8 You have feared the sword; and I will bring the sword on you," says the Lord Yahweh. 9"I will bring you out of the middle of it, and deliver you into the hands of strangers, and will execute judgments among you. 10 You will fall by the sword. I will judge you in the border of Israel. Then you will know that I am Yahweh. 11 This will not be your cauldron, neither will you be the meat in the middle of it. I will judge you in the border of Israel. 12 You will know that I am Yahweh, for you have not walked in my statutes. You have not executed my ordinances, but have done after the ordinances of the nations that are around you."'" 13 When I prophesied, Pelatiah the son of Benaiah died. Then I fell down on my face, and cried with a loud voice, and said, "Ah Lord Yahweh! Will you make a full end of the remnant of Israel?" 14 Yahweh's word came to me, saying, 15"Son of man, your brothers, even your brothers, the men of your relatives, and all the house of Israel, all of them, are the ones to whom the inhabitants of Jerusalem have said, 'Go far away from Yahweh. This land has been given to us for a possession.' 16"Therefore say, 'The Lord Yahweh says: "Whereas I have removed them far off among the nations, and

whereas I have scattered them among the countries, yet I will be to them a sanctuary for a little while in the countries where they have come."' 17"Therefore say, 'The Lord Yahweh says: "I will gather you from the peoples, and assemble you out of the countries where you have been scattered, and I will give you the land of Israel." 18"'They will come there, and they will take away all its detestable things and all its abominations from there. 19 I will give them one heart, and I will put a new spirit within them. I will take the stony heart out of their flesh, and will give them a heart of flesh, 20 that they may walk in my statutes, and keep my ordinances, and do them. They will be my people, and I will be their God. 21 But as for them whose heart walks after the heart of their detestable things and their abominations, I will bring their way on their own heads,' says the Lord Yahweh." 22 Then the cherubim lifted up their wings, and the wheels were beside them. The glory of the God of Israel was over them above. 23 Yahweh's glory went up from the middle of the city, and stood on the mountain which is on the east side of the city. 24 The Spirit lifted me up, and brought me in the vision by the Spirit of God into Chaldea, to the captives. So the vision that I had seen went up from me. 25 Then I spoke to the captives all the things that Yahweh had shown me.

12

1 Yahweh's word also came to me, saying, 2"Son of man, you dwell in the middle of the rebellious house, who have eyes to see, and don't see, who have ears to hear, and don't hear; for they are a rebellious house. 3"Therefore, you son of man, prepare your baggage for moving, and move by day in their sight. You shall move from your place to another place in their sight. It may be they will consider, though they are a rebellious house. 4 You shall bring out your baggage by day in their sight, as baggage for moving. You shall go out yourself at evening in their sight, as when men go out into exile. 5 Dig through the wall in their sight, and carry your baggage out that way. 6 In their sight you shall bear it on your shoulder, and carry it out in the dark. You shall cover your face, so that you don't see the land, for I have set you for a sign to the house of Israel." 7 I did so as I was commanded. I brought out my baggage by day, as baggage for moving, and in the evening I dug through the wall with my hand. I brought it out in the dark, and bore it on my shoulder in their sight. 8 In the morning, Yahweh's word came to me, saying, 9"Son of man, hasn't the house of Israel, the rebellious house, said to you, 'What are you doing?' 10"Say to them, 'The Lord Yahweh says: "This burden concerns

the prince in Jerusalem, and all the house of Israel among whom they are.'"

11"Say, 'I am your sign. As I have done, so will it be done to them. They will go into exile, into captivity. 12"'The prince who is among them will bear his baggage on his shoulder in the dark, and will go out. They will dig through the wall to carry things out that way. He will cover his face, because he will not see the land with his eyes. 13 I will also spread my net on him, and he will be taken in my snare. I will bring him to Babylon to the land of the Chaldeans; yet he will not see it, though he will die there. 14 I will scatter toward every wind all who are around him to help him, and all his bands. I will draw out the sword after them. 15"'They will know that I am Yahweh when I disperse them among the nations and scatter them through the countries. 16 But I will leave a few men of them from the sword, from the famine, and from the pestilence, that they may declare all their abominations among the nations where they come. Then they will know that I am Yahweh.'" 17 Moreover Yahweh's word came to me, saying, 18"Son of man, eat your bread with quaking, and drink your water with trembling and with fearfulness. 19 Tell the people of the land, 'The Lord Yahweh says concerning the inhabitants of Jerusalem and the land of Israel: "They will eat their bread with fearfulness and drink their water in dismay, that her land may be desolate, and all that is therein, because of the violence of all those who dwell therein. 20 The cities that are inhabited will be laid waste, and the land will be a desolation. Then you will know that I am Yahweh."'" 21 Yahweh's word came to me, saying, 22"Son of man, what is this proverb that you have in the land of Israel, saying, 'The days are prolonged, and every vision fails'? 23 Tell them therefore, 'The Lord Yahweh says: "I will make this proverb to cease, and they will no more use it as a proverb in Israel;"' but tell them, '"The days are at hand, and the fulfillment of every vision. 24 For there will be no more any false vision nor flattering divination within the house of Israel. 25 For I am Yahweh. I will speak, and the word that I speak will be performed. It will be no more deferred; for in your days, rebellious house, I will speak the word and will perform it," says the Lord Yahweh.'" 26 Again Yahweh's word came to me, saying, 27"Son of man, behold, they of the house of Israel say, 'The vision that he sees is for many days to come, and he prophesies of times that are far off.' 28" Therefore tell them, 'The Lord Yahweh says: "None of my words will be deferred any more, but the word which I speak will be performed," says the Lord Yahweh.'"

13

1 Yahweh's word came to me, saying, 2"Son of man, prophesy against the prophets of Israel who prophesy, and say to those who prophesy out of their own heart, 'Hear Yahweh's word: 3 The Lord Yahweh says, "Woe to the foolish prophets, who follow their own spirit, and have seen nothing! 4 Israel, your prophets have been like foxes in the waste places. 5 You have not gone up into the gaps or built up the wall for the house of Israel, to stand in the battle in Yahweh's day. 6 They have seen falsehood and lying divination, who say, 'Yahweh says;' but Yahweh has not sent them. They have made men to hope that the word would be confirmed. 7 Haven't you seen a false vision, and haven't you spoken a lying divination, in that you say, 'Yahweh says;' but I have not spoken?" 8"Therefore the Lord Yahweh says: "Because you have spoken falsehood and seen lies, therefore, behold, I am against you," says the Lord Yahweh. 9"My hand will be against the prophets who see false visions and who utter lying divinations. They will not be in the council of my people, neither will they be written in the writing of the house of Israel, neither will they enter into the land of Israel. Then you will know that I am the Lord Yahweh." 10"'Because, even because they have seduced my people, saying, "Peace;" and there is no peace. When one builds up a wall, behold, they plaster it with whitewash. 11 Tell those who plaster it with whitewash that it will fall. There will be an overflowing shower; and you, great hailstones, will fall. A stormy wind will tear it. 12 Behold, when the wall has fallen, won't it be said to you, "Where is the plaster with which you have plastered it?" 13"'Therefore the Lord Yahweh says: "I will even tear it with a stormy wind in my wrath. There will be an overflowing shower in my anger, and great hailstones in wrath to consume it. 14 So I will break down the wall that you have plastered with whitewash, and bring it down to the ground, so that its foundation will be uncovered. It will fall, and you will be consumed in the middle of it. Then you will know that I am Yahweh. 15 Thus I will accomplish my wrath on the wall, and on those who have plastered it with whitewash. I will tell you, 'The wall is no more, nor those who plastered it— 16 to wit, the prophets of Israel who prophesy concerning Jerusalem, and who see visions of peace for her, and there is no peace,'" says the Lord Yahweh.'" 17 You, son of man, set your face against the daughters of your people, who prophesy out of their own heart; and prophesy against them, 18 and say, "The Lord Yahweh says: 'Woe to the women who sew magic bands on all elbows and make veils for the head of persons of every stature to hunt souls! Will you hunt the souls of my people and save souls alive for yourselves? 19 You have profaned me

among my people for handfuls of barley and for pieces of bread, to kill the souls who should not die and to save the souls alive who should not live, by your lying to my people who listen to lies.' 20"Therefore the Lord Yahweh says: 'Behold, I am against your magic bands, with which you hunt the souls to make them fly, and I will tear them from your arms. I will let the souls fly free, even the souls whom you ensnare like birds. 21 I will also tear your veils and deliver my people out of your hand; and they will no longer be in your hand to be ensnared. Then you will know that I am Yahweh. 22 Because with lies you have grieved the heart of the righteous, whom I have not made sad; and strengthened the hands of the wicked, that he should not return from his wicked way, and be saved alive. 23 Therefore you shall no more see false visions nor practice divination. I will deliver my people out of your hand. Then you will know that I am Yahweh.'"

14

1 Then some of the elders of Israel came to me and sat before me. 2 Yahweh's word came to me, saying, 3"Son of man, these men have taken their idols into their heart, and put the stumbling block of their iniquity before their face. Should I be inquired of at all by them? 4 Therefore speak to them and tell them, 'The Lord Yahweh says: "Every man of the house of Israel who takes his idols into his heart and puts the stumbling block of his iniquity before his face then comes to the prophet, I Yahweh will answer him there according to the multitude of his idols, 5 that I may take the house of Israel in their own heart, because they are all estranged from me through their idols."' 6"Therefore tell the house of Israel, 'The Lord Yahweh says: "Return, and turn yourselves from your idols! Turn away your faces from all your abominations. 7""For everyone of the house of Israel, or of the strangers who live in Israel, who separates himself from me and takes his idols into his heart, and puts the stumbling block of his iniquity before his face, and comes to the prophet to inquire for himself of me, I Yahweh will answer him by myself. 8 I will set my face against that man and will make him an astonishment, for a sign and a proverb, and I will cut him off from among my people. Then you will know that I am Yahweh. 9""If the prophet is deceived and speaks a word, I, Yahweh, have deceived that prophet, and I will stretch out my hand on him, and will destroy him from among my people Israel. 10 They will bear their iniquity. The iniquity of the prophet will be even as the iniquity of him who seeks him, 11 that the house of Israel may no more go astray from me, neither defile themselves any more with all their

transgressions; but that they may be my people, and I may be their God,” says the Lord Yahweh.’” ¹² Yahweh’s word came to me, saying, ¹³“Son of man, when a land sins against me by committing a trespass, and I stretch out my hand on it, and break the staff of its bread and send famine on it, and cut off from it man and animal— ¹⁴ though these three men, Noah, Daniel, and Job, were in it, they would deliver only their own souls by their righteousness,” says the Lord Yahweh. ¹⁵“If I cause evil animals to pass through the land, and they ravage it and it is made desolate, so that no man may pass through because of the animals— ¹⁶ though these three men were in it, as I live,” says the Lord Yahweh, “they would deliver neither sons nor daughters. They only would be delivered, but the land would be desolate. ¹⁷“Or if I bring a sword on that land, and say, ‘Sword, go through the land, so that I cut off from it man and animal’— ¹⁸ though these three men were in it, as I live,” says the Lord Yahweh, “they would deliver neither sons nor daughters, but they only would be delivered themselves. ¹⁹“Or if I send a pestilence into that land, and pour out my wrath on it in blood, to cut off from it man and animal— ²⁰ though Noah, Daniel, and Job, were in it, as I live,” says the Lord Yahweh, “they would deliver neither son nor daughter; they would deliver only their own souls by their righteousness.” ²¹ For the Lord Yahweh says: “How much more when I send my four severe judgments on Jerusalem—the sword, the famine, the evil animals, and the pestilence—to cut off from it man and animal! ²² Yet, behold, there will be left a remnant in it that will be carried out, both sons and daughters. Behold, they will come out to you, and you will see their way and their doings. Then you will be comforted concerning the evil that I have brought on Jerusalem, even concerning all that I have brought on it. ²³ They will comfort you, when you see their way and their doings; then you will know that I have not done all that I have done in it without cause,” says the Lord Yahweh.

15

¹ Yahweh’s word came to me, saying, ²“Son of man, what is the vine tree more than any tree, the vine branch which is among the trees of the forest? ³ Will wood be taken of it to make anything? Will men take a pin of it to hang any vessel on it? ⁴ Behold, it is cast into the fire for fuel; the fire has devoured both its ends, and the middle of it is burned. Is it profitable for any work? ⁵ Behold, when it was whole, it was suitable for no work. How much less, when the fire has devoured it, and it has been burned, will it yet be suitable for any work?” ⁶ Therefore the Lord Yahweh says: “As the vine wood among

the trees of the forest, which I have given to the fire for fuel, so I will give the inhabitants of Jerusalem. 7 I will set my face against them. They will go out from the fire, but the fire will still devour them. Then you will know that I am Yahweh, when I set my face against them. 8 I will make the land desolate, because they have acted unfaithfully," says the Lord Yahweh.

16

1 Again Yahweh's word came to me, saying, 2"Son of man, cause Jerusalem to know her abominations; 3 and say, 'The Lord Yahweh says to Jerusalem: "Your origin and your birth is of the land of the Canaanite. An Amorite was your father, and your mother was a Hittite. 4 As for your birth, in the day you were born your navel was not cut. You weren't washed in water to cleanse you. You weren't salted at all, nor wrapped in blankets at all. 5 No eye pitied you, to do any of these things to you, to have compassion on you; but you were cast out in the open field, because you were abhorred in the day that you were born. 6"""When I passed by you, and saw you wallowing in your blood, I said to you, 'Though you are in your blood, live!' Yes, I said to you, 'Though you are in your blood, live!' 7 I caused you to multiply as that which grows in the field, and you increased and grew great, and you attained to excellent beauty. Your breasts were formed, and your hair grew; yet you were naked and bare. 8"""Now when I passed by you, and looked at you, behold, your time was the time of love; and I spread my garment over you and covered your nakedness. Yes, I pledged myself to you and entered into a covenant with you," says the Lord Yahweh, "and you became mine. 9"""Then I washed you with water. Yes, I thoroughly washed away your blood from you, and I anointed you with oil. 10 I clothed you also with embroidered work and put leather sandals on you. I dressed you with fine linen and covered you with silk. 11 I decked you with ornaments, put bracelets on your hands, and put a chain on your neck. 12 I put a ring on your nose, earrings in your ears, and a beautiful crown on your head. 13 Thus you were decked with gold and silver. Your clothing was of fine linen, silk, and embroidered work. You ate fine flour, honey, and oil. You were exceedingly beautiful, and you prospered to royal estate. 14 Your renown went out among the nations for your beauty; for it was perfect, through my majesty which I had put on you," says the Lord Yahweh. 15"""But you trusted in your beauty, and played the prostitute because of your renown, and poured out your prostitution on everyone who passed by. It was his. 16 You took some of your garments, and made for yourselves high places decked with various colors, and played the prostitute

on them. This shouldn't happen, neither shall it be. 17 You also took your beautiful jewels of my gold and of my silver, which I had given you, and made for yourself images of men, and played the prostitute with them. 18 You took your embroidered garments, covered them, and set my oil and my incense before them. 19 My bread also which I gave you, fine flour, oil, and honey, with which I fed you, you even set it before them for a pleasant aroma; and so it was," says the Lord Yahweh. 20""Moreover you have taken your sons and your daughters, whom you have borne to me, and you have sacrificed these to them to be devoured. Was your prostitution a small matter, 21 that you have slain my children and delivered them up, in causing them to pass through the fire to them? 22 In all your abominations and your prostitution you have not remembered the days of your youth, when you were naked and bare, and were wallowing in your blood. 23""It has happened after all your wickedness—woe, woe to you!" says the Lord Yahweh— 24"that you have built for yourselves a vaulted place, and have made yourselves a lofty place in every street. 25 You have built your lofty place at the head of every way, and have made your beauty an abomination, and have opened your feet to everyone who passed by, and multiplied your prostitution. 26 You have also committed sexual immorality with the Egyptians, your neighbors, great of flesh; and have multiplied your prostitution, to provoke me to anger. 27 See therefore, I have stretched out my hand over you, and have diminished your portion, and delivered you to the will of those who hate you, the daughters of the Philistines, who are ashamed of your lewd way. 28 You have played the prostitute also with the Assyrians, because you were insatiable; yes, you have played the prostitute with them, and yet you weren't satisfied. 29 You have moreover multiplied your prostitution to the land of merchants, to Chaldea; and yet you weren't satisfied with this. 30""How weak is your heart," says the Lord Yahweh, "since you do all these things, the work of an impudent prostitute; 31 in that you build your vaulted place at the head of every way, and make your lofty place in every street, and have not been as a prostitute, in that you scorn pay. 32""Adulterous wife, who takes strangers instead of her husband! 33 People give gifts to all prostitutes; but you give your gifts to all your lovers, and bribe them, that they may come to you on every side for your prostitution. 34 You are different from other women in your prostitution, in that no one follows you to play the prostitute; and whereas you give hire, and no hire is given to you, therefore you are different."' 35"Therefore, prostitute, hear Yahweh's word: 36'The Lord Yahweh says, "Because your

200

filthiness was poured out, and your nakedness uncovered through your prostitution with your lovers; and because of all the idols of your abominations, and for the blood of your children, that you gave to them; ³⁷ therefore see, I will gather all your lovers, with whom you have taken pleasure, and all those whom you have loved, with all those whom you have hated. I will even gather them against you on every side, and will uncover your nakedness to them, that they may see all your nakedness. ³⁸ I will judge you as women who break wedlock and shed blood are judged; and I will bring on you the blood of wrath and jealousy. ³⁹ I will also give you into their hand, and they will throw down your vaulted place, and break down your lofty places. They will strip you of your clothes and take your beautiful jewels. They will leave you naked and bare. ⁴⁰ They will also bring up a company against you, and they will stone you with stones, and thrust you through with their swords. ⁴¹ They will burn your houses with fire, and execute judgments on you in the sight of many women. I will cause you to cease from playing the prostitute, and you will also give no hire any more. ⁴² So I will cause my wrath toward you to rest, and my jealousy will depart from you. I will be quiet, and will not be angry any more. ⁴³ "Because you have not remembered the days of your youth, but have raged against me in all these things; therefore, behold, I also will bring your way on your head," says the Lord Yahweh: "and you shall not commit this lewdness with all your abominations. ⁴⁴ "Behold, everyone who uses proverbs will use this proverb against you, saying, 'As is the mother, so is her daughter.' ⁴⁵ You are the daughter of your mother, who loathes her husband and her children; and you are the sister of your sisters, who loathed their husbands and their children. Your mother was a Hittite, and your father an Amorite. ⁴⁶ Your elder sister is Samaria, who dwells at your left hand, she and her daughters; and your younger sister, who dwells at your right hand, is Sodom with her daughters. ⁴⁷ Yet you have not walked in their ways, nor done their abominations; but soon you were more corrupt than they in all your ways. ⁴⁸ As I live," says the Lord Yahweh, "Sodom your sister has not done, she nor her daughters, as you have done, you and your daughters. ⁴⁹ "Behold, this was the iniquity of your sister Sodom: pride, fullness of bread, and prosperous ease was in her and in her daughters. She also didn't strengthen the hand of the poor and needy. ⁵⁰ They were arrogant and committed abomination before me. Therefore I took them away when I saw it. ⁵¹ Samaria hasn't committed half of your sins; but you have multiplied your abominations more than they, and have justified your sisters by all your abominations which you have done. 52 You also bear your own shame yourself, in that you have given judgment for your sisters; through your sins that you have committed more abominable than they, they are more righteous than you. Yes, be also confounded, and bear your shame, in that you have justified your sisters. 53""I will reverse their captivity, the captivity of Sodom and her daughters, and the captivity of Samaria and her daughters, and the captivity of your captives among them; 54 that you may bear your own shame, and may be ashamed because of all that you have done, in that you are a comfort to them. 55 Your sisters, Sodom and her daughters, will return to their former estate; and Samaria and her daughters will return to their former estate; and you and your daughters will return to your former estate. 56 For your sister Sodom was not mentioned by your mouth in the day of your pride, 57 before your wickedness was uncovered, as at the time of the reproach of the daughters of Syria, and of all who are around her, the daughters of the Philistines, who despise you all around. 58 You have borne your lewdness and your abominations," says Yahweh. 59"'For the Lord Yahweh says: "I will also deal with you as you have done, who have despised the oath in breaking the covenant. 60 Nevertheless I will remember my covenant with you in the days of your youth, and I will establish an everlasting covenant with you. 61 Then you will remember your ways and be ashamed when you receive your sisters, your elder sisters and your younger; and I will give them to you for daughters, but not by your covenant. 62 I will establish my covenant with you. Then you will know that I am Yahweh; 63 that you may remember, and be confounded, and never open your mouth any more because of your shame, when I have forgiven you all that you have done," says the Lord Yahweh.'"

17

1 Yahweh's word came to me, saying, 2"Son of man, tell a riddle, and speak a parable to the house of Israel; 3 and say, 'The Lord Yahweh says: "A great eagle with great wings and long feathers, full of feathers which had various colors, came to Lebanon and took the top of the cedar. 4 He cropped off the topmost of its young twigs, and carried it to a land of traffic. He planted it in a city of merchants. 5""He also took some of the seed of the land and planted it in fruitful soil. He placed it beside many waters. He set it as a willow tree. 6 It grew and became a spreading vine of low stature, whose branches turned toward him, and its roots were under him. So it became a vine, produced branches, and shot out sprigs. 7"""There was also another great eagle with

great wings and many feathers. Behold, this vine bent its roots toward him, and shot out its branches toward him, from the ground where it was planted, that he might water it. 8 It was planted in a good soil by many waters, that it might produce branches and that it might bear fruit, that it might be a good vine."' 9"Say, 'The Lord Yahweh says: "Will it prosper? Won't he pull up its roots and cut off its fruit, that it may wither, that all its fresh springing leaves may wither? It can't be raised from its roots by a strong arm or many people. 10 Yes, behold, being planted, will it prosper? Won't it utterly wither when the east wind touches it? It will wither in the ground where it grew."'" 11 Moreover Yahweh's word came to me, saying, 12"Say now to the rebellious house, 'Don't you know what these things mean?' Tell them, 'Behold, the king of Babylon came to Jerusalem, and took its king, and its princes, and brought them to him to Babylon. 13 He took one of the royal offspring, and made a covenant with him. He also brought him under an oath, and took away the mighty of the land, 14 that the kingdom might be brought low, that it might not lift itself up, but that by keeping his covenant it might stand. 15 But he rebelled against him in sending his ambassadors into Egypt, that they might give him horses and many people. Will he prosper? Will he who does such things escape? Will he break the covenant, and still escape? 16"'As I live,' says the Lord Yahweh, 'surely in the place where the king dwells who made him king, whose oath he despised, and whose covenant he broke, even with him in the middle of Babylon he will die. 17 Pharaoh with his mighty army and great company won't help him in the war, when they cast up mounds and build forts to cut off many persons. 18 For he has despised the oath by breaking the covenant; and behold, he had given his hand, and yet has done all these things. He won't escape. 19"Therefore the Lord Yahweh says: 'As I live, I will surely bring on his own head my oath that he has despised and my covenant that he has broken. 20 I will spread my net on him, and he will be taken in my snare. I will bring him to Babylon, and will enter into judgment with him there for his trespass that he has trespassed against me. 21 All his fugitives in all his bands will fall by the sword, and those who remain will be scattered toward every wind. Then you will know that I, Yahweh, have spoken it.' 22"The Lord Yahweh says: 'I will also take some of the lofty top of the cedar, and will plant it. I will crop off from the topmost of its young twigs a tender one, and I will plant it on a high and lofty mountain. 23 I will plant it in the mountain of the height of Israel; and it will produce boughs, and bear fruit, and be a good cedar. Birds of every kind will dwell in the shade of its branches. 24 All the trees of the field will know that I, Yahweh, have brought down the high tree, have exalted the low tree, have dried up the green tree, and have made the dry tree flourish. "'I, Yahweh, have spoken and have done it.'"

18

1 Yahweh's word came to me again, saying, 2"What do you mean, that you use this proverb concerning the land of Israel, saying, 'The fathers have eaten sour grapes, and the children's teeth are set on edge'? 3"As I live," says the Lord Yahweh, "you shall not use this proverb any more in Israel. 4 Behold, all souls are mine; as the soul of the father, so also the soul of the son is mine. The soul who sins, he shall die. 5"But if a man is just, and does that which is lawful and right, 6 and has not eaten on the mountains, hasn't lifted up his eyes to the idols of the house of Israel, hasn't defiled his neighbor's wife, hasn't come near a woman in her impurity, 7 and has not wronged any, but has restored to the debtor his pledge, has taken nothing by robbery, has given his bread to the hungry, and has covered the naked with a garment; 8 he who hasn't lent to them with interest, hasn't taken any increase from them, who has withdrawn his hand from iniquity, has executed true justice between man and man, 9 has walked in my statutes, and has kept my ordinances, to deal truly; he is just, he shall surely live," says the Lord Yahweh. 10"If he fathers a son who is a robber who sheds blood, and who does any one of these things, 11 or who does not do any of those things but has eaten at the mountain shrines and defiled his neighbor's wife, 12 has wronged the poor and needy, has taken by robbery, has not restored the pledge, and has lifted up his eyes to the idols, has committed abomination, 13 has lent with interest, and has taken increase from the poor, shall he then live? He shall not live. He has done all these abominations. He shall surely die. His blood will be on him. 14"Now, behold, if he fathers a son who sees all his father's sins which he has done, and fears, and doesn't do likewise, 15 who hasn't eaten on the mountains, hasn't lifted up his eyes to the idols of the house of Israel, hasn't defiled his neighbor's wife, 16 hasn't wronged any, hasn't taken anything to pledge, hasn't taken by robbery, but has given his bread to the hungry, and has covered the naked with a garment; 17 who has withdrawn his hand from the poor, who hasn't received interest or increase, has executed my ordinances, has walked in my statutes; he shall not die for the iniquity of his father. He shall surely live. 18 As for his father, because he cruelly oppressed, robbed his brother, and did that which is not good among his people, behold, he will die

in his iniquity. ¹⁹"Yet you say, 'Why doesn't the son bear the iniquity of the father?' When the son has done that which is lawful and right, and has kept all my statutes, and has done them, he will surely live. ²⁰ The soul who sins, he shall die. The son shall not bear the iniquity of the father, neither shall the father bear the iniquity of the son. The righteousness of the righteous shall be on him, and the wickedness of the wicked shall be on him. ²¹"But if the wicked turns from all his sins that he has committed, and keeps all my statutes, and does that which is lawful and right, he shall surely live. He shall not die. ²² None of his transgressions that he has committed will be remembered against him. In his righteousness that he has done, he shall live. ²³ Have I any pleasure in the death of the wicked?" says the Lord Yahweh, "and not rather that he should return from his way, and live? ²⁴"But when the righteous turns away from his righteousness, and commits iniquity, and does according to all the abominations that the wicked man does, should he live? None of his righteous deeds that he has done will be remembered. In his trespass that he has trespassed, and in his sin that he has sinned, in them he shall die. ²⁵"Yet you say, 'The way of the Lord is not equal.' Hear now, house of Israel: Is my way not equal? Aren't your ways unequal? ²⁶ When the righteous man turns away from his righteousness, and commits iniquity, and dies in it, then he dies in his iniquity that he has done. ²⁷ Again, when the wicked man turns away from his wickedness that he has committed, and does that which is lawful and right, he will save his soul alive. ²⁸ Because he considers, and turns away from all his transgressions that he has committed, he shall surely live. He shall not die. ²⁹ Yet the house of Israel says, 'The way of the Lord is not fair.' House of Israel, aren't my ways fair? Aren't your ways unfair? ³⁰"Therefore I will judge you, house of Israel, everyone according to his ways," says the Lord Yahweh. "Return, and turn yourselves from all your transgressions, so iniquity will not be your ruin. ³¹ Cast away from you all your transgressions in which you have transgressed; and make yourself a new heart and a new spirit. For why will you die, house of Israel? ³² For I have no pleasure in the death of him who dies," says the Lord Yahweh. "Therefore turn yourselves, and live!

19

¹"Moreover, take up a lamentation for the princes of Israel, ² and say, 'What was your mother? A lioness. She couched among lions, in the middle of the young lions she nourished her cubs. ³ She brought up one of her cubs. He became a young lion. He learned to catch the prey. He devoured men. ⁴ The

nations also heard of him. He was taken in their pit; and they brought him with hooks to the land of Egypt. ⁵"'Now when she saw that she had waited, and her hope was lost, then she took another of her cubs, and made him a young lion. ⁶ He went up and down among the lions. He became a young lion. He learned to catch the prey. He devoured men. ⁷ He knew their palaces, and laid waste their cities. The land was desolate with its fullness, because of the noise of his roaring. ⁸ Then the nations attacked him on every side from the provinces. They spread their net over him. He was taken in their pit. ⁹ They put him in a cage with hooks, and brought him to the king of Babylon. They brought him into strongholds, so that his voice should no more be heard on the mountains of Israel. ¹⁰"'Your mother was like a vine in your blood, planted by the waters. It was fruitful and full of branches by reason of many waters. ¹¹ It had strong branches for the scepters of those who ruled. Their stature was exalted among the thick boughs. They were seen in their height with the multitude of their branches. ¹² But it was plucked up in fury. It was cast down to the ground, and the east wind dried up its fruit. Its strong branches were broken off and withered. The fire consumed them. ¹³ Now it is planted in the wilderness, in a dry and thirsty land. ¹⁴ Fire has gone out of its branches. It has devoured its fruit, so that there is in it no strong branch to be a scepter to rule.' This is a lamentation, and shall be for a lamentation."

20

¹ In the seventh year, in the fifth month, the tenth day of the month, some of the elders of Israel came to inquire of Yahweh, and sat before me. ² Yahweh's word came to me, saying, ³"Son of man, speak to the elders of Israel, and tell them, 'The Lord Yahweh says: "Is it to inquire of me that you have come? As I live," says the Lord Yahweh, "I will not be inquired of by you."' ⁴"Will you judge them, son of man? Will you judge them? Cause them to know the abominations of their fathers. ⁵ Tell them, 'The Lord Yahweh says: "In the day when I chose Israel, and swore to the offspring of the house of Jacob, and made myself known to them in the land of Egypt, when I swore to them, saying, 'I am Yahweh your God;' ⁶ in that day I swore to them to bring them out of the land of Egypt into a land that I had searched out for them, flowing with milk and honey, which is the glory of all lands. ⁷ I said to them, 'Each of you throw away the abominations of his eyes. Don't defile yourselves with the idols of Egypt. I am Yahweh your God.' ⁸"'But they rebelled against me and wouldn't listen to me. They didn't all throw away the abominations of their eyes. They also didn't forsake the idols of Egypt. Then

I said I would pour out my wrath on them, to accomplish my anger against them in the middle of the land of Egypt. 9 But I worked for my name's sake, that it should not be profaned in the sight of the nations among which they were, in whose sight I made myself known to them in bringing them out of the land of Egypt. 10 So I caused them to go out of the land of Egypt and brought them into the wilderness. 11 I gave them my statutes and showed them my ordinances, which if a man does, he will live in them. 12 Moreover also I gave them my Sabbaths, to be a sign between me and them, that they might know that I am Yahweh who sanctifies them. 13 "'"But the house of Israel rebelled against me in the wilderness. They didn't walk in my statutes and they rejected my ordinances, which if a man keeps, he shall live in them. They greatly profaned my Sabbaths. Then I said I would pour out my wrath on them in the wilderness, to consume them. 14 But I worked for my name's sake, that it should not be profaned in the sight of the nations, in whose sight I brought them out. 15 Moreover also I swore to them in the wilderness that I would not bring them into the land which I had given them, flowing with milk and honey, which is the glory of all lands, 16 because they rejected my ordinances, and didn't walk in my statutes, and profaned my Sabbaths; for their heart went after their idols. 17 Nevertheless my eye spared them, and I didn't destroy them. I didn't make a full end of them in the wilderness. 18 I said to their children in the wilderness, 'Don't walk in the statutes of your fathers. Don't observe their ordinances or defile yourselves with their idols. 19 I am Yahweh your God. Walk in my statutes, keep my ordinances, and do them. 20 Make my Sabbaths holy. They shall be a sign between me and you, that you may know that I am Yahweh your God.' 21 "'"But the children rebelled against me. They didn't walk in my statutes, and didn't keep my ordinances to do them, which if a man does, he shall live in them. They profaned my Sabbaths. Then I said I would pour out my wrath on them, to accomplish my anger against them in the wilderness. 22 Nevertheless I withdrew my hand and worked for my name's sake, that it should not be profaned in the sight of the nations, in whose sight I brought them out. 23 Moreover I swore to them in the wilderness, that I would scatter them among the nations and disperse them through the countries, 24 because they had not executed my ordinances, but had rejected my statutes, and had profaned my Sabbaths, and their eyes were after their fathers' idols. 25 Moreover also I gave them statutes that were not good, and ordinances in which they couldn't live. 26 I polluted them in their own gifts, in that they caused all that opens the womb to pass through the fire, that I might make them desolate, to the end that they might know that I am Yahweh.'" 27"Therefore, son of man, speak to the house of Israel, and tell them, 'The Lord Yahweh says: "Moreover, in this your fathers have blasphemed me, in that they have committed a trespass against me. 28 For when I had brought them into the land which I swore to give to them, then they saw every high hill and every thick tree, and they offered there their sacrifices, and there they presented the provocation of their offering. There they also made their pleasant aroma, and there they poured out their drink offerings. 29 Then I said to them, 'What does the high place where you go mean?' So its name is called Bamah to this day."' 30"Therefore tell the house of Israel, 'The Lord Yahweh says: "Do you pollute yourselves in the way of your fathers? Do you play the prostitute after their abominations? 31 When you offer your gifts, when you make your sons pass through the fire, do you pollute yourselves with all your idols to this day? Should I be inquired of by you, house of Israel? As I live, says the Lord Yahweh, I will not be inquired of by you! 32""That which comes into your mind will not be at all, in that you say, 'We will be as the nations, as the families of the countries, to serve wood and stone.' 33 As I live," says the Lord Yahweh, "surely with a mighty hand, with an outstretched arm, and with wrath poured out, I will be king over you. 34 I will bring you out from the peoples, and will gather you out of the countries in which you are scattered with a mighty hand, with an outstretched arm, and with wrath poured out. 35 I will bring you into the wilderness of the peoples, and there I will enter into judgment with you face to face. 36 Just as I entered into judgment with your fathers in the wilderness of the land of Egypt, so I will enter into judgment with you," says the Lord Yahweh. 37"I will cause you to pass under the rod, and I will bring you into the bond of the covenant. 38 I will purge out from among you the rebels and those who disobey me. I will bring them out of the land where they live, but they shall not enter into the land of Israel. Then you will know that I am Yahweh." 39"'As for you, house of Israel, the Lord Yahweh says: "Go, everyone serve his idols, and hereafter also, if you will not listen to me; but you shall no more profane my holy name with your gifts and with your idols. 40 For in my holy mountain, in the mountain of the height of Israel," says the Lord Yahweh, "there all the house of Israel, all of them, shall serve me in the land. There I will accept them, and there I will require your offerings and the first fruits of your offerings, with all your holy things. 41 I will accept you as a pleasant aroma when I bring you out from the peoples and gather you out of the countries in which you have been scattered. I will be sanctified in you in the sight of the nations. 42 You will know that I am Yahweh when I bring you into the land of Israel, into the country which I swore to give to your fathers. 43 There you will remember your ways, and all your deeds in which you have polluted yourselves. Then you will loathe yourselves in your own sight for all your evils that you have committed. 44 You will know that I am Yahweh, when I have dealt with you for my name's sake, not according to your evil ways, nor according to your corrupt doings, you house of Israel," says the Lord Yahweh.'" 45 Yahweh's word came to me, saying, 46"Son of man, set your face toward the south, and preach toward the south, and prophesy against the forest of the field in the south. 47 Tell the forest of the south, 'Hear Yahweh's word: The Lord Yahweh says, "Behold, I will kindle a fire in you, and it will devour every green tree in you, and every dry tree. The burning flame will not be quenched, and all faces from the south to the north will be burned by it. 48 All flesh will see that I, Yahweh, have kindled it. It will not be quenched."'" 49 Then I said, "Ah Lord Yahweh! They say of me, 'Isn't he a speaker of parables?'"

21

1 Yahweh's word came to me, saying, 2"Son of man, set your face toward Jerusalem, and preach toward the sanctuaries, and prophesy against the land of Israel. 3 Tell the land of Israel, 'Yahweh says: "Behold, I am against you, and will draw my sword out of its sheath, and will cut off from you the righteous and the wicked. 4 Seeing then that I will cut off from you the righteous and the wicked, therefore my sword will go out of its sheath against all flesh from the south to the north. 5 All flesh will know that I, Yahweh, have drawn my sword out of its sheath. It will not return any more."' 6"Therefore sigh, you son of man. You shall sigh before their eyes with a broken heart and with bitterness. 7 It shall be, when they ask you, 'Why do you sigh?' that you shall say, 'Because of the news, for it comes! Every heart will melt, all hands will be feeble, every spirit will faint, and all knees will be weak as water. Behold, it comes, and it shall be done, says the Lord Yahweh.'" 8 Yahweh's word came to me, saying, 9"Son of man, prophesy, and say, 'Yahweh says: "A sword! A sword! It is sharpened, and also polished. 10 It is sharpened that it may make a slaughter. It is polished that it may be as lightning. Should we then make mirth? The rod of my son condemns every tree. 11 It is given to be polished, that it may be handled. The

sword is sharpened. Yes, it is polished to give it into the hand of the killer."' ¹² Cry and wail, son of man; for it is on my people. It is on all the princes of Israel. They are delivered over to the sword with my people. Therefore beat your thigh. ¹³"For there is a trial. What if even the rod that condemns will be no more?" says the Lord Yahweh. ¹⁴"You therefore, son of man, prophesy, and strike your hands together. Let the sword be doubled the third time, the sword of the fatally wounded. It is the sword of the great one who is fatally wounded, which enters into their rooms. ¹⁵ I have set the threatening sword against all their gates, that their heart may melt, and their stumblings be multiplied. Ah! It is made as lightning. It is pointed for slaughter. ¹⁶ Gather yourselves together. Go to the right. Set yourselves in array. Go to the left, wherever your face is set. ¹⁷ I will also strike my hands together, and I will cause my wrath to rest. I, Yahweh, have spoken it." ¹⁸ Yahweh's word came to me again, saying, ¹⁹"Also, you son of man, appoint two ways, that the sword of the king of Babylon may come. They both will come out of one land, and mark out a place. Mark it out at the head of the way to the city. ²⁰ You shall appoint a way for the sword to come to Rabbah of the children of Ammon, and to Judah in Jerusalem the fortified. ²¹ For the king of Babylon stood at the parting of the way, at the head of the two ways, to use divination. He shook the arrows back and forth. He consulted the teraphim. He looked in the liver. ²² In his right hand was the lot for Jerusalem, to set battering rams, to open the mouth in the slaughter, to lift up the voice with shouting, to set battering rams against the gates, to cast up mounds, and to build forts. ²³ It will be to them as a false divination in their sight, who have sworn oaths to them; but he brings iniquity to memory, that they may be taken. ²⁴"Therefore the Lord Yahweh says: 'Because you have caused your iniquity to be remembered, in that your transgressions are uncovered, so that in all your doings your sins appear; because you have come to memory, you will be taken with the hand. ²⁵"'You, deadly wounded wicked one, the prince of Israel, whose day has come, in the time of the iniquity of the end, ²⁶ the Lord Yahweh says: "Remove the turban, and take off the crown. This will not be as it was. Exalt that which is low, and humble that which is high. ²⁷ I will overturn, overturn, overturn it. This also will be no more, until he comes whose right it is; and I will give it."' ²⁸"You, son of man, prophesy and say, 'The Lord Yahweh says this concerning the children of Ammon, and concerning their reproach: "A sword! A sword is drawn! It is polished for the slaughter, to cause it to devour, that it may be as lightning; ²⁹ while they see for you false visions, while they divine lies to you, to lay you on the necks of the wicked who are deadly wounded, whose day has come in the time of the iniquity of the end. 30 Cause it to return into its sheath. In the place where you were created, in the land of your birth, I will judge you. 31 I will pour out my indignation on you. I will blow on you with the fire of my wrath. I will deliver you into the hand of brutish men, skillful to destroy. 32 You will be for fuel to the fire. Your blood will be in the middle of the land. You will be remembered no more; for I, Yahweh, have spoken it.""'

22

1 Moreover Yahweh's word came to me, saying, 2"You, son of man, will you judge? Will you judge the bloody city? Then cause her to know all her abominations. 3 You shall say, 'The Lord Yahweh says: "A city that sheds blood within herself, that her time may come, and that makes idols against herself to defile her! 4 You have become guilty in your blood that you have shed, and are defiled in your idols which you have made! You have caused your days to draw near, and have come to the end of your years. Therefore I have made you a reproach to the nations, and a mocking to all the countries. 5 Those who are near and those who are far from you will mock you, you infamous one, full of tumult. 6"""Behold, the princes of Israel, everyone according to his power, have been in you to shed blood. 7 In you have they treated father and mother with contempt. Among you they have oppressed the foreigner. In you they have wronged the fatherless and the widow. 8 You have despised my holy things, and have profaned my Sabbaths. 9 Slanderous men have been in you to shed blood. In you they have eaten on the mountains. They have committed lewdness among you. 10 In you have they uncovered their fathers' nakedness. In you have they humbled her who was unclean in her impurity. 11 One has committed abomination with his neighbor's wife, and another has lewdly defiled his daughter-in-law. Another in you has humbled his sister, his father's daughter. 12 In you have they taken bribes to shed blood. You have taken interest and increase, and you have greedily gained of your neighbors by oppression, and have forgotten me," says the Lord Yahweh. 13"""Behold, therefore I have struck my hand at your dishonest gain which you have made, and at the blood which has been shed within you. 14 Can your heart endure, or can your hands be strong, in the days that I will deal with you? I, Yahweh, have spoken it, and will do it. 15 I will scatter you among the nations, and disperse you through the countries. I will purge your filthiness out of you. 16 You will be profaned in yourself in the sight of the

nations. Then you will know that I am Yahweh.""" 17 Yahweh's word came to me, saying, 18"Son of man, the house of Israel has become dross to me. All of them are bronze, tin, iron, and lead in the middle of the furnace. They are the dross of silver. 19 Therefore the Lord Yahweh says: 'Because you have all become dross, therefore, behold, I will gather you into the middle of Jerusalem. 20 As they gather silver, bronze, iron, lead, and tin into the middle of the furnace, to blow the fire on it, to melt it, so I will gather you in my anger and in my wrath, and I will lay you there and melt you. 21 Yes, I will gather you, and blow on you with the fire of my wrath, and you will be melted in the middle of it. 22 As silver is melted in the middle of the furnace, so you will be melted in the middle of it; and you will know that I, Yahweh, have poured out my wrath on you.'" 23 Yahweh's word came to me, saying, 24"Son of man, tell her, 'You are a land that is not cleansed nor rained on in the day of indignation.' 25 There is a conspiracy of her prophets within it, like a roaring lion ravening the prey. They have devoured souls. They take treasure and precious things. They have made many widows within it. 26 Her priests have done violence to my law and have profaned my holy things. They have made no distinction between the holy and the common, neither have they caused men to discern between the unclean and the clean, and have hidden their eyes from my Sabbaths. So I am profaned among them. 27 Her princes within it are like wolves ravening the prey, to shed blood and to destroy souls, that they may get dishonest gain. 28 Her prophets have plastered for them with whitewash, seeing false visions, and divining lies to them, saying, 'The Lord Yahweh says,' when Yahweh has not spoken. 29 The people of the land have used oppression and exercised robbery. Yes, they have troubled the poor and needy, and have oppressed the foreigner wrongfully. 30"I sought for a man among them who would build up the wall and stand in the gap before me for the land, that I would not destroy it; but I found no one. 31 Therefore I have poured out my indignation on them. I have consumed them with the fire of my wrath. I have brought their own way on their heads," says the Lord Yahweh.

23

1 Yahweh's word came again to me, saying, 2"Son of man, there were two women, the daughters of one mother. 3 They played the prostitute in Egypt. They played the prostitute in their youth. Their breasts were fondled there, and their youthful nipples were caressed there. 4 Their names were Oholah the elder, and Oholibah her sister. They became mine, and they bore sons and

daughters. As for their names, Samaria is Oholah, and Jerusalem Oholibah. 5"Oholah played the prostitute when she was mine. She doted on her lovers, on the Assyrians her neighbors, 6 who were clothed with blue—governors and rulers, all of them desirable young men, horsemen riding on horses. 7 She gave herself as a prostitute to them, all of them the choicest men of Assyria. She defiled herself with the idols of whomever she lusted after. 8 She hasn't left her prostitution since leaving Egypt; for in her youth they lay with her. They caressed her youthful nipples and they poured out their prostitution on her. 9"Therefore I delivered her into the hand of her lovers, into the hand of the Assyrians on whom she doted. 10 These uncovered her nakedness. They took her sons and her daughters, and they killed her with the sword. She became a byword among women; for they executed judgments on her. 11"Her sister Oholibah saw this, yet she was more corrupt in her lusting than she, and in her prostitution which was more depraved than the prostitution of her sister. 12 She lusted after the Assyrians, governors and rulers—her neighbors, clothed most gorgeously, horsemen riding on horses, all of them desirable young men. 13 I saw that she was defiled. They both went the same way. 14"She increased her prostitution; for she saw men portrayed on the wall, the images of the Chaldeans portrayed with red, 15 dressed with belts on their waists, with flowing turbans on their heads, all of them looking like princes, after the likeness of the Babylonians in Chaldea, the land of their birth. 16 As soon as she saw them, she lusted after them and sent messengers to them into Chaldea. 17 The Babylonians came to her into the bed of love, and they defiled her with their prostitution. She was polluted with them, and her soul was alienated from them. 18 So she uncovered her prostitution and uncovered her nakedness. Then my soul was alienated from her, just like my soul was alienated from her sister. 19 Yet she multiplied her prostitution, remembering the days of her youth, in which she had played the prostitute in the land of Egypt. 20 She lusted after their lovers, whose flesh is as the flesh of donkeys, and whose issue is like the issue of horses. 21 Thus you called to memory the lewdness of your youth, in the caressing of your nipples by the Egyptians because of your youthful breasts. 22"Therefore, Oholibah, the Lord Yahweh says: 'Behold, I will raise up your lovers against you, from whom your soul is alienated, and I will bring them against you on every side: 23 the Babylonians and all the Chaldeans, Pekod, Shoa, Koa, and all the Assyrians with them; all of them desirable young men, governors and rulers, princes and men of renown, all of them riding on horses. 24 They will come against you with weapons, chariots, and wagons, and with a company of peoples. They will set themselves against you with buckler, shield, and helmet all around. I will commit the judgment to them, and they will judge you according to their judgments. 25 I will set my jealousy against you, and they will deal with you in fury. They will take away your nose and your ears. Your remnant will fall by the sword. They will take your sons and your daughters; and the rest of you will be devoured by the fire. 26 They will also strip you of your clothes and take away your beautiful jewels. 27 Thus I will make your lewdness to cease from you, and remove your prostitution from the land of Egypt, so that you will not lift up your eyes to them, nor remember Egypt any more.' 28"For the Lord Yahweh says: 'Behold, I will deliver you into the hand of them whom you hate, into the hand of them from whom your soul is alienated. 29 They will deal with you in hatred, and will take away all your labor, and will leave you naked and bare. The nakedness of your prostitution will be uncovered, both your lewdness and your prostitution. 30 These things will be done to you because you have played the prostitute after the nations, and because you are polluted with their idols. 31 You have walked in the way of your sister; therefore I will give her cup into your hand.' 32"The Lord Yahweh says: 'You will drink of your sister's cup, which is deep and large. You will be ridiculed and held in derision. It contains much. 33 You will be filled with drunkenness and sorrow, with the cup of astonishment and desolation, with the cup of your sister Samaria. 34 You will even drink it and drain it out. You will gnaw the broken pieces of it, and will tear your breasts; for I have spoken it,' says the Lord Yahweh. 35"Therefore the Lord Yahweh says: 'Because you have forgotten me and cast me behind your back, therefore you also bear your lewdness and your prostitution.'" 36 Yahweh said moreover to me: "Son of man, will you judge Oholah and Oholibah? Then declare to them their abominations. 37 For they have committed adultery, and blood is in their hands. They have committed adultery with their idols. They have also caused their sons, whom they bore to me, to pass through the fire to them to be devoured. 38 Moreover this they have done to me: they have defiled my sanctuary in the same day, and have profaned my Sabbaths. 39 For when they had slain their children to their idols, then they came the same day into my sanctuary to profane it; and behold, they have done this in the middle of my house. 40"Furthermore you sisters have sent for men who come from far away, to whom a messenger was sent, and behold, they came; for whom you washed yourself, painted your eyes, decorated yourself with ornaments,

41 and sat on a stately bed, with a table prepared before it, whereupon you set my incense and my oil. 42"The voice of a multitude being at ease was with her. With men of the common sort were brought drunkards from the wilderness; and they put bracelets on their hands, and beautiful crowns on their heads. 43 Then I said of her who was old in adulteries, 'Now they will play the prostitute with her, and she with them.' 44 They went in to her, as they go in to a prostitute. So they went in to Oholah and to Oholibah, the lewd women. 45 Righteous men will judge them with the judgment of adulteresses and with the judgment of women who shed blood, because they are adulteresses, and blood is in their hands. 46"For the Lord Yahweh says: 'I will bring up a mob against them, and will give them to be tossed back and forth and robbed. 47 The company will stone them with stones and dispatch them with their swords. They will kill their sons and their daughters, and burn up their houses with fire. 48"'Thus I will cause lewdness to cease out of the land, that all women may be taught not to be lewd like you. 49 They will recompense your lewdness on you, and you will bear the sins of your idols. Then you will know that I am the Lord Yahweh.'"

24

1 Again, in the ninth year, in the tenth month, in the tenth day of the month, Yahweh's word came to me, saying, 2"Son of man, write the name of the day, this same day. The king of Babylon drew close to Jerusalem this same day. 3 Utter a parable to the rebellious house, and tell them, 'The Lord Yahweh says, "Put the cauldron on the fire. Put it on, and also pour water into it. 4 Gather its pieces into it, even every good piece: the thigh and the shoulder. Fill it with the choice bones. 5 Take the choice of the flock, and also a pile of wood for the bones under the cauldron. Make it boil well. Yes, let its bones be boiled within it." 6"'Therefore the Lord Yahweh says: "Woe to the bloody city, to the cauldron whose rust is in it, and whose rust hasn't gone out of it! Take out of it piece after piece without casting lots for it. 7"'"For the blood she shed is in the middle of her. She set it on the bare rock. She didn't pour it on the ground, to cover it with dust. 8 That it may cause wrath to come up to take vengeance, I have set her blood on the bare rock, that it should not be covered." 9"'Therefore the Lord Yahweh says: "Woe to the bloody city! I also will make the pile great. 10 Heap on the wood. Make the fire hot. Boil the meat well. Make the broth thick, and let the bones be burned. 11 Then set it empty on its coals, that it may be hot, and its bronze may burn, and that its filthiness may be molten in it, that its rust may be consumed. 12 She is weary

with toil; yet her great rust, rust by fire, doesn't leave her. 13""In your filthiness is lewdness. Because I have cleansed you and you weren't cleansed, you won't be cleansed from your filthiness any more, until I have caused my wrath toward you to rest. 14""I, Yahweh, have spoken it. It will happen, and I will do it. I won't go back. I won't spare. I won't repent. According to your ways and according to your doings, they will judge you," says the Lord Yahweh.'" 15 Also Yahweh's word came to me, saying, 16"Son of man, behold, I will take away from you the desire of your eyes with one stroke; yet you shall neither mourn nor weep, neither shall your tears run down. 17 Sigh, but not aloud. Make no mourning for the dead. Bind your headdress on you, and put your sandals on your feet. Don't cover your lips, and don't eat mourner's bread." 18 So I spoke to the people in the morning, and at evening my wife died. So I did in the morning as I was commanded. 19 The people asked me, "Won't you tell us what these things mean to us, that you act like this?" 20 Then I said to them, "Yahweh's word came to me, saying, 21'Speak to the house of Israel, "The Lord Yahweh says: 'Behold, I will profane my sanctuary, the pride of your power, the desire of your eyes, and that which your soul pities; and your sons and your daughters whom you have left behind will fall by the sword. 22 You will do as I have done. You won't cover your lips or eat mourner's bread. 23 Your turbans will be on your heads, and your sandals on your feet. You won't mourn or weep; but you will pine away in your iniquities, and moan one toward another. 24 Thus Ezekiel will be a sign to you; according to all that he has done, you will do. When this comes, then you will know that I am the Lord Yahweh.'"" 25"You, son of man, shouldn't it be in the day when I take from them their strength, the joy of their glory, the desire of their eyes, and that whereupon they set their heart— their sons and their daughters— 26 that in that day he who escapes will come to you, to cause you to hear it with your ears? 27 In that day your mouth will be opened to him who has escaped, and you will speak and be no more mute. So you will be a sign to them. Then they will know that I am Yahweh."

25

1 Yahweh's word came to me, saying, 2"Son of man, set your face toward the children of Ammon, and prophesy against them. 3 Tell the children of Ammon, 'Hear the word of the Lord Yahweh! The Lord Yahweh says, "Because you said, 'Aha!' against my sanctuary when it was profaned, and against the land of Israel when it was made desolate, and against the house of Judah when they went into captivity, 4 therefore, behold, I will deliver you to

the children of the east for a possession. They will set their encampments in you and make their dwellings in you. They will eat your fruit and they will drink your milk. 5 I will make Rabbah a stable for camels and the children of Ammon a resting place for flocks. Then you will know that I am Yahweh." 6 For the Lord Yahweh says: "Because you have clapped your hands, stamped with the feet, and rejoiced with all the contempt of your soul against the land of Israel, 7 therefore, behold, I have stretched out my hand on you, and will deliver you for a plunder to the nations. I will cut you off from the peoples, and I will cause you to perish out of the countries. I will destroy you. Then you will know that I am Yahweh." 8 "The Lord Yahweh says: "Because Moab and Seir say, 'Behold, the house of Judah is like all the nations,' 9 therefore, behold, I will open the side of Moab from the cities, from his cities which are on its frontiers, the glory of the country, Beth Jeshimoth, Baal Meon, and Kiriathaim, 10 to the children of the east, to go against the children of Ammon; and I will give them for a possession, that the children of Ammon may not be remembered among the nations. 11 I will execute judgments on Moab. Then they will know that I am Yahweh." 12 "The Lord Yahweh says: "Because Edom has dealt against the house of Judah by taking vengeance, and has greatly offended, and taken revenge on them," 13 therefore the Lord Yahweh says, "I will stretch out my hand on Edom, and will cut off man and animal from it; and I will make it desolate from Teman. They will fall by the sword even to Dedan. 14 I will lay my vengeance on Edom by the hand of my people Israel. They will do in Edom according to my anger and according to my wrath. Then they will know my vengeance," says the Lord Yahweh. 15 "The Lord Yahweh says: "Because the Philistines have taken revenge, and have taken vengeance with contempt of soul to destroy with perpetual hostility," 16 therefore the Lord Yahweh says, "Behold, I will stretch out my hand on the Philistines, and I will cut off the Cherethites, and destroy the remnant of the sea coast. 17 I will execute great vengeance on them with wrathful rebukes. Then they will know that I am Yahweh, when I lay my vengeance on them.""""

26

1 In the eleventh year, in the first of the month, Yahweh's word came to me, saying, 2 "Son of man, because Tyre has said against Jerusalem, 'Aha! She is broken! She who was the gateway of the peoples has been returned to me. I will be replenished, now that she is laid waste;' 3 therefore the Lord Yahweh says, 'Behold, I am against you, Tyre, and will cause many nations to come

up against you, as the sea causes its waves to come up. 4 They will destroy the walls of Tyre, and break down her towers. I will also scrape her dust from her, and make her a bare rock. 5 She will be a place for the spreading of nets in the middle of the sea; for I have spoken it,' says the Lord Yahweh. 'She will become plunder for the nations. 6 Her daughters who are in the field will be slain with the sword. Then they will know that I am Yahweh.' 7"For the Lord Yahweh says: 'Behold, I will bring on Tyre Nebuchadnezzar king of Babylon, king of kings, from the north, with horses, with chariots, with horsemen, and an army with many people. 8 He will kill your daughters in the field with the sword. He will make forts against you, cast up a mound against you, and raise up the buckler against you. 9 He will set his battering engines against your walls, and with his axes he will break down your towers. 10 By reason of the abundance of his horses, their dust will cover you. Your walls will shake at the noise of the horsemen, of the wagons, and of the chariots, when he enters into your gates, as men enter into a city which is broken open. 11 He will tread down all your streets with the hoofs of his horses. He will kill your people with the sword. The pillars of your strength will go down to the ground. 12 They will make a plunder of your riches and make a prey of your merchandise. They will break down your walls and destroy your pleasant houses. They will lay your stones, your timber, and your dust in the middle of the waters. 13 I will cause the noise of your songs to cease. The sound of your harps won't be heard any more. 14 I will make you a bare rock. You will be a place for the spreading of nets. You will be built no more; for I Yahweh have spoken it,' says the Lord Yahweh. 15"The Lord Yahweh says to Tyre: 'Won't the islands shake at the sound of your fall, when the wounded groan, when the slaughter is made within you? 16 Then all the princes of the sea will come down from their thrones, and lay aside their robes, and strip off their embroidered garments. They will clothe themselves with trembling. They will sit on the ground, and will tremble every moment, and be astonished at you. 17 They will take up a lamentation over you, and tell you, "How you are destroyed, who were inhabited by seafaring men, the renowned city, who was strong in the sea, she and her inhabitants, who caused their terror to be on all who lived there!" 18 Now the islands will tremble in the day of your fall. Yes, the islands that are in the sea will be dismayed at your departure.' 19"For the Lord Yahweh says: 'When I make you a desolate city, like the cities that are not inhabited, when I bring up the deep on you, and the great waters cover you, 20 then I will bring you down with those who descend into the pit, to the people of old time, and will make you dwell in the lower parts of the earth, in the places that are desolate of old, with those who go down to the pit, that you be not inhabited; and I will set glory in the land of the living. 21 I will make you a terror, and you will no more have any being. Though you are sought for, yet you will never be found again,' says the Lord Yahweh."

27

1 Yahweh's word came again to me, saying, 2"You, son of man, take up a lamentation over Tyre; 3 and tell Tyre, 'You who dwell at the entry of the sea, who are the merchant of the peoples to many islands, the Lord Yahweh says: "You, Tyre, have said, 'I am perfect in beauty.' 4 Your borders are in the heart of the seas. Your builders have perfected your beauty. 5 They have made all your planks of cypress trees from Senir. They have taken a cedar from Lebanon to make a mast for you. 6 They have made your oars of the oaks of Bashan. They have made your benches of ivory inlaid in cypress wood from the islands of Kittim. 7 Your sail was of fine linen with embroidered work from Egypt, that it might be to you for a banner. Blue and purple from the islands of Elishah was your awning. 8 The inhabitants of Sidon and Arvad were your rowers. Your wise men, Tyre, were in you. They were your pilots. 9 The old men of Gebal and its wise men were your repairers of ship seams in you. All the ships of the sea with their mariners were in you to deal in your merchandise. 10""Persia, Lud, and Put were in your army, your men of war. They hung the shield and helmet in you. They showed your beauty. 11 The men of Arvad with your army were on your walls all around, and valiant men were in your towers. They hung their shields on your walls all around. They have perfected your beauty. 12""Tarshish was your merchant by reason of the multitude of all kinds of riches. They traded for your wares with silver, iron, tin, and lead. 13""Javan, Tubal, and Meshech were your traders. They traded the persons of men and vessels of bronze for your merchandise. 14""They of the house of Togarmah traded for your wares with horses, war horses, and mules. 15""The men of Dedan traded with you. Many islands were the market of your hand. They brought you horns of ivory and ebony in exchange. 16""Syria was your merchant by reason of the multitude of your handiworks. They traded for your wares with emeralds, purple, embroidered work, fine linen, coral, and rubies. 17""Judah and the land of Israel were your traders. They traded wheat of Minnith, confections, honey, oil, and balm for your merchandise. 18""Damascus was your merchant for the multitude of your handiworks by reason of the multitude of

all kinds of riches, with the wine of Helbon, and white wool. ¹⁹""Vedan and Javan traded with yarn for your wares; wrought iron, cassia, and calamus were among your merchandise. ²⁰""Dedan was your merchant in precious saddle blankets for riding. ²¹""Arabia and all the princes of Kedar were your favorite dealers in lambs, rams, and goats. In these, they were your merchants. ²²""The traders of Sheba and Raamah were your traders. They traded for your wares with the best of all spices, all precious stones, and gold. ²³""Haran, Canneh, Eden, the traders of Sheba, Asshur and Chilmad, were your traders. ²⁴ These were your traders in choice wares, in wrappings of blue and embroidered work, and in cedar chests of rich clothing bound with cords, among your merchandise. ²⁵""The ships of Tarshish were your caravans for your merchandise. You were replenished and made very glorious in the heart of the seas. ²⁶ Your rowers have brought you into great waters. The east wind has broken you in the heart of the seas. ²⁷ Your riches, your wares, your merchandise, your mariners, your pilots, your repairers of ship seams, the dealers in your merchandise, and all your men of war who are in you, with all your company which is among you, will fall into the heart of the seas in the day of your ruin. ²⁸ At the sound of the cry of your pilots, the pasture lands will shake. ²⁹ All who handle the oars, the mariners and all the pilots of the sea, will come down from their ships. They will stand on the land, ³⁰ and will cause their voice to be heard over you, and will cry bitterly. They will cast up dust on their heads. They will wallow in the ashes. ³¹ They will make themselves bald for you, and clothe themselves with sackcloth. They will weep for you in bitterness of soul, with bitter mourning. ³² In their wailing they will take up a lamentation for you, and lament over you, saying, 'Who is there like Tyre, like her who is brought to silence in the middle of the sea?' ³³ When your wares came from the seas, you filled many peoples. You enriched the kings of the earth with the multitude of your riches and of your merchandise. ³⁴ In the time that you were broken by the seas, in the depths of the waters, your merchandise and all your company fell within you. ³⁵ All the inhabitants of the islands are astonished at you, and their kings are horribly afraid. They are troubled in their face. ³⁶ The merchants among the peoples hiss at you. You have come to a terrible end, and you will be no more."""

28

¹ Yahweh's word came again to me, saying, ²"Son of man, tell the prince of Tyre, 'The Lord Yahweh says: "Because your heart is lifted up, and you have said, 'I am a god, I sit in the seat of God, in the middle of the seas;' yet you

are man, and no god, though you set your heart as the heart of a god— ³ behold, you are wiser than Daniel. There is no secret that is hidden from you. ⁴ By your wisdom and by your understanding you have gotten yourself riches, and have gotten gold and silver into your treasuries. ⁵ By your great wisdom and by your trading you have increased your riches, and your heart is lifted up because of your riches—" ⁶"'therefore the Lord Yahweh says: "Because you have set your heart as the heart of God, ⁷ therefore, behold, I will bring strangers on you, the terrible of the nations. They will draw their swords against the beauty of your wisdom. They will defile your brightness. ⁸ They will bring you down to the pit. You will die the death of those who are slain in the heart of the seas. ⁹ Will you yet say before him who kills you, 'I am God'? But you are man, and not God, in the hand of him who wounds you. ¹⁰ You will die the death of the uncircumcised by the hand of strangers; for I have spoken it," says the Lord Yahweh.'" ¹¹ Moreover Yahweh's word came to me, saying, ¹²"Son of man, take up a lamentation over the king of Tyre, and tell him, 'The Lord Yahweh says: "You were the seal of full measure, full of wisdom, and perfect in beauty. ¹³ You were in Eden, the garden of God. Every precious stone adorned you: ruby, topaz, emerald, chrysolite, onyx, jasper, sapphire, turquoise, and beryl. Gold work of tambourines and of pipes was in you. They were prepared in the day that you were created. ¹⁴ You were the anointed cherub who covers. Then I set you up on the holy mountain of God. You have walked up and down in the middle of the stones of fire. ¹⁵ You were perfect in your ways from the day that you were created, until unrighteousness was found in you. ¹⁶ By the abundance of your commerce, your insides were filled with violence, and you have sinned. Therefore I have cast you as profane out of God's mountain. I have destroyed you, covering cherub, from the middle of the stones of fire. ¹⁷ Your heart was lifted up because of your beauty. You have corrupted your wisdom by reason of your splendor. I have cast you to the ground. I have laid you before kings, that they may see you. ¹⁸ By the multitude of your iniquities, in the unrighteousness of your commerce, you have profaned your sanctuaries. Therefore I have brought out a fire from the middle of you. It has devoured you. I have turned you to ashes on the earth in the sight of all those who see you. ¹⁹ All those who know you among the peoples will be astonished at you. You have become a terror, and you will exist no more."'" ²⁰ Yahweh's word came to me, saying, ²¹"Son of man, set your face toward Sidon, and prophesy against it, ²² and say, 'The Lord Yahweh says: "Behold, I am against you,

Sidon. I will be glorified among you. Then they will know that I am Yahweh, when I have executed judgments in her, and am sanctified in her. 23 For I will send pestilence into her, and blood into her streets. The wounded will fall within her, with the sword on her on every side. Then they will know that I am Yahweh. 24"""There will no longer be a pricking brier to the house of Israel, nor a hurting thorn of any that are around them that scorned them. Then they will know that I am the Lord Yahweh." 25"'The Lord Yahweh says: "When I have gathered the house of Israel from the peoples among whom they are scattered, and am shown as holy among them in the sight of the nations, then they will dwell in their own land which I gave to my servant Jacob. 26 They will dwell in it securely. Yes, they will build houses, plant vineyards, and will dwell securely when I have executed judgments on all those around them who have treated them with contempt. Then they will know that I am Yahweh their God.""" **29** 1 In the tenth year, in the tenth month, on the twelfth day of the month, Yahweh's word came to me, saying, 2"Son of man, set your face against Pharaoh king of Egypt, and prophesy against him and against all Egypt. 3 Speak and say, 'The Lord Yahweh says: "Behold, I am against you, Pharaoh king of Egypt, the great monster that lies in the middle of his rivers, that has said, 'My river is my own, and I have made it for myself.' 4 I will put hooks in your jaws, and I will make the fish of your rivers stick to your scales. I will bring you up out of the middle of your rivers, with all the fish of your rivers which stick to your scales. 5 I'll cast you out into the wilderness, you and all the fish of your rivers. You'll fall on the open field. You won't be brought together or gathered. I have given you for food to the animals of the earth and to the birds of the sky. 6"""All the inhabitants of Egypt will know that I am Yahweh, because they have been a staff of reed to the house of Israel. 7 When they took hold of you by your hand, you broke and tore all their shoulders. When they leaned on you, you broke and paralyzed all of their thighs." 8"'Therefore the Lord Yahweh says: "Behold, I will bring a sword on you, and will cut off man and animal from you. 9 The land of Egypt will be a desolation and a waste. Then they will know that I am Yahweh. """Because he has said, 'The river is mine, and I have made it,' 10 therefore, behold, I am against you and against your rivers. I will make the land of Egypt an utter waste and desolation, from the tower of Seveneh even to the border of Ethiopia. 11 No foot of man will pass through it, nor will any animal foot pass through it. It won't be inhabited for forty years. 12 I will make the land of Egypt a desolation in the middle of the countries that are desolate. Her cities among the cities that are laid waste will be a desolation forty years. I will scatter the Egyptians among the nations, and will disperse them through the countries." 13"'For the Lord Yahweh says: "At the end of forty years I will gather the Egyptians from the peoples where they were scattered. 14 I will reverse the captivity of Egypt, and will cause them to return into the land of Pathros, into the land of their birth. There they will be a lowly kingdom. 15 It will be the lowest of the kingdoms. It won't lift itself up above the nations any more. I will diminish them so that they will no longer rule over the nations. 16 It will no longer be the confidence of the house of Israel, bringing iniquity to memory, when they turn to look after them. Then they will know that I am the Lord Yahweh."'" 17 It came to pass in the twenty-seventh year, in the first month, in the first day of the month, Yahweh's word came to me, saying, 18"Son of man, Nebuchadnezzar king of Babylon caused his army to serve a great service against Tyre. Every head was made bald, and every shoulder was worn; yet he had no wages, nor did his army, from Tyre, for the service that he had served against it. 19 Therefore the Lord Yahweh says: 'Behold, I will give the land of Egypt to Nebuchadnezzar king of Babylon. He will carry off her multitude, take her plunder, and take her prey. That will be the wages for his army. 20 I have given him the land of Egypt as his payment for which he served, because they worked for me,' says the Lord Yahweh. 21" In that day I will cause a horn to sprout for the house of Israel, and I will open your mouth among them. Then they will know that I am Yahweh."

30

1 Yahweh's word came again to me, saying, 2"Son of man, prophesy, and say, 'The Lord Yahweh says: "Wail, 'Alas for the day!' 3 For the day is near, even Yahweh's day is near. It will be a day of clouds, a time of the nations. 4 A sword will come on Egypt, and anguish will be in Ethiopia, when the slain fall in Egypt. They take away her multitude, and her foundations are broken down. 5""Ethiopia, Put, Lud, all the mixed people, Cub, and the children of the land that is allied with them, will fall with them by the sword." 6"'Yahweh says: "They also who uphold Egypt will fall. The pride of her power will come down. They will fall by the sword in it from the tower of Seveneh," says the Lord Yahweh. 7"They will be desolate in the middle of the countries that are desolate. Her cities will be among the cities that are wasted. 8 They will know that I am Yahweh when I have set a fire in Egypt, and all

her helpers are destroyed. ⁹"""In that day messengers will go out from before me in ships to make the careless Ethiopians afraid. There will be anguish on them, as in the day of Egypt; for, behold, it comes." ¹⁰"The Lord Yahweh says: "I will also make the multitude of Egypt to cease, by the hand of Nebuchadnezzar king of Babylon. ¹¹ He and his people with him, the terrible of the nations, will be brought in to destroy the land. They will draw their swords against Egypt, and fill the land with the slain. ¹² I will make the rivers dry, and will sell the land into the hand of evil men. I will make the land desolate, and all that is therein, by the hand of foreigners. I, Yahweh, have spoken it." ¹³"The Lord Yahweh says: "I will also destroy the idols, and I will cause the images to cease from Memphis. There will be no more a prince from the land of Egypt. I will put a fear in the land of Egypt. ¹⁴ I will make Pathros desolate, and will set a fire in Zoan, and will execute judgments on No. ¹⁵ I will pour my wrath on Sin, the stronghold of Egypt. I will cut off the multitude of No. ¹⁶ I will set a fire in Egypt Sin will be in great anguish. No will be broken up. Memphis will have adversaries in the daytime. ¹⁷ The young men of Aven and of Pibeseth will fall by the sword. They will go into captivity. ¹⁸ At Tehaphnehes also the day will withdraw itself, when I break the yokes of Egypt there. The pride of her power will cease in her. As for her, a cloud will cover her, and her daughters will go into captivity. ¹⁹ Thus I will execute judgments on Egypt. Then they will know that I am Yahweh."" ²⁰ In the eleventh year, in the first month, in the seventh day of the month, Yahweh's word came to me, saying, ²¹"Son of man, I have broken the arm of Pharaoh king of Egypt. Behold, it has not been bound up, to apply medicines, to put a bandage to bind it, that it may become strong to hold the sword. ²² Therefore the Lord Yahweh says: 'Behold, I am against Pharaoh king of Egypt, and will break his arms, the strong arm, and that which was broken. I will cause the sword to fall out of his hand. ²³ I will scatter the Egyptians among the nations, and will disperse them through the countries. ²⁴ I will strengthen the arms of the king of Babylon, and put my sword in his hand; but I will break the arms of Pharaoh, and he will groan before the king of Babylon with the groaning of a mortally wounded man. ²⁵ I will hold up the arms of the king of Babylon, but the arms of Pharaoh will fall down. Then they will know that I am Yahweh when I put my sword into the hand of the king of Babylon, and he stretches it out on the land of Egypt. ²⁶ I will scatter the Egyptians among the nations and disperse them through the countries. Then they will know that I am Yahweh.'"

31

1 In the eleventh year, in the third month, in the first day of the month, Yahweh's word came to me, saying, 2 "Son of man, tell Pharaoh king of Egypt and his multitude: 'Whom are you like in your greatness? 3 Behold, the Assyrian was a cedar in Lebanon with beautiful branches, and with a forest-like shade, of high stature; and its top was among the thick boughs. 4 The waters nourished it. The deep made it to grow. Its rivers ran all around its plantation. It sent out its channels to all the trees of the field. 5 Therefore its stature was exalted above all the trees of the field; and its boughs were multiplied. Its branches became long by reason of many waters, when it spread them out. 6 All the birds of the sky made their nests in its boughs. Under its branches, all the animals of the field gave birth to their young. All great nations lived under its shadow. 7 Thus it was beautiful in its greatness, in the length of its branches; for its root was by many waters. 8 The cedars in the garden of God could not hide it. The cypress trees were not like its branches. The pine trees were not like its branches; nor was any tree in the garden of God like it in its beauty. 9 I made it beautiful by the multitude of its branches, so that all the trees of Eden, that were in the garden of God, envied it.' 10 "Therefore thus said the Lord Yahweh: 'Because he is exalted in stature, and he has set his top among the thick branches, and his heart is lifted up in his height, 11 I will deliver him into the hand of the mighty one of the nations. He will surely deal with him. I have driven him out for his wickedness. 12 Foreigners, the tyrants of the nations, have cut him off and have left him. His branches have fallen on the mountains and in all the valleys, and his boughs are broken by all the watercourses of the land. All the peoples of the earth have gone down from his shadow and have left him. 13 All the birds of the sky will dwell on his ruin, and all the animals of the field will be on his branches, 14 to the end that none of all the trees by the waters exalt themselves in their stature, and don't set their top among the thick boughs. Their mighty ones don't stand up on their height, even all who drink water; for they are all delivered to death, to the lower parts of the earth, among the children of men, with those who go down to the pit.' 15 "The Lord Yahweh says: 'In the day when he went down to Sheol, I caused a mourning. I covered the deep for him, and I restrained its rivers. The great waters were stopped. I caused Lebanon to mourn for him, and all the trees of the field fainted for him. 16 I made the nations to shake at the sound of his fall, when I cast him down to Sheol with those who descend into the pit. All the trees of Eden, the choice

and best of Lebanon, all that drink water, were comforted in the lower parts of the earth. 17 They also went down into Sheol with him to those who are slain by the sword; yes, those who were his arm, who lived under his shadow in the middle of the nations. 18"'To whom are you thus like in glory and in greatness among the trees of Eden? Yet you will be brought down with the trees of Eden to the lower parts of the earth. You will lie in the middle of the uncircumcised, with those who are slain by the sword. "'This is Pharaoh and all his multitude,' says the Lord Yahweh."

32

1 In the twelfth year, in the twelfth month, in the first day of the month, "Yahweh's word came to me, saying, 2'Son of man, take up a lamentation over Pharaoh king of Egypt, and tell him, "You were likened to a young lion of the nations; yet you are as a monster in the seas. You broke out with your rivers, and troubled the waters with your feet, and fouled their rivers." 3 The Lord Yahweh says: "I will spread out my net on you with a company of many peoples. They will bring you up in my net. 4 I will leave you on the land. I will cast you out on the open field, and will cause all the birds of the sky to settle on you. I will satisfy the animals of the whole earth with you. 5 I will lay your flesh on the mountains, and fill the valleys with your height. 6 I will also water the land in which you swim with your blood, even to the mountains. The watercourses will be full of you. 7 When I extinguish you, I will cover the heavens and make its stars dark. I will cover the sun with a cloud, and the moon won't give its light. 8 I will make all the bright lights of the sky dark over you, and set darkness on your land," says the Lord Yahweh. 9"I will also trouble the hearts of many peoples, when I bring your destruction among the nations, into the countries which you have not known. 10 Yes, I will make many peoples amazed at you, and their kings will be horribly afraid for you, when I brandish my sword before them. They will tremble at every moment, every man for his own life, in the day of your fall." 11 For the Lord Yahweh says: "The sword of the king of Babylon will come on you. 12 I will cause your multitude to fall by the swords of the mighty. They are all the ruthless of the nations. They will bring the pride of Egypt to nothing, and all its multitude will be destroyed. 13 I will destroy also all its animals from beside many waters. The foot of man won't trouble them any more, nor will the hoofs of animals trouble them. 14 Then I will make their waters clear, and cause their rivers to run like oil," says the Lord Yahweh. 15"When I make the land of Egypt desolate and waste, a land destitute of that of which it was full,

when I strike all those who dwell therein, then they will know that I am Yahweh. 16""This is the lamentation with which they will lament. The daughters of the nations will lament with this. They will lament with it over Egypt, and over all her multitude," says the Lord Yahweh.'" 17 Also in the twelfth year, in the fifteenth day of the month, Yahweh's word came to me, saying, 18"Son of man, wail for the multitude of Egypt, and cast them down, even her and the daughters of the famous nations, to the lower parts of the earth, with those who go down into the pit. 19 Whom do you pass in beauty? Go down, and be laid with the uncircumcised. 20 They will fall among those who are slain by the sword. She is delivered to the sword. Draw her away with all her multitudes. 21 The strong among the mighty will speak to him out of the middle of Sheol with those who help him. They have gone down. The uncircumcised lie still, slain by the sword. 22"Asshur is there with all her company. Her graves are all around her. All of them are slain, fallen by the sword, 23 whose graves are set in the uttermost parts of the pit, and her company is around her grave, all of them slain, fallen by the sword, who caused terror in the land of the living. 24"There is Elam and all her multitude around her grave; all of them slain, fallen by the sword, who have gone down uncircumcised into the lower parts of the earth, who caused their terror in the land of the living, and have borne their shame with those who go down to the pit. 25 They have made Elam a bed among the slain with all her multitude. Her graves are around her, all of them uncircumcised, slain by the sword; for their terror was caused in the land of the living, and they have borne their shame with those who go down to the pit. He is put among those who are slain. 26"There is Meshech, Tubal, and all their multitude. Their graves are around them, all of them uncircumcised, slain by the sword; for they caused their terror in the land of the living. 27 They will not lie with the mighty who are fallen of the uncircumcised, who have gone down to Sheol with their weapons of war and have laid their swords under their heads. Their iniquities are on their bones; for they were the terror of the mighty in the land of the living. 28"But you will be broken among the uncircumcised, and will lie with those who are slain by the sword. 29"There is Edom, her kings, and all her princes, who in their might are laid with those who are slain by the sword. They will lie with the uncircumcised, and with those who go down to the pit. 30"There are the princes of the north, all of them, and all the Sidonians, who have gone down with the slain. They are put to shame in the terror which they caused by their might. They lie uncircumcised with those who are slain by the sword, and bear their shame with those who go down to the pit. 31"Pharaoh will see them and will be comforted over all his multitude, even Pharaoh and all his army, slain by the sword," says the Lord Yahweh. 32" For I have put his terror in the land of the living. He will be laid among the uncircumcised, with those who are slain by the sword, even Pharaoh and all his multitude," says the Lord Yahweh.

33

1 Yahweh's word came to me, saying, 2"Son of man, speak to the children of your people, and tell them, 'When I bring the sword on a land, and the people of the land take a man from among them, and set him for their watchman, 3 if, when he sees the sword come on the land, he blows the trumpet and warns the people, 4 then whoever hears the sound of the trumpet and doesn't heed the warning, if the sword comes and takes him away, his blood will be on his own head. 5 He heard the sound of the trumpet and didn't take warning. His blood will be on him; whereas if he had heeded the warning, he would have delivered his soul. 6 But if the watchman sees the sword come and doesn't blow the trumpet, and the people aren't warned, and the sword comes and takes any person from among them, he is taken away in his iniquity, but his blood I will require at the watchman's hand.' 7"So you, son of man, I have set you a watchman to the house of Israel. Therefore hear the word from my mouth, and give them warnings from me. 8 When I tell the wicked, 'O wicked man, you will surely die,' and you don't speak to warn the wicked from his way, that wicked man will die in his iniquity, but I will require his blood at your hand. 9 Nevertheless, if you warn the wicked of his way to turn from it, and he doesn't turn from his way; he will die in his iniquity, but you have delivered your soul. 10"You, son of man, tell the house of Israel: 'You say this, "Our transgressions and our sins are on us, and we pine away in them. How then can we live?"' 11 Tell them, '"As I live," says the Lord Yahweh, "I have no pleasure in the death of the wicked, but that the wicked turn from his way and live. Turn, turn from your evil ways! For why will you die, house of Israel?"' 12"You, son of man, tell the children of your people, 'The righteousness of the righteous will not deliver him in the day of his disobedience. And as for the wickedness of the wicked, he will not fall by it in the day that he turns from his wickedness; neither will he who is righteous be able to live by it in the day that he sins. 13 When I tell the righteous that he will surely live, if he trusts in his righteousness and commits iniquity, none of his righteous deeds will be remembered; but he will die in his iniquity that he

has committed. 14 Again, when I say to the wicked, "You will surely die," if he turns from his sin and does that which is lawful and right, 15 if the wicked restore the pledge, give again that which he had taken by robbery, walk in the statutes of life, committing no iniquity, he will surely live. He will not die. 16 None of his sins that he has committed will be remembered against him. He has done that which is lawful and right. He will surely live. 17"Yet the children of your people say, "The way of the Lord is not fair;" but as for them, their way is not fair. 18 When the righteous turns from his righteousness and commits iniquity, he will even die therein. 19 When the wicked turns from his wickedness and does that which is lawful and right, he will live by it. 20 Yet you say, "The way of the Lord is not fair." House of Israel, I will judge every one of you after his ways.'" 21 In the twelfth year of our captivity, in the tenth month, in the fifth day of the month, one who had escaped out of Jerusalem came to me, saying, "The city has been defeated!" 22 Now Yahweh's hand had been on me in the evening, before he who had escaped came; and he had opened my mouth until he came to me in the morning; and my mouth was opened, and I was no longer mute. 23 Yahweh's word came to me, saying, 24"Son of man, those who inhabit the waste places in the land of Israel speak, saying, 'Abraham was one, and he inherited the land; but we are many. The land is given us for inheritance.' 25 Therefore tell them, 'The Lord Yahweh says: "You eat with the blood, and lift up your eyes to your idols, and shed blood. So should you possess the land? 26 You stand on your sword, you work abomination, and every one of you defiles his neighbor's wife. So should you possess the land?"' 27"You shall tell them, 'The Lord Yahweh says: "As I live, surely those who are in the waste places will fall by the sword. I will give whoever is in the open field to the animals to be devoured, and those who are in the strongholds and in the caves will die of the pestilence. 28 I will make the land a desolation and an astonishment. The pride of her power will cease. The mountains of Israel will be desolate, so that no one will pass through. 29 Then they will know that I am Yahweh, when I have made the land a desolation and an astonishment because of all their abominations which they have committed."' 30"As for you, son of man, the children of your people talk about you by the walls and in the doors of the houses, and speak to one another, everyone to his brother, saying, 'Please come and hear what the word is that comes out from Yahweh.' 31 They come to you as the people come, and they sit before you as my people, and they hear your words, but don't do them; for with their mouth they show much love, but their heart goes after their gain. ³² Behold, you are to them as a very lovely song of one who has a pleasant voice, and can play well on an instrument; for they hear your words, but they don't do them. ³³"When this comes to pass—behold, it comes—then they will know that a prophet has been among them."

34

¹ Yahweh's word came to me, saying, ²"Son of man, prophesy against the shepherds of Israel. Prophesy, and tell them, even the shepherds, 'The Lord Yahweh says: "Woe to the shepherds of Israel who feed themselves! Shouldn't the shepherds feed the sheep? ³ You eat the fat. You clothe yourself with the wool. You kill the fatlings, but you don't feed the sheep. ⁴ You haven't strengthened the diseased. You haven't healed that which was sick. You haven't bound up that which was broken. You haven't brought back that which was driven away. You haven't sought that which was lost, but you have ruled over them with force and with rigor. ⁵ They were scattered, because there was no shepherd. They became food to all the animals of the field, and were scattered. ⁶ My sheep wandered through all the mountains and on every high hill. Yes, my sheep were scattered on all the surface of the earth. There was no one who searched or sought." ⁷"'Therefore, you shepherds, hear Yahweh's word: ⁸"As I live," says the Lord Yahweh, "surely because my sheep became a prey, and my sheep became food to all the animals of the field, because there was no shepherd, and my shepherds didn't search for my sheep, but the shepherds fed themselves, and didn't feed my sheep, ⁹ therefore, you shepherds, hear Yahweh's word!" ¹⁰ The Lord Yahweh says: "Behold, I am against the shepherds. I will require my sheep at their hand, and cause them to cease from feeding the sheep. The shepherds won't feed themselves any more. I will deliver my sheep from their mouth, that they may not be food for them." ¹¹"'For the Lord Yahweh says: "Behold, I myself, even I, will search for my sheep, and will seek them out. ¹² As a shepherd seeks out his flock in the day that he is among his sheep that are scattered abroad, so I will seek out my sheep. I will deliver them out of all places where they have been scattered in the cloudy and dark day. ¹³ I will bring them out from the peoples, and gather them from the countries, and will bring them into their own land. I will feed them on the mountains of Israel, by the watercourses, and in all the inhabited places of the country. ¹⁴ I will feed them with good pasture, and their fold will be on the mountains of the height of Israel. There they will lie down in a good fold. They will feed on

rich pasture on the mountains of Israel. 15 I myself will be the shepherd of my sheep, and I will cause them to lie down," says the Lord Yahweh. 16"I will seek that which was lost, and will bring back that which was driven away, and will bind up that which was broken, and will strengthen that which was sick; but I will destroy the fat and the strong. I will feed them in justice.'" 17"As for you, O my flock, the Lord Yahweh says: 'Behold, I judge between sheep and sheep, the rams and the male goats. 18 Does it seem a small thing to you to have fed on the good pasture, but you must tread down with your feet the residue of your pasture? And to have drunk of the clear waters, but must you foul the residue with your feet? 19 As for my sheep, they eat that which you have trodden with your feet, and they drink that which you have fouled with your feet.' 20"Therefore the Lord Yahweh says to them: 'Behold, I, even I, will judge between the fat sheep and the lean sheep. 21 Because you thrust with side and with shoulder, and push all the diseased with your horns, until you have scattered them abroad, 22 therefore I will save my flock, and they will no more be a prey. I will judge between sheep and sheep. 23 I will set up one shepherd over them, and he will feed them, even my servant David. He will feed them, and he will be their shepherd. 24 I, Yahweh, will be their God, and my servant David prince among them. I, Yahweh, have spoken it. 25"'I will make with them a covenant of peace, and will cause evil animals to cease out of the land. They will dwell securely in the wilderness and sleep in the woods. 26 I will make them and the places around my hill a blessing. I will cause the shower to come down in its season. There will be showers of blessing. 27 The tree of the field will yield its fruit, and the earth will yield its increase, and they will be secure in their land. Then they will know that I am Yahweh, when I have broken the bars of their yoke, and have delivered them out of the hand of those who made slaves of them. 28 They will no more be a prey to the nations, neither will the animals of the earth devour them; but they will dwell securely, and no one will make them afraid. 29 I will raise up to them a plantation for renown, and they will no more be consumed with famine in the land, and not bear the shame of the nations any more. 30 They will know that I, Yahweh, their God am with them, and that they, the house of Israel, are my people, says the Lord Yahweh. 31 You my sheep, the sheep of my pasture, are men, and I am your God,' says the Lord Yahweh."

35

1 Moreover Yahweh's word came to me, saying, 2"Son of man, set your face against Mount Seir, and prophesy against it, 3 and tell it, 'The Lord Yahweh

says: "Behold, I am against you, Mount Seir, and I will stretch out my hand against you. I will make you a desolation and an astonishment. ⁴ I will lay your cities waste, and you will be desolate. Then you will know that I am Yahweh. ⁵ "Because you have had a perpetual hostility, and have given over the children of Israel to the power of the sword in the time of their calamity, in the time of the iniquity of the end, ⁶ therefore, as I live," says the Lord Yahweh, "I will prepare you for blood, and blood will pursue you. Since you have not hated blood, therefore blood will pursue you. ⁷ Thus I will make Mount Seir an astonishment and a desolation. I will cut off from it him who passes through and him who returns. ⁸ I will fill its mountains with its slain. The slain with the sword will fall in your hills and in your valleys and in all your watercourses. ⁹ I will make you a perpetual desolation, and your cities will not be inhabited. Then you will know that I am Yahweh. ¹⁰ "Because you have said, 'These two nations and these two countries will be mine, and we will possess it,' although Yahweh was there, ¹¹ therefore, as I live," says the Lord Yahweh, "I will do according to your anger, and according to your envy which you have shown out of your hatred against them; and I will make myself known among them when I judge you. ¹² You will know that I, Yahweh, have heard all your insults which you have spoken against the mountains of Israel, saying, 'They have been laid desolate. They have been given to us to devour.' ¹³ You have magnified yourselves against me with your mouth, and have multiplied your words against me. I have heard it." ¹⁴ The Lord Yahweh says: "When the whole earth rejoices, I will make you desolate. ¹⁵ As you rejoiced over the inheritance of the house of Israel because it was desolate, so I will do to you. You will be desolate, Mount Seir, and all Edom, even all of it. Then they will know that I am Yahweh.'"

36

¹ You, son of man, prophesy to the mountains of Israel, and say, "You mountains of Israel, hear Yahweh's word. ² The Lord Yahweh says: 'Because the enemy has said against you, "Aha!" and, "The ancient high places are ours in possession!"' ³ therefore prophesy, and say, 'The Lord Yahweh says: "Because, even because they have made you desolate, and swallowed you up on every side, that you might be a possession to the residue of the nations, and you are taken up in the lips of talkers, and the evil report of the people;" ⁴ therefore, you mountains of Israel, hear the word of the Lord Yahweh: The Lord Yahweh says to the mountains and to the hills, to the watercourses and to the valleys, to the desolate wastes and to the cities that are forsaken, which

have become a prey and derision to the residue of the nations that are all around; 5 therefore the Lord Yahweh says: "Surely in the fire of my jealousy I have spoken against the residue of the nations, and against all Edom, that have appointed my land to themselves for a possession with the joy of all their heart, with despite of soul, to cast it out for a prey."' 6 Therefore prophesy concerning the land of Israel, and tell the mountains, the hills, the watercourses and the valleys, 'The Lord Yahweh says: "Behold, I have spoken in my jealousy and in my wrath, because you have borne the shame of the nations." 7 Therefore the Lord Yahweh says: "I have sworn, 'Surely the nations that are around you will bear their shame.' 8""But you, mountains of Israel, you shall shoot out your branches and yield your fruit to my people Israel; for they are at hand to come. 9 For, behold, I am for you, and I will come to you, and you will be tilled and sown. 10 I will multiply men on you, all the house of Israel, even all of it. The cities will be inhabited and the waste places will be built. 11 I will multiply man and animal on you. They will increase and be fruitful. I will cause you to be inhabited as you were before, and you will do better than at your beginnings. Then you will know that I am Yahweh. 12 Yes, I will cause men to walk on you, even my people Israel. They will possess you, and you will be their inheritance, and you will never again bereave them of their children." 13"'The Lord Yahweh says: "Because they say to you, 'You are a devourer of men, and have been a bereaver of your nation;' 14 therefore you shall devour men no more, and not bereave your nation any more," says the Lord Yahweh. 15"I won't let you hear the shame of the nations any more. You won't bear the reproach of the peoples any more, and you won't cause your nation to stumble any more," says the Lord Yahweh.'" 16 Moreover Yahweh's word came to me, saying, 17"Son of man, when the house of Israel lived in their own land, they defiled it by their ways and by their deeds. Their way before me was as the uncleanness of a woman in her impurity. 18 Therefore I poured out my wrath on them for the blood which they had poured out on the land, and because they had defiled it with their idols. 19 I scattered them among the nations, and they were dispersed through the countries. I judged them according to their way and according to their deeds. 20 When they came to the nations where they went, they profaned my holy name, in that men said of them, 'These are Yahweh's people, and have left his land.' 21 But I had respect for my holy name, which the house of Israel had profaned among the nations where they went. 22"Therefore tell the house of Israel, 'The Lord Yahweh says: "I don't do this for your sake, house of Israel, but for my holy name, which you have profaned among the nations where you went. 23 I will sanctify my great name, which has been profaned among the nations, which you have profaned among them. Then the nations will know that I am Yahweh," says the Lord Yahweh, "when I am proven holy in you before their eyes. 24""For I will take you from among the nations and gather you out of all the countries, and will bring you into your own land. 25 I will sprinkle clean water on you, and you will be clean. I will cleanse you from all your filthiness and from all your idols. 26 I will also give you a new heart, and I will put a new spirit within you. I will take away the stony heart out of your flesh, and I will give you a heart of flesh. 27 I will put my Spirit within you, and cause you to walk in my statutes. You will keep my ordinances and do them. 28 You will dwell in the land that I gave to your fathers. You will be my people, and I will be your God. 29 I will save you from all your uncleanness. I will call for the grain and will multiply it, and lay no famine on you. 30 I will multiply the fruit of the tree and the increase of the field, that you may receive no more the reproach of famine among the nations. 31""Then you will remember your evil ways, and your deeds that were not good; and you will loathe yourselves in your own sight for your iniquities and for your abominations. 32 I don't do this for your sake," says the Lord Yahweh. "Let it be known to you. Be ashamed and confounded for your ways, house of Israel." 33"'The Lord Yahweh says: "In the day that I cleanse you from all your iniquities, I will cause the cities to be inhabited and the waste places will be built. 34 The land that was desolate will be tilled instead of being a desolation in the sight of all who passed by. 35 They will say, 'This land that was desolate has become like the garden of Eden. The waste, desolate, and ruined cities are fortified and inhabited.' 36 Then the nations that are left around you will know that I, Yahweh, have built the ruined places and planted that which was desolate. I, Yahweh, have spoken it, and I will do it." 37"'The Lord Yahweh says: "For this, moreover, I will be inquired of by the house of Israel, to do it for them: I will increase them with men like a flock. 38 As the flock for sacrifice, as the flock of Jerusalem in her appointed feasts, so the waste cities will be filled with flocks of men. Then they will know that I am Yahweh.'"

37

1 Yahweh's hand was on me, and he brought me out in Yahweh's Spirit, and set me down in the middle of the valley; and it was full of bones. 2 He caused me to pass by them all around; and behold, there were very many in the open

valley, and behold, they were very dry. ³ He said to me, "Son of man, can these bones live?" I answered, "Lord Yahweh, you know." ⁴ Again he said to me, "Prophesy over these bones, and tell them, 'You dry bones, hear Yahweh's word. ⁵ The Lord Yahweh says to these bones: "Behold, I will cause breath to enter into you, and you will live. ⁶ I will lay sinews on you, and will bring up flesh on you, and cover you with skin, and put breath in you, and you will live. Then you will know that I am Yahweh."'" ⁷ So I prophesied as I was commanded. As I prophesied, there was a noise, and behold, there was an earthquake. Then the bones came together, bone to its bone. ⁸ I saw, and, behold, there were sinews on them, and flesh came up, and skin covered them above; but there was no breath in them. ⁹ Then he said to me, "Prophesy to the wind, prophesy, son of man, and tell the wind, 'The Lord Yahweh says: "Come from the four winds, breath, and breathe on these slain, that they may live."'" ¹⁰ So I prophesied as he commanded me, and the breath came into them, and they lived, and stood up on their feet, an exceedingly great army. ¹¹ Then he said to me, "Son of man, these bones are the whole house of Israel. Behold, they say, 'Our bones are dried up, and our hope is lost. We are completely cut off.' ¹² Therefore prophesy, and tell them, 'The Lord Yahweh says: "Behold, I will open your graves, and cause you to come up out of your graves, my people; and I will bring you into the land of Israel. ¹³ You will know that I am Yahweh, when I have opened your graves and caused you to come up out of your graves, my people. ¹⁴ I will put my Spirit in you, and you will live. Then I will place you in your own land; and you will know that I, Yahweh, have spoken it and performed it," says Yahweh.'" ¹⁵ Yahweh's word came again to me, saying, ¹⁶"You, son of man, take one stick and write on it, 'For Judah, and for the children of Israel his companions.' Then take another stick, and write on it, 'For Joseph, the stick of Ephraim, and for all the house of Israel his companions.' ¹⁷ Then join them for yourself to one another into one stick, that they may become one in your hand. ¹⁸"When the children of your people speak to you, saying, 'Won't you show us what you mean by these?' ¹⁹ tell them, 'The Lord Yahweh says: "Behold, I will take the stick of Joseph, which is in the hand of Ephraim, and the tribes of Israel his companions; and I will put them with it, with the stick of Judah, and make them one stick, and they will be one in my hand. ²⁰ The sticks on which you write will be in your hand before their eyes."' ²¹ Say to them, 'The Lord Yahweh says: "Behold, I will take the children of Israel from among the nations where they have gone, and will gather them on every side, and bring them into their own land. 22 I will make them one nation in the land, on the mountains of Israel. One king will be king to them all. They will no longer be two nations. They won't be divided into two kingdoms any more at all. 23 They won't defile themselves any more with their idols, nor with their detestable things, nor with any of their transgressions; but I will save them out of all their dwelling places in which they have sinned, and will cleanse them. So they will be my people, and I will be their God. 24""My servant David will be king over them. They all will have one shepherd. They will also walk in my ordinances and observe my statutes, and do them. 25 They will dwell in the land that I have given to Jacob my servant, in which your fathers lived. They will dwell therein, they, and their children, and their children's children, forever. David my servant will be their prince forever. 26 Moreover I will make a covenant of peace with them. It will be an everlasting covenant with them. I will place them, multiply them, and will set my sanctuary among them forever more. 27 My tent also will be with them. I will be their God, and they will be my people. 28 The nations will know that I am Yahweh who sanctifies Israel, when my sanctuary is among them forever more.""

38

1 Yahweh's word came to me, saying, 2"Son of man, set your face toward Gog, of the land of Magog, the prince of Rosh, Meshech, and Tubal, and prophesy against him, 3 and say, 'The Lord Yahweh says: "Behold, I am against you, Gog, prince of Rosh, Meshech, and Tubal. 4 I will turn you around, and put hooks into your jaws, and I will bring you out, with all your army, horses and horsemen, all of them clothed in full armor, a great company with buckler and shield, all of them handling swords; 5 Persia, Cush, and Put with them, all of them with shield and helmet; 6 Gomer, and all his hordes; the house of Togarmah in the uttermost parts of the north, and all his hordes—even many peoples with you. 7""Be prepared, yes, prepare yourself, you, and all your companies who are assembled to you, and be a guard to them. 8 After many days you will be visited. In the latter years you will come into the land that is brought back from the sword, that is gathered out of many peoples, on the mountains of Israel, which have been a continual waste; but it is brought out of the peoples and they will dwell securely, all of them. 9 You will ascend. You will come like a storm. You will be like a cloud to cover the land, you and all your hordes, and many peoples with you." 10"'The Lord Yahweh says: "It will happen in that day that things will come

into your mind, and you will devise an evil plan. ¹¹ You will say, 'I will go up to the land of unwalled villages. I will go to those who are at rest, who dwell securely, all of them dwelling without walls, and having neither bars nor gates, ¹² to take the plunder and to take prey; to turn your hand against the waste places that are inhabited, and against the people who are gathered out of the nations, who have gotten livestock and goods, who dwell in the middle of the earth.' ¹³ Sheba, Dedan, and the merchants of Tarshish, with all its young lions, will ask you, 'Have you come to take the plunder? Have you assembled your company to take the prey, to carry away silver and gold, to take away livestock and goods, to take great plunder?'" ¹⁴"Therefore, son of man, prophesy, and tell Gog, 'The Lord Yahweh says: "In that day when my people Israel dwells securely, will you not know it? ¹⁵ You will come from your place out of the uttermost parts of the north, you, and many peoples with you, all of them riding on horses, a great company and a mighty army. ¹⁶ You will come up against my people Israel as a cloud to cover the land. It will happen in the latter days that I will bring you against my land, that the nations may know me when I am sanctified in you, Gog, before their eyes." ¹⁷"'The Lord Yahweh says: "Are you he of whom I spoke in old time by my servants the prophets of Israel, who prophesied in those days for years that I would bring you against them? ¹⁸ It will happen in that day, when Gog comes against the land of Israel," says the Lord Yahweh, "that my wrath will come up into my nostrils. ¹⁹ For in my jealousy and in the fire of my wrath I have spoken. Surely in that day there will be a great shaking in the land of Israel, ²⁰ so that the fish of the sea, the birds of the sky, the animals of the field, all creeping things who creep on the earth, and all the men who are on the surface of the earth will shake at my presence. Then the mountains will be thrown down, the steep places will fall, and every wall will fall to the ground. ²¹ I will call for a sword against him to all my mountains," says the Lord Yahweh. "Every man's sword will be against his brother. ²² I will enter into judgment with him with pestilence and with blood. I will rain on him, on his hordes, and on the many peoples who are with him, torrential rains with great hailstones, fire, and sulfur. ²³ I will magnify myself and sanctify myself, and I will make myself known in the eyes of many nations. Then they will know that I am Yahweh.'"

39

¹"You, son of man, prophesy against Gog, and say, 'The Lord Yahweh says: "Behold, I am against you, Gog, prince of Rosh, Meshech, and Tubal. ² I will

turn you around, will lead you on, and will cause you to come up from the uttermost parts of the north; and I will bring you onto the mountains of Israel. 3 I will strike your bow out of your left hand, and will cause your arrows to fall out of your right hand. 4 You will fall on the mountains of Israel, you, and all your hordes, and the peoples who are with you. I will give you to the ravenous birds of every sort and to the animals of the field to be devoured. 5 You will fall on the open field, for I have spoken it," says the Lord Yahweh. 6"I will send a fire on Magog and on those who dwell securely in the islands. Then they will know that I am Yahweh. 7""I will make my holy name known among my people Israel. I won't allow my holy name to be profaned any more. Then the nations will know that I am Yahweh, the Holy One in Israel. 8 Behold, it comes, and it will be done," says the Lord Yahweh. "This is the day about which I have spoken. 9"""Those who dwell in the cities of Israel will go out and will make fires of the weapons and burn them, both the shields and the bucklers, the bows and the arrows, and the war clubs and the spears, and they will make fires with them for seven years; 10 so that they will take no wood out of the field, and not cut down any out of the forests; for they will make fires with the weapons. They will plunder those who plundered them, and rob those who robbed them," says the Lord Yahweh. 11"""It will happen in that day, that I will give to Gog a place for burial in Israel, the valley of those who pass through on the east of the sea; and it will stop those who pass through. They will bury Gog and all his multitude there, and they will call it 'The valley of Hamon Gog'. 12"""The house of Israel will be burying them for seven months, that they may cleanse the land. 13 Yes, all the people of the land will bury them; and they will become famous in the day that I will be glorified," says the Lord Yahweh. 14"""They will set apart men of continual employment who will pass through the land. Those who pass through will go with those who bury those who remain on the surface of the land, to cleanse it. After the end of seven months they will search. 15 Those who search through the land will pass through; and when anyone sees a man's bone, then he will set up a sign by it, until the undertakers have buried it in the valley of Hamon Gog. 16 Hamonah will also be the name of a city. Thus they will cleanse the land."' 17"You, son of man, the Lord Yahweh says: 'Speak to the birds of every sort, and to every animal of the field, "Assemble yourselves, and come; gather yourselves on every side to my sacrifice that I sacrifice for you, even a great sacrifice on the mountains of Israel, that you may eat meat and drink blood. 18 You shall eat the flesh of the mighty, and drink the blood of the princes of the earth, of rams, of lambs, and of goats, of bulls, all of them fatlings of Bashan. 19 You shall eat fat until you are full, and drink blood until you are drunk, of my sacrifice which I have sacrificed for you. 20 You shall be filled at my table with horses and charioteers, with mighty men, and with all men of war," says the Lord Yahweh.' 21"I will set my glory among the nations. Then all the nations will see my judgment that I have executed, and my hand that I have laid on them. 22 So the house of Israel will know that I am Yahweh their God, from that day and forward. 23 The nations will know that the house of Israel went into captivity for their iniquity, because they trespassed against me, and I hid my face from them; so I gave them into the hand of their adversaries, and they all fell by the sword. 24 I did to them according to their uncleanness and according to their transgressions. I hid my face from them. 25"Therefore the Lord Yahweh says: 'Now I will reverse the captivity of Jacob and have mercy on the whole house of Israel. I will be jealous for my holy name. 26 They will forget their shame and all their trespasses by which they have trespassed against me, when they dwell securely in their land. No one will make them afraid 27 when I have brought them back from the peoples, gathered them out of their enemies' lands, and am shown holy among them in the sight of many nations. 28 They will know that I am Yahweh their God, in that I caused them to go into captivity among the nations, and have gathered them to their own land. Then I will leave none of them captive any more. 29 I won't hide my face from them any more, for I have poured out my Spirit on the house of Israel,' says the Lord Yahweh."

40

1 In the twenty-fifth year of our captivity, in the beginning of the year, in the tenth day of the month, in the fourteenth year after the city was struck, in the same day, Yahweh's hand was on me, and he brought me there. 2 In the visions of God he brought me into the land of Israel, and set me down on a very high mountain, on which was something like the frame of a city to the south. 3 He brought me there; and, behold, there was a man whose appearance was like the appearance of bronze, with a line of flax in his hand and a measuring reed; and he stood in the gate. 4 The man said to me, "Son of man, see with your eyes, and hear with your ears, and set your heart on all that I will show you; for you have been brought here so that I may show them to you. Declare all that you see to the house of Israel." 5 Behold, there was a wall on the outside of the house all around, and in the man's hand a

measuring reed six cubits long, of a cubit and a hand width each. So he measured the thickness of the building, one reed; and the height, one reed. 6 Then he came to the gate which looks toward the east, and went up its steps. He measured the threshold of the gate, one reed wide; and the other threshold, one reed wide. 7 Every lodge was one reed long and one reed wide. Between the lodges was five cubits. The threshold of the gate by the porch of the gate toward the house was one reed. 8 He measured also the porch of the gate toward the house, one reed. 9 Then he measured the porch of the gate, eight cubits; and its posts, two cubits; and the porch of the gate was toward the house. 10 The side rooms of the gate eastward were three on this side, and three on that side. The three of them were of one measure. The posts had one measure on this side and on that side. 11 He measured the width of the opening of the gate, ten cubits; and the length of the gate, thirteen cubits; 12 and a border before the lodges, one cubit on this side, and a border, one cubit on that side; and the side rooms, six cubits on this side, and six cubits on that side. 13 He measured the gate from the roof of the one side room to the roof of the other, a width of twenty-five cubits, door against door. 14 He also made posts, sixty cubits; and the court reached to the posts, around the gate. 15 From the forefront of the gate at the entrance to the forefront of the inner porch of the gate were fifty cubits. 16 There were closed windows to the side rooms, and to their posts within the gate all around, and likewise to the arches. Windows were around inward. Palm trees were on each post. 17 Then he brought me into the outer court. Behold, there were rooms and a pavement made for the court all around. Thirty rooms were on the pavement. 18 The pavement was by the side of the gates, corresponding to the length of the gates, even the lower pavement. 19 Then he measured the width from the forefront of the lower gate to the forefront of the inner court outside, one hundred cubits, both on the east and on the north. 20 He measured the length and width of the gate of the outer court which faces toward the north. 21 The lodges of it were three on this side and three on that side. Its posts and its arches were the same as the measure of the first gate: its length was fifty cubits, and the width twenty-five cubits. 22 Its windows, its arches, and its palm trees were the same as the measure of the gate which faces toward the east. They went up to it by seven steps. Its arches were before them. 23 There was a gate to the inner court facing the other gate, on the north and on the east. He measured one hundred cubits from gate to gate. 24 He led me toward the south; and behold, there was a gate toward the south. He measured its posts and its arches according to these measurements. 25 There were windows in it and in its arches all around, like the other windows: the length was fifty cubits, and the width twenty-five cubits. 26 There were seven steps to go up to it, and its arches were before them. It had palm trees, one on this side, and another on that side, on its posts. 27 There was a gate to the inner court toward the south. He measured one hundred cubits from gate to gate toward the south. 28 Then he brought me to the inner court by the south gate. He measured the south gate according to these measurements; 29 with its lodges, its posts, and its arches, according to these measurements. There were windows in it and in its arches all around. It was fifty cubits long, and twenty-five cubits wide. 30 There were arches all around, twenty-five cubits long and five cubits wide. 31 Its arches were toward the outer court. Palm trees were on its posts. The ascent to it had eight steps. 32 He brought me into the inner court toward the east. He measured the gate according to these measurements; 33 with its lodges, its posts, and its arches, according to these measurements. There were windows in it and in its arches all around. It was fifty cubits long, and twenty-five cubits wide. 34 Its arches were toward the outer court. Palm trees were on its posts on this side and on that side. The ascent to it had eight steps. 35 He brought me to the north gate, and he measured it according to these measurements— 36 its lodges, its posts, and its arches. There were windows in it all around. The length was fifty cubits and the width twenty-five cubits. 37 Its posts were toward the outer court. Palm trees were on its posts on this side and on that side. The ascent to it had eight steps. 38 A room with its door was by the posts at the gates. They washed the burnt offering there. 39 In the porch of the gate were two tables on this side and two tables on that side, on which to kill the burnt offering, the sin offering, and the trespass offering. 40 On the one side outside, as one goes up to the entry of the gate toward the north, were two tables; and on the other side, which belonged to the porch of the gate, were two tables. 41 Four tables were on this side, and four tables on that side, by the side of the gate: eight tables, on which they killed the sacrifices. 42 There were four cut stone tables for the burnt offering, a cubit and a half long, a cubit and a half wide, and one cubit high. They laid the instruments with which they killed the burnt offering and the sacrifice on them. 43 The hooks, a hand width long, were fastened within all around. The meat of the offering was on the tables. 44 Outside of the inner gate were rooms for the singers in the inner court, which was at the side of the north gate. They faced toward the south. One at the side of the east gate faced toward the north. ⁴⁵ He said to me, "This room, which faces toward the south, is for the priests who perform the duty of the house. ⁴⁶ The room which faces toward the north is for the priests who perform the duty of the altar. These are the sons of Zadok, who from among the sons of Levi come near to Yahweh to minister to him." ⁴⁷ He measured the court, one hundred cubits long and one hundred cubits wide, square. The altar was before the house. ⁴⁸ Then he brought me to the porch of the house, and measured each post of the porch, five cubits on this side, and five cubits on that side. The width of the gate was three cubits on this side and three cubits on that side. ⁴⁹ The length of the porch was twenty cubits and the width eleven cubits, even by the steps by which they went up to it. There were pillars by the posts, one on this side, and another on that side.

41

¹ He brought me to the nave and measured the posts, six cubits wide on the one side and six cubits wide on the other side, which was the width of the tent. ² The width of the entrance was ten cubits, and the sides of the entrance were five cubits on the one side, and five cubits on the other side. He measured its length, forty cubits, and the width, twenty cubits. ³ Then he went inward and measured each post of the entrance, two cubits; and the entrance, six cubits; and the width of the entrance, seven cubits. ⁴ He measured its length, twenty cubits, and the width, twenty cubits, before the nave. He said to me, "This is the most holy place." ⁵ Then he measured the wall of the house, six cubits; and the width of every side room, four cubits, all around the house on every side. ⁶ The side rooms were in three stories, one over another, and thirty in each story. They entered into the wall which belonged to the house for the side rooms all around, that they might be supported and not penetrate the wall of the house. ⁷ The side rooms were wider on the higher levels, because the walls were narrower at the higher levels. Therefore the width of the house increased upward; and so one went up from the lowest level to the highest through the middle level. ⁸ I saw also that the house had a raised base all around. The foundations of the side rooms were a full reed of six great cubits. ⁹ The thickness of the outer wall of the side rooms was five cubits. That which was left was the place of the side rooms that belonged to the house. ¹⁰ Between the rooms was a width of twenty cubits around the house on every side. ¹¹ The doors of the side rooms were toward an open area that was left, one door toward the north, and another door toward the south. The width of the open area was five cubits all around. ¹² The building that

was before the separate place at the side toward the west was seventy cubits wide; and the wall of the building was five cubits thick all around, and its length ninety cubits. 13 So he measured the temple, one hundred cubits long; and the separate place, and the building, with its walls, one hundred cubits long; 14 also the width of the face of the temple, and of the separate place toward the east, one hundred cubits. 15 He measured the length of the building before the separate place which was at its back, and its galleries on the one side and on the other side, one hundred cubits from the inner temple, and the porches of the court, 16 the thresholds, and the closed windows, and the galleries around on their three stories, opposite the threshold, with wood ceilings all around, and from the ground up to the windows, (now the windows were covered), 17 to the space above the door, even to the inner house, and outside, and by all the wall all around inside and outside, by measure. 18 It was made with cherubim and palm trees. A palm tree was between cherub and cherub, and every cherub had two faces, 19 so that there was the face of a man toward the palm tree on the one side, and the face of a young lion toward the palm tree on the other side. It was made like this through all the house all around. 20 Cherubim and palm trees were made from the ground to above the door. The wall of the temple was like this. 21 The door posts of the nave were squared. As for the face of the nave, its appearance was as the appearance of the temple. 22 The altar was of wood, three cubits high, and its length two cubits. Its corners, its base, and its walls were of wood. He said to me, "This is the table that is before Yahweh." 23 The temple and the sanctuary had two doors. 24 The doors had two leaves each, two turning leaves: two for the one door, and two leaves for the other. 25 There were made on them, on the doors of the nave, cherubim and palm trees, like those made on the walls. There was a threshold of wood on the face of the porch outside. 26 There were closed windows and palm trees on the one side and on the other side, on the sides of the porch. This is how the side rooms of the temple and the thresholds were arranged.

42

1 Then he brought me out into the outer court, the way toward the north. Then he brought me into the room that was opposite the separate place, and which was opposite the building toward the north. 2 Facing the length of one hundred cubits was the north door, and the width was fifty cubits. 3 Opposite the twenty cubits which belonged to the inner court, and opposite the pavement which belonged to the outer court, was gallery against gallery in

the three stories. 4 Before the rooms was a walk of ten cubits' width inward, a way of one cubit; and their doors were toward the north. 5 Now the upper rooms were shorter; for the galleries took away from these more than from the lower and the middle in the building. 6 For they were in three stories, and they didn't have pillars as the pillars of the courts. Therefore the uppermost was set back more than the lowest and the middle from the ground. 7 The wall that was outside by the side of the rooms, toward the outer court before the rooms, was fifty cubits long. 8 For the length of the rooms that were in the outer court was fifty cubits. Behold, those facing the temple were one hundred cubits. 9 From under these rooms was the entry on the east side, as one goes into them from the outer court. 10 In the thickness of the wall of the court toward the east, before the separate place, and before the building, there were rooms. 11 The way before them was like the appearance of the rooms which were toward the north. Their length and width were the same. All their exits had the same arrangement and doors. 12 Like the doors of the rooms that were toward the south was a door at the head of the way, even the way directly before the wall toward the east, as one enters into them. 13 Then he said to me, "The north rooms and the south rooms, which are opposite the separate place, are the holy rooms, where the priests who are near to Yahweh shall eat the most holy things. There they shall lay the most holy things, with the meal offering, the sin offering, and the trespass offering; for the place is holy. 14 When the priests enter in, then they shall not go out of the holy place into the outer court until they lay their garments in which they minister there; for they are holy. Then they shall put on other garments, and shall approach that which is for the people." 15 Now when he had finished measuring the inner house, he brought me out by the way of the gate which faces toward the east, and measured it all around. 16 He measured on the east side with the measuring reed five hundred reeds, with the measuring reed all around. 17 He measured on the north side five hundred reeds with the measuring reed all around. 18 He measured on the south side five hundred reeds with the measuring reed. 19 He turned about to the west side, and measured five hundred reeds with the measuring reed. 20 He measured it on the four sides. It had a wall around it, the length five hundred cubits, and the width five hundred cubits, to make a separation between that which was holy and that which was common.

43

1 Afterward he brought me to the gate, even the gate that looks toward the

east. 2 Behold, the glory of the God of Israel came from the way of the east. His voice was like the sound of many waters; and the earth was illuminated with his glory. 3 It was like the appearance of the vision which I saw, even according to the vision that I saw when I came to destroy the city; and the visions were like the vision that I saw by the river Chebar; and I fell on my face. 4 Yahweh's glory came into the house by the way of the gate which faces toward the east. 5 The Spirit took me up and brought me into the inner court; and behold, Yahweh's glory filled the house. 6 I heard one speaking to me out of the house, and a man stood by me. 7 He said to me, "Son of man, this is the place of my throne and the place of the soles of my feet, where I will dwell among the children of Israel forever. The house of Israel will no more defile my holy name, neither they nor their kings, by their prostitution and by the dead bodies of their kings in their high places; 8 in their setting of their threshold by my threshold and their door post beside my door post. There was a wall between me and them; and they have defiled my holy name by their abominations which they have committed. Therefore I have consumed them in my anger. 9 Now let them put away their prostitution, and the dead bodies of their kings far from me. Then I will dwell among them forever. 10 "You, son of man, show the house to the house of Israel, that they may be ashamed of their iniquities; and let them measure the pattern. 11 If they are ashamed of all that they have done, make known to them the form of the house, its fashion, its exits, its entrances, its structure, all its ordinances, all its forms, and all its laws; and write it in their sight, that they may keep the whole form of it, and all its ordinances, and do them. 12 "This is the law of the house. On the top of the mountain the whole limit around it shall be most holy. Behold, this is the law of the house. 13 "These are the measurements of the altar by cubits (the cubit is a cubit and a hand width): the bottom shall be a cubit, and the width a cubit, and its border around its edge a span; and this shall be the base of the altar. 14 From the bottom on the ground to the lower ledge shall be two cubits, and the width one cubit; and from the lesser ledge to the greater ledge shall be four cubits, and the width a cubit. 15 The upper altar shall be four cubits; and from the altar hearth and upward there shall be four horns. 16 The altar hearth shall be twelve cubits long by twelve wide, square in its four sides. 17 The ledge shall be fourteen cubits long by fourteen wide in its four sides; and the border about it shall be half a cubit; and its bottom shall be a cubit around; and its steps shall look toward the east." 18 He said to me, "Son of man, the Lord Yahweh says: 'These are the ordinances of the altar in the day when they make it, to offer burnt offerings on it, and to sprinkle blood on it. 19 You shall give to the Levitical priests who are of the offspring of Zadok, who are near to me, to minister to me,' says the Lord Yahweh, 'a young bull for a sin offering. 20 You shall take of its blood and put it on its four horns, and on the four corners of the ledge, and on the border all around. You shall cleanse it and make atonement for it that way. 21 You shall also take the bull of the sin offering, and it shall be burned in the appointed place of the house, outside of the sanctuary. 22"On the second day you shall offer a male goat without defect for a sin offering; and they shall cleanse the altar, as they cleansed it with the bull. 23 When you have finished cleansing it, you shall offer a young bull without defect and a ram out of the flock without defect. 24 You shall bring them near to Yahweh, and the priests shall cast salt on them, and they shall offer them up for a burnt offering to Yahweh. 25"Seven days you shall prepare every day a goat for a sin offering. They shall also prepare a young bull and a ram out of the flock, without defect. 26 Seven days shall they make atonement for the altar and purify it. So shall they consecrate it. 27 When they have accomplished the days, it shall be that on the eighth day and onward, the priests shall make your burnt offerings on the altar and your peace offerings. Then I will accept you,' says the Lord Yahweh."

44

1 Then he brought me back by the way of the outer gate of the sanctuary, which looks toward the east; and it was shut. 2 Yahweh said to me, "This gate shall be shut. It shall not be opened, no man shall enter in by it; for Yahweh, the God of Israel, has entered in by it. Therefore it shall be shut. 3 As for the prince, he shall sit in it as prince to eat bread before Yahweh. He shall enter by the way of the porch of the gate, and shall go out the same way." 4 Then he brought me by the way of the north gate before the house; and I looked, and behold, Yahweh's glory filled Yahweh's house; so I fell on my face. 5 Yahweh said to me, "Son of man, mark well, and see with your eyes, and hear with your ears all that I tell you concerning all the ordinances of Yahweh's house and all its laws; and mark well the entrance of the house, with every exit of the sanctuary. 6 You shall tell the rebellious, even the house of Israel, 'The Lord Yahweh says: "You house of Israel, let that be enough of all your abominations, 7 in that you have brought in foreigners, uncircumcised in heart and uncircumcised in flesh, to be in my sanctuary, to profane it, even my house, when you offer my bread, the fat and the blood; and they have

broken my covenant, to add to all your abominations. 8 You have not performed the duty of my holy things; but you have set performers of my duty in my sanctuary for yourselves." 9 The Lord Yahweh says, "No foreigner, uncircumcised in heart and uncircumcised in flesh, shall enter into my sanctuary, of any foreigners who are among the children of Israel. 10""But the Levites who went far from me when Israel went astray, who went astray from me after their idols, they will bear their iniquity. 11 Yet they shall be ministers in my sanctuary, having oversight at the gates of the house, and ministering in the house. They shall kill the burnt offering and the sacrifice for the people, and they shall stand before them to minister to them. 12 Because they ministered to them before their idols, and became a stumbling block of iniquity to the house of Israel, therefore I have lifted up my hand against them," says the Lord Yahweh, "and they will bear their iniquity. 13 They shall not come near to me, to execute the office of priest to me, nor to come near to any of my holy things, to the things that are most holy; but they will bear their shame and their abominations which they have committed. 14 Yet I will make them performers of the duty of the house, for all its service and for all that will be done therein. 15""But the Levitical priests, the sons of Zadok, who performed the duty of my sanctuary when the children of Israel went astray from me, shall come near to me to minister to me. They shall stand before me to offer to me the fat and the blood," says the Lord Yahweh. 16"They shall enter into my sanctuary, and they shall come near to my table, to minister to me, and they shall keep my instruction. 17""It will be that when they enter in at the gates of the inner court, they shall be clothed with linen garments. No wool shall come on them while they minister in the gates of the inner court, and within. 18 They shall have linen turbans on their heads, and shall have linen trousers on their waists. They shall not clothe themselves with anything that makes them sweat. 19 When they go out into the outer court, even into the outer court to the people, they shall put off their garments in which they minister and lay them in the holy rooms. They shall put on other garments, that they not sanctify the people with their garments. 20""They shall not shave their heads, or allow their locks to grow long. They shall only cut off the hair of their heads. 21 None of the priests shall drink wine when they enter into the inner court. 22 They shall not take for their wives a widow, or her who is put away; but they shall take virgins of the offspring of the house of Israel, or a widow who is the widow of a priest. 23 They shall teach my people the difference between the holy and the common, and cause them to discern between the unclean and the clean. ²⁴"'In a controversy they shall stand to judge. They shall judge it according to my ordinances. They shall keep my laws and my statutes in all my appointed feasts. They shall make my Sabbaths holy. ²⁵"'"They shall go in to no dead person to defile themselves; but for father, or for mother, or for son, or for daughter, for brother, or for sister who has had no husband, they may defile themselves. ²⁶ After he is cleansed, they shall reckon to him seven days. ²⁷ In the day that he goes into the sanctuary, into the inner court, to minister in the sanctuary, he shall offer his sin offering," says the Lord Yahweh. ²⁸"'They shall have an inheritance: I am their inheritance; and you shall give them no possession in Israel. I am their possession. ²⁹ They shall eat the meal offering, and the sin offering, and the trespass offering; and every devoted thing in Israel shall be theirs. ³⁰ The first of all the first fruits of every thing, and every offering of everything, of all your offerings, shall be for the priest. You shall also give to the priests the first of your dough, to cause a blessing to rest on your house. ³¹ The priests shall not eat of anything that dies of itself or is torn, whether it is bird or animal.

45

¹"'"Moreover, when you divide by lot the land for inheritance, you shall offer an offering to Yahweh, a holy portion of the land. The length shall be the length of twenty-five thousand reeds, and the width shall be ten thousand. It shall be holy in all its border all around. ² Of this there shall be a five hundred by five hundred square for the holy place, and fifty cubits for its pasture lands all around. ³ Of this measure you shall measure a length of twenty-five thousand, and a width of ten thousand. In it shall be the sanctuary, which is most holy. ⁴ It is a holy portion of the land; it shall be for the priests, the ministers of the sanctuary, who come near to minister to Yahweh. It shall be a place for their houses and a holy place for the sanctuary. ⁵ Twenty-five thousand cubits in length and ten thousand in width shall be for the Levites, the ministers of the house, as a possession for themselves, for twenty rooms. ⁶"'"You shall appoint the possession of the city five thousand cubits wide and twenty-five thousand long, side by side with the offering of the holy portion. It shall be for the whole house of Israel. ⁷"'"What is for the prince shall be on the one side and on the other side of the holy allotment and of the possession of the city, in front of the holy allotment and in front of the possession of the city, on the west side westward, and on the east side eastward, and in length corresponding to one of the portions,

from the west border to the east border. 8 In the land it shall be to him for a possession in Israel. My princes shall no more oppress my people, but they shall give the land to the house of Israel according to their tribes." 9"The Lord Yahweh says: "Enough you, princes of Israel! Remove violence and plunder, and execute justice and righteousness! Stop dispossessing my people!" says the Lord Yahweh. 10"You shall have just balances, a just ephah, and a just bath. 11 The ephah and the bath shall be of one measure, that the bath may contain one tenth of a homer, and the ephah one tenth of a homer. Its measure shall be the same as the homer. 12 The shekel shall be twenty gerahs. Twenty shekels plus twenty-five shekels plus fifteen shekels shall be your mina. 13""This is the offering that you shall offer: the sixth part of an ephah from a homer of wheat, and you shall give the sixth part of an ephah from a homer of barley, 14 and the set portion of oil, of the bath of oil, one tenth of a bath out of the cor, which is ten baths, even a homer (for ten baths are a homer), 15 and one lamb of the flock out of two hundred, from the well-watered pastures of Israel—for a meal offering, for a burnt offering, and for peace offerings, to make atonement for them," says the Lord Yahweh. 16"All the people of the land shall give to this offering for the prince in Israel. 17 It shall be the prince's part to give the burnt offerings, the meal offerings, and the drink offerings, in the feasts, and on the new moons, and on the Sabbaths, in all the appointed feasts of the house of Israel. He shall prepare the sin offering, the meal offering, the burnt offering, and the peace offerings, to make atonement for the house of Israel." 18"'The Lord Yahweh says: "In the first month, on the first day of the month, you shall take a young bull without defect, and you shall cleanse the sanctuary. 19 The priest shall take of the blood of the sin offering and put it on the door posts of the house, and on the four corners of the ledge of the altar, and on the posts of the gate of the inner court. 20 So you shall do on the seventh day of the month for everyone who errs, and for him who is simple. So you shall make atonement for the house. 21"""In the first month, on the fourteenth day of the month, you shall have the Passover, a feast of seven days; unleavened bread shall be eaten. 22 On that day the prince shall prepare for himself and for all the people of the land a bull for a sin offering. 23 The seven days of the feast he shall prepare a burnt offering to Yahweh, seven bulls and seven rams without defect daily the seven days; and a male goat daily for a sin offering. 24 He shall prepare a meal offering, an ephah for a bull, an ephah for a ram, and a hin of oil to an ephah. 25"""In the seventh month, on the fifteenth day of the month, during the feast, he shall do like that for seven days. He shall make the same provision for sin offering, the burnt offering, the meal offering, and the oil."

46

¹"'The Lord Yahweh says: "The gate of the inner court that looks toward the east shall be shut the six working days; but on the Sabbath day it shall be opened, and on the day of the new moon it shall be opened. ² The prince shall enter by the way of the porch of the gate outside, and shall stand by the post of the gate; and the priests shall prepare his burnt offering and his peace offerings, and he shall worship at the threshold of the gate. Then he shall go out, but the gate shall not be shut until the evening. ³ The people of the land shall worship at the door of that gate before Yahweh on the Sabbaths and on the new moons. ⁴ The burnt offering that the prince shall offer to Yahweh shall be on the Sabbath day, six lambs without defect and a ram without defect; ⁵ and the meal offering shall be an ephah for the ram, and the meal offering for the lambs as he is able to give, and a hin of oil to an ephah. ⁶ On the day of the new moon it shall be a young bull without defect, six lambs, and a ram. They shall be without defect. ⁷ He shall prepare a meal offering: an ephah for the bull, and an ephah for the ram, and for the lambs according as he is able, and a hin of oil to an ephah. ⁸ When the prince enters, he shall go in by the way of the porch of the gate, and he shall go out by its way.

⁹"'"But when the people of the land come before Yahweh in the appointed feasts, he who enters by the way of the north gate to worship shall go out by the way of the south gate; and he who enters by the way of the south gate shall go out by the way of the north gate. He shall not return by the way of the gate by which he came in, but shall go out straight before him. ¹⁰ The prince shall go in with them when they go in. When they go out, he shall go out. ¹¹"'"In the feasts and in the appointed holidays, the meal offering shall be an ephah for a bull, and an ephah for a ram, and for the lambs as he is able to give, and a hin of oil to an ephah. ¹² When the prince prepares a free will offering, a burnt offering or peace offerings as a free will offering to Yahweh, one shall open for him the gate that looks toward the east; and he shall prepare his burnt offering and his peace offerings, as he does on the Sabbath day. Then he shall go out; and after his going out one shall shut the gate. ¹³"'"You shall prepare a lamb a year old without defect for a burnt offering to Yahweh daily. Morning by morning you shall prepare it. ¹⁴ You shall prepare a meal offering with it morning by morning, the sixth part of an ephah, and the third part of a hin of oil to moisten the fine flour; a meal offering to

Yahweh continually by a perpetual ordinance. 15 Thus they shall prepare the lamb, the meal offering, and the oil, morning by morning, for a continual burnt offering." 16 "The Lord Yahweh says: "If the prince gives a gift to any of his sons, it is his inheritance. It shall belong to his sons. It is their possession by inheritance. 17 But if he gives of his inheritance a gift to one of his servants, it shall be his to the year of liberty; then it shall return to the prince; but as for his inheritance, it shall be for his sons. 18 Moreover the prince shall not take of the people's inheritance, to thrust them out of their possession. He shall give inheritance to his sons out of his own possession, that my people not each be scattered from his possession.""" 19 Then he brought me through the entry, which was at the side of the gate, into the holy rooms for the priests, which looked toward the north. Behold, there was a place on the back part westward. 20 He said to me, "This is the place where the priests shall boil the trespass offering and the sin offering, and where they shall bake the meal offering, that they not bring them out into the outer court, to sanctify the people." 21 Then he brought me out into the outer court and caused me to pass by the four corners of the court; and behold, in every corner of the court there was a court. 22 In the four corners of the court there were courts enclosed, forty cubits long and thirty wide. These four in the corners were the same size. 23 There was a wall around in them, around the four, and boiling places were made under the walls all around. 24 Then he said to me, "These are the boiling houses, where the ministers of the house shall boil the sacrifice of the people."

47

1 He brought me back to the door of the temple; and behold, waters flowed out from under the threshold of the temple eastward, for the front of the temple faced toward the east. The waters came down from underneath, from the right side of the temple, on the south of the altar. 2 Then he brought me out by the way of the gate northward, and led me around by the way outside to the outer gate, by the way of the gate that looks toward the east. Behold, waters ran out on the right side. 3 When the man went out eastward with the line in his hand, he measured one thousand cubits, and he caused me to pass through the waters, waters that were to the ankles. 4 Again he measured one thousand, and caused me to pass through the waters, waters that were to the knees. Again he measured one thousand, and caused me to pass through waters that were to the waist. 5 Afterward he measured one thousand; and it was a river that I could not pass through, for the waters had risen, waters to

251

swim in, a river that could not be walked through. 6 He said to me, "Son of man, have you seen this?" Then he brought me and caused me to return to the bank of the river. 7 Now when I had returned, behold, on the bank of the river were very many trees on the one side and on the other. 8 Then he said to me, "These waters flow out toward the eastern region and will go down into the Arabah. Then they will go toward the sea and flow into the sea which will be made to flow out; and the waters will be healed. 9 It will happen that every living creature which swarms, in every place where the rivers come, will live. Then there will be a very great multitude of fish; for these waters have come there, and the waters of the sea will be healed, and everything will live wherever the river comes. 10 It will happen that fishermen will stand by it. From En Gedi even to En Eglaim will be a place for the spreading of nets. Their fish will be after their kinds, as the fish of the great sea, exceedingly many. 11 But its swamps and marshes will not be healed. They will be given up to salt. 12 By the river banks, on both sides, will grow every tree for food, whose leaf won't wither, neither will its fruit fail. It will produce new fruit every month, because its waters issue out of the sanctuary. Its fruit will be for food, and its leaf for healing." 13 The Lord Yahweh says: "This shall be the border by which you shall divide the land for inheritance according to the twelve tribes of Israel. Joseph shall have two portions. 14 You shall inherit it, one as well as another; for I swore to give it to your fathers. This land will fall to you for inheritance. 15"This shall be the border of the land: "On the north side, from the great sea, by the way of Hethlon, to the entrance of Zedad; 16 Hamath, Berothah, Sibraim (which is between the border of Damascus and the border of Hamath), to Hazer Hatticon, which is by the border of Hauran. 17 The border from the sea shall be Hazar Enon at the border of Damascus; and on the north northward is the border of Hamath. This is the north side. 18"The east side, between Hauran, Damascus, Gilead, and the land of Israel, shall be the Jordan; from the north border to the east sea you shall measure. This is the east side. 19"The south side southward shall be from Tamar as far as the waters of Meriboth Kadesh, to the brook, to the great sea. This is the south side southward. 20"The west side shall be the great sea, from the south border as far as opposite the entrance of Hamath. This is the west side. 21"So you shall divide this land to yourselves according to the tribes of Israel. 22 You shall divide it by lot for an inheritance to you and to the aliens who live among you, who will father children among you. Then they shall be to you as the native-born among the children of Israel. They shall have inheritance with you among the tribes of Israel. 23 In whatever tribe the stranger lives, there you shall give him his inheritance," says the Lord Yahweh.

48

1"Now these are the names of the tribes: From the north end, beside the way of Hethlon to the entrance of Hamath, Hazar Enan at the border of Damascus, northward beside Hamath (and they shall have their sides east and west), Dan, one portion. 2"By the border of Dan, from the east side to the west side, Asher, one portion. 3"By the border of Asher, from the east side even to the west side, Naphtali, one portion. 4"By the border of Naphtali, from the east side to the west side, Manasseh, one portion. 5"By the border of Manasseh, from the east side to the west side, Ephraim, one portion. 6"By the border of Ephraim, from the east side even to the west side, Reuben, one portion. 7"By the border of Reuben, from the east side to the west side, Judah, one portion. 8"By the border of Judah, from the east side to the west side, shall be the offering which you shall offer, twenty-five thousand reeds in width, and in length as one of the portions, from the east side to the west side; and the sanctuary shall be in the middle of it. 9"The offering that you shall offer to Yahweh shall be twenty-five thousand reeds in length, and ten thousand in width. 10 For these, even for the priests, shall be the holy offering: toward the north twenty-five thousand in length, and toward the west ten thousand in width, and toward the east ten thousand in width, and toward the south twenty-five thousand in length; and the sanctuary of Yahweh shall be in the middle of it. 11 It shall be for the priests who are sanctified of the sons of Zadok, who have kept my instruction, who didn't go astray when the children of Israel went astray, as the Levites went astray. 12 It shall be to them an offering from the offering of the land, a most holy thing, by the border of the Levites. 13"Alongside the border of the priests, the Levites shall have twenty-five thousand cubits in length and ten thousand in width. All the length shall be twenty-five thousand, and the width ten thousand. 14 They shall sell none of it, nor exchange it, nor shall the first fruits of the land be alienated, for it is holy to Yahweh. 15"The five thousand cubits that are left in the width, in front of the twenty-five thousand, shall be for common use, for the city, for dwelling and for pasture lands; and the city shall be in the middle of it. 16 These shall be its measurements: the north side four thousand and five hundred, and the south side four thousand and five hundred, and on the east side four thousand and five hundred, and the west side four thousand and five hundred. 17 The city shall have pasture lands: toward the north two hundred fifty, and toward the south two hundred fifty, and toward the east two hundred fifty, and toward the west two hundred fifty. 18 The remainder of the length, alongside the holy offering, shall be ten thousand eastward and ten thousand westward; and it shall be alongside the holy offering. Its increase shall be for food to those who labor in the city. 19 Those who labor in the city, out of all the tribes of Israel, shall cultivate it. 20 All the offering shall be a square of twenty-five thousand by twenty-five thousand. You shall offer it as a holy offering, with the possession of the city. 21"The remainder shall be for the prince, on the one side and on the other of the holy offering and of the possession of the city; in front of the twenty-five thousand of the offering toward the east border, and westward in front of the twenty-five thousand toward the west border, alongside the portions, it shall be for the prince. The holy offering and the sanctuary of the house shall be in the middle of it. 22 Moreover, from the possession of the Levites, and from the possession of the city, being in the middle of that which is the prince's, between the border of Judah and the border of Benjamin, shall be for the prince. 23"As for the rest of the tribes: from the east side to the west side, Benjamin, one portion. 24"By the border of Benjamin, from the east side to the west side, Simeon, one portion. 25"By the border of Simeon, from the east side to the west side, Issachar, one portion. 26"By the border of Issachar, from the east side to the west side, Zebulun, one portion. 27"By the border of Zebulun, from the east side to the west side, Gad, one portion. 28"By the border of Gad, at the south side southward, the border shall be even from Tamar to the waters of Meribath Kadesh, to the brook, to the great sea. 29"This is the land which you shall divide by lot to the tribes of Israel for inheritance, and these are their several portions, says the Lord Yahweh. 30"These are the exits of the city: On the north side four thousand five hundred reeds by measure; 31 and the gates of the city shall be named after the tribes of Israel, three gates northward: the gate of Reuben, one; the gate of Judah, one; the gate of Levi, one. 32"At the east side four thousand five hundred reeds, and three gates: even the gate of Joseph, one; the gate of Benjamin, one; the gate of Dan, one. 33"At the south side four thousand five hundred reeds by measure, and three gates: the gate of Simeon, one; the gate of Issachar, one; the gate of Zebulun, one. 34"At the west side four thousand five hundred reeds, with their three gates: the gate of Gad, one; the gate of Asher, one; the gate of Naphtali, one.

35"It shall be eighteen thousand reeds in circumference; and the name of the city from that day shall be, 'Yahweh is there.'

The Book of Daniel

1

1 In the third year of the reign of Jehoiakim king of Judah, Nebuchadnezzar king of Babylon came to Jerusalem and besieged it. 2 The Lord gave Jehoiakim king of Judah into his hand, with some of the vessels of the house of God; and he carried them into the land of Shinar to the house of his god. He brought the vessels into the treasure house of his god. 3 The king spoke to Ashpenaz, the master of his eunuchs, that he should bring in some of the children of Israel, even of the royal offspring and of the nobles: 4 youths in whom was no defect, but well-favored, skillful in all wisdom, endowed with knowledge, understanding science, and who had the ability to stand in the king's palace; and that he should teach them the learning and the language of the Chaldeans. 5 The king appointed for them a daily portion of the king's delicacies and of the wine which he drank, and that they should be nourished three years, that at its end they should stand before the king. 6 Now among these of the children of Judah were Daniel, Hananiah, Mishael, and Azariah. 7 The prince of the eunuchs gave names to them: to Daniel he gave the name Belteshazzar; to Hananiah, Shadrach; to Mishael, Meshach; and to Azariah, Abednego. 8 But Daniel purposed in his heart that he would not defile himself with the king's delicacies, nor with the wine which he drank. Therefore he requested of the prince of the eunuchs that he might not defile himself. 9 Now God made Daniel find kindness and compassion in the sight of the prince of the eunuchs. 10 The prince of the eunuchs said to Daniel, "I fear my lord the king, who has appointed your food and your drink. For why should he see your faces worse looking than the youths who are of your own age? Then you would endanger my head with the king." 11 Then Daniel said to the steward whom the prince of the eunuchs had appointed over Daniel, Hananiah, Mishael, and Azariah: 12"Test your servants, I beg you, ten days; and let them give us vegetables to eat and water to drink. 13 Then let our faces be examined before you, and the face of the youths who eat of the king's delicacies; and as you see, deal with your servants." 14 So he listened to them in this matter, and tested them for ten days. 15 At the end of ten days, their faces appeared fairer and they were fatter in flesh than all the youths who ate of the king's delicacies. 16 So the steward took away their delicacies and the wine that they were given to drink, and gave them vegetables. 17 Now as for these four youths, God gave them knowledge and skill in all learning and wisdom; and

Daniel had understanding in all visions and dreams. 18 At the end of the days which the king had appointed for bringing them in, the prince of the eunuchs brought them in before Nebuchadnezzar. 19 The king talked with them; and among them all was found no one like Daniel, Hananiah, Mishael, and Azariah. Therefore stood they before the king. 20 In every matter of wisdom and understanding concerning which the king inquired of them, he found them ten times better than all the magicians and enchanters who were in all his realm. 21 Daniel continued even to the first year of King Cyrus.

2

1 In the second year of the reign of Nebuchadnezzar, Nebuchadnezzar dreamed dreams; and his spirit was troubled, and his sleep went from him. 2 Then the king commanded that the magicians, the enchanters, the sorcerers, and the Chaldeans be called to tell the king his dreams. So they came in and stood before the king. 3 The king said to them, "I have dreamed a dream, and my spirit is troubled to know the dream." 4 Then the Chaldeans spoke to the king in the Syrian language, "O king, live forever! Tell your servants the dream, and we will show the interpretation." 5 The king answered the Chaldeans, "The thing has gone from me. If you don't make known to me the dream and its interpretation, you will be cut in pieces, and your houses will be made a dunghill. 6 But if you show the dream and its interpretation, you will receive from me gifts, rewards, and great honor. Therefore show me the dream and its interpretation." 7 They answered the second time and said, "Let the king tell his servants the dream, and we will show the interpretation." 8 The king answered, "I know of a certainty that you are trying to gain time, because you see the thing has gone from me. 9 But if you don't make known to me the dream, there is but one law for you; for you have prepared lying and corrupt words to speak before me, until the situation changes. Therefore tell me the dream, and I will know that you can show me its interpretation." 10 The Chaldeans answered the king and said, "There is not a man on the earth who can show the king's matter, because no king, lord, or ruler has asked such a thing of any magician, enchanter, or Chaldean. 11 It is a rare thing that the king requires, and there is no other who can show it before the king except the gods, whose dwelling is not with flesh." 12 Because of this, the king was angry and very furious, and commanded that all the wise men of Babylon be destroyed. 13 So the decree went out, and the wise men were to be slain. They sought Daniel and his companions to be slain. 14 Then Daniel returned answer with counsel and prudence to Arioch the captain of the

king's guard, who had gone out to kill the wise men of Babylon. ¹⁵ He answered Arioch the king's captain, "Why is the decree so urgent from the king?" Then Arioch made the thing known to Daniel. ¹⁶ Daniel went in, and desired of the king that he would appoint him a time, and he would show the king the interpretation. ¹⁷ Then Daniel went to his house and made the thing known to Hananiah, Mishael, and Azariah, his companions: ¹⁸ that they would desire mercies of the God of heaven concerning this secret, that Daniel and his companions would not perish with the rest of the wise men of Babylon. ¹⁹ Then the secret was revealed to Daniel in a vision of the night. Then Daniel blessed the God of heaven. ²⁰ Daniel answered, "Blessed be the name of God forever and ever; for wisdom and might are his. ²¹ He changes the times and the seasons. He removes kings and sets up kings. He gives wisdom to the wise, and knowledge to those who have understanding. ²² He reveals the deep and secret things. He knows what is in the darkness, and the light dwells with him. ²³ I thank you and praise you, O God of my fathers, who have given me wisdom and might, and have now made known to me what we desired of you; for you have made known to us the king's matter." ²⁴ Therefore Daniel went in to Arioch, whom the king had appointed to destroy the wise men of Babylon. He went and said this to him: "Don't destroy the wise men of Babylon. Bring me in before the king, and I will show to the king the interpretation." ²⁵ Then Arioch brought in Daniel before the king in haste, and said this to him: "I have found a man of the children of the captivity of Judah who will make known to the king the interpretation." ²⁶ The king answered Daniel, whose name was Belteshazzar, "Are you able to make known to me the dream which I have seen, and its interpretation?" ²⁷ Daniel answered before the king, and said, "The secret which the king has demanded can't be shown to the king by wise men, enchanters, magicians, or soothsayers; ²⁸ but there is a God in heaven who reveals secrets, and he has made known to King Nebuchadnezzar what will be in the latter days. Your dream and the visions of your head on your bed are these: ²⁹"As for you, O king, your thoughts came on your bed, what should happen hereafter; and he who reveals secrets has made known to you what will happen. ³⁰ But as for me, this secret is not revealed to me for any wisdom that I have more than any living, but to the intent that the interpretation may be made known to the king, and that you may know the thoughts of your heart. ³¹"You, O king, saw, and behold, a great image. This image, which was mighty, and whose brightness was excellent, stood before you; and its appearance was terrifying.

³² As for this image, its head was of fine gold, its chest and its arms of silver, its belly and its thighs of bronze, ³³ its legs of iron, its feet part of iron and part of clay. ³⁴ You saw until a stone was cut out without hands, which struck the image on its feet that were of iron and clay, and broke them in pieces. ³⁵ Then the iron, the clay, the bronze, the silver, and the gold were broken in pieces together, and became like the chaff of the summer threshing floors. The wind carried them away, so that no place was found for them. The stone that struck the image became a great mountain and filled the whole earth. ³⁶"This is the dream; and we will tell its interpretation before the king. ³⁷ You, O king, are king of kings, to whom the God of heaven has given the kingdom, the power, the strength, and the glory. ³⁸ Wherever the children of men dwell, he has given the animals of the field and the birds of the sky into your hand, and has made you rule over them all. You are the head of gold. ³⁹"After you, another kingdom will arise that is inferior to you; and another third kingdom of bronze, which will rule over all the earth. ⁴⁰ The fourth kingdom will be strong as iron, because iron breaks in pieces and subdues all things; and as iron that crushes all these, it will break in pieces and crush. ⁴¹ Whereas you saw the feet and toes, part of potters' clay and part of iron, it will be a divided kingdom; but there will be in it of the strength of the iron, because you saw the iron mixed with miry clay. ⁴² As the toes of the feet were part of iron, and part of clay, so the kingdom will be partly strong and partly brittle. ⁴³ Whereas you saw the iron mixed with miry clay, they will mingle themselves with the seed of men; but they won't cling to one another, even as iron does not mix with clay. ⁴⁴"In the days of those kings the God of heaven will set up a kingdom which will never be destroyed, nor will its sovereignty be left to another people; but it will break in pieces and consume all these kingdoms, and it will stand forever. ⁴⁵ Because you saw that a stone was cut out of the mountain without hands, and that it broke in pieces the iron, the bronze, the clay, the silver, and the gold, the great God has made known to the king what will happen hereafter. The dream is certain, and its interpretation sure." ⁴⁶ Then King Nebuchadnezzar fell on his face, worshiped Daniel, and commanded that they should offer an offering and sweet odors to him. ⁴⁷ The king answered to Daniel, and said, "Of a truth your God is the God of gods, and the Lord of kings, and a revealer of secrets, since you have been able to reveal this secret." ⁴⁸ Then the king made Daniel great and gave him many great gifts, and made him rule over the whole province of Babylon and to be chief governor over all the wise men of Babylon. ⁴⁹ Daniel

requested of the king, and he appointed Shadrach, Meshach, and Abednego over the affairs of the province of Babylon, but Daniel was in the king's gate.

3

1 Nebuchadnezzar the king made an image of gold, whose height was sixty cubits and its width six cubits. He set it up in the plain of Dura, in the province of Babylon. 2 Then Nebuchadnezzar the king sent to gather together the local governors, the deputies, and the governors, the judges, the treasurers, the counselors, the sheriffs, and all the rulers of the provinces, to come to the dedication of the image which Nebuchadnezzar the king had set up. 3 Then the local governors, the deputies, and the governors, the judges, the treasurers, the counselors, the sheriffs, and all the rulers of the provinces were gathered together to the dedication of the image that Nebuchadnezzar the king had set up; and they stood before the image that Nebuchadnezzar had set up. 4 Then the herald cried aloud, "To you it is commanded, peoples, nations, and languages, 5 that whenever you hear the sound of the horn, flute, zither, lyre, harp, pipe, and all kinds of music, you fall down and worship the golden image that Nebuchadnezzar the king has set up. 6 Whoever doesn't fall down and worship shall be cast into the middle of a burning fiery furnace the same hour." 7 Therefore at that time, when all the peoples heard the sound of the horn, flute, zither, lyre, harp, pipe, and all kinds of music, all the peoples, the nations, and the languages fell down and worshiped the golden image that Nebuchadnezzar the king had set up. 8 Therefore at that time certain Chaldeans came near and brought accusation against the Jews. 9 They answered Nebuchadnezzar the king, "O king, live for ever! 10 You, O king, have made a decree that every man who hears the sound of the horn, flute, zither, lyre, harp, pipe, and all kinds of music shall fall down and worship the golden image; 11 and whoever doesn't fall down and worship shall be cast into the middle of a burning fiery furnace. 12 There are certain Jews whom you have appointed over the affairs of the province of Babylon: Shadrach, Meshach, and Abednego. These men, O king, have not respected you. They don't serve your gods, and don't worship the golden image which you have set up." 13 Then Nebuchadnezzar in rage and fury commanded that Shadrach, Meshach, and Abednego be brought. Then these men were brought before the king. 14 Nebuchadnezzar answered them, "Is it true, Shadrach, Meshach, and Abednego, that you don't serve my gods and you don't worship the golden image which I have set up? 15 Now if you are ready whenever you hear the sound of the horn, flute, zither, lyre, harp, pipe, and all kinds of music to fall

down and worship the image which I have made, good; but if you don't worship, you shall be cast the same hour into the middle of a burning fiery furnace. Who is that god who will deliver you out of my hands?" 16 Shadrach, Meshach, and Abednego answered the king, "Nebuchadnezzar, we have no need to answer you in this matter. 17 If it happens, our God whom we serve is able to deliver us from the burning fiery furnace; and he will deliver us out of your hand, O king. 18 But if not, let it be known to you, O king, that we will not serve your gods or worship the golden image which you have set up." 19 Then Nebuchadnezzar was full of fury, and the form of his appearance was changed against Shadrach, Meshach, and Abednego. He spoke, and commanded that they should heat the furnace seven times more than it was usually heated. 20 He commanded certain mighty men who were in his army to bind Shadrach, Meshach, and Abednego, and to cast them into the burning fiery furnace. 21 Then these men were bound in their pants, their tunics, and their mantles, and their other clothes, and were cast into the middle of the burning fiery furnace. 22 Therefore because the king's commandment was urgent and the furnace exceedingly hot, the flame of the fire killed those men who took up Shadrach, Meshach, and Abednego. 23 These three men, Shadrach, Meshach, and Abednego, fell down bound into the middle of the burning fiery furnace. 24 Then Nebuchadnezzar the king was astonished and rose up in haste. He spoke and said to his counselors, "Didn't we cast three men bound into the middle of the fire?" They answered the king, "True, O king." 25 He answered, "Look, I see four men loose, walking in the middle of the fire, and they are unharmed. The appearance of the fourth is like a son of the gods." 26 Then Nebuchadnezzar came near to the mouth of the burning fiery furnace. He spoke and said, "Shadrach, Meshach, and Abednego, you servants of the Most High God, come out, and come here!" Then Shadrach, Meshach, and Abednego came out of the middle of the fire. 27 The local governors, the deputies, and the governors, and the king's counselors, being gathered together, saw these men, that the fire had no power on their bodies. The hair of their head wasn't singed. Their pants weren't changed. The smell of fire wasn't even on them. 28 Nebuchadnezzar spoke and said, "Blessed be the God of Shadrach, Meshach, and Abednego, who has sent his angel and delivered his servants who trusted in him, and have changed the king's word, and have yielded their bodies, that they might not serve nor worship any god except their own God. 29 Therefore I make a decree that every people, nation, and language which speak anything evil against the God of Shadrach,

Meshach, and Abednego shall be cut in pieces, and their houses shall be made a dunghill, because there is no other god who is able to deliver like this." 30 Then the king promoted Shadrach, Meshach, and Abednego in the province of Babylon.

4

1 Nebuchadnezzar the king, to all the peoples, nations, and languages, who dwell in all the earth: Peace be multiplied to you. 2 It has seemed good to me to show the signs and wonders that the Most High God has worked toward me. 3 How great are his signs! How mighty are his wonders! His kingdom is an everlasting kingdom. His dominion is from generation to generation. 4 I, Nebuchadnezzar, was at rest in my house, and flourishing in my palace. 5 I saw a dream which made me afraid; and the thoughts on my bed and the visions of my head troubled me. 6 Therefore I made a decree to bring in all the wise men of Babylon before me, that they might make known to me the interpretation of the dream. 7 Then the magicians, the enchanters, the Chaldeans, and the soothsayers came in; and I told them the dream, but they didn't make known to me its interpretation. 8 But at last, Daniel came in before me, whose name was Belteshazzar according to the name of my god, and in whom is the spirit of the holy gods. I told the dream before him, saying, 9"Belteshazzar, master of the magicians, because I know that the spirit of the holy gods is in you and no secret troubles you, tell me the visions of my dream that I have seen, and its interpretation. 10 These were the visions of my head on my bed: I saw, and behold, a tree in the middle of the earth; and its height was great. 11 The tree grew and was strong. Its height reached to the sky and its sight to the end of all the earth. 12 Its leaves were beautiful, and it had much fruit, and in it was food for all. The animals of the field had shade under it, and the birds of the sky lived in its branches, and all flesh was fed from it. 13"I saw in the visions of my head on my bed, and behold, a holy watcher came down from the sky. 14 He cried aloud and said this: 'Cut down the tree, and cut off its branches! Shake off its leaves and scatter its fruit! Let the animals get away from under it and the birds from its branches. 15 Nevertheless leave the stump of its roots in the earth, even with a band of iron and bronze, in the tender grass of the field; and let it be wet with the dew of the sky. Let his portion be with the animals in the grass of the earth. 16 Let his heart be changed from man's, and let an animal's heart be given to him. Then let seven times pass over him. 17"'The sentence is by the decree of the watchers and the demand by the word of the holy ones, to the intent that the

living may know that the Most High rules in the kingdom of men, and gives it to whomever he will, and sets up over it the lowest of men.' 18"This dream I, King Nebuchadnezzar, have seen; and you, Belteshazzar, declare the interpretation, because all the wise men of my kingdom are not able to make known to me the interpretation; but you are able, for the spirit of the holy gods is in you." 19 Then Daniel, whose name was Belteshazzar, was stricken mute for a while, and his thoughts troubled him. The king answered, "Belteshazzar, don't let the dream or the interpretation, trouble you." Belteshazzar answered, "My lord, may the dream be for those who hate you, and its interpretation to your adversaries. 20 The tree that you saw, which grew and was strong, whose height reached to the sky and its sight to all the earth; 21 whose leaves were beautiful and its fruit plentiful, and in it was food for all; under which the animals of the field lived, and on whose branches the birds of the sky had their habitation— 22 it is you, O king, that have grown and become strong; for your greatness has grown, and reaches to the sky, and your dominion to the end of the earth. 23"Whereas the king saw a holy watcher coming down from the sky and saying, 'Cut down the tree, and destroy it; nevertheless leave the stump of its roots in the earth, even with a band of iron and bronze, in the tender grass of the field, and let it be wet with the dew of the sky. Let his portion be with the animals of the field, until seven times pass over him.' 24"This is the interpretation, O king, and it is the decree of the Most High, which has come on my lord the king: 25 You will be driven from men and your dwelling shall be with the animals of the field. You will be made to eat grass as oxen, and will be wet with the dew of the sky, and seven times shall pass over you, until you know that the Most High rules in the kingdom of men, and gives it to whomever he will. 26 Whereas it was commanded to leave the stump of the roots of the tree, your kingdom shall be sure to you after you know that Heaven rules. 27 Therefore, O king, let my counsel be acceptable to you, and break off your sins by righteousness, and your iniquities by showing mercy to the poor. Perhaps there may be a lengthening of your tranquility." 28 All this came on the King Nebuchadnezzar. 29 At the end of twelve months he was walking in the royal palace of Babylon. 30 The king spoke and said, "Is not this great Babylon, which I have built for the royal dwelling place by the might of my power and for the glory of my majesty?" 31 While the word was in the king's mouth, a voice came from the sky, saying, "O King Nebuchadnezzar, to you it is spoken: 'The kingdom has departed from you. 32 You shall be driven from men, and your dwelling shall be with the animals of the field. You shall be made to eat grass like oxen. Seven times shall pass over you, until you know that the Most High rules in the kingdom of men, and gives it to whomever he will.'" 33 This was fulfilled the same hour on Nebuchadnezzar. He was driven from men and ate grass like oxen; and his body was wet with the dew of the sky until his hair had grown like eagles' feathers, and his nails like birds' claws. 34 At the end of the days I, Nebuchadnezzar, lifted up my eyes to heaven, and my understanding returned to me; and I blessed the Most High, and I praised and honored him who lives forever, for his dominion is an everlasting dominion, and his kingdom from generation to generation. 35 All the inhabitants of the earth are reputed as nothing; and he does according to his will in the army of heaven, and among the inhabitants of the earth; and no one can stop his hand, or ask him, "What are you doing?" 36 At the same time my understanding returned to me; and for the glory of my kingdom, my majesty and brightness returned to me. My counselors and my lords sought me; and I was established in my kingdom, and excellent greatness was added to me. 37 Now I, Nebuchadnezzar, praise and extol and honor the King of heaven; for all his works are truth, and his ways justice; and those who walk in pride he is able to abase.

5

1 Belshazzar the king made a great feast to a thousand of his lords, and drank wine before the thousand. 2 Belshazzar, while he tasted the wine, commanded that the golden and silver vessels which Nebuchadnezzar his father had taken out of the temple which was in Jerusalem be brought to him, that the king and his lords, his wives and his concubines, might drink from them. 3 Then they brought the golden vessels that were taken out of the temple of God's house which was at Jerusalem; and the king and his lords, his wives and his concubines, drank from them. 4 They drank wine, and praised the gods of gold, and of silver, of bronze, of iron, of wood, and of stone. 5 In the same hour, the fingers of a man's hand came out and wrote near the lamp stand on the plaster of the wall of the king's palace. The king saw the part of the hand that wrote. 6 Then the king's face was changed in him, and his thoughts troubled him; and the joints of his thighs were loosened, and his knees struck one against another. 7 The king cried aloud to bring in the enchanters, the Chaldeans, and the soothsayers. The king spoke and said to the wise men of Babylon, "Whoever reads this writing and shows me its interpretation shall be clothed with purple, and have a chain of gold about his neck, and shall be

the third ruler in the kingdom." 8 Then all the king's wise men came in; but they could not read the writing, and couldn't make known to the king the interpretation. 9 Then King Belshazzar was greatly troubled, and his face was changed in him, and his lords were perplexed. 10 The queen by reason of the words of the king and his lords came into the banquet house. The queen spoke and said, "O king, live forever; don't let your thoughts trouble you, nor let your face be changed. 11 There is a man in your kingdom in whom is the spirit of the holy gods; and in the days of your father, light and understanding and wisdom, like the wisdom of the gods, were found in him. The king, Nebuchadnezzar, your father—yes, the king, your father—made him master of the magicians, enchanters, Chaldeans, and soothsayers, 12 because an excellent spirit, knowledge, understanding, interpreting of dreams, showing of dark sentences, and dissolving of doubts were found in the same Daniel, whom the king named Belteshazzar. Now let Daniel be called, and he will show the interpretation." 13 Then Daniel was brought in before the king. The king spoke and said to Daniel, "Are you that Daniel of the children of the captivity of Judah, whom the king my father brought out of Judah? 14 I have heard of you, that the spirit of the gods is in you and that light, understanding, and excellent wisdom are found in you. 15 Now the wise men, the enchanters, have been brought in before me, that they should read this writing, and make known to me its interpretation; but they could not show the interpretation of the thing. 16 But I have heard of you, that you can give interpretations and dissolve doubts. Now if you can read the writing and make known to me its interpretation, you shall be clothed with purple, and have a chain of gold around your neck, and shall be the third ruler in the kingdom." 17 Then Daniel answered before the king, "Let your gifts be to yourself, and give your rewards to another. Nevertheless, I will read the writing to the king, and make known to him the interpretation. 18"To you, king, the Most High God gave Nebuchadnezzar your father the kingdom, and greatness, and glory, and majesty. 19 Because of the greatness that he gave him, all the peoples, nations, and languages trembled and feared before him. He killed whom he wanted to, and he kept alive whom he wanted to. He raised up whom he wanted to, and he put down whom he wanted to. 20 But when his heart was lifted up, and his spirit was hardened so that he dealt proudly, he was deposed from his kingly throne, and they took his glory from him. 21 He was driven from the sons of men, and his heart was made like the animals', and his dwelling was with the wild donkeys. He was fed with grass like oxen, and his body was wet with the dew of the sky, until he knew that the Most High God rules in the kingdom of men, and that he sets up over it whomever he will. 22"You, his son, Belshazzar, have not humbled your heart, though you knew all this, 23 but have lifted up yourself against the Lord of heaven; and they have brought the vessels of his house before you, and you and your lords, your wives, and your concubines, have drunk wine from them. You have praised the gods of silver and gold, of bronze, iron, wood, and stone, which don't see, or hear, or know; and you have not glorified the God in whose hand your breath is, and whose are all your ways. 24 Then the part of the hand was sent from before him, and this writing was inscribed. 25"This is the writing that was inscribed: 'MENE, MENE, TEKEL, UPHARSIN.' 26"This is the interpretation of the thing: MENE: God has counted your kingdom, and brought it to an end. 27 TEKEL: you are weighed in the balances, and are found wanting. 28 PERES: your kingdom is divided, and given to the Medes and Persians." 29 Then Belshazzar commanded, and they clothed Daniel with purple, and put a chain of gold about his neck, and made proclamation concerning him, that he should be the third ruler in the kingdom. 30 In that night Belshazzar the Chaldean King was slain. 31 Darius the Mede received the kingdom, being about sixty-two years old.

6

1 It pleased Darius to set over the kingdom one hundred twenty local governors, who should be throughout the whole kingdom; 2 and over them three presidents, of whom Daniel was one, that these local governors might give account to them, and that the king should suffer no loss. 3 Then this Daniel was distinguished above the presidents and the local governors, because an excellent spirit was in him; and the king thought to set him over the whole realm. 4 Then the presidents and the local governors sought to find occasion against Daniel as touching the kingdom; but they could find no occasion or fault, because he was faithful. There wasn't any error or fault found in him. 5 Then these men said, "We won't find any occasion against this Daniel, unless we find it against him concerning the law of his God." 6 Then these presidents and local governors assembled together to the king, and said this to him, "King Darius, live forever! 7 All the presidents of the kingdom, the deputies and the local governors, the counselors and the governors, have consulted together to establish a royal statute and to make a strong decree, that whoever asks a petition of any god or man for thirty days, except of you, O king, he shall be cast into the den of lions. 8 Now, O king,

establish the decree and sign the writing, that it not be changed, according to the law of the Medes and Persians, which doesn't alter." 9 Therefore King Darius signed the writing and the decree. 10 When Daniel knew that the writing was signed, he went into his house (now his windows were open in his room toward Jerusalem) and he kneeled on his knees three times a day, and prayed, and gave thanks before his God, as he did before. 11 Then these men assembled together, and found Daniel making petition and supplication before his God. 12 Then they came near, and spoke before the king concerning the king's decree: "Haven't you signed a decree that every man who makes a petition to any god or man within thirty days, except to you, O king, shall be cast into the den of lions?" The king answered, "This thing is true, according to the law of the Medes and Persians, which doesn't alter." 13 Then they answered and said before the king, "That Daniel, who is of the children of the captivity of Judah, doesn't respect you, O king, nor the decree that you have signed, but makes his petition three times a day." 14 Then the king, when he heard these words, was very displeased, and set his heart on Daniel to deliver him; and he labored until the going down of the sun to rescue him. 15 Then these men assembled together to the king, and said to the king, "Know, O king, that it is a law of the Medes and Persians, that no decree nor statute which the king establishes may be changed." 16 Then the king commanded, and they brought Daniel and cast him into the den of lions. The king spoke and said to Daniel, "Your God whom you serve continually, he will deliver you." 17 A stone was brought, and laid on the mouth of the den; and the king sealed it with his own signet, and with the signet of his lords; that nothing might be changed concerning Daniel. 18 Then the king went to his palace, and passed the night fasting. No musical instruments were brought before him; and his sleep fled from him. 19 Then the king arose very early in the morning, and went in haste to the den of lions. 20 When he came near to the den to Daniel, he cried with a troubled voice. The king spoke and said to Daniel, "Daniel, servant of the living God, is your God, whom you serve continually, able to deliver you from the lions?" 21 Then Daniel said to the king, "O king, live forever! 22 My God has sent his angel, and has shut the lions' mouths, and they have not hurt me, because innocence was found in me before him; and also before you, O king, I have done no harm." 23 Then the king was exceedingly glad, and commanded that they should take Daniel up out of the den. So Daniel was taken up out of the den, and no kind of harm was found on him, because he had trusted in his God. 24 The king commanded, and they brought those men who had accused Daniel, and they cast them into the den of lions—them, their children, and their wives; and the lions mauled them, and broke all their bones in pieces before they came to the bottom of the den. 25 Then King Darius wrote to all the peoples, nations, and languages who dwell in all the earth: "Peace be multiplied to you. 26"I make a decree that in all the dominion of my kingdom men tremble and fear before the God of Daniel. "For he is the living God, and steadfast forever. His kingdom is that which will not be destroyed. His dominion will be even to the end. 27 He delivers and rescues. He works signs and wonders in heaven and in earth, who has delivered Daniel from the power of the lions." 28 So this Daniel prospered in the reign of Darius and in the reign of Cyrus the Persian.

7

1 In the first year of Belshazzar king of Babylon, Daniel had a dream and visions of his head while on his bed. Then he wrote the dream and told the sum of the matters. 2 Daniel spoke and said, "I saw in my vision by night, and, behold, the four winds of the sky broke out on the great sea. 3 Four great animals came up from the sea, different from one another. 4"The first was like a lion, and had eagle's wings. I watched until its wings were plucked, and it was lifted up from the earth and made to stand on two feet as a man. A man's heart was given to it. 5"Behold, there was another animal, a second, like a bear. It was raised up on one side, and three ribs were in its mouth between its teeth. They said this to it: 'Arise! Devour much flesh!' 6"After this I saw, and behold, another, like a leopard, which had on its back four wings of a bird. The animal also had four heads; and dominion was given to it. 7"After this I saw in the night visions, and, behold, there was a fourth animal, awesome, powerful, and exceedingly strong. It had great iron teeth. It devoured and broke in pieces, and stamped the residue with its feet. It was different from all the animals that were before it. It had ten horns. 8"I considered the horns, and behold, there came up among them another horn, a little one, before which three of the first horns were plucked up by the roots; and behold, in this horn were eyes like the eyes of a man, and a mouth speaking arrogantly. 9"I watched until thrones were placed, and one who was Ancient of Days sat. His clothing was white as snow, and the hair of his head like pure wool. His throne was fiery flames, and its wheels burning fire. 10 A fiery stream issued and came out from before him. Thousands of thousands ministered to him. Ten thousand times ten thousand stood before him. The judgment was set. The books were opened. 11"I watched at that time because

of the voice of the arrogant words which the horn spoke. I watched even until the animal was slain, and its body destroyed, and it was given to be burned with fire. 12 As for the rest of the animals, their dominion was taken away; yet their lives were prolonged for a season and a time. 13"I saw in the night visions, and behold, there came with the clouds of the sky one like a son of man, and he came even to the Ancient of Days, and they brought him near before him. 14 Dominion was given him, and glory, and a kingdom, that all the peoples, nations, and languages should serve him. His dominion is an everlasting dominion, which will not pass away, and his kingdom one that will not be destroyed. 15"As for me, Daniel, my spirit was grieved within my body, and the visions of my head troubled me. 16 I came near to one of those who stood by, and asked him the truth concerning all this. "So he told me, and made me know the interpretation of the things. 17'These great animals, which are four, are four kings, who will arise out of the earth. 18 But the saints of the Most High will receive the kingdom, and possess the kingdom forever, even forever and ever.' 19"Then I desired to know the truth concerning the fourth animal, which was different from all of them, exceedingly terrible, whose teeth were of iron, and its nails of bronze; which devoured, broke in pieces, and stamped the residue with its feet; 20 and concerning the ten horns that were on its head and the other horn which came up, and before which three fell, even that horn that had eyes and a mouth that spoke arrogantly, whose look was more stout than its fellows. 21 I saw, and the same horn made war with the saints, and prevailed against them, 22 until the Ancient of Days came, and judgment was given to the saints of the Most High, and the time came that the saints possessed the kingdom. 23"So he said, 'The fourth animal will be a fourth kingdom on earth, which will be different from all the kingdoms, and will devour the whole earth, and will tread it down and break it in pieces. 24 As for the ten horns, ten kings will arise out of this kingdom. Another will arise after them; and he will be different from the former, and he will put down three kings. 25 He will speak words against the Most High, and will wear out the saints of the Most High. He will plan to change the times and the law; and they will be given into his hand until a time and times and half a time. 26"'But the judgment will be set, and they will take away his dominion, to consume and to destroy it to the end. 27 The kingdom and the dominion, and the greatness of the kingdoms under the whole sky, will be given to the people of the saints of the Most High. His kingdom is an everlasting kingdom, and all dominions will serve and obey him.' 28"Here is the end of the matter. As for me, Daniel, my thoughts troubled me greatly, and my face was changed in me; but I kept the matter in my heart."

8

1 In the third year of the reign of King Belshazzar, a vision appeared to me, even to me, Daniel, after that which appeared to me at the first. 2 I saw the vision. Now it was so, that when I saw, I was in the citadel of Susa, which is in the province of Elam. I saw in the vision, and I was by the river Ulai. 3 Then I lifted up my eyes and saw, and behold, a ram which had two horns stood before the river. The two horns were high, but one was higher than the other, and the higher came up last. 4 I saw the ram pushing westward, northward, and southward. No animals could stand before him. There wasn't any who could deliver out of his hand, but he did according to his will, and magnified himself. 5 As I was considering, behold, a male goat came from the west over the surface of the whole earth, and didn't touch the ground. The goat had a notable horn between his eyes. 6 He came to the ram that had the two horns, which I saw standing before the river, and ran on him in the fury of his power. 7 I saw him come close to the ram, and he was moved with anger against him, and struck the ram, and broke his two horns. There was no power in the ram to stand before him; but he cast him down to the ground and trampled on him. There was no one who could deliver the ram out of his hand. 8 The male goat magnified himself exceedingly. When he was strong, the great horn was broken; and instead of it there came up four notable horns toward the four winds of the sky. 9 Out of one of them came out a little horn which grew exceedingly great—toward the south, and toward the east, and toward the glorious land. 10 It grew great, even to the army of the sky; and it cast down some of the army and of the stars to the ground and trampled on them. 11 Yes, it magnified itself, even to the prince of the army; and it took away from him the continual burnt offering, and the place of his sanctuary was cast down. 12 The army was given over to it together with the continual burnt offering through disobedience. It cast down truth to the ground, and it did its pleasure and prospered. 13 Then I heard a holy one speaking; and another holy one said to that certain one who spoke, "How long will the vision about the continual burnt offering, and the disobedience that makes desolate, to give both the sanctuary and the army to be trodden under foot be?" 14 He said to me, "To two thousand and three hundred evenings and mornings. Then the sanctuary will be cleansed." 15 When I, even I Daniel, had seen the vision, I sought to understand it. Then behold, there stood before me

someone with the appearance of a man. 16 I heard a man's voice between the banks of the Ulai, which called and said, "Gabriel, make this man understand the vision." 17 So he came near where I stood; and when he came, I was frightened, and fell on my face; but he said to me, "Understand, son of man, for the vision belongs to the time of the end." 18 Now as he was speaking with me, I fell into a deep sleep with my face toward the ground; but he touched me and set me upright. 19 He said, "Behold, I will make you know what will be in the latter time of the indignation, for it belongs to the appointed time of the end. 20 The ram which you saw, that had the two horns, they are the kings of Media and Persia. 21 The rough male goat is the king of Greece. The great horn that is between his eyes is the first king. 22 As for that which was broken, in the place where four stood up, four kingdoms will stand up out of the nation, but not with his power. 23"In the latter time of their kingdom, when the transgressors have come to the full, a king of fierce face, and understanding riddles, will stand up. 24 His power will be mighty, but not by his own power. He will destroy awesomely, and will prosper in what he does. He will destroy the mighty ones and the holy people. 25 Through his policy he will cause deceit to prosper in his hand. He will magnify himself in his heart, and he will destroy many in their security. He will also stand up against the prince of princes, but he will be broken without human hands. 26"The vision of the evenings and mornings which has been told is true; but seal up the vision, for it belongs to many days to come." 27 I, Daniel, fainted, and was sick for some days. Then I rose up and did the king's business. I wondered at the vision, but no one understood it.

9

1 In the first year of Darius the son of Ahasuerus, of the offspring of the Medes, who was made king over the realm of the Chaldeans— 2 in the first year of his reign I, Daniel, understood by the books the number of the years about which Yahweh's word came to Jeremiah the prophet for the accomplishing of the desolations of Jerusalem, even seventy years. 3 I set my face to the Lord God, to seek by prayer and petitions, with fasting and sackcloth and ashes. 4 I prayed to Yahweh my God, and made confession, and said, "Oh, Lord, the great and dreadful God, who keeps covenant and loving kindness with those who love him and keep his commandments, 5 we have sinned, and have dealt perversely, and have done wickedly, and have rebelled, even turning aside from your precepts and from your ordinances. 6 We haven't listened to your servants the prophets, who spoke in your name to

our kings, our princes, and our fathers, and to all the people of the land. 7"Lord, righteousness belongs to you, but to us confusion of face, as it is today; to the men of Judah, and to the inhabitants of Jerusalem, and to all Israel, who are near and who are far off, through all the countries where you have driven them, because of their trespass that they have trespassed against you. 8 Lord, to us belongs confusion of face, to our kings, to our princes, and to our fathers, because we have sinned against you. 9 To the Lord our God belong mercies and forgiveness, for we have rebelled against him. 10 We haven't obeyed Yahweh our God's voice, to walk in his laws, which he set before us by his servants the prophets. 11 Yes, all Israel have transgressed your law, turning aside, that they should not obey your voice. "Therefore the curse and the oath written in the law of Moses the servant of God has been poured out on us, for we have sinned against him. 12 He has confirmed his words, which he spoke against us and against our judges who judged us, by bringing on us a great evil; for under the whole sky, such has not been done as has been done to Jerusalem. 13 As it is written in the law of Moses, all this evil has come on us. Yet we have not entreated the favor of Yahweh our God, that we should turn from our iniquities and have discernment in your truth. 14 Therefore Yahweh has watched over the evil, and brought it on us; for Yahweh our God is righteous in all his works which he does, and we have not obeyed his voice. 15"Now, Lord our God, who has brought your people out of the land of Egypt with a mighty hand, and have gotten yourself renown, as it is today, we have sinned. We have done wickedly. 16 Lord, according to all your righteousness, please let your anger and your wrath be turned away from your city Jerusalem, your holy mountain; because for our sins and for the iniquities of our fathers, Jerusalem and your people have become a reproach to all who are around us. 17"Now therefore, our God, listen to the prayer of your servant and to his petitions, and cause your face to shine on your sanctuary that is desolate, for the Lord's sake. 18 My God, turn your ear and hear. Open your eyes and see our desolations, and the city which is called by your name; for we do not present our petitions before you for our righteousness, but for your great mercies' sake. 19 Lord, hear. Lord, forgive. Lord, listen and do. Don't defer, for your own sake, my God, because your city and your people are called by your name." 20 While I was speaking, praying, and confessing my sin and the sin of my people Israel, and presenting my supplication before Yahweh my God for the holy mountain of my God— 21 yes, while I was speaking in prayer—the man Gabriel, whom I had seen in the vision at the beginning, being caused to fly swiftly, touched me about the time of the evening offering. 22 He instructed me and talked with me, and said, "Daniel, I have now come to give you wisdom and understanding. 23 At the beginning of your petitions the commandment went out, and I have come to tell you, for you are greatly beloved. Therefore consider the matter and understand the vision. 24"Seventy weeks are decreed on your people and on your holy city, to finish disobedience, to make an end of sins, to make reconciliation for iniquity, to bring in everlasting righteousness, to seal up vision and prophecy, and to anoint the most holy. 25"Know therefore and discern that from the going out of the commandment to restore and build Jerusalem to the Anointed One, the prince, will be seven weeks and sixty-two weeks. It will be built again, with street and moat, even in troubled times. 26 After the sixty-two weeks the Anointed One will be cut off, and will have nothing. The people of the prince who come will destroy the city and the sanctuary. Its end will be with a flood, and war will be even to the end. Desolations are determined. 27 He will make a firm covenant with many for one week. In the middle of the week he will cause the sacrifice and the offering to cease. On the wing of abominations will come one who makes desolate; and even to the decreed full end, wrath will be poured out on the desolate."

10

1 In the third year of Cyrus king of Persia a message was revealed to Daniel, whose name was called Belteshazzar; and the message was true, even a great warfare. He understood the message, and had understanding of the vision. 2 In those days I, Daniel, was mourning three whole weeks. 3 I ate no pleasant food. No meat or wine came into my mouth. I didn't anoint myself at all, until three whole weeks were fulfilled. 4 In the twenty-fourth day of the first month, as I was by the side of the great river, which is Hiddekel, 5 I lifted up my eyes and looked, and behold, there was a man clothed in linen, whose waist was adorned with pure gold of Uphaz. 6 His body also was like beryl, and his face as the appearance of lightning, and his eyes as flaming torches. His arms and his feet were like burnished bronze. The voice of his words was like the voice of a multitude. 7 I, Daniel, alone saw the vision, for the men who were with me didn't see the vision, but a great quaking fell on them, and they fled to hide themselves. 8 So I was left alone and saw this great vision. No strength remained in me; for my face grew deathly pale, and I retained no strength. 9 Yet I heard the voice of his words. When I heard the voice of his

words, then I fell into a deep sleep on my face, with my face toward the ground. 10 Behold, a hand touched me, which set me on my knees and on the palms of my hands. 11 He said to me, "Daniel, you greatly beloved man, understand the words that I speak to you, and stand upright, for I have been sent to you, now." When he had spoken this word to me, I stood trembling. 12 Then he said to me, "Don't be afraid, Daniel; for from the first day that you set your heart to understand, and to humble yourself before your God, your words were heard. I have come for your words' sake. 13 But the prince of the kingdom of Persia withstood me twenty-one days; but, behold, Michael, one of the chief princes, came to help me because I remained there with the kings of Persia. 14 Now I have come to make you understand what will happen to your people in the latter days, for the vision is yet for many days." 15 When he had spoken these words to me, I set my face toward the ground and was mute. 16 Behold, one in the likeness of the sons of men touched my lips. Then I opened my mouth, and spoke and said to him who stood before me, "My lord, by reason of the vision my sorrows have overtaken me, and I retain no strength. 17 For how can the servant of this my lord talk with this my lord? For as for me, immediately there remained no strength in me. There was no breath left in me." 18 Then one like the appearance of a man touched me again, and he strengthened me. 19 He said, "Greatly beloved man, don't be afraid. Peace be to you. Be strong. Yes, be strong." When he spoke to me, I was strengthened, and said, "Let my lord speak, for you have strengthened me." 20 Then he said, "Do you know why I have come to you? Now I will return to fight with the prince of Persia. When I go out, behold, the prince of Greece will come. 21 But I will tell you that which is inscribed in the writing of truth. There is no one who holds with me against these but Michael your prince.

11

1"As for me, in the first year of Darius the Mede, I stood up to confirm and strengthen him. 2"Now I will show you the truth. Behold, three more kings will stand up in Persia. The fourth will be far richer than all of them. When he has grown strong through his riches, he will stir up all against the realm of Greece. 3 A mighty king will stand up, who will rule with great dominion, and do according to his will. 4 When he stands up, his kingdom will be broken and will be divided toward the four winds of the sky, but not to his posterity, nor according to his dominion with which he ruled; for his kingdom will be plucked up, even for others besides these. 5"The king of the south will be strong. One of his princes will become stronger than him, and have dominion. His dominion will be a great dominion. 6 At the end of years they will join themselves together; and the daughter of the king of the south will come to the king of the north to make an agreement, but she will not retain the strength of her arm. He will also not stand, nor will his arm; but she will be given up, with those who brought her, and he who became the father of her, and he who strengthened her in those times. 7"But out of a shoot from her roots one will stand up in his place, who will come to the army and will enter into the fortress of the king of the north, and will deal against them and will prevail. 8 He will also carry their gods with their molten images, and with their goodly vessels of silver and of gold, captive into Egypt. He will refrain some years from the king of the north. 9 He will come into the realm of the king of the south, but he will return into his own land. 10 His sons will wage war, and will assemble a multitude of great forces which will come on, and overflow, and pass through. They will return and wage war, even to his fortress. 11"The king of the south will be moved with anger and will come out and fight with him, even with the king of the north. He will send out a great multitude, and the multitude will be given into his hand. 12 The multitude will be carried off, and his heart will be exalted. He will cast down tens of thousands, but he won't prevail. 13 The king of the north will return, and will send out a multitude greater than the former. He will come on at the end of the times, even of years, with a great army and with abundant supplies. 14"In those times many will stand up against the king of the south. Also the children of the violent among your people will lift themselves up to establish the vision, but they will fall. 15 So the king of the north will come and cast up a mound, and take a well-fortified city. The forces of the south won't stand, neither will his select troops, neither will there be any strength to stand. 16 But he who comes against him will do according to his own will, and no one will stand before him. He will stand in the glorious land, and destruction will be in his hand. 17 He will set his face to come with the strength of his whole kingdom, and with him equitable conditions. He will perform them. He will give him the daughter of women, to destroy the kingdom, but she will not stand, and won't be for him. 18 After this he will turn his face to the islands, and will take many, but a prince will cause the reproach offered by him to cease. Yes, moreover, he will cause his reproach to turn on him. 19 Then he will turn his face toward the fortresses of his own land; but he will stumble and fall, and won't be found. 20"Then one who will cause a tax collector to pass through the kingdom to maintain its glory will stand up in his place; but within few days he shall be destroyed, not in anger, and not in battle. 21"In his place a contemptible person will stand up, to whom they had not given the honor of the kingdom; but he will come in time of security, and will obtain the kingdom by flatteries. 22 The overwhelming forces will be overwhelmed from before him, and will be broken. Yes, also the prince of the covenant. 23 After the treaty made with him he will work deceitfully; for he will come up and will become strong with few people. 24 In time of security he will come even on the fattest places of the province. He will do that which his fathers have not done, nor his fathers' fathers. He will scatter among them prey, plunder, and wealth. Yes, he will devise his plans against the strongholds, but only for a time. 25"He will stir up his power and his courage against the king of the south with a great army; and the king of the south will wage war in battle with an exceedingly great and mighty army, but he won't stand; for they will devise plans against him. 26 Yes, those who eat of his delicacies will destroy him, and his army will be swept away. Many will fall down slain. 27 As for both these kings, their hearts will be to do evil, and they will speak lies at one table; but it won't prosper, for the end will still be at the appointed time. 28 Then he will return into his land with great wealth. His heart will be against the holy covenant. He will take action, and return to his own land. 29"He will return at the appointed time and come into the south; but it won't be in the latter time as it was in the former. 30 For ships of Kittim will come against him. Therefore he will be grieved, and will return, and have indignation against the holy covenant, and will take action. He will even return, and have regard to those who forsake the holy covenant. 31"Forces from him will profane the sanctuary, even the fortress, and will take away the continual burnt offering. Then they will set up the abomination that makes desolate. 32 He will corrupt those who do wickedly against the covenant by flatteries; but the people who know their God will be strong and take action. 33"Those who are wise among the people will instruct many; yet they will fall by the sword and by flame, by captivity and by plunder, many days. 34 Now when they fall, they will be helped with a little help; but many will join themselves to them with flatteries. 35 Some of those who are wise will fall— to refine them, and to purify, and to make them white, even to the time of the end, because it is yet for the time appointed. 36"The king will do according to his will. He will exalt himself and magnify himself above every god, and will speak marvelous things against the God of gods. He will prosper until the indignation is accomplished, for that which is determined will be done. 37 He won't regard the gods of his fathers, or the desire of women, or regard any god; for he will magnify himself above all. 38 But in their place, he will honor the god of fortresses. He will honor a god whom his fathers didn't know with gold, silver, and with precious stones and pleasant things. 39 He will deal with the strongest fortresses by the help of a foreign god. He will increase with glory whoever acknowledges him. He will cause them to rule over many, and will divide the land for a price. 40 "At the time of the end the king of the south will contend with him; and the king of the north will come against him like a whirlwind, with chariots, with horsemen, and with many ships. He will enter into the countries, and will overflow and pass through. 41 He will enter also into the glorious land, and many countries will be overthrown; but these will be delivered out of his hand: Edom, Moab, and the chief of the children of Ammon. 42 He will also stretch out his hand on the countries. The land of Egypt won't escape. 43 But he will have power over the treasures of gold and of silver, and over all the precious things of Egypt. The Libyans and the Ethiopians will follow his steps. 44 But news out of the east and out of the north will trouble him; and he will go out with great fury to destroy and utterly to sweep away many. 45 He will plant the tents of his palace between the sea and the glorious holy mountain; yet he will come to his end, and no one will help him.

12

1"At that time Michael will stand up, the great prince who stands for the children of your people; and there will be a time of trouble, such as never was since there was a nation even to that same time. At that time your people will be delivered, everyone who is found written in the book. 2 Many of those who sleep in the dust of the earth will awake, some to everlasting life, and some to shame and everlasting contempt. 3 Those who are wise will shine as the brightness of the expanse. Those who turn many to righteousness will shine as the stars forever and ever. 4 But you, Daniel, shut up the words and seal the book, even to the time of the end. Many will run back and forth, and knowledge will be increased." 5 Then I, Daniel, looked, and behold, two others stood, one on the river bank on this side, and the other on the river bank on that side. 6 One said to the man clothed in linen, who was above the waters of the river, "How long will it be to the end of these wonders?" 7 I heard the man clothed in linen, who was above the waters of the river, when he held up his right hand and his left hand to heaven, and swore by him who lives forever that it will be for a time, times, and a half; and when they have finished breaking in pieces the power of the holy people, all these things will be finished. 8 I heard, but I didn't understand. Then I said, "My lord, what will be the outcome of these things?" 9 He said, "Go your way, Daniel; for the words are shut up and sealed until the time of the end. 10 Many will purify themselves, and make themselves white, and be refined, but the wicked will do wickedly; and none of the wicked will understand, but those who are wise will understand. 11"From the time that the continual burnt offering is taken away and the abomination that makes desolate set up, there will be one thousand two hundred ninety days. 12 Blessed is he who waits, and comes to the one thousand three hundred thirty-five days. 13"But go your way until the end; for you will rest, and will stand in your inheritance at the end of the days."

The Book of Daniel with Greek Portions
1

1 In the third year of the reign of Jehoiakim king of Judah, Nebuchadnezzar king of Babylon came to Jerusalem and besieged it. 2 The Lord gave Jehoiakim king of Judah into his hand, with part of the vessels of the house of God; and he carried them into the land of Shinar to the house of his god. He brought the vessels into the treasure house of his god. 3 The king spoke to Ashpenaz the master of his eunuchs, that he should bring in some of the children of Israel, even of the royal offspring and of the nobles— 4 youths in whom was no defect, but well-favored, and skillful in all wisdom, and endowed with knowledge, and understanding science, and who had the ability to serve in the king's palace; and that he should teach them the learning and the language of the Chaldeans. 5 The king appointed for them a daily portion of the king's delicacies, and of the wine which he drank, and that they should be nourished three years; that at its end they should serve the king. 6 Now among these were of the children of Judah: Daniel, Hananiah, Mishael, and Azariah. 7 The prince of the eunuchs gave names to them: to Daniel he gave the name Belteshazzar; to Hananiah, Shadrach; to Mishael, Meshach; and to Azariah, Abednego. 8 But Daniel purposed in his heart that he would not defile himself with the king's delicacies, nor with the wine which he drank. Therefore he requested of the prince of the eunuchs that he might not defile himself. 9 Now God made Daniel find kindness and

compassion in the sight of the prince of the eunuchs. 10 The prince of the eunuchs said to Daniel, "I fear my lord the king, who has appointed your food and your drink. For why should he see your faces worse looking than the youths who are of your own age? Then you would endanger my head with the king." 11 Then Daniel said to the steward whom the prince of the eunuchs had appointed over Daniel, Hananiah, Mishael, and Azariah: 12"Test your servants, I beg you, ten days; and let them give us vegetables to eat and water to drink. 13 Then let our faces be examined before you, and the face of the youths who eat of the king's delicacies; and as you see, deal with your servants." 14 So he listened to them in this matter, and tested them for ten days. 15 At the end of ten days, their faces appeared fairer, and they were fatter in flesh, than all the youths who ate of the king's delicacies. 16 So the steward took away their delicacies, and the wine that they would drink, and gave them vegetables. 17 Now as for these four youths, God gave them knowledge and skill in all learning and wisdom; and Daniel had understanding in all visions and dreams. 18 At the end of the days which the king had appointed for bringing them in, the prince of the eunuchs brought them in before Nebuchadnezzar. 19 The king talked with them; and among them all was found no one like Daniel, Hananiah, Mishael, and Azariah. Therefore they served the king. 20 In every matter of wisdom and understanding concerning which the king inquired of them, he found them ten times better than all the magicians and enchanters who were in all his realm. 21 Daniel continued serving even to the first year of King Cyrus.

2

1 In the second year of the reign of Nebuchadnezzar, Nebuchadnezzar dreamed dreams; and his spirit was troubled, and his sleep went from him. 2 Then the king commanded that the magicians, the enchanters, the sorcerers, and the Chaldeans be called to tell the king his dreams. So they came in and stood before the king. 3 The king said to them, "I have dreamed a dream, and my spirit is troubled to know the dream." 4 Then the Chaldeans spoke to the king in the Syrian language, "O king, live forever! Tell your servants the dream, and we will show the interpretation." 5 The king answered the Chaldeans, "The thing has gone from me. If you don't make known to me the dream and its interpretation, you will be cut in pieces, and your houses will be made a dunghill. 6 But if you show the dream and its interpretation, you will receive from me gifts, rewards, and great honor. Therefore show me the dream and its interpretation." 7 They answered the second time and said, "Let

the king tell his servants the dream, and we will show the interpretation." 8 The king answered, "I know of a certainty that you are trying to gain time, because you see the thing has gone from me. 9 But if you don't make known to me the dream, there is but one law for you; for you have prepared lying and corrupt words to speak before me, until the situation changes. Therefore tell me the dream, and I will know that you can show me its interpretation." 10 The Chaldeans answered before the king, and said, "There is not a man on the earth who can show the king's matter, because no king, lord, or ruler, has asked such a thing of any magician, enchanter, or Chaldean. 11 It is a rare thing that the king requires, and there is no other who can show it before the king, except the gods, whose dwelling is not with flesh." 12 Because of this, the king was angry and very furious, and commanded that all the wise men of Babylon be destroyed. 13 So the decree went out, and the wise men were to be slain. They sought Daniel and his companions to be slain. 14 Then Daniel returned answer with counsel and prudence to Arioch the captain of the king's guard, who had gone out to kill the wise men of Babylon. 15 He answered Arioch the king's captain, "Why is the decree so urgent from the king?" Then Arioch made the thing known to Daniel. 16 Daniel went in, and desired of the king that he would appoint him a time, and he would show the king the interpretation. 17 Then Daniel went to his house and made the thing known to Hananiah, Mishael, and Azariah, his companions, 18 that they would desire mercies of the God of heaven concerning this secret, and that Daniel and his companions would not perish with the rest of the wise men of Babylon. 19 Then the secret was revealed to Daniel in a vision of the night. Then Daniel blessed the God of heaven. 20 Daniel answered, "Blessed be the name of God forever and ever; for wisdom and might are his. 21 He changes the times and the seasons. He removes kings and sets up kings. He gives wisdom to the wise, and knowledge to those who have understanding. 22 He reveals the deep and secret things. He knows what is in the darkness, and the light dwells with him. 23 I thank you and praise you, O God of my fathers, who have given me wisdom and might, and have now made known to me what we desired of you; for you have made known to us the king's matter." 24 Therefore Daniel went in to Arioch, whom the king had appointed to destroy the wise men of Babylon. He went and said this to him: "Don't destroy the wise men of Babylon. Bring me in before the king, and I will show to the king the interpretation." 25 Then Arioch brought in Daniel before the king in haste, and said this to him: "I have found a man of the children of the captivity of Judah who will make known to the king the interpretation." 26 The king answered Daniel, whose name was Belteshazzar, "Are you able to make known to me the dream which I have seen, and its interpretation?" 27 Daniel answered before the king, and said, "The secret which the king has demanded can't be shown to the king by wise men, enchanters, magicians, or soothsayers; 28 but there is a God in heaven who reveals secrets, and he has made known to King Nebuchadnezzar what will be in the latter days. Your dream, and the visions of your head on your bed, are these: 29"As for you, O king, your thoughts came on your bed, what should happen hereafter; and he who reveals secrets has made known to you what will happen. 30 But as for me, this secret is not revealed to me for any wisdom that I have more than any living, but to the intent that the interpretation may be made known to the king, and that you may know the thoughts of your heart. 31"You, O king, saw, and behold, a great image. This image, which was mighty, and whose brightness was excellent, stood before you; and its appearance was terrifying. 32 As for this image, its head was of fine gold, its chest and its arms of silver, its belly and its thighs of bronze, 33 its legs of iron, its feet part of iron, and part of clay. 34 You saw until a stone was cut out without hands, which struck the image on its feet that were of iron and clay, and broke them in pieces. 35 Then the iron, the clay, the bronze, the silver, and the gold were broken in pieces together, and became like the chaff of the summer threshing floors. The wind carried them away, so that no place was found for them. The stone that struck the image became a great mountain, and filled the whole earth. 36"This is the dream; and we will tell its interpretation before the king. 37 You, O king, are king of kings, to whom the God of heaven has given the kingdom, the power, the strength, and the glory. 38 Wherever the children of men dwell, he has given the animals of the field and the birds of the sky into your hand, and has made you rule over them all. You are the head of gold. 39"After you, another kingdom will arise that is inferior to you; and a third kingdom of bronze, which will rule over all the earth. 40 The fourth kingdom will be strong as iron, because iron breaks in pieces and subdues all things; and as iron that crushes all these, it will break in pieces and crush. 41 Whereas you saw the feet and toes, part of potters' clay, and part of iron, it will be a divided kingdom; but there will be in it of the strength of the iron, because you saw the iron mixed with miry clay. 42 As the toes of the feet were part of iron, and part of clay, so the kingdom will be partly strong, and partly brittle. 43 Whereas you saw the iron mixed with miry clay, they will mingle themselves with the seed of men; but they won't cling to one another, even as iron does not mix with clay. 44"In the days of those kings the God of heaven will set up a kingdom which will never be destroyed, nor will its sovereignty be left to another people; but it will break in pieces and consume all these kingdoms, and it will stand forever. 45 Because you saw that a stone was cut out of the mountain without hands, and that it broke in pieces the iron, the bronze, the clay, the silver, and the gold. The great God has made known to the king what will happen hereafter. The dream is certain, and its interpretation sure." 46 Then King Nebuchadnezzar fell on his face, worshiped Daniel, and commanded that they should offer an offering and sweet odors to him. 47 The king answered to Daniel, and said, "Of a truth your God is the God of gods, and the Lord of kings, and a revealer of secrets, since you have been able to reveal this secret." 48 Then the king made Daniel great, and gave him many great gifts, and made him rule over the whole province of Babylon, and to be chief governor over all the wise men of Babylon. 49 Daniel requested of the king, and he appointed Shadrach, Meshach, and Abednego over the affairs of the province of Babylon; but Daniel was in the king's gate.

3

1 Nebuchadnezzar the king made an image of gold, whose height was sixty cubits, and its width six cubits. He set it up in the plain of Dura, in the province of Babylon. 2 Then Nebuchadnezzar the king sent to gather together the local governors, the deputies, and the governors, the judges, the treasurers, the counselors, the sheriffs, and all the rulers of the provinces, to come to the dedication of the image which Nebuchadnezzar the king had set up. 3 Then the local governors, the deputies, and the governors, the judges, the treasurers, the counselors, the sheriffs, and all the rulers of the provinces, were gathered together to the dedication of the image that Nebuchadnezzar the king had set up; and they stood before the image that Nebuchadnezzar had set up. 4 Then the herald cried aloud, "To you it is commanded, peoples, nations, and languages, 5 that whenever you hear the sound of the horn, flute, zither, lyre, harp, pipe, and all kinds of music, you fall down and worship the golden image that Nebuchadnezzar the king has set up. 6 Whoever doesn't fall down and worship shall be cast into the middle of a burning fiery furnace the same hour." 7 Therefore at that time, when all the peoples heard the sound of the horn, flute, zither, lyre, harp, pipe, and all kinds of music, all the peoples, the nations, and the languages, fell down and worshiped the golden image that Nebuchadnezzar the king had set up. 8 Therefore at that time certain

Chaldeans came near, and brought accusation against the Jews. 9 They answered Nebuchadnezzar the king, "O king, live for ever! 10 You, O king, have made a decree that every man who hears the sound of the horn, flute, zither, lyre, harp, pipe, and all kinds of music shall fall down and worship the golden image; 11 and whoever doesn't fall down and worship shall be cast into the middle of a burning fiery furnace. 12 There are certain Jews whom you have appointed over the affairs of the province of Babylon: Shadrach, Meshach, and Abednego. These men, O king, have not respected you. They don't serve your gods, and don't worship the golden image which you have set up." 13 Then Nebuchadnezzar in rage and fury commanded that Shadrach, Meshach, and Abednego be brought. Then these men were brought before the king. 14 Nebuchadnezzar answered them, "Is it on purpose, Shadrach, Meshach, and Abednego, that you don't serve my god, nor worship the golden image which I have set up? 15 Now if you are ready whenever you hear the sound of the horn, flute, zither, lyre, harp, pipe, and all kinds of music to fall down and worship the image which I have made, good; but if you don't worship, you shall be cast the same hour into the middle of a burning fiery furnace. Who is that god who will deliver you out of my hands?" 16 Shadrach, Meshach, and Abednego answered the king, "Nebuchadnezzar, we have no need to answer you in this matter. 17 If it happens, our God whom we serve is able to deliver us from the burning fiery furnace; and he will deliver us out of your hand, O king. 18 But if not, let it be known to you, O king, that we will not serve your gods or worship the golden image which you have set up." 19 Then Nebuchadnezzar was full of fury, and the form of his appearance was changed against Shadrach, Meshach, and Abednego. He spoke, and commanded that they should heat the furnace seven times more than it was usually heated. 20 He commanded certain mighty men who were in his army to bind Shadrach, Meshach, and Abednego, and to cast them into the burning fiery furnace. 21 Then these men were bound in their pants, their tunics, their mantles, and their other clothes, and were cast into the middle of the burning fiery furnace. 22 Therefore because the king's commandment was urgent, and the furnace exceedingly hot, the flame of the fire killed those men who took up Shadrach, Meshach, and Abednego. 23 These three men, Shadrach, Meshach, and Abednego, fell down bound into the middle of the burning fiery furnace.

The Song of the Three Holy Children, or The Prayer of Azariah
Continuation of Daniel with Greek Portions
3

24 They walked in the midst of the fire, praising God, and blessing the Lord. 25 Then Azarias stood, and prayed like this. Opening his mouth in the midst of the fire he said, 26"Blessed are you, O Lord, you God of our fathers! Your name is worthy to be praised and glorified for evermore; 27 for you are righteous in all the things that you have done. Yes, all your works are true. Your ways are right, and all your judgments are truth. 28 In all the things that you have brought upon us, and upon the holy city of our fathers, Jerusalem, you have executed true judgments. For according to truth and justice you have brought all these things upon us because of our sins. 29 For we have sinned and committed iniquity in departing from you. 30 In all things we have trespassed, and not obeyed your commandments or kept them. We haven't done as you have commanded us, that it might go well with us. 31 Therefore all that you have brought upon us, and everything that you have done to us, you have done in true judgment. 32 You delivered us into the hands of lawless enemies, most hateful rebels, and to an unjust king who is the most wicked in all the world. 33 And now we can't open our mouth. Shame and reproach have come on your servants and those who worship you. 34 Don't utterly deliver us up, for your name's sake. Don't annul your covenant. 35 Don't cause your mercy to depart from us, for the sake of Abraham who is loved by you, and for the sake of Isaac your servant, and Israel your holy one, 36 to whom you promised that you would multiply their offspring as the stars of the sky, and as the sand that is on the sea shore. 37 For we, O Lord, have become less than any nation, and are brought low this day in all the world because of our sins. 38 There isn't at this time prince, or prophet, or leader, or burnt offering, or sacrifice, or oblation, or incense, or place to offer before you, and to find mercy. 39 Nevertheless in a contrite heart and a humble spirit let us be accepted, 40 like the burnt offerings of rams and bullocks, and like ten thousands of fat lambs. So let our sacrifice be in your sight this day, that we may wholly go after you, for they shall not be ashamed who put their trust in you. 41 And now we follow you with all our heart. We fear you, and seek your face. 42 Put us not to shame; but deal with us after your kindness, and according to the multitude of your mercy. 43 Deliver us also according to your

marvelous works, and give glory to your name, O Lord. Let all those who harm your servants be confounded. 44 Let them be ashamed of all their power and might, and let their strength be broken. 45 Let them know that you are the Lord, the only God, and glorious over the whole world." 46 The king's servants who put them in didn't stop making the furnace hot with naphtha, pitch, tinder, and small wood, 47 so that the flame streamed out forty nine cubits above the furnace. 48 It spread and burned those Chaldeans whom it found around the furnace. 49 But the angel of the Lord came down into the furnace together with Azarias and his fellows, and he struck the flame of the fire out of the furnace, 50 and made the midst of the furnace as it had been a moist whistling wind, so that the fire didn't touch them at all. It neither hurt nor troubled them. 51 Then the three, as out of one mouth, praised, glorified, and blessed God in the furnace, saying, 52 "Blessed are you, O Lord, you God of our fathers, to be praised and exalted above all forever! 53 Blessed is your glorious and holy name, to be praised and exalted above all forever! 54 Blessed are you in the temple of your holy glory, to be praised and glorified above all forever! 55 Blessed are you who see the depths and sit upon the cherubim, to be praised and exalted above all forever. 56 Blessed are you on the throne of your kingdom, to be praised and extolled above all forever! 57 Blessed are you in the firmament of heaven, to be praised and glorified forever! 58 O all you works of the Lord, bless the Lord! Praise and exalt him above all forever! 59 O you heavens, bless the Lord! Praise and exalt him above all for ever! 60 O you angels of the Lord, bless the Lord! Praise and exalt him above all forever! 61 O all you waters that are above the sky, bless the Lord! Praise and exalt him above all forever! 62 O all you powers of the Lord, bless the Lord! Praise and exalt him above all forever! 63 O you sun and moon, bless the Lord! Praise and exalt him above all forever! 64 O you stars of heaven, bless the Lord! Praise and exalt him above all forever! 65 O every shower and dew, bless the Lord! Praise and exalt him above all forever! 66 O all you winds, bless the Lord! Praise and exalt him above all forever! 67 O you fire and heat, bless the Lord! Praise and exalt him above all forever! 68 O you dews and storms of snow, bless the Lord! Praise and exalt him above all forever! 69 O you nights and days, bless the Lord! Praise and exalt him above all forever! 70 O you light and darkness, bless the Lord! Praise and exalt him above all forever! 71 O you cold and heat, bless the Lord! Praise and exalt him above all forever! 72 O you frost and snow, bless the Lord! Praise and exalt him above all forever! 73 O you lightnings and clouds, bless the Lord! Praise and exalt him above all forever! 74 O let the earth bless the Lord! Let it praise and exalt him above all forever! 75 O you mountains and hills, bless the Lord! Praise and exalt him above all forever! 76 O all you things that grow on the earth, bless the Lord! Praise and exalt him above all forever! 77 O sea and rivers, bless the Lord! Praise and exalt him above all forever! 78 O you springs, bless the Lord! Praise and exalt him above all forever! 79 O you whales and all that move in the waters, bless the Lord! Praise and exalt him above all forever! 80 O all you birds of the air, bless the Lord! Praise and exalt him above all forever! 81 O all you beasts and cattle, bless the Lord! Praise and exalt him above all forever! 82 O you children of men, bless the Lord! Praise and exalt him above all forever! 83 O let Israel bless the Lord! Praise and exalt him above all forever. 84 O you priests of the Lord, bless the Lord! Praise and exalt him above all forever! 85 O you servants of the Lord, bless the Lord! Praise and exalt him above all forever! 86 O you spirits and souls of the righteous, bless the Lord! Praise and exalt him above all forever! 87 O you who are holy and humble of heart, bless the Lord! Praise and exalt him above all forever! 88 O Hananiah, Mishael, and Azariah, bless the Lord! Praise and exalt him above all forever; for he has rescued us from Hades, and saved us from the hand of death! He has delivered us out of the midst of the furnace and burning flame. He has delivered us out of the midst of the fire. 89 O give thanks to the Lord, for he is good; for his mercy is forever. 90 O all you who worship the Lord, bless the God of gods, praise him, and give him thanks; for his mercy is forever!"

Deliverance from the Furnace

91   Then Nebuchadnezzar the king was astonished and rose up in haste. He spoke and said to his counselors, "Didn't we cast three men bound into the middle of the fire?" They answered the king, "True, O king." 92 He answered, "Look, I see four men loose, walking in the middle of the fire, and they are unharmed. The appearance of the fourth is like a son of the gods." 93 Then Nebuchadnezzar came near to the mouth of the burning fiery furnace. He spoke and said, "Shadrach, Meshach, and Abednego, you servants of the Most High God, come out, and come here!" Then Shadrach, Meshach, and Abednego came out of the middle of the fire. 94 The local governors, the deputies, and the governors, and the king's counselors, being gathered together, saw these men, that the fire had no power on their bodies. The hair of their head wasn't singed. Their pants weren't changed. The smell of fire wasn't even on them. 95 Nebuchadnezzar spoke and said, "Blessed be the God

of Shadrach, Meshach, and Abednego, who has sent his angel and delivered his servants who trusted in him, and have changed the king's word, and have yielded their bodies, that they might not serve nor worship any god, except their own God. 96 Therefore I make a decree, that every people, nation, and language, who speak anything evil against the God of Shadrach, Meshach, and Abednego, shall be cut in pieces, and their houses shall be made a dunghill, because there is no other god who is able to deliver like this." 97 Then the king promoted Shadrach, Meshach, and Abednego in the province of Babylon.

4

1 Nebuchadnezzar the king, to all the peoples, nations, and languages, who dwell in all the earth: Peace be multiplied to you. 2 It has seemed good to me to show the signs and wonders that the Most High God has worked toward me. 3 How great are his signs! How mighty are his wonders! His kingdom is an everlasting kingdom. His dominion is from generation to generation. 4 I, Nebuchadnezzar, was at rest in my house, and flourishing in my palace. 5 I saw a dream which made me afraid; and the thoughts on my bed and the visions of my head troubled me. 6 Therefore I made a decree to bring in all the wise men of Babylon before me, that they might make known to me the interpretation of the dream. 7 Then the magicians, the enchanters, the Chaldeans, and the soothsayers came in; and I told the dream before them; but they didn't make known to me its interpretation. 8 But at the last Daniel came in before me, whose name was Belteshazzar, according to the name of my god, and in whom is the spirit of the holy gods. I told the dream before him, saying, 9 "Belteshazzar, master of the magicians, because I know that the spirit of the holy gods is in you, and no secret troubles you, tell me the visions of my dream that I have seen, and its interpretation. 10 These were the visions of my head on my bed: I saw, and behold, a tree in the middle of the earth; and its height was great. 11 The tree grew, and was strong, and its height reached to the sky, and its sight to the end of all the earth. 12 Its leaves were beautiful, and it had much fruit, and in it was food for all. The animals of the field had shade under it, and the birds of the sky lived in its branches, and all flesh was fed from it. 13 "I saw in the visions of my head on my bed, and behold, a watcher and a holy one came down from the sky. 14 He cried aloud, and said this, 'Cut down the tree and cut off its branches! Shake off its leaves and scatter its fruit! Let the animals get away from under it, and the fowls from its branches. 15 Nevertheless leave the stump of its roots in the earth,

even with a band of iron and bronze, in the tender grass of the field; and let it be wet with the dew of the sky. Let his portion be with the animals in the grass of the earth. 16 Let his heart be changed from man's, and let an animal's heart be given to him. Then let seven times pass over him. 17 "The sentence is by the decree of the watchers, and the demand by the word of the holy ones, to the intent that the living may know that the Most High rules in the kingdom of men, and gives it to whomever he will, and sets up over it the lowest of men.' 18 "This dream I, King Nebuchadnezzar, have seen; and you, Belteshazzar, declare the interpretation, because all the wise men of my kingdom are not able to make known to me the interpretation; but you are able, for the spirit of the holy gods is in you." 19 Then Daniel, whose name was Belteshazzar, was stricken mute for a while, and his thoughts troubled him. The king answered, "Belteshazzar, don't let the dream, or the interpretation, trouble you." Belteshazzar answered, "My lord, may the dream be for those who hate you, and its interpretation to your adversaries. 20 The tree that you saw, which grew and was strong, whose height reached to the sky, and its sight to all the earth; 21 whose leaves were beautiful, and its fruit plentiful, and in it was food for all; under which the animals of the field lived, and on whose branches the birds of the sky had their habitation— 22 it is you, O king, who have grown and become strong; for your greatness has grown, and reaches to the sky, and your dominion to the end of the earth. 23 "Whereas the king saw a watcher and a holy one coming down from the sky, and saying, 'Cut down the tree, and destroy it; nevertheless leave the stump of its roots in the earth, even with a band of iron and bronze, in the tender grass of the field, and let it be wet with the dew of the sky. Let his portion be with the animals of the field, until seven times pass over him.' 24 "This is the interpretation, O king, and it is the decree of the Most High, which has come on my lord the king: 25 that you shall be driven from men, and your dwelling shall be with the animals of the field. You shall be made to eat grass as oxen, and shall be wet with the dew of the sky, and seven times shall pass over you; until you know that the Most High rules in the kingdom of men, and gives it to whomever he will. 26 Their command to leave the stump of the roots of the tree means your kingdom will be sure to you, after you will have known that the heavens do rule. 27 Therefore, O king, let my counsel be acceptable to you, and break off your sins by righteousness, and your iniquities by showing mercy to the poor. Perhaps there may be a lengthening of your tranquility." 28 All this came on the King Nebuchadnezzar. 29 At the end of twelve months he was walking in the royal palace of Babylon. ³⁰ The king spoke and said, "Is not this great Babylon, which I have built for the royal dwelling place, by the might of my power and for the glory of my majesty?" ³¹ While the word was in the king's mouth, a voice came from the sky, saying, "O King Nebuchadnezzar, to you it is spoken: 'The kingdom has departed from you. ³² You shall be driven from men, and your dwelling shall be with the animals of the field. You shall be made to eat grass as oxen. Seven times shall pass over you, until you know that the Most High rules in the kingdom of men, and gives it to whomever he will.'" ³³ This was fulfilled the same hour on Nebuchadnezzar. He was driven from men, and ate grass as oxen, and his body was wet with the dew of the sky, until his hair had grown like eagles' feathers, and his nails like birds' claws. ³⁴ At the end of the days I, Nebuchadnezzar, lifted up my eyes to heaven, and my understanding returned to me, and I blessed the Most High, and I praised and honored him who lives forever. For his dominion is an everlasting dominion, and his kingdom from generation to generation. ³⁵ All the inhabitants of the earth are reputed as nothing; and he does according to his will in the army of heaven, and among the inhabitants of the earth; and no one can stop his hand, or ask him, "What are you doing?" ³⁶ At the same time my understanding returned to me; and for the glory of my kingdom, my majesty and brightness returned to me. My counselors and my lords sought me; and I was established in my kingdom, and excellent greatness was added to me. ³⁷ Now I, Nebuchadnezzar, praise and extol and honor the King of heaven; for all his works are right and his ways just; and those who walk in pride he is able to humble.

5

¹ Belshazzar the king made a great feast to a thousand of his lords, and drank wine before the thousand. ² Belshazzar, while he tasted the wine, commanded that the golden and silver vessels which Nebuchadnezzar his father had taken out of the temple which was in Jerusalem be brought to him, that the king and his lords, his wives and his concubines, might drink from them. ³ Then they brought the golden vessels that were taken out of the temple of God's house which was at Jerusalem; and the king and his lords, his wives and his concubines, drank from them. ⁴ They drank wine, and praised the gods of gold, and of silver, of bronze, of iron, of wood, and of stone. ⁵ In the same hour, the fingers of a man's hand came out and wrote near the lamp stand on the plaster of the wall of the king's palace. The king saw the part of the hand that wrote. ⁶ Then the king's face was changed in him, and his thoughts

troubled him; and the joints of his thighs were loosened, and his knees struck one against another. 7 The king cried aloud to bring in the enchanters, the Chaldeans, and the soothsayers. The king spoke and said to the wise men of Babylon, "Whoever reads this writing and shows me its interpretation shall be clothed with purple, and have a chain of gold about his neck, and shall be the third ruler in the kingdom." 8 Then all the king's wise men came in; but they could not read the writing and couldn't make known to the king the interpretation. 9 Then King Belshazzar was greatly troubled. His face was changed in him, and his lords were perplexed. 10 The queen by reason of the words of the king and his lords came into the banquet house. The queen spoke and said, "O king, live forever; don't let your thoughts trouble you, nor let your face be changed. 11 There is a man in your kingdom in whom is the spirit of the holy gods. In the days of your father, light, understanding, and wisdom like the wisdom of the gods were found in him. The king, Nebuchadnezzar, your father—yes, the king, your father—made him master of the magicians, enchanters, Chaldeans, and soothsayers 12 because an excellent spirit, knowledge, understanding, interpreting of dreams, showing of dark sentences, and dissolving of doubts were found in the same Daniel, whom the king named Belteshazzar. Now let Daniel be called, and he will show the interpretation." 13 Then Daniel was brought in before the king. The king spoke and said to Daniel, "Are you that Daniel of the children of the captivity of Judah, whom the king my father brought out of Judah? 14 I have heard of you, that the spirit of the gods is in you, and that light, understanding, and excellent wisdom are found in you. 15 Now the wise men, the enchanters, have been brought in before me to read this writing, and make known to me its interpretation; but they could not show the interpretation of the thing. 16 But I have heard of you, that you can give interpretations and dissolve doubts. Now if you can read the writing, and make known to me its interpretation, you shall be clothed with purple, and have a chain of gold around your neck, and shall be the third ruler in the kingdom." 17 Then Daniel answered the king, "Let your gifts be to yourself, and give your rewards to another. Nevertheless, I will read the writing to the king, and make known to him the interpretation. 18"To you, king, the Most High God gave Nebuchadnezzar your father the kingdom, and greatness, and glory, and majesty. 19 Because of the greatness that he gave him, all the peoples, nations, and languages trembled and feared before him. He killed whom he wanted to, and he kept alive whom he wanted to. He raised up whom he wanted to, and he put down whom he wanted to. ²⁰ But when his heart was lifted up, and his spirit was hardened so that he dealt proudly, he was deposed from his kingly throne, and they took his glory from him. ²¹ He was driven from the sons of men and his heart was made like the animals', and his dwelling was with the wild donkeys. He was fed with grass like oxen, and his body was wet with the dew of the sky, until he knew that the Most High God rules in the kingdom of men, and that he sets up over it whomever he will. ²²"You, his son, Belshazzar, have not humbled your heart, though you knew all this, ²³ but have lifted up yourself against the Lord of heaven; and they have brought the vessels of his house before you, and you and your lords, your wives, and your concubines, have drunk wine from them. You have praised the gods of silver, gold, bronze, iron, wood, and stone, which don't see, hear, or know; and you have not glorified the God in whose hand is your breath and whose are all your ways. ²⁴ Then the part of the hand was sent from before him, and this writing was inscribed. ²⁵"This is the writing that was inscribed: 'MENE, MENE, TEKEL, UPHARSIN.' ²⁶"This is the interpretation of the thing: MENE: God has counted your kingdom, and brought it to an end. ²⁷ TEKEL: you are weighed in the balances, and are found wanting. ²⁸ PERES: your kingdom is divided, and given to the Medes and Persians." ²⁹ Then Belshazzar commanded, and they clothed Daniel with purple, and put a chain of gold about his neck, and proclaimed that he should be the third highest ruler in the kingdom. ³⁰ In that night Belshazzar the Chaldean King was slain. ³¹ Darius the Mede received the kingdom, being about sixty-two years old.

6

¹ It pleased Darius to set over the kingdom one hundred twenty local governors, who should be throughout the whole kingdom; ² and over them three presidents, of whom Daniel was one; that these local governors might give account to them, and that the king should suffer no loss. ³ Then this Daniel was distinguished above the presidents and the local governors, because an excellent spirit was in him; and the king thought to set him over the whole realm. ⁴ Then the presidents and the local governors sought to find occasion against Daniel as touching the kingdom; but they could find no occasion or fault, because he was faithful. There wasn't any error or fault found in him. ⁵ Then these men said, "We won't find any occasion against this Daniel, unless we find it against him concerning the law of his God." ⁶ Then these presidents and local governors assembled together to the king, and said this to him, "King Darius, live forever! ⁷ All the presidents of the

kingdom, the deputies and the local governors, the counselors and the governors, have consulted together to establish a royal statute, and to make a strong decree, that whoever asks a petition of any god or man for thirty days, except of you, O king, he shall be cast into the den of lions. 8 Now, O king, establish the decree, and sign the writing, that it not be changed, according to the law of the Medes and Persians, which doesn't alter." 9 Therefore King Darius signed the writing and the decree. 10 When Daniel knew that the writing was signed, he went into his house (now his windows were open in his room toward Jerusalem) and he kneeled on his knees three times a day, and prayed, and gave thanks before his God, as he did before. 11 Then these men assembled together, and found Daniel making petition and supplication before his God. 12 Then they came near, and spoke before the king concerning the king's decree: "Haven't you signed a decree that every man who makes a petition to any god or man within thirty days, except to you, O king, shall be cast into the den of lions?" The king answered, "This thing is true, according to the law of the Medes and Persians, which doesn't alter." 13 Then they answered and said before the king, "That Daniel, who is of the children of the captivity of Judah, doesn't respect you, O king, nor the decree that you have signed, but makes his petition three times a day." 14 Then the king, when he heard these words, was very displeased, and set his heart on Daniel to deliver him; and he labored until the going down of the sun to rescue him. 15 Then these men assembled together to the king, and said to the king, "Know, O king, that it is a law of the Medes and Persians, that no decree nor statute which the king establishes may be changed." 16 Then the king commanded, and they brought Daniel, and cast him into the den of lions. The king spoke and said to Daniel, "Your God whom you serve continually, he will deliver you." 17 A stone was brought, and laid on the mouth of the den; and the king sealed it with his own signet, and with the signet of his lords, that nothing might be changed concerning Daniel. 18 Then the king went to his palace, and passed the night fasting. No musical instruments were brought before him; and his sleep fled from him. 19 Then the king arose very early in the morning, and went in haste to the den of lions. 20 When he came near to the den to Daniel, he cried with a troubled voice. The king spoke and said to Daniel, "Daniel, servant of the living God, is your God, whom you serve continually, able to deliver you from the lions?" 21 Then Daniel said to the king, "O king, live forever! 22 My God has sent his angel, and has shut the lions' mouths, and they have not hurt me; because I am innocent in his sight. Also before you, O king, I have done no harm." 23 Then the king was exceedingly glad, and commanded that they should take Daniel up out of the den. So Daniel was taken up out of the den, and no kind of harm was found on him, because he had trusted in his God. 24 The king commanded, and they brought those men who had accused Daniel, and they cast them into the den of lions—them, their children, and their wives; and the lions mauled them and broke all their bones in pieces before they came to the bottom of the den. 25 Then King Darius wrote to all the peoples, nations, and languages, who dwell in all the earth: "Peace be multiplied to you. 26"I make a decree that in all the dominion of my kingdom men tremble and fear before the God of Daniel; "for he is the living God, and steadfast forever. His kingdom is that which will not be destroyed. His dominion will be even to the end. 27 He delivers and rescues. He works signs and wonders in heaven and in earth, who has delivered Daniel from the power of the lions." 28 So this Daniel prospered in the reign of Darius, and in the reign of Cyrus the Persian.

7

1 In the first year of Belshazzar king of Babylon, Daniel had a dream and visions of his head on his bed. Then he wrote the dream and told the sum of the matters. 2 Daniel spoke and said, "I saw in my vision by night and behold, the four winds of the sky broke out on the great sea. 3 Four great animals came up from the sea, different from one another. 4"The first was like a lion, and had eagle's wings. I watched until its wings were plucked, and it was lifted up from the earth, and made to stand on two feet as a man. A man's heart was given to it. 5"Behold, there was another animal, a second, like a bear. It was raised up on one side, and three ribs were in its mouth between its teeth. They said this to it: 'Arise! Devour much flesh!' 6"After this I saw, and behold, another, like a leopard, which had on its back four wings of a bird. The animal also had four heads; and dominion was given to it. 7"After this I saw in the night visions, and, behold, there was a fourth animal, awesome and powerful, and exceedingly strong. It had great iron teeth. It devoured and broke in pieces, and stamped the residue with its feet. It was different from all the animals that were before it. It had ten horns. 8"I considered the horns, and behold, another horn came up among them, a little one, before which three of the first horns were plucked up by the roots: and behold, in this horn were eyes like the eyes of a man, and a mouth speaking great things. 9"I watched until thrones were placed, and one who was Ancient of Days sat. His clothing was white as snow, and the hair of his head like

pure wool. His throne was fiery flames, and its wheels burning fire. 10 A fiery stream issued and came out from before him. Thousands of thousands ministered to him. Ten thousand times ten thousand stood before him. The judgment was set. The books were opened. 11"I watched at that time because of the voice of the great words which the horn spoke. I watched even until the animal was slain, its body destroyed, and it was given to be burned with fire. 12 As for the rest of the animals, their dominion was taken away; yet their lives were prolonged for a season and a time. 13"I saw in the night visions, and behold, one like a son of man came with the clouds, and he came to the Ancient of Days, and they brought him near before him. 14 Dominion was given him, with glory and a kingdom, that all the peoples, nations, and languages should serve him. His dominion is an everlasting dominion, which will not pass away, and his kingdom will not be destroyed. 15"As for me, Daniel, my spirit was grieved within my body, and the visions of my head troubled me. 16 I came near to one of those who stood by, and asked him the truth concerning all this. "So he told me, and made me know the interpretation of the things. 17'These great animals, which are four, are four kings, who will arise out of the earth. 18 But the saints of the Most High will receive the kingdom, and possess the kingdom forever, even forever and ever.' 19"Then I desired to know the truth concerning the fourth animal, which was different from all of them, exceedingly terrible, whose teeth were of iron, and its nails of bronze; which devoured, broke in pieces, and stamped the residue with its feet; 20 and concerning the ten horns that were on its head, and the other horn which came up, and before which three fell, even that horn that had eyes, and a mouth that spoke great things, whose look was more stout than its fellows. 21 I saw, and the same horn made war with the saints and prevailed against them 22 until the Ancient of Days came, and judgment was given to the saints of the Most High, and the time came that the saints possessed the kingdom. 23"So he said, 'The fourth animal will be a fourth kingdom on earth, which will be different from all the kingdoms, and will devour the whole earth, and will tread it down, and break it in pieces. 24 As for the ten horns, ten kings will arise out of this kingdom. Another will arise after them; and he will be different from the former, and he will put down three kings. 25 He will speak words against the Most High, and will wear out the saints of the Most High. He will plan to change the times and the law; and they will be given into his hand until a time and times and half a time. 26"'But the judgment will be set, and they will take away his dominion, to consume and to destroy it to the end. 27 The kingdom and the dominion, and the greatness of the kingdoms under the whole sky, will be given to the people of the saints of the Most High. His kingdom is an everlasting kingdom, and all dominions will serve and obey him.' 28 "Here is the end of the matter. As for me, Daniel, my thoughts troubled me greatly, and my face was changed in me; but I kept the matter in my heart."

8

1 In the third year of the reign of King Belshazzar, a vision appeared to me, even to me, Daniel, after that which appeared to me at the first. 2 I saw the vision. Now it was so, that when I saw, I was in the citadel of Susa, which is in the province of Elam. I saw in the vision, and I was by the river Ulai. 3 Then I lifted up my eyes, and saw, and behold, a ram which had two horns stood before the river. The two horns were high; but one was higher than the other, and the higher came up last. 4 I saw the ram pushing westward, northward, and southward. No animals could stand before him. There wasn't anyone who could deliver out of his hand; but he did according to his will, and magnified himself. 5 As I was considering, behold, a male goat came from the west over the surface of the whole earth, and didn't touch the ground. The goat had a notable horn between his eyes. 6 He came to the ram that had the two horns, which I saw standing before the river, and ran on him in the fury of his power. 7 I saw him come close to the ram, and he was moved with anger against him, and struck the ram, and broke his two horns. There was no power in the ram to stand before him; but he cast him down to the ground, and trampled on him. There was no one who could deliver the ram out of his hand. 8 The male goat magnified himself exceedingly. When he was strong, the great horn was broken; and instead of it there came up four notable horns toward the four winds of the sky. 9 Out of one of them came out a little horn, which grew exceedingly great, toward the south, and toward the east, and toward the glorious land. 10 It grew great, even to the army of the sky; and it cast down some of the army and of the stars to the ground, and trampled on them. 11 Yes, it magnified itself, even to the prince of the army; and it took away from him the continual burnt offering, and the place of his sanctuary was cast down. 12 The army was given over to it together with the continual burnt offering through disobedience. It cast down truth to the ground, and it did its pleasure and prospered. 13 Then I heard a holy one speaking; and another holy one said to that certain one who spoke, "How long will the vision about the continual burnt offering, and the disobedience

that makes desolate, to give both the sanctuary and the army to be trodden under foot be?" 14 He said to me, "To two thousand and three hundred evenings and mornings. Then the sanctuary will be cleansed." 15 When I, even I Daniel, had seen the vision, I sought to understand it. Then behold, there stood before me something like the appearance of a man. 16 I heard a man's voice between the banks of the Ulai, which called, and said, "Gabriel, make this man understand the vision." 17 So he came near where I stood; and when he came, I was frightened, and fell on my face; but he said to me, "Understand, son of man; for the vision belongs to the time of the end." 18 Now as he was speaking with me, I fell into a deep sleep with my face toward the ground; but he touched me, and set me upright. 19 He said, "Behold, I will make you know what will be in the latter time of the indignation; for it belongs to the appointed time of the end. 20 The ram which you saw, that had the two horns, they are the kings of Media and Persia. 21 The rough male goat is the king of Greece. The great horn that is between his eyes is the first king. 22 As for that which was broken, in the place where four stood up, four kingdoms will stand up out of the nation, but not with his power. 23 "In the latter time of their kingdom, when the transgressors have come to the full, a king of fierce face, and understanding dark sentences, will stand up. 24 His power will be mighty, but not by his own power. He will destroy awesomely, and will prosper in what he does. He will destroy the mighty ones and the holy people. 25 Through his policy he will cause deceit to prosper in his hand. He will magnify himself in his heart, and he will destroy many in their security. He will also stand up against the prince of princes; but he will be broken without human power. 26 "The vision of the evenings and mornings which has been told is true; but seal up the vision, for it belongs to many days to come." 27 I, Daniel, fainted, and was sick for some days. Then I rose up, and did the king's business. I wondered at the vision, but no one understood it.

9

1 In the first year of Darius the son of Ahasuerus, of the offspring of the Medes, who was made king over the realm of the Chaldeans, 2 in the first year of his reign I, Daniel, understood by the books the number of the years about which Yahweh's word came to Jeremiah the prophet, for the accomplishing of the desolations of Jerusalem, even seventy years. 3 I set my face to the Lord God, to seek by prayer and petitions, with fasting in sackcloth and ashes. 4 I prayed to Yahweh my God, and made confession, and said, "Oh,

Lord, the great and dreadful God, who keeps covenant and loving kindness with those who love him and keep his commandments, 5 we have sinned, and have dealt perversely, and have done wickedly, and have rebelled, even turning aside from your precepts and from your ordinances. 6 We haven't listened to your servants the prophets, who spoke in your name to our kings, our princes, and our fathers, and to all the people of the land. 7"Lord, righteousness belongs to you, but to us confusion of face, as it is today—to the men of Judah, and to the inhabitants of Jerusalem, and to all Israel, who are near, and who are far off, through all the countries where you have driven them, because of their trespass that they have trespassed against you. 8 Lord, to us belongs confusion of face, to our kings, to our princes, and to our fathers, because we have sinned against you. 9 To the Lord our God belong mercies and forgiveness; for we have rebelled against him. 10 We haven't obeyed Yahweh our God's voice, to walk in his laws, which he set before us by his servants the prophets. 11 Yes, all Israel have transgressed your law, turning aside, that they wouldn't obey your voice. "Therefore the curse and the oath written in the law of Moses the servant of God has been poured out on us; for we have sinned against him. 12 He has confirmed his words, which he spoke against us, and against our judges who judged us, by bringing on us a great evil; for under the whole sky, such has not been done as has been done to Jerusalem. 13 As it is written in the law of Moses, all this evil has come on us. Yet we have not entreated the favor of Yahweh our God, that we should turn from our iniquities and have discernment in your truth. 14 Therefore Yahweh has watched over the evil, and brought it on us; for Yahweh our God is righteous in all his works which he does, and we have not obeyed his voice. 15"Now, Lord our God, who has brought your people out of the land of Egypt with a mighty hand, and have gotten yourself renown, as it is today, we have sinned. We have done wickedly. 16 Lord, according to all your righteousness, please let your anger and your wrath be turned away from your city Jerusalem, your holy mountain, because for our sins, and for the iniquities of our fathers, Jerusalem and your people have become a reproach to all who are around us. 17"Now therefore, our God, listen to the prayer of your servant, and to his petitions, and cause your face to shine on your sanctuary that is desolate, for the Lord's sake. 18 My God, turn your ear and hear. Open your eyes and see our desolations and the city which is called by your name; for we don't present our petitions before you for our righteousness, but for your great mercies' sake. 19 Lord, hear. Lord, forgive.

Lord, listen and do. Don't defer, for your own sake, my God, because your city and your people are called by your name." 20 While I was speaking, praying, and confessing my sin and the sin of my people Israel, and presenting my supplication before Yahweh my God for the holy mountain of my God— 21 yes, while I was speaking in prayer, the man Gabriel, whom I had seen in the vision at the beginning, being caused to fly swiftly, touched me about the time of the evening offering. 22 He instructed me and talked with me, and said, "Daniel, I have now come to give you wisdom and understanding. 23 At the beginning of your petitions the commandment went out and I have come to tell you, for you are greatly beloved. Therefore consider the matter and understand the vision. 24 "Seventy weeks are decreed on your people and on your holy city, to finish disobedience, to put an end to sin, to make reconciliation for iniquity, to bring in everlasting righteousness, to seal up vision and prophecy, and to anoint the most holy. 25 "Know therefore and discern that from the going out of the commandment to restore and to build Jerusalem to the Anointed One, the prince, will be seven weeks and sixty-two weeks. It will be built again with street and moat, even in troubled times. 26 After the sixty-two weeks the Anointed One will be cut off and will have nothing. The people of the prince who come will destroy the city and the sanctuary. Its end will be with a flood, and war will be even to the end. Desolations are determined. 27 He will make a firm covenant with many for one week. In the middle of the week he will cause the sacrifice and the offering to cease. On the wing of abominations will come one who makes desolate. Even to the full end that is decreed, wrath will be poured out on the desolate."

10

1 In the third year of Cyrus king of Persia a revelation was revealed to Daniel, whose name was called Belteshazzar. The revelation was true, even a great warfare. He understood the revelation, and had understanding of the vision. 2 In those days I, Daniel, was mourning three whole weeks. 3 I ate no pleasant bread. No meat or wine came into my mouth. I didn't anoint myself at all, until three whole weeks were fulfilled. 4 In the twenty-fourth day of the first month, as I was by the side of the great river, which is Hiddekel, 5 I lifted up my eyes and looked, and behold, there was a man clothed in linen, whose thighs were adorned with pure gold of Uphaz. 6 His body also was like beryl, and his face like the appearance of lightning, and his eyes like flaming torches. His arms and his feet were like burnished bronze. The voice of his

words was like the voice of a multitude. 7 I, Daniel, alone saw the vision; for the men who were with me didn't see the vision; but a great quaking fell on them, and they fled to hide themselves. 8 So I was left alone, and saw this great vision. No strength remained in me; for my face grew deathly pale, and I retained no strength. 9 Yet I heard the voice of his words. When I heard the voice of his words, then I fell into a deep sleep on my face, with my face toward the ground. 10 Behold, a hand touched me, which set me on my knees and on the palms of my hands. 11 He said to me, "Daniel, you greatly beloved man, understand the words that I speak to you. Stand upright, for I have been sent to you, now." When he had spoken this word to me, I stood trembling. 12 Then he said to me, "Don't be afraid, Daniel; for from the first day that you set your heart to understand, and to humble yourself before your God, your words were heard. I have come for your words' sake. 13 But the prince of the kingdom of Persia withstood me twenty-one days; but, behold, Michael, one of the chief princes, came to help me because I remained there with the kings of Persia. 14 Now I have come to make you understand what will happen to your people in the latter days; for the vision is yet for many days." 15 When he had spoken these words to me, I set my face toward the ground, and was mute. 16 Behold, one in the likeness of the sons of men touched my lips. Then I opened my mouth, and spoke and said to him who stood before me, "My lord, by reason of the vision my sorrows have overtaken me, and I retain no strength. 17 For how can the servant of my lord talk with my lord? For as for me, immediately there remained no strength in me. There was no breath left in me." 18 Then one like the appearance of a man touched me again, and he strengthened me. 19 He said, "Greatly beloved man, don't be afraid. Peace be to you. Be strong. Yes, be strong." When he spoke to me, I was strengthened, and said, "Let my lord speak; for you have strengthened me." 20 Then he said, "Do you know why I have come to you? Now I will return to fight with the prince of Persia. When I go out, behold, the prince of Greece will come. 21 But I will tell you what is inscribed in the writing of truth. There is no one who supports me against these except Michael, your prince.

11

1 "As for me, in the first year of Darius the Mede, I stood up to confirm and strengthen him. 2 "Now I will show you the truth. Behold, three more kings will stand up in Persia. The fourth will be far richer than all of them. When he has grown strong through his riches, he will stir up all against the realm of Greece. 3 A mighty king will stand up who will rule with great dominion, and

do according to his will. 4 When he stands up, his kingdom will be broken, and will be divided toward the four winds of the sky, but not to his posterity, nor according to his dominion with which he ruled; for his kingdom will be plucked up, even for others besides these. 5 "The king of the south will be strong. One of his princes will become stronger than him and have dominion. His dominion will be a great dominion. 6 At the end of years they will join themselves together. The daughter of the king of the south will come to the king of the north to make an agreement, but she will not retain the strength of her arm. He will also not stand, nor will his arm; but she will be given up, with those who brought her and he who became her father, and he who strengthened her in those times. 7 "But out of a shoot from her roots one will stand up in his place who will come to the army and will enter into the fortress of the king of the north, and will deal against them and will prevail. 8 He will also carry their gods, with their molten images and their precious vessels of silver and of gold, captive into Egypt. He will refrain some years from the king of the north. 9 He will come into the realm of the king of the south, but he will return into his own land. 10 His sons will wage war and will assemble a multitude of great forces which will keep coming and overflow and pass through. They will return and wage war, even to his fortress. 11 "The king of the south will be moved with anger and will come out and fight with him, even with the king of the north. He will send out a great multitude, and the multitude will be given into his hand. 12 The multitude will be lifted up, and his heart will be exalted. He will cast down tens of thousands, but he won't prevail. 13 The king of the north will return, and will send out a multitude greater than the former. He will come on at the end of the times, even of years, with a great army and with abundant supplies. 14 "In those times many will stand up against the king of the south. Also the children of the violent among your people will lift themselves up to establish the vision; but they will fall. 15 So the king of the north will come and cast up a mound, and take a well-fortified city. The forces of the south won't stand, neither will his chosen people, neither will there be any strength to stand. 16 But he who comes against him will do according to his own will, and no one will stand before him. He will stand in the glorious land, and destruction will be in his hand. 17 He will set his face to come with the strength of his whole kingdom, and with him equitable conditions. He will perform them. He will give him the daughter of women to corrupt her; but she will not stand, and won't be for him. 18 After this he will turn his face to the islands, and will take many; but a prince will cause the reproach offered by him to cease. Yes, moreover, he will cause his reproach to turn on him. 19 Then he will turn his face toward the fortresses of his own land; but he will stumble and fall, and won't be found. 20"Then one who will cause a tax collector to pass through the kingdom to maintain its glory will stand up in his place; but within few days he shall be destroyed, not in anger, and not in battle. 21"In his place, a contemptible person will stand up, to whom they had not given the honor of the kingdom; but he will come in time of security, and will obtain the kingdom by flatteries. 22 The overwhelming forces will be overwhelmed from before him, and will be broken. Yes, also the prince of the covenant. 23 After the treaty is made with him, he will work deceitfully; for he will come up, and will become strong with a small people. 24 In time of security, he will come even on the fattest places of the province. He will do that which his fathers have not done, nor his fathers' fathers. He will scatter among them prey, plunder, and substance. Yes, he will devise his plans against the strongholds, even for a time. 25"He will stir up his power and his courage against the king of the south with a great army; and the king of the south will wage war in battle with an exceedingly great and mighty army; but he won't stand, for they will devise plans against him. 26 Yes, those who eat of his delicacies will destroy him, and his army will be swept away. Many will fall down slain. 27 As for both these kings, their hearts will be to do mischief, and they will speak lies at one table; but it won't prosper, for the end will still be at the appointed time. 28 Then he will return into his land with great wealth. His heart will be against the holy covenant. He will take action and return to his own land. 29"He will return at the appointed time and come into the south; but it won't be in the latter time as it was in the former. 30 For ships of Kittim will come against him. Therefore he will be grieved, and will return, and have indignation against the holy covenant, and will take action. He will even return, and have regard to those who forsake the holy covenant. 31"Forces will stand on his part and they will profane the sanctuary, even the fortress, and will take away the continual burnt offering. Then they will set up the abomination that makes desolate. 32 He will corrupt those who do wickedly against the covenant by flatteries; but the people who know their God will be strong and take action. 33"Those who are wise among the people will instruct many; yet they will fall by the sword and by flame, by captivity and by plunder, many days. 34 Now when they fall, they will be helped with a little help; but many will join themselves to them with flatteries. 35 Some of those who are wise will fall, to refine them, and to purify, and to make them white, even to the time of the end; because it is yet for the appointed time. ³⁶"The king will do according to his will. He will exalt himself, and magnify himself above every god, and will speak marvelous things against the God of gods. He will prosper until the indignation is accomplished; for what is determined will be done. ³⁷ He won't regard the gods of his fathers, or the desire of women, or regard any god; for he will magnify himself above all. ³⁸ But in his place he will honor the god of fortresses. He will honor a god whom his fathers didn't know with gold, silver, precious stones, and pleasant things. ³⁹ He will deal with the strongest fortresses by the help of a foreign god. He will increase with glory whoever acknowledges him. He will cause them to rule over many, and will divide the land for a price. ⁴⁰"At the time of the end, the king of the south will contend with him; and the king of the north will come against him like a whirlwind, with chariots, with horsemen, and with many ships. He will enter into the countries, and will overflow and pass through. ⁴¹ He will enter also into the glorious land, and many countries will be overthrown; but these will be delivered out of his hand: Edom, Moab, and the chief of the children of Ammon. ⁴² He will also stretch out his hand against the countries. The land of Egypt won't escape. ⁴³ But he will have power over the treasures of gold and of silver, and over all the precious things of Egypt. The Libyans and the Ethiopians will be at his steps. ⁴⁴ But news out of the east and out of the north will trouble him; and he will go out with great fury to destroy and utterly to sweep away many. ⁴⁵ He will plant the tents of his palace between the sea and the glorious holy mountain; yet he will come to his end, and no one will help him.

12

¹"At that time Michael will stand up, the great prince who stands for the children of your people. There will be a time of trouble, such as never was since there was a nation even to that same time. At that time, your people will be delivered—everyone who is found written in the book. ² Many of those who sleep in the dust of the earth will awake, some to everlasting life, and some to shame and everlasting contempt. ³ Those who are wise will shine as the brightness of the expanse. Those who turn many to righteousness will shine like the stars forever and ever. ⁴ But you, Daniel, shut up the words and seal the book, even to the time of the end. Many will run back and forth, and knowledge will be increased."

⁵ Then I, Daniel, looked, and behold, two others stood, one on the river bank

on this side, and the other on the river bank on that side. 6 One said to the man clothed in linen, who was above the waters of the river, "How long will it be to the end of these wonders?" 7 I heard the man clothed in linen, who was above the waters of the river, when he held up his right hand and his left hand to heaven, and swore by him who lives forever that it will be for a time, times, and a half; and when they have finished breaking in pieces the power of the holy people, all these things will be finished. 8 I heard, but I didn't understand. Then I said, "My lord, what will be the outcome of these things?" 9 He said, "Go your way, Daniel; for the words are shut up and sealed until the time of the end. 10 Many will purify themselves, make themselves white, and be refined; but the wicked will do wickedly. None of the wicked will understand; but those who are wise will understand. 11"From the time that the continual burnt offering is taken away and the abomination that makes desolate set up, there will be one thousand two hundred ninety days. 12 Blessed is he who waits and comes to the one thousand three hundred thirty-five days. 13"But go your way until the end; for you will rest and will stand in your inheritance at the end of the days."

The History of Susanna

13

¹ A man lived in Babylon, and his name was Joakim. ² He took a wife, whose name was Susanna, the daughter of Helkias, a very fair woman, and one who feared the Lord. ³ Her parents were also righteous, and taught their daughter according to the law of Moses. ⁴ Now Joakim was a great rich man, and had a beautiful garden next to his house. The Jews used to come to him, because he was more honorable than all others. ⁵ The same year, two of the elders of the people were appointed to be judges, such as the Lord spoke of, that wickedness came from Babylon from elders who were judges, who were supposed to govern the people. ⁶ These were often at Joakim's house. All that had any lawsuits came to them. ⁷ When the people departed away at noon, Susanna went into her husband's garden to walk. ⁸ The two elders saw her going in every day and walking; and they were inflamed with lust for her. ⁹ They perverted their own mind and turned away their eyes, that they might not look to heaven, nor remember just judgments. ¹⁰ And although they both were wounded with lust for her, yet dared not show the other his grief. ¹¹ For they were ashamed to declare their lust, what they desired to do with her. ¹² Yet they watched eagerly from day to day to see her. ¹³ The one said to the other, "Let's go home, now; for it is dinner time." ¹⁴ So when they had gone out, they parted company, and turning back again, they came to the same place. After they had asked one another the cause, they acknowledged their lust. Then they appointed a time both together, when they might find her alone. ¹⁵ It happened, as they watched on an opportune day, she went in as before with only two maids, and she desired to wash herself in the garden; for it was hot. ¹⁶ There was nobody there except the two elders who had hid themselves and watched her. ¹⁷ Then she said to her maids, "Bring me olive oil and ointment, and shut the garden doors, that I may wash myself." ¹⁸ They did as she asked them and shut the garden doors, and went out themselves at the side doors to fetch the things that she had commanded them. They didn't see the elders, because they were hidden. ¹⁹ Now when the maids had gone out, the two elders rose up and ran to her, saying, ²⁰"Behold, the garden doors are shut, that no man can see us, and we are in love with you. Therefore consent to us, and lie with us. ²¹ If you will not, we will testify against you, that a young man was with you; therefore you sent your maids away from you." ²² Then Susanna sighed, and said, "I am trapped; for if I do this thing, it

is death to me. If I don't do it, I can't escape your hands. 23 It is better for me to fall into your hands, and not do it, than to sin in the sight of the Lord." 24 With that Susanna cried with a loud voice; and the two elders cried out against her. 25 Then one of them ran and opened the garden doors. 26 So when the servants of the house heard the cry in the garden, they rushed in at the side door to see what had happened to her. 27 But when the elders had told their tale, the servants were greatly ashamed; for there was never such a report made of Susanna. 28 It came to pass on the next day, when the people assembled to her husband Joakim, the two elders came full of their wicked intent against Susanna to put her to death, 29 and said before the people, "Send for Susanna, the daughter of Helkias, Joakim's wife." So they sent; 30 and she came with her father and mother, her children, and all her kindred. 31 Now Susanna was a very delicate woman, and beautiful to behold. 32 These wicked men commanded her to be unveiled, for she was veiled, that they might be filled with her beauty. 33 Therefore her friends and all who saw her wept. 34 Then the two elders stood up in the midst of the people and laid their hands upon her head. 35 She, weeping, looked up toward heaven; for her heart trusted in the Lord. 36 The elders said, "As we walked in the garden alone, this woman came in with two maids, shut the garden doors, and sent the maids away. 37 Then a young man who was hidden there came to her and lay with her. 38 And we, being in a corner of the garden, saw this wickedness and ran to them. 39 And when we saw them together, we couldn't hold the man; for he was stronger than we, and opened the doors, and leaped out. 40 But having taken this woman, we asked who the young man was, but she would not tell us. We testify these things. 41 Then the assembly believed them, as those who were elders of the people and judges; so they condemned her to death. 42 Then Susanna cried out with a loud voice, and said, "O everlasting God, you know the secrets, and know all things before they happen. 43 You know that they have testified falsely against me. Behold, I must die, even though I never did such things as these men have maliciously invented against me." 44 The Lord heard her voice. 45 Therefore when she was led away to be put to death, God raised up the holy spirit of a young youth, whose name was Daniel. 46 He cried with a loud voice, "I am clear from the blood of this woman!" 47 Then all the people turned them toward him, and said, "What do these words that you have spoken mean?" 48 So he, standing in the midst of them, said, "Are you all such fools, you sons of Israel, that without examination or knowledge of the truth you have condemned a daughter of Israel? 49 Return again to the place of judgment; for these have testified falsely against her." 50 Therefore all the people turned again in haste, and the elders said to him, "Come, sit down among us, and show it to us, seeing God has given you the honor of an elder." 51 Then Daniel said to them, "Put them far apart from each another, and I will examine them." 52 So when they were put apart one from another, he called one of them, and said to him, "O you who have become old in wickedness, now your sins have returned which you have committed before, 53 in pronouncing unjust judgment, condemning the innocent, and letting the guilty go free; although the Lord says, 'You shall not kill the innocent and righteous.' 54 Now then, if you saw her, tell me, under which tree did you see them companying together?" He answered, "Under a mastick tree." 55 And Daniel said, "You have certainly lied against your own head; for even now the angel of God has received the sentence of God and will cut you in two." 56 So he put him aside, and commanded to bring the other, and said to him, "O you seed of Canaan, and not of Judah, beauty has deceived you, and lust has perverted your heart. 57 Thus you have dealt with the daughters of Israel, and they for fear were intimate with you; but the daughter of Judah would not tolerate your wickedness. 58 Now therefore tell me, under which tree did you take them being intimate together?" He answered, "Under an evergreen oak tree." 59 Then Daniel said to him, "You have also certainly lied against your own head; for the angel of God waits with the sword to cut you in two, that he may destroy you." 60 With that, all the assembly cried out with a loud voice, and blessed God, who saves those who hope in him. 61 Then they arose against the two elders, for Daniel had convicted them of false testimony out of their own mouth. 62 According to the law of Moses they did to them what they maliciously intended to do to their neighbor. They put them to death, and the innocent blood was saved the same day. 63 Therefore Helkias and his wife praised God for their daughter Susanna, with Joakim her husband, and all the kindred, because there was no dishonesty found in her. 64 And from that day forth, Daniel had a great reputation in the sight of the people.

Bel and the Dragon

14

1 King Astyages was gathered to his fathers, and Cyrus the Persian received his kingdom. 2 Daniel lived with the king, and was honored above all his friends. 3 Now the Babylonians had an idol called Bel, and every day twelve great measures of fine flour, forty sheep, and six firkins of wine were spent on it. 4 The king honored it and went daily to worship it; but Daniel worshiped his own God. The king said to him, "Why don't you worship Bel?" 5 He said, "Because I may not honor idols made with hands, but only the living God, who has created the sky and the earth, and has sovereignty over all flesh." 6 Then the king said to him, "Don't you think that Bel is a living god? Don't you see how much he eats and drinks every day?" 7 Then Daniel laughed, and said, "O king, don't be deceived; for this is just clay inside, and brass outside, and never ate or drank anything." 8 So the king was angry, and called for his priests, and said to them, "If you don't tell me who this is who devours these expenses, you shall die. 9 But if you can show me that Bel devours them, then Daniel shall die; for he has spoken blasphemy against Bel." Daniel said to the king, "Let it be according to your word." 10 Now there were seventy priests of Bel, besides their wives and children. The king went with Daniel into Bel's temple. 11 So Bel's priests said, "Behold, we will leave; but you, O king, set out the food, and mix the wine and set it out, shut the door securely, and seal it with your own signet. 12 When you come in the morning, if you don't find that Bel has eaten everything, we will suffer death, or else Daniel, who speaks falsely against us." 13 They weren't concerned, for under the table they had made a secret entrance, by which they entered in continually, and consumed those things. 14 It happened, when they had gone out, the king set the food before Bel. Now Daniel had commanded his servants to bring ashes, and they scattered them all over the temple in the presence of the king alone. Then they went out, shut the door, sealed it with the king's signet, and so departed. 15 Now in the night, the priests came with their wives and children, as they usually did, and ate and drank it all. 16 In the morning, the king arose, and Daniel with him. 17 The king said, "Daniel, are the seals whole?" He said, "Yes, O king, they are whole." 18 And as soon as he had opened the door, the king looked at the table, and cried with a loud voice, "You are great, O Bel, and with you is no deceit at all!" 19 Then Daniel laughed, and held the king that he should not go in, and said, "Behold now the pavement, and mark well

whose footsteps these are." 20 The king said, "I see the footsteps of men, women, and children." Then the king was angry, 21 and took the priests with their wives and children, who showed him the secret doors, where they came in and consumed the things that were on the table. 22 Therefore the king killed them, and delivered Bel into Daniel's power, who overthrew it and its temple. 23 In that same place there was a great dragon which the people of Babylon worshiped. 24 The king said to Daniel, "Will you also say that this is of brass? Behold, he lives, eats and drinks. You can't say that he is no living god. Therefore worship him." 25 Then Daniel said, "I will worship the Lord my God; for he is a living God. 26 But allow me, O king, and I will kill this dragon without sword or staff." The king said, "I allow you." 27 Then Daniel took pitch, fat, and hair, and melted them together, and made lumps of them. He put these in the dragon's mouth, so the dragon ate and burst apart. Daniel said, "Behold, these are the gods you all worship." 28 When the people of Babylon heard that, they took great indignation, and conspired against the king, saying, "The king has become a Jew. He has pulled down Bel, slain the dragon, and put the priests to the sword." 29 So they came to the king, and said, "Deliver Daniel to us, or else we will destroy you and your house." 30 Now when the king saw that they trapped him, being constrained, the king delivered Daniel to them. 31 They cast him into the lion's den, where he was six days. 32 There were seven lions in the den, and they had been giving them two carcasses and two sheep every day, which then were not given to them, intending that they would devour Daniel. 33 Now there was in Jewry the prophet Habakkuk, who had made stew, and had broken bread into a bowl. He was going into the field to bring it to the reapers. 34 But the angel of the Lord said to Habakkuk, "Go carry the dinner that you have into Babylon to Daniel, in the lions' den." 35 Habakkuk said, "Lord, I never saw Babylon. I don't know where the den is." 36 Then the angel of the Lord took him by the crown, and lifted him up by the hair of his head, and with the blast of his breath set him in Babylon over the den. 37 Habakkuk cried, saying, "O Daniel, Daniel, take the dinner which God has sent you." 38 Daniel said, "You have remembered me, O God! You haven't forsaken those who love you!" 39 So Daniel arose and ate; and the angel of God set Habakkuk in his own place again immediately. 40 On the seventh day, the king came to mourn for Daniel. When he came to the den, he looked in, and, behold, Daniel was sitting. 41 Then the king cried with a loud voice, saying, "Great are you, O Lord, you God of Daniel, and there is none other beside you!" 42 So he drew him out, and cast those that were the cause of his destruction into the den; and they were devoured in a moment before his face.

The Book of Hosea

1

¹ Yahweh's word that came to Hosea the son of Beeri, in the days of Uzziah, Jotham, Ahaz, and Hezekiah, kings of Judah, and in the days of Jeroboam the son of Joash, king of Israel. ² When Yahweh spoke at first by Hosea, Yahweh said to Hosea, "Go, take for yourself a wife of prostitution and children of unfaithfulness; for the land commits great adultery, forsaking Yahweh." ³ So he went and took Gomer the daughter of Diblaim; and she conceived, and bore him a son. ⁴ Yahweh said to him, "Call his name Jezreel, for yet a little while, and I will avenge the blood of Jezreel on the house of Jehu, and will cause the kingdom of the house of Israel to cease. ⁵ It will happen in that day that I will break the bow of Israel in the valley of Jezreel." ⁶ She conceived again, and bore a daughter. Then he said to him, "Call her name Lo-Ruhamah, for I will no longer have mercy on the house of Israel, that I should in any way pardon them. ⁷ But I will have mercy on the house of Judah, and will save them by Yahweh their God, and will not save them by bow, sword, battle, horses, or horsemen." ⁸ Now when she had weaned Lo-Ruhamah, she conceived, and bore a son. ⁹ He said, "Call his name Lo-Ammi, for you are not my people, and I will not be yours. ¹⁰ Yet the number of the children of Israel will be as the sand of the sea, which can't be measured or counted; and it will come to pass that, in the place where it was said to them, 'You are not my people,' they will be called 'sons of the living God.' ¹¹ The children of Judah and the children of Israel will be gathered together, and they will appoint themselves one head, and will go up from the land; for great will be the day of Jezreel.

2

¹"Say to your brothers, 'My people!' and to your sisters, 'My loved one!' ² Contend with your mother! Contend, for she is not my wife, neither am I her husband; and let her put away her prostitution from her face, and her adulteries from between her breasts; ³ lest I strip her naked, and make her bare as in the day that she was born, and make her like a wilderness, and set her like a dry land, and kill her with thirst. ⁴ Indeed, on her children I will have no mercy, for they are children of unfaithfulness. ⁵ For their mother has played the prostitute. She who conceived them has done shamefully; for she said, 'I will go after my lovers, who give me my bread and my water, my wool and my flax, my oil and my drink.' ⁶ Therefore behold, I will hedge up

your way with thorns, and I will build a wall against her, that she can't find her way. ⁷ She will follow after her lovers, but she won't overtake them; and she will seek them, but won't find them. Then she will say, 'I will go and return to my first husband, for then it was better with me than now.' ⁸ For she didn't know that I gave her the grain, the new wine, and the oil, and multiplied to her silver and gold, which they used for Baal. ⁹ Therefore I will take back my grain in its time, and my new wine in its season, and will pluck away my wool and my flax which should have covered her nakedness. ¹⁰ Now I will uncover her lewdness in the sight of her lovers, and no one will deliver her out of my hand. ¹¹ I will also cause all her celebrations to cease: her feasts, her new moons, her Sabbaths, and all her solemn assemblies. ¹² I will lay waste her vines and her fig trees, about which she has said, 'These are my wages that my lovers have given me,' and I will make them a forest, and the animals of the field shall eat them. ¹³ I will visit on her the days of the Baals, to which she burned incense when she decked herself with her earrings and her jewels, and went after her lovers and forgot me," says Yahweh. ¹⁴"Therefore behold, I will allure her, and bring her into the wilderness, and speak tenderly to her. ¹⁵ I will give her vineyards from there, and the valley of Achor for a door of hope; and she will respond there as in the days of her youth, and as in the day when she came up out of the land of Egypt. ¹⁶ It will be in that day," says Yahweh, "that you will call me 'my husband,' and no longer call me 'my master.' ¹⁷ For I will take away the names of the Baals out of her mouth, and they will no longer be mentioned by name. ¹⁸ In that day I will make a covenant for them with the animals of the field, and with the birds of the sky, and with the creeping things of the ground. I will break the bow, the sword, and the battle out of the land, and will make them lie down safely. ¹⁹ I will betroth you to me forever. Yes, I will betroth you to me in righteousness, in justice, in loving kindness, and in compassion. ²⁰ I will even betroth you to me in faithfulness; and you shall know Yahweh. ²¹ It will happen in that day, that I will respond," says Yahweh. "I will respond to the heavens, and they will respond to the earth; ²² and the earth will respond to the grain, and the new wine, and the oil; and they will respond to Jezreel. ²³ I will sow her to me in the earth; and I will have mercy on her who had not obtained mercy; and I will tell those who were not my people, 'You are my people;' and they will say, 'You are My God!'"

3

¹ Yahweh said to me, "Go again, love a woman loved by another, and an

adulteress, even as Yahweh loves the children of Israel, though they turn to other gods, and love cakes of raisins." 2 So I bought her for myself for fifteen pieces of silver and a homer and a half of barley. 3 I said to her, "You shall stay with me many days. You shall not play the prostitute, and you shall not be with any other man. I will also be so toward you." 4 For the children of Israel shall live many days without king, without prince, without sacrifice, without sacred stone, and without ephod or idols. 5 Afterward the children of Israel shall return and seek Yahweh their God, and David their king, and shall come with trembling to Yahweh and to his blessings in the last days.

4

1 Hear Yahweh's word, you children of Israel, for Yahweh has a charge against the inhabitants of the land: "Indeed there is no truth, nor goodness, nor knowledge of God in the land. 2 There is cursing, lying, murder, stealing, and committing adultery; they break boundaries, and bloodshed causes bloodshed. 3 Therefore the land will mourn, and everyone who dwells in it will waste away, with all living things in her, even the animals of the field and the birds of the sky; yes, the fish of the sea also die. 4 "Yet let no man bring a charge, neither let any man accuse; for your people are like those who bring charges against a priest. 5 You will stumble in the day, and the prophet will also stumble with you in the night; and I will destroy your mother. 6 My people are destroyed for lack of knowledge. Because you have rejected knowledge, I will also reject you, that you may be no priest to me. Because you have forgotten your God's law, I will also forget your children. 7 As they were multiplied, so they sinned against me. I will change their glory into shame. 8 They feed on the sin of my people, and set their heart on their iniquity. 9 It will be like people, like priest; and I will punish them for their ways, and will repay them for their deeds. 10 They will eat, and not have enough. They will play the prostitute, and will not increase; because they have abandoned listening to Yahweh. 11 Prostitution, wine, and new wine take away understanding. 12 My people consult with their wooden idol, and answer to a stick of wood. Indeed the spirit of prostitution has led them astray, and they have been unfaithful to their God. 13 They sacrifice on the tops of the mountains, and burn incense on the hills, under oaks, poplars, and terebinths, because its shade is good. Therefore your daughters play the prostitute, and your brides commit adultery. 14 I will not punish your daughters when they play the prostitute, nor your brides when they commit adultery; because the men consort with prostitutes, and they sacrifice with the shrine prostitutes; so

the people without understanding will come to ruin. 15"Though you, Israel, play the prostitute, yet don't let Judah offend; and don't come to Gilgal, neither go up to Beth Aven, nor swear, 'As Yahweh lives.' 16 For Israel has behaved extremely stubbornly, like a stubborn heifer. Then how will Yahweh feed them like a lamb in a meadow? 17 Ephraim is joined to idols. Leave him alone! 18 Their drink has become sour. They play the prostitute continually. Her rulers dearly love their shameful way. 19 The wind has wrapped her up in its wings; and they shall be disappointed because of their sacrifices.

5

1"Listen to this, you priests! Listen, house of Israel, and give ear, house of the king! For the judgment is against you; for you have been a snare at Mizpah, and a net spread on Tabor. 2 The rebels are deep in slaughter, but I discipline all of them. 3 I know Ephraim, and Israel is not hidden from me; for now, Ephraim, you have played the prostitute. Israel is defiled. 4 Their deeds won't allow them to turn to their God, for the spirit of prostitution is within them, and they don't know Yahweh. 5 The pride of Israel testifies to his face. Therefore Israel and Ephraim will stumble in their iniquity. Judah also will stumble with them. 6 They will go with their flocks and with their herds to seek Yahweh, but they won't find him. He has withdrawn himself from them. 7 They are unfaithful to Yahweh; for they have borne illegitimate children. Now the new moon will devour them with their fields. 8"Blow the cornet in Gibeah, and the trumpet in Ramah! Sound a battle cry at Beth Aven, behind you, Benjamin! 9 Ephraim will become a desolation in the day of rebuke. Among the tribes of Israel, I have made known that which will surely be. 10 The princes of Judah are like those who remove a landmark. I will pour out my wrath on them like water. 11 Ephraim is oppressed, he is crushed in judgment, because he is intent in his pursuit of idols. 12 Therefore I am to Ephraim like a moth, and to the house of Judah like rottenness. 13"When Ephraim saw his sickness, and Judah his wound, then Ephraim went to Assyria, and sent to King Jareb: but he is not able to heal you, neither will he cure you of your wound. 14 For I will be to Ephraim like a lion, and like a young lion to the house of Judah. I myself will tear in pieces and go away. I will carry off, and there will be no one to deliver. 15 I will go and return to my place, until they acknowledge their offense, and seek my face. In their affliction they will seek me earnestly."

6

1"Come! Let's return to Yahweh; for he has torn us to pieces, and he will heal us; he has injured us, and he will bind up our wounds. 2 After two days he will revive us. On the third day he will raise us up, and we will live before him. 3 Let's acknowledge Yahweh. Let's press on to know Yahweh. As surely as the sun rises, Yahweh will appear. He will come to us like the rain, like the spring rain that waters the earth." 4"Ephraim, what shall I do to you? Judah, what shall I do to you? For your love is like a morning cloud, and like the dew that disappears early. 5 Therefore I have cut them to pieces with the prophets; I killed them with the words of my mouth. Your judgments are like a flash of lightning. 6 For I desire mercy, and not sacrifice; and the knowledge of God more than burnt offerings. 7 But they, like Adam, have broken the covenant. They were unfaithful to me there. 8 Gilead is a city of those who work iniquity; it is stained with blood. 9 As gangs of robbers wait to ambush a man, so the company of priests murder on the path toward Shechem, committing shameful crimes. 10 In the house of Israel I have seen a horrible thing. There is prostitution in Ephraim. Israel is defiled. 11"Also, Judah, there is a harvest appointed for you, when I restore the fortunes of my people.

7

1 When I would heal Israel, then the iniquity of Ephraim is uncovered, also the wickedness of Samaria; for they commit falsehood, and the thief enters in, and the gang of robbers ravages outside. 2 They don't consider in their hearts that I remember all their wickedness. Now their own deeds have engulfed them. They are before my face. 3 They make the king glad with their wickedness, and the princes with their lies. 4 They are all adulterers. They are burning like an oven that the baker stops stirring, from the kneading of the dough, until it is leavened. 5 On the day of our king, the princes made themselves sick with the heat of wine. He joined his hand with mockers. 6 For they have prepared their heart like an oven, while they lie in wait. Their anger smolders all night. In the morning it burns as a flaming fire. 7 They are all hot as an oven, and devour their judges. All their kings have fallen. There is no one among them who calls to me. 8 Ephraim mixes himself among the nations. Ephraim is a pancake not turned over. 9 Strangers have devoured his strength, and he doesn't realize it. Indeed, gray hairs are here and there on him, and he doesn't realize it. 10 The pride of Israel testifies to his face; yet they haven't returned to Yahweh their God, nor sought him, for all this. 11"Ephraim is like an easily deceived dove, without understanding. They call to Egypt. They go to Assyria. 12 When they go, I will spread my net on them.

I will bring them down like the birds of the sky. I will chastise them, as their congregation has heard. ¹³ Woe to them! For they have wandered from me. Destruction to them! For they have trespassed against me. Though I would redeem them, yet they have spoken lies against me. ¹⁴ They haven't cried to me with their heart, but they howl on their beds. They assemble themselves for grain and new wine. They turn away from me. ¹⁵ Though I have taught and strengthened their arms, yet they plot evil against me. ¹⁶ They return, but not to the Most High. They are like a faulty bow. Their princes will fall by the sword for the rage of their tongue. This will be their derision in the land of Egypt.

8

¹"Put the trumpet to your lips! Something like an eagle is over Yahweh's house, because they have broken my covenant and rebelled against my law. ² They cry to me, 'My God, we, Israel, acknowledge you!' ³ Israel has cast off that which is good. The enemy will pursue him. ⁴ They have set up kings, but not by me. They have made princes, and I didn't approve. Of their silver and their gold they have made themselves idols, that they may be cut off. ⁵ Let Samaria throw out his calf idol! My anger burns against them! How long will it be until they are capable of purity? ⁶ For this is even from Israel! The workman made it, and it is no God; indeed, the calf of Samaria shall be broken in pieces. ⁷ For they sow the wind, and they will reap the whirlwind. He has no standing grain. The stalk will yield no head. If it does yield, strangers will swallow it up. ⁸ Israel is swallowed up. Now they are among the nations like a worthless thing. ⁹ For they have gone up to Assyria, like a wild donkey wandering alone. Ephraim has hired lovers for himself. ¹⁰ But although they sold themselves among the nations, I will now gather them; and they begin to waste away because of the oppression of the king of mighty ones. ¹¹ Because Ephraim has multiplied altars for sinning, they became for him altars for sinning. ¹² I wrote for him the many things of my law, but they were regarded as a strange thing. ¹³ As for the sacrifices of my offerings, they sacrifice meat and eat it, but Yahweh doesn't accept them. Now he will remember their iniquity, and punish their sins. They will return to Egypt. ¹⁴ For Israel has forgotten his Maker and built palaces; and Judah has multiplied fortified cities; but I will send a fire on his cities, and it will devour its fortresses."

9

1 Don't rejoice, Israel, to jubilation like the nations; for you were unfaithful to your God. You love the wages of a prostitute at every grain threshing floor. 2 The threshing floor and the wine press won't feed them, and the new wine will fail her. 3 They won't dwell in Yahweh's land; but Ephraim will return to Egypt, and they will eat unclean food in Assyria. 4 They won't pour out wine offerings to Yahweh, neither will they be pleasing to him. Their sacrifices will be to them like the bread of mourners; all who eat of it will be polluted; for their bread will be for their appetite. It will not come into Yahweh's house. 5 What will you do in the day of solemn assembly, and in the day of the feast of Yahweh? 6 For, behold, when they flee destruction, Egypt will gather them up. Memphis will bury them. Nettles will possess their pleasant things of silver. Thorns will be in their tents. 7 The days of visitation have come. The days of reckoning have come. Israel will consider the prophet to be a fool, and the man who is inspired to be insane, because of the abundance of your sins, and because your hostility is great. 8 A prophet watches over Ephraim with my God. A fowler's snare is on all of his paths, and hostility in the house of his God. 9 They have deeply corrupted themselves, as in the days of Gibeah. He will remember their iniquity. He will punish them for their sins. 10 I found Israel like grapes in the wilderness. I saw your fathers as the first ripe in the fig tree at its first season; but they came to Baal Peor, and consecrated themselves to the shameful thing, and became abominable like that which they loved. 11 As for Ephraim, their glory will fly away like a bird. There will be no birth, no one with child, and no conception. 12 Though they bring up their children, yet I will bereave them, so that not a man shall be left. Indeed, woe also to them when I depart from them! 13 I have seen Ephraim, like Tyre, planted in a pleasant place; but Ephraim will bring out his children to the murderer. 14 Give them—Yahweh what will you give? Give them a miscarrying womb and dry breasts. 15"All their wickedness is in Gilgal; for there I hated them. Because of the wickedness of their deeds, I will drive them out of my house! I will love them no more. All their princes are rebels. 16 Ephraim is struck. Their root has dried up. They will bear no fruit. Even though they give birth, yet I will kill the beloved ones of their womb." 17 My God will cast them away, because they didn't listen to him; and they will be wanderers among the nations.

10

1 Israel is a luxuriant vine that produces his fruit. According to the abundance of his fruit he has multiplied his altars. As their land has

prospered, they have adorned their sacred stones. 2 Their heart is divided. Now they will be found guilty. He will demolish their altars. He will destroy their sacred stones. 3 Surely now they will say, "We have no king; for we don't fear Yahweh; and the king, what can he do for us?" 4 They make promises, swearing falsely in making covenants. Therefore judgment springs up like poisonous weeds in the furrows of the field. 5 The inhabitants of Samaria will be in terror for the calves of Beth Aven, for its people will mourn over it, along with its priests who rejoiced over it, for its glory, because it has departed from it. 6 It also will be carried to Assyria for a present to a great king. Ephraim will receive shame, and Israel will be ashamed of his own counsel. 7 Samaria and her king float away like a twig on the water. 8 The high places also of Aven, the sin of Israel, will be destroyed. The thorn and the thistle will come up on their altars. They will tell the mountains, "Cover us!" and the hills, "Fall on us!" 9"Israel, you have sinned from the days of Gibeah. There they remained. The battle against the children of iniquity doesn't overtake them in Gibeah. 10 When it is my desire, I will chastise them; and the nations will be gathered against them when they are bound to their two transgressions. 11 Ephraim is a trained heifer that loves to thresh, so I will put a yoke on her beautiful neck. I will set a rider on Ephraim. Judah will plow. Jacob will break his clods. 12 Sow to yourselves in righteousness, reap according to kindness. Break up your fallow ground, for it is time to seek Yahweh, until he comes and rains righteousness on you. 13 You have plowed wickedness. You have reaped iniquity. You have eaten the fruit of lies, for you trusted in your way, in the multitude of your mighty men. 14 Therefore a battle roar will arise among your people, and all your fortresses will be destroyed, as Shalman destroyed Beth Arbel in the day of battle. The mother was dashed in pieces with her children. 15 So Bethel will do to you because of your great wickedness. At daybreak the king of Israel will be destroyed.

11

1"When Israel was a child, then I loved him, and called my son out of Egypt. 2 They called to them, so they went from them. They sacrificed to the Baals, and burned incense to engraved images. 3 Yet I taught Ephraim to walk. I took them by their arms, but they didn't know that I healed them. 4 I drew them with cords of a man, with ties of love; and I was to them like those who lift up the yoke on their necks; and I bent down to him and I fed him. 5"They won't return into the land of Egypt; but the Assyrian will be their king, because they refused to repent. 6 The sword will fall on their cities, and will destroy the bars of their gates, and will put an end to their plans. 7 My people are determined to turn from me. Though they call to the Most High, he certainly won't exalt them. 8"How can I give you up, Ephraim? How can I hand you over, Israel? How can I make you like Admah? How can I make you like Zeboiim? My heart is turned within me, my compassion is aroused. 9 I will not execute the fierceness of my anger. I will not return to destroy Ephraim, for I am God, and not man—the Holy One among you. I will not come in wrath. 10 They will walk after Yahweh, who will roar like a lion; for he will roar, and the children will come trembling from the west. 11 They will come trembling like a bird out of Egypt, and like a dove out of the land of Assyria; and I will settle them in their houses," says Yahweh. 12 Ephraim surrounds me with falsehood, and the house of Israel with deceit. Judah still strays from God, and is unfaithful to the Holy One.

12

1 Ephraim feeds on wind, and chases the east wind. He continually multiplies lies and desolation. They make a covenant with Assyria, and oil is carried into Egypt. 2 Yahweh also has a controversy with Judah, and will punish Jacob according to his ways; according to his deeds he will repay him. 3 In the womb he took his brother by the heel, and in his manhood he contended with God. 4 Indeed, he struggled with the angel, and prevailed; he wept, and made supplication to him. He found him at Bethel, and there he spoke with us — 5 even Yahweh, the God of Armies. Yahweh is his name of renown! 6 Therefore turn to your God. Keep kindness and justice, and wait continually for your God. 7 A merchant has dishonest scales in his hand. He loves to defraud. 8 Ephraim said, "Surely I have become rich. I have found myself wealth. In all my wealth they won't find in me any iniquity that is sin." 9"But I am Yahweh your God from the land of Egypt. I will yet again make you dwell in tents, as in the days of the solemn feast. 10 I have also spoken to the prophets, and I have multiplied visions; and by the ministry of the prophets I have used parables. 11 If Gilead is wicked, surely they are worthless. In Gilgal they sacrifice bulls. Indeed, their altars are like heaps in the furrows of the field. 12 Jacob fled into the country of Aram. Israel served to get a wife. For a wife he tended flocks and herds. 13 By a prophet Yahweh brought Israel up out of Egypt, and by a prophet he was preserved. 14 Ephraim has bitterly provoked anger. Therefore his blood will be left on him, and his Lord will repay his contempt.

13

1 When Ephraim spoke, there was trembling. He exalted himself in Israel, but when he became guilty through Baal, he died. 2 Now they sin more and more, and have made themselves molten images of their silver, even idols according to their own understanding, all of them the work of the craftsmen. They say of them, 'They offer human sacrifice and kiss the calves.' 3 Therefore they will be like the morning mist, like the dew that passes away early, like the chaff that is driven with the whirlwind out of the threshing floor, and like the smoke out of the chimney. 4 "Yet I am Yahweh your God from the land of Egypt; and you shall acknowledge no god but me, and besides me there is no savior. 5 I knew you in the wilderness, in the land of great drought. 6 According to their pasture, so were they filled; they were filled, and their heart was exalted. Therefore they have forgotten me. 7 Therefore I am like a lion to them. Like a leopard, I will lurk by the path. 8 I will meet them like a bear that is bereaved of her cubs, and will tear the covering of their heart. There I will devour them like a lioness. The wild animal will tear them. 9 You are destroyed, Israel, because you are against me, against your helper. 10 Where is your king now, that he may save you in all your cities? And your judges, of whom you said, 'Give me a king and princes'? 11 I have given you a king in my anger, and have taken him away in my wrath. 12 The guilt of Ephraim is stored up. His sin is stored up. 13 The sorrows of a travailing woman will come on him. He is an unwise son, for when it is time, he doesn't come to the opening of the womb. 14 I will ransom them from the power of Sheol. I will redeem them from death! Death, where are your plagues? Sheol, where is your destruction? "Compassion will be hidden from my eyes. 15 Though he is fruitful among his brothers, an east wind will come, the breath of Yahweh coming up from the wilderness; and his spring will become dry, and his fountain will be dried up. He will plunder the storehouse of treasure. 16 Samaria will bear her guilt, for she has rebelled against her God. They will fall by the sword. Their infants will be dashed in pieces, and their pregnant women will be ripped open."

14

1 Israel, return to Yahweh your God; for you have fallen because of your sin. 2 Take words with you, and return to Yahweh. Tell him, "Forgive all our sins, and accept that which is good; so we offer bulls as we vowed of our lips. 3 Assyria can't save us. We won't ride on horses; neither will we say any more

to the work of our hands, 'Our gods!' for in you the fatherless finds mercy."
⁴"I will heal their waywardness. I will love them freely; for my anger is turned away from them. ⁵ I will be like the dew to Israel. He will blossom like the lily, and send down his roots like Lebanon. ⁶ His branches will spread, and his beauty will be like the olive tree, and his fragrance like Lebanon. ⁷ Men will dwell in his shade. They will revive like the grain, and blossom like the vine. Their fragrance will be like the wine of Lebanon. ⁸ Ephraim, what have I to do any more with idols? I answer, and will take care of him. I am like a green cypress tree; from me your fruit is found." ⁹ Who is wise, that he may understand these things? Who is prudent, that he may know them? For the ways of Yahweh are right, and the righteous walk in them, but the rebellious stumble in them.

The Book of Joel

1

1 Yahweh's word that came to Joel, the son of Pethuel. 2 Hear this, you elders, and listen, all you inhabitants of the land! Has this ever happened in your days, or in the days of your fathers? 3 Tell your children about it, and have your children tell their children, and their children, another generation. 4 What the swarming locust has left, the great locust has eaten. What the great locust has left, the grasshopper has eaten. What the grasshopper has left, the caterpillar has eaten. 5 Wake up, you drunkards, and weep! Wail, all you drinkers of wine, because of the sweet wine, for it is cut off from your mouth. 6 For a nation has come up on my land, strong, and without number. His teeth are the teeth of a lion, and he has the fangs of a lioness. 7 He has laid my vine waste, and stripped my fig tree. He has stripped its bark, and thrown it away. Its branches are made white. 8 Mourn like a virgin dressed in sackcloth for the husband of her youth! 9 The meal offering and the drink offering are cut off from Yahweh's house. The priests, Yahweh's ministers, mourn. 10 The field is laid waste. The land mourns, for the grain is destroyed, The new wine has dried up, and the oil languishes. 11 Be confounded, you farmers! Wail, you vineyard keepers, for the wheat and for the barley; for the harvest of the field has perished. 12 The vine has dried up, and the fig tree withered— the pomegranate tree, the palm tree also, and the apple tree, even all of the trees of the field are withered; for joy has withered away from the sons of men. 13 Put on sackcloth and mourn, you priests! Wail, you ministers of the altar. Come, lie all night in sackcloth, you ministers of my God, for the meal offering and the drink offering are withheld from your God's house. 14 Sanctify a fast. Call a solemn assembly. Gather the elders and all the inhabitants of the land to the house of Yahweh, your God, and cry to Yahweh. 15 Alas for the day! For the day of Yahweh is at hand, and it will come as destruction from the Almighty. 16 Isn't the food cut off before our eyes, joy and gladness from the house of our God? 17 The seeds rot under their clods. The granaries are laid desolate. The barns are broken down, for the grain has withered. 18 How the animals groan! The herds of livestock are perplexed, because they have no pasture. Yes, the flocks of sheep are made desolate. 19 Yahweh, I cry to you, for the fire has devoured the pastures of the wilderness, and the flame has burned all the trees of the field. 20 Yes, the animals of the field pant to you, for the water brooks have dried up, and the

fire has devoured the pastures of the wilderness.

2

1 Blow the trumpet in Zion, and sound an alarm in my holy mountain! Let all the inhabitants of the land tremble, for the day of Yahweh comes, for it is close at hand: 2 A day of darkness and gloominess, a day of clouds and thick darkness. As the dawn spreading on the mountains, a great and strong people; there has never been the like, neither will there be any more after them, even to the years of many generations. 3 A fire devours before them, and behind them, a flame burns. The land is as the garden of Eden before them, and behind them, a desolate wilderness. Yes, and no one has escaped them. 4 Their appearance is as the appearance of horses, and they run as horsemen. 5 Like the noise of chariots on the tops of the mountains, they leap, like the noise of a flame of fire that devours the stubble, like a strong people set in battle array. 6 At their presence the peoples are in anguish. All faces have grown pale. 7 They run like mighty men. They climb the wall like warriors. They each march in his line, and they don't swerve off course. 8 One doesn't jostle another. They each march in their own path. They burst through the defenses and don't break ranks. 9 They rush on the city. They run on the wall. They climb up into the houses. They enter in at the windows like thieves. 10 The earth quakes before them. The heavens tremble. The sun and the moon are darkened, and the stars withdraw their shining. 11 Yahweh thunders his voice before his army, for his forces are very great; for he is strong who obeys his command; for the day of Yahweh is great and very awesome, and who can endure it? 12"Yet even now," says Yahweh, "turn to me with all your heart, and with fasting, and with weeping, and with mourning." 13 Tear your heart and not your garments, and turn to Yahweh, your God; for he is gracious and merciful, slow to anger, and abundant in loving kindness, and relents from sending calamity. 14 Who knows? He may turn and relent, and leave a blessing behind him, even a meal offering and a drink offering to Yahweh, your God. 15 Blow the trumpet in Zion! Sanctify a fast. Call a solemn assembly. 16 Gather the people.Sanctify the assembly. Assemble the elders. Gather the children, and those who nurse from breasts. Let the bridegroom go out of his room, and the bride out of her chamber. 17 Let the priests, the ministers of Yahweh, weep between the porch and the altar, and let them say, "Spare your people, Yahweh, and don't give your heritage to reproach, that the nations should rule over them. Why should they say among the peoples, 'Where is their God?'" 18 Then Yahweh was jealous for his land,

and had pity on his people. ¹⁹ Yahweh answered his people, "Behold, I will send you grain, new wine, and oil, and you will be satisfied with them; and I will no more make you a reproach among the nations. ²⁰ But I will remove the northern army far away from you, and will drive it into a barren and desolate land, its front into the eastern sea, and its back into the western sea; and its stench will come up, and its bad smell will rise." Surely he has done great things. ²¹ Land, don't be afraid. Be glad and rejoice, for Yahweh has done great things. ²² Don't be afraid, you animals of the field; for the pastures of the wilderness spring up, for the tree bears its fruit. The fig tree and the vine yield their strength. ²³"Be glad then, you children of Zion, and rejoice in Yahweh, your God; for he gives you the early rain in just measure, and he causes the rain to come down for you, the early rain and the latter rain, as before. ²⁴ The threshing floors will be full of wheat, and the vats will overflow with new wine and oil. ²⁵ I will restore to you the years that the swarming locust has eaten, the great locust, the grasshopper, and the caterpillar, my great army, which I sent among you. ²⁶ You will have plenty to eat and be satisfied, and will praise the name of Yahweh, your God, who has dealt wondrously with you; and my people will never again be disappointed. ²⁷ You will know that I am among Israel, and that I am Yahweh, your God, and there is no one else; and my people will never again be disappointed. ²⁸"It will happen afterward, that I will pour out my Spirit on all flesh; and your sons and your daughters will prophesy. Your old men will dream dreams. Your young men will see visions. ²⁹ And also on the servants and on the handmaids in those days, I will pour out my Spirit. ³⁰ I will show wonders in the heavens and in the earth: blood, fire, and pillars of smoke. ³¹ The sun will be turned into darkness, and the moon into blood, before the great and terrible day of Yahweh comes. ³² It will happen that whoever will call on Yahweh's name shall be saved; for in Mount Zion and in Jerusalem there will be those who escape, as Yahweh has said, and among the remnant, those whom Yahweh calls.

3

¹"For, behold, in those days, and in that time, when I restore the fortunes of Judah and Jerusalem, ² I will gather all nations, and will bring them down into the valley of Jehoshaphat; and I will execute judgment on them there for my people, and for my heritage, Israel, whom they have scattered among the nations. They have divided my land, ³ and have cast lots for my people, and have given a boy for a prostitute, and sold a girl for wine, that they may

drink. 4"Yes, and what are you to me, Tyre and Sidon, and all the regions of Philistia? Will you repay me? And if you repay me, I will swiftly and speedily return your repayment on your own head. 5 Because you have taken my silver and my gold, and have carried my finest treasures into your temples, 6 and have sold the children of Judah and the children of Jerusalem to the sons of the Greeks, that you may remove them far from their border. 7 Behold, I will stir them up out of the place where you have sold them, and will return your repayment on your own head; 8 and I will sell your sons and your daughters into the hands of the children of Judah, and they will sell them to the men of Sheba, to a faraway nation, for Yahweh has spoken it." 9 Proclaim this among the nations: "Prepare for war! Stir up the mighty men. Let all the warriors draw near. Let them come up. 10 Beat your plowshares into swords, and your pruning hooks into spears. Let the weak say, 'I am strong.' 11 Hurry and come, all you surrounding nations, and gather yourselves together." Cause your mighty ones to come down there, Yahweh. 12"Let the nations arouse themselves, and come up to the valley of Jehoshaphat; for there I will sit to judge all the surrounding nations. 13 Put in the sickle; for the harvest is ripe. Come, tread, for the wine press is full, the vats overflow, for their wickedness is great." 14 Multitudes, multitudes in the valley of decision! For the day of Yahweh is near in the valley of decision. 15 The sun and the moon are darkened, and the stars withdraw their shining. 16 Yahweh will roar from Zion, and thunder from Jerusalem; and the heavens and the earth will shake; but Yahweh will be a refuge to his people, and a stronghold to the children of Israel. 17"So you will know that I am Yahweh, your God, dwelling in Zion, my holy mountain. Then Jerusalem will be holy, and no strangers will pass through her any more. 18 It will happen in that day, that the mountains will drop down sweet wine, the hills will flow with milk, all the brooks of Judah will flow with waters; and a fountain will flow out from Yahweh's house, and will water the valley of Shittim. 19 Egypt will be a desolation and Edom will be a desolate wilderness, for the violence done to the children of Judah, because they have shed innocent blood in their land. 20 But Judah will be inhabited forever, and Jerusalem from generation to generation. 21 I will cleanse their blood that I have not cleansed, for Yahweh dwells in Zion."

The Book of Amos

1

1 The words of Amos, who was among the herdsmen of Tekoa, which he saw concerning Israel in the days of Uzziah king of Judah and in the days of Jeroboam the son of Joash, king of Israel, two years before the earthquake. 2 He said: "Yahweh will roar from Zion, and utter his voice from Jerusalem; and the pastures of the shepherds will mourn, and the top of Carmel will wither." 3 Yahweh says: "For three transgressions of Damascus, yes, for four, I will not turn away its punishment, because they have threshed Gilead with threshing instruments of iron; 4 but I will send a fire into the house of Hazael, and it will devour the palaces of Ben Hadad. 5 I will break the bar of Damascus, and cut off the inhabitant from the valley of Aven, and him who holds the scepter from the house of Eden; and the people of Syria shall go into captivity to Kir," says Yahweh. 6 Yahweh says: "For three transgressions of Gaza, yes, for four, I will not turn away its punishment, because they carried away captive the whole community, to deliver them up to Edom; 7 but I will send a fire on the wall of Gaza, and it will devour its palaces. 8 I will cut off the inhabitant from Ashdod, and him who holds the scepter from Ashkelon; and I will turn my hand against Ekron; and the remnant of the Philistines will perish," says the Lord Yahweh. 9 Yahweh says: "For three transgressions of Tyre, yes, for four, I will not turn away its punishment; because they delivered up the whole community to Edom, and didn't remember the brotherly covenant; 10 but I will send a fire on the wall of Tyre, and it will devour its palaces." 11 Yahweh says: "For three transgressions of Edom, yes, for four, I will not turn away its punishment, because he pursued his brother with the sword and cast off all pity, and his anger raged continually, and he kept his wrath forever; 12 but I will send a fire on Teman, and it will devour the palaces of Bozrah." 13 Yahweh says: "For three transgressions of the children of Ammon, yes, for four, I will not turn away its punishment, because they have ripped open the pregnant women of Gilead, that they may enlarge their border. 14 But I will kindle a fire in the wall of Rabbah, and it will devour its palaces, with shouting in the day of battle, with a storm in the day of the whirlwind; 15 and their king will go into captivity, he and his princes together," says Yahweh.

2

1 Yahweh says: "For three transgressions of Moab, yes, for four, I will not

turn away its punishment, because he burned the bones of the king of Edom into lime; 2 but I will send a fire on Moab, and it will devour the palaces of Kerioth; and Moab will die with tumult, with shouting, and with the sound of the trumpet; 3 and I will cut off the judge from among them, and will kill all its princes with him," says Yahweh. 4 Yahweh says: "For three transgressions of Judah, yes, for four, I will not turn away its punishment, because they have rejected Yahweh's law, and have not kept his statutes, and their lies have led them astray, after which their fathers walked; 5 but I will send a fire on Judah, and it will devour the palaces of Jerusalem." 6 Yahweh says: "For three transgressions of Israel, yes, for four, I will not turn away its punishment, because they have sold the righteous for silver, and the needy for a pair of sandals; 7 They trample the heads of the poor into the dust of the earth and deny justice to the oppressed. A man and his father use the same maiden, to profane my holy name. 8 They lay themselves down beside every altar on clothes taken in pledge. In the house of their God they drink the wine of those who have been fined. 9 Yet I destroyed the Amorite before them, whose height was like the height of the cedars, and he was strong as the oaks; yet I destroyed his fruit from above, and his roots from beneath. 10 Also I brought you up out of the land of Egypt and led you forty years in the wilderness, to possess the land of the Amorite. 11 I raised up some of your sons for prophets, and some of your young men for Nazirites. Isn't this true, you children of Israel?" says Yahweh. 12"But you gave the Nazirites wine to drink, and commanded the prophets, saying, 'Don't prophesy!' 13 Behold, I will crush you in your place, as a cart crushes that is full of grain. 14 Flight will perish from the swift. The strong won't strengthen his force. The mighty won't deliver himself. 15 He who handles the bow won't stand. He who is swift of foot won't escape. He who rides the horse won't deliver himself. 16 He who is courageous among the mighty will flee away naked on that day," says Yahweh.

3

1 Hear this word that Yahweh has spoken against you, children of Israel, against the whole family which I brought up out of the land of Egypt, saying: 2"I have only chosen you of all the families of the earth. Therefore I will punish you for all of your sins." 3 Do two walk together, unless they have agreed? 4 Will a lion roar in the thicket, when he has no prey? Does a young lion cry out of his den, if he has caught nothing? 5 Can a bird fall in a trap on the earth, where no snare is set for him? Does a snare spring up from the

ground, when there is nothing to catch? 6 Does the trumpet alarm sound in a city, without the people being afraid? Does evil happen to a city, and Yahweh hasn't done it? 7 Surely the Lord Yahweh will do nothing, unless he reveals his secret to his servants the prophets. 8 The lion has roared. Who will not fear? The Lord Yahweh has spoken. Who can but prophesy? 9 Proclaim in the palaces at Ashdod, and in the palaces in the land of Egypt, and say, "Assemble yourselves on the mountains of Samaria, and see what unrest is in her, and what oppression is among them." 10"Indeed they don't know to do right," says Yahweh, "Who hoard plunder and loot in their palaces." 11 Therefore the Lord Yahweh says: "An adversary will overrun the land; and he will pull down your strongholds, and your fortresses will be plundered." 12 Yahweh says: "As the shepherd rescues out of the mouth of the lion two legs, or a piece of an ear, so shall the children of Israel be rescued who sit in Samaria on the corner of a couch, and on the silken cushions of a bed." 13"Listen, and testify against the house of Jacob," says the Lord Yahweh, the God of Armies. 14"For in the day that I visit the transgressions of Israel on him, I will also visit the altars of Bethel; and the horns of the altar will be cut off, and fall to the ground. 15 I will strike the winter house with the summer house; and the houses of ivory will perish, and the great houses will have an end," says Yahweh.

4

1 Listen to this word, you cows of Bashan, who are on the mountain of Samaria, who oppress the poor, who crush the needy, who tell their husbands, "Bring us drinks!" 2 The Lord Yahweh has sworn by his holiness, "Behold, the days shall come on you that they will take you away with hooks, and the last of you with fish hooks. 3 You will go out at the breaks in the wall, everyone straight before her; and you will cast yourselves into Harmon," says Yahweh. 4"Go to Bethel, and sin; to Gilgal, and sin more. Bring your sacrifices every morning, your tithes every three days, 5 offer a sacrifice of thanksgiving of that which is leavened, and proclaim free will offerings and brag about them; for this pleases you, you children of Israel," says the Lord Yahweh. 6"I also have given you cleanness of teeth in all your cities, and lack of bread in every town; yet you haven't returned to me," says Yahweh. 7"I also have withheld the rain from you, when there were yet three months to the harvest; and I caused it to rain on one city, and caused it not to rain on another city. One field was rained on, and the field where it didn't rain withered. 8 So two or three cities staggered to one city to drink water, and

were not satisfied; yet you haven't returned to me," says Yahweh. 9"I struck you with blight and mildew many times in your gardens and your vineyards, and the swarming locusts have devoured your fig trees and your olive trees; yet you haven't returned to me," says Yahweh. 10"I sent plagues among you like I did Egypt. I have slain your young men with the sword, and have carried away your horses. I filled your nostrils with the stench of your camp, yet you haven't returned to me," says Yahweh. 11"I have overthrown some of you, as when God overthrew Sodom and Gomorrah, and you were like a burning stick plucked out of the fire; yet you haven't returned to me," says Yahweh. 12"Therefore I will do this to you, Israel; because I will do this to you, prepare to meet your God, Israel. 13 For, behold, he who forms the mountains, creates the wind, declares to man what is his thought, who makes the morning darkness, and treads on the high places of the earth: Yahweh, the God of Armies, is his name."

5

1 Listen to this word which I take up for a lamentation over you, O house of Israel: 2"The virgin of Israel has fallen; She shall rise no more. She is cast down on her land; there is no one to raise her up." 3 For the Lord Yahweh says: "The city that went out a thousand shall have a hundred left, and that which went out one hundred shall have ten left to the house of Israel." 4 For Yahweh says to the house of Israel: "Seek me, and you will live; 5 but don't seek Bethel, nor enter into Gilgal, and don't pass to Beersheba; for Gilgal shall surely go into captivity, and Bethel shall come to nothing. 6 Seek Yahweh, and you will live, lest he break out like fire in the house of Joseph, and it devour, and there be no one to quench it in Bethel. 7 You who turn justice to wormwood, and cast down righteousness to the earth! 8 Seek him who made the Pleiades and Orion, and turns the shadow of death into the morning, and makes the day dark with night; who calls for the waters of the sea, and pours them out on the surface of the earth, Yahweh is his name, 9 who brings sudden destruction on the strong, so that destruction comes on the fortress. 10 They hate him who reproves in the gate, and they abhor him who speaks blamelessly. 11 Therefore, because you trample on the poor and take taxes from him of wheat, you have built houses of cut stone, but you will not dwell in them. You have planted pleasant vineyards, but you shall not drink their wine. 12 For I know how many are your offenses, and how great are your sins— you who afflict the just, who take a bribe, and who turn away the needy in the courts. 13 Therefore a prudent person keeps silent in such a time,

for it is an evil time. 14 Seek good, and not evil, that you may live; and so Yahweh, the God of Armies, will be with you, as you say. 15 Hate evil, love good, and establish justice in the courts. It may be that Yahweh, the God of Armies, will be gracious to the remnant of Joseph." 16 Therefore Yahweh, the God of Armies, the Lord, says: "Wailing will be in all the wide ways. They will say in all the streets, 'Alas! Alas!' They will call the farmer to mourning, and those who are skillful in lamentation to wailing. 17 In all vineyards there will be wailing, for I will pass through the middle of you," says Yahweh. 18"Woe to you who desire the day of Yahweh! Why do you long for the day of Yahweh? It is darkness, and not light. 19 As if a man fled from a lion, and a bear met him; or he went into the house and leaned his hand on the wall, and a snake bit him. 20 Won't the day of Yahweh be darkness, and not light? Even very dark, and no brightness in it? 21 I hate, I despise your feasts, and I can't stand your solemn assemblies. 22 Yes, though you offer me your burnt offerings and meal offerings, I will not accept them; neither will I regard the peace offerings of your fat animals. 23 Take away from me the noise of your songs! I will not listen to the music of your harps. 24 But let justice roll on like rivers, and righteousness like a mighty stream. 25"Did you bring to me sacrifices and offerings in the wilderness forty years, house of Israel? 26 You also carried the tent of your king and the shrine of your images, the star of your god, which you made for yourselves. 27 Therefore I will cause you to go into captivity beyond Damascus," says Yahweh, whose name is the God of Armies.

6

1 Woe to those who are at ease in Zion, and to those who are secure on the mountain of Samaria, the notable men of the chief of the nations, to whom the house of Israel come! 2 Go to Calneh, and see. From there go to Hamath the great. Then go down to Gath of the Philistines. Are they better than these kingdoms? Is their border greater than your border? 3 Alas for you who put far away the evil day, and cause the seat of violence to come near, 4 who lie on beds of ivory, and stretch themselves on their couches, and eat the lambs out of the flock, and the calves out of the middle of the stall, 5 who strum on the strings of a harp, who invent for themselves instruments of music, like David; 6 who drink wine in bowls, and anoint themselves with the best oils, but they are not grieved for the affliction of Joseph. 7 Therefore they will now go captive with the first who go captive. The feasting and lounging will end. 8"The Lord Yahweh has sworn by himself," says Yahweh, the God of

Armies: "I abhor the pride of Jacob, and detest his fortresses. Therefore I will deliver up the city with all that is in it. 9 It will happen that if ten men remain in one house, they will die. 10"When a man's relative carries him, even he who burns him, to bring bodies out of the house, and asks him who is in the innermost parts of the house, 'Is there yet any with you?' And he says, 'No;' then he will say, 'Hush! Indeed we must not mention Yahweh's name.' 11"For, behold, Yahweh commands, and the great house will be smashed to pieces, and the little house into bits. 12 Do horses run on the rocky crags? Does one plow there with oxen? But you have turned justice into poison, and the fruit of righteousness into bitterness, 13 you who rejoice in a thing of nothing, who say, 'Haven't we taken for ourselves horns by our own strength?' 14 For, behold, I will raise up against you a nation, house of Israel," says Yahweh, the God of Armies; "and they will afflict you from the entrance of Hamath to the brook of the Arabah."

7

1 Thus the Lord Yahweh showed me: behold, he formed locusts in the beginning of the shooting up of the latter growth; and behold, it was the latter growth after the king's harvest. 2 When they finished eating the grass of the land, then I said, "Lord Yahweh, forgive, I beg you! How could Jacob stand? For he is small." 3 Yahweh relented concerning this. "It shall not be," says Yahweh. 4 Thus the Lord Yahweh showed me: behold, the Lord Yahweh called for judgment by fire; and it dried up the great deep, and would have devoured the land. 5 Then I said, "Lord Yahweh, stop, I beg you! How could Jacob stand? For he is small." 6 Yahweh relented concerning this. "This also shall not be," says the Lord Yahweh. 7 Thus he showed me: behold, the Lord stood beside a wall made by a plumb line, with a plumb line in his hand. 8 Yahweh said to me, "Amos, what do you see?" I said, "A plumb line." Then the Lord said, "Behold, I will set a plumb line in the middle of my people Israel. I will not again pass by them any more. 9 The high places of Isaac will be desolate, the sanctuaries of Israel will be laid waste; and I will rise against the house of Jeroboam with the sword." 10 Then Amaziah the priest of Bethel sent to Jeroboam king of Israel, saying, "Amos has conspired against you in the middle of the house of Israel. The land is not able to bear all his words. 11 For Amos says, 'Jeroboam will die by the sword, and Israel shall surely be led away captive out of his land.'" 12 Amaziah also said to Amos, "You seer, go, flee away into the land of Judah, and there eat bread, and prophesy there, 13 but don't prophesy again any more at Bethel; for it is the king's sanctuary,

and it is a royal house!" 14 Then Amos answered Amaziah, "I was no prophet, neither was I a prophet's son, but I was a herdsman, and a farmer of sycamore figs; 15 and Yahweh took me from following the flock, and Yahweh said to me, 'Go, prophesy to my people Israel.' 16 Now therefore listen to Yahweh's word: 'You say, Don't prophesy against Israel, and don't preach against the house of Isaac.' 17 Therefore Yahweh says: 'Your wife shall be a prostitute in the city, and your sons and your daughters shall fall by the sword, and your land shall be divided by line; and you yourself shall die in a land that is unclean, and Israel shall surely be led away captive out of his land.'"

8

1 Thus the Lord Yahweh showed me: behold, a basket of summer fruit. 2 He said, "Amos, what do you see?" I said, "A basket of summer fruit." Then Yahweh said to me, "The end has come on my people Israel. I will not again pass by them any more. 3 The songs of the temple will be wailing in that day," says the Lord Yahweh. "The dead bodies will be many. In every place they will throw them out with silence. 4 Hear this, you who desire to swallow up the needy, and cause the poor of the land to fail, 5 saying, 'When will the new moon be gone, that we may sell grain? And the Sabbath, that we may market wheat, making the ephah small, and the shekel large, and dealing falsely with balances of deceit; 6 that we may buy the poor for silver, and the needy for a pair of sandals, and sell the sweepings with the wheat?'" 7 Yahweh has sworn by the pride of Jacob, "Surely I will never forget any of their works. 8 Won't the land tremble for this, and everyone mourn who dwells in it? Yes, it will rise up wholly like the River; and it will be stirred up and sink again, like the River of Egypt. 9 It will happen in that day," says the Lord Yahweh, "that I will cause the sun to go down at noon, and I will darken the earth in the clear day. 10 I will turn your feasts into mourning, and all your songs into lamentation; and I will make you wear sackcloth on all your bodies, and baldness on every head. I will make it like the mourning for an only son, and its end like a bitter day. 11 Behold, the days come," says the Lord Yahweh, "that I will send a famine in the land, not a famine of bread, nor a thirst for water, but of hearing Yahweh's words. 12 They will wander from sea to sea, and from the north even to the east; they will run back and forth to seek Yahweh's word, and will not find it. 13 In that day the beautiful virgins and the young men will faint for thirst. 14 Those who swear by the sin of Samaria, and say, 'As your god, Dan, lives,' and, 'As the way of

Beersheba lives,' they will fall, and never rise up again."

9

1 I saw the Lord standing beside the altar, and he said, "Strike the tops of the pillars, that the thresholds may shake. Break them in pieces on the head of all of them. I will kill the last of them with the sword. Not one of them will flee away. Not one of them will escape. 2 Though they dig into Sheol, there my hand will take them; and though they climb up to heaven, there I will bring them down. 3 Though they hide themselves in the top of Carmel, I will search and take them out from there; and though they be hidden from my sight in the bottom of the sea, there I will command the serpent, and it will bite them. 4 Though they go into captivity before their enemies, there I will command the sword, and it will kill them. I will set my eyes on them for evil, and not for good. 5 For the Lord, Yahweh of Armies, is he who touches the land and it melts, and all who dwell in it will mourn; and it will rise up wholly like the River, and will sink again, like the River of Egypt. 6 It is he who builds his rooms in the heavens, and has founded his vault on the earth; he who calls for the waters of the sea, and pours them out on the surface of the earth— Yahweh is his name. 7 Are you not like the children of the Ethiopians to me, children of Israel?" says Yahweh. "Haven't I brought up Israel out of the land of Egypt, and the Philistines from Caphtor, and the Syrians from Kir? 8 Behold, the eyes of the Lord Yahweh are on the sinful kingdom, and I will destroy it from off the surface of the earth, except that I will not utterly destroy the house of Jacob," says Yahweh. 9"For behold, I will command, and I will sift the house of Israel among all the nations as grain is sifted in a sieve, yet not the least kernel will fall on the earth. 10 All the sinners of my people will die by the sword, who say, 'Evil won't overtake nor meet us.' 11 In that day I will raise up the tent of David who is fallen and close up its breaches, and I will raise up its ruins, and I will build it as in the days of old, 12 that they may possess the remnant of Edom and all the nations who are called by my name," says Yahweh who does this. 13"Behold, the days come," says Yahweh, "that the plowman shall overtake the reaper, and the one treading grapes him who sows seed; and sweet wine will drip from the mountains, and flow from the hills. 14 I will bring my people Israel back from captivity, and they will rebuild the ruined cities, and inhabit them; and they will plant vineyards, and drink wine from them. They shall also make gardens, and eat their fruit. 15 I will plant them on their land, and they will no more be plucked up out of their land which I have given them," says Yahweh

your God.

The Book of Obadiah

1

1 The vision of Obadiah. This is what the Lord Yahweh says about Edom. We have heard news from Yahweh, and an ambassador is sent among the nations, saying, "Arise, and let's rise up against her in battle. 2 Behold, I have made you small among the nations. You are greatly despised. 3 The pride of your heart has deceived you, you who dwell in the clefts of the rock, whose habitation is high, who says in his heart, 'Who will bring me down to the ground?' 4 Though you mount on high as the eagle, and though your nest is set among the stars, I will bring you down from there," says Yahweh. 5"If thieves came to you, if robbers by night—oh, what disaster awaits you— wouldn't they only steal until they had enough? If grape pickers came to you, wouldn't they leave some gleaning grapes? 6 How Esau will be ransacked! How his hidden treasures are sought out! 7 All the men of your alliance have brought you on your way, even to the border. The men who were at peace with you have deceived you, and prevailed against you. Friends who eat your bread lay a snare under you. There is no understanding in him." 8"Won't I in that day", says Yahweh, "destroy the wise men out of Edom, and understanding out of the mountain of Esau? 9 Your mighty men, Teman, will be dismayed, to the end that everyone may be cut off from the mountain of Esau by slaughter. 10 For the violence done to your brother Jacob, shame will cover you, and you will be cut off forever. 11 In the day that you stood on the other side, in the day that strangers carried away his substance and foreigners entered into his gates and cast lots for Jerusalem, even you were like one of them. 12 But don't look down on your brother in the day of his disaster, and don't rejoice over the children of Judah in the day of their destruction. Don't speak proudly in the day of distress. 13 Don't enter into the gate of my people in the day of their calamity. Don't look down on their affliction in the day of their calamity, neither seize their wealth on the day of their calamity. 14 Don't stand in the crossroads to cut off those of his who escape. Don't deliver up those of his who remain in the day of distress. 15 For the day of Yahweh is near all the nations! As you have done, it will be done to you. Your deeds will return upon your own head. 16 For as you have drunk on my holy mountain, so all the nations will drink continually. Yes, they will drink, swallow down, and will be as though they had not been. 17 But in Mount Zion, there will be those who escape, and it will be holy. The house of Jacob

will possess their possessions. **18** The house of Jacob will be a fire, the house of Joseph a flame, and the house of Esau for stubble. They will burn among them and devour them. There will not be any remaining to the house of Esau." Indeed, Yahweh has spoken. **19** Those of the South will possess the mountain of Esau, and those of the lowland, the Philistines. They will possess the field of Ephraim, and the field of Samaria. Benjamin will possess Gilead. **20** The captives of this army of the children of Israel, who are among the Canaanites, will possess even to Zarephath; and the captives of Jerusalem, who are in Sepharad, will possess the cities of the Negev. **21** Saviors will go up on Mount Zion to judge the mountains of Esau, and the kingdom will be Yahweh's.

The Book of Jonah

1

1 Now Yahweh's word came to Jonah the son of Amittai, saying, 2"Arise, go to Nineveh, that great city, and preach against it, for their wickedness has come up before me." 3 But Jonah rose up to flee to Tarshish from the presence of Yahweh. He went down to Joppa, and found a ship going to Tarshish; so he paid its fare, and went down into it, to go with them to Tarshish from the presence of Yahweh. 4 But Yahweh sent out a great wind on the sea, and there was a mighty storm on the sea, so that the ship was likely to break up. 5 Then the mariners were afraid, and every man cried to his god. They threw the cargo that was in the ship into the sea to lighten the ship. But Jonah had gone down into the innermost parts of the ship and he was laying down, and was fast asleep. 6 So the ship master came to him, and said to him, "What do you mean, sleeper? Arise, call on your God! Maybe your God will notice us, so that we won't perish." 7 They all said to each other, "Come! Let's cast lots, that we may know who is responsible for this evil that is on us." So they cast lots, and the lot fell on Jonah. 8 Then they asked him, "Tell us, please, for whose cause this evil is on us. What is your occupation? Where do you come from? What is your country? Of what people are you?" 9 He said to them, "I am a Hebrew, and I fear Yahweh, the God of heaven, who has made the sea and the dry land." 10 Then the men were exceedingly afraid, and said to him, "What have you done?" For the men knew that he was fleeing from the presence of Yahweh, because he had told them. 11 Then they said to him, "What shall we do to you, that the sea may be calm to us?" For the sea grew more and more stormy. 12 He said to them, "Take me up, and throw me into the sea. Then the sea will be calm for you; for I know that because of me this great storm is on you." 13 Nevertheless the men rowed hard to get them back to the land; but they could not, for the sea grew more and more stormy against them. 14 Therefore they cried to Yahweh, and said, "We beg you, Yahweh, we beg you, don't let us die for this man's life, and don't lay on us innocent blood; for you, Yahweh, have done as it pleased you." 15 So they took up Jonah and threw him into the sea; and the sea ceased its raging. 16 Then the men feared Yahweh exceedingly; and they offered a sacrifice to Yahweh and made vows. 17 Yahweh prepared a huge fish to swallow up Jonah, and Jonah was in the belly of the fish three days and three nights.

2

1 Then Jonah prayed to Yahweh, his God, out of the fish's belly. 2 He said, "I called because of my affliction to Yahweh. He answered me. Out of the belly of Sheol I cried. You heard my voice. 3 For you threw me into the depths, in the heart of the seas. The flood was all around me. All your waves and your billows passed over me. 4 I said, 'I have been banished from your sight; yet I will look again toward your holy temple.' 5 The waters surrounded me, even to the soul. The deep was around me. The weeds were wrapped around my head. 6 I went down to the bottoms of the mountains. The earth barred me in forever; yet you have brought my life up from the pit, Yahweh my God. 7"When my soul fainted within me, I remembered Yahweh. My prayer came in to you, into your holy temple. 8 Those who regard vain idols forsake their own mercy. 9 But I will sacrifice to you with the voice of thanksgiving. I will pay that which I have vowed. Salvation belongs to Yahweh." 10 Then Yahweh spoke to the fish, and it vomited out Jonah on the dry land.

3

1 Yahweh's word came to Jonah the second time, saying, 2"Arise, go to Nineveh, that great city, and preach to it the message that I give you." 3 So Jonah arose, and went to Nineveh, according to Yahweh's word. Now Nineveh was an exceedingly great city, three days' journey across. 4 Jonah began to enter into the city a day's journey, and he cried out, and said, "In forty days, Nineveh will be overthrown!" 5 The people of Nineveh believed God; and they proclaimed a fast and put on sackcloth, from their greatest even to their least. 6 The news reached the king of Nineveh, and he arose from his throne, took off his royal robe, covered himself with sackcloth, and sat in ashes. 7 He made a proclamation and published through Nineveh by the decree of the king and his nobles, saying, "Let neither man nor animal, herd nor flock, taste anything; let them not feed, nor drink water; 8 but let them be covered with sackcloth, both man and animal, and let them cry mightily to God. Yes, let them turn everyone from his evil way and from the violence that is in his hands. 9 Who knows whether God will not turn and relent, and turn away from his fierce anger, so that we might not perish?" 10 God saw their works, that they turned from their evil way. God relented of the disaster which he said he would do to them, and he didn't do it.

4

1 But it displeased Jonah exceedingly, and he was angry. 2 He prayed to

Yahweh, and said, "Please, Yahweh, wasn't this what I said when I was still in my own country? Therefore I hurried to flee to Tarshish, for I knew that you are a gracious God and merciful, slow to anger, and abundant in loving kindness, and you relent of doing harm. 3 Therefore now, Yahweh, take, I beg you, my life from me, for it is better for me to die than to live." 4 Yahweh said, "Is it right for you to be angry?" 5 Then Jonah went out of the city and sat on the east side of the city, and there made himself a booth and sat under it in the shade, until he might see what would become of the city. 6 Yahweh God prepared a vine and made it to come up over Jonah, that it might be a shade over his head to deliver him from his discomfort. So Jonah was exceedingly glad because of the vine. 7 But God prepared a worm at dawn the next day, and it chewed on the vine so that it withered. 8 When the sun arose, God prepared a sultry east wind; and the sun beat on Jonah's head, so that he was faint and requested for himself that he might die. He said, "It is better for me to die than to live." 9 God said to Jonah, "Is it right for you to be angry about the vine?" He said, "I am right to be angry, even to death." 10 Yahweh said, "You have been concerned for the vine, for which you have not labored, neither made it grow; which came up in a night and perished in a night. 11 Shouldn't I be concerned for Nineveh, that great city, in which are more than one hundred twenty thousand persons who can't discern between their right hand and their left hand, and also many animals?"

The Book of Micah

1

1 Yahweh's word that came to Micah of Morasheth in the days of Jotham, Ahaz, and Hezekiah, kings of Judah, which he saw concerning Samaria and Jerusalem. 2 Hear, you peoples, all of you! Listen, O earth, and all that is therein. Let the Lord Yahweh be witness against you, the Lord from his holy temple. 3 For behold, Yahweh comes out of his place, and will come down and tread on the high places of the earth. 4 The mountains melt under him, and the valleys split apart like wax before the fire, like waters that are poured down a steep place. 5"All this is for the disobedience of Jacob, and for the sins of the house of Israel. What is the disobedience of Jacob? Isn't it Samaria? And what are the high places of Judah? Aren't they Jerusalem? 6 Therefore I will make Samaria like a rubble heap of the field, like places for planting vineyards; and I will pour down its stones into the valley, and I will uncover its foundations. 7 All her idols will be beaten to pieces, all her temple gifts will be burned with fire, and I will destroy all her images; for of the hire of a prostitute has she gathered them, and to the hire of a prostitute shall they return." 8 For this I will lament and wail. I will go stripped and naked. I will howl like the jackals and mourn like the ostriches. 9 For her wounds are incurable; for it has come even to Judah. It reaches to the gate of my people, even to Jerusalem. 10 Don't tell it in Gath. Don't weep at all. At Beth Ophrah I have rolled myself in the dust. 11 Pass on, inhabitant of Shaphir, in nakedness and shame. The inhabitant of Zaanan won't come out. The wailing of Beth Ezel will take from you his protection. 12 For the inhabitant of Maroth waits anxiously for good, because evil has come down from Yahweh to the gate of Jerusalem. 13 Harness the chariot to the swift steed, inhabitant of Lachish. She was the beginning of sin to the daughter of Zion; for the transgressions of Israel were found in you. 14 Therefore you will give a parting gift to Moresheth Gath. The houses of Achzib will be a deceitful thing to the kings of Israel. 15 I will yet bring a conqueror to you, inhabitants of Mareshah. The glory of Israel will come to Adullam. 16 Shave your heads, and cut off your hair for the children of your delight. Enlarge your baldness like the vulture, for they have gone into captivity from you!

2

1 Woe to those who devise iniquity and work evil on their beds! When the morning is light, they practice it, because it is in the power of their hand. 2

They covet fields and seize them, and houses, then take them away. They oppress a man and his house, even a man and his heritage. ³ Therefore Yahweh says: "Behold, I am planning against these people a disaster, from which you will not remove your necks, neither will you walk haughtily, for it is an evil time. ⁴ In that day they will take up a parable against you, and lament with a doleful lamentation, saying, 'We are utterly ruined! My people's possession is divided up. Indeed he takes it from me and assigns our fields to traitors!'" ⁵ Therefore you will have no one who divides the land by lot in Yahweh's assembly. ⁶"Don't prophesy!"—they prophesy— "Don't prophesy about these things. Disgrace won't overtake us." ⁷ Shall it be said, O house of Jacob, "Is Yahweh's Spirit angry? Are these his doings? Don't my words do good to him who walks blamelessly?" ⁸ But lately my people have risen up as an enemy. You strip the robe and clothing from those who pass by without a care, returning from battle. ⁹ You drive the women of my people out from their pleasant houses; from their young children you take away my blessing forever. ¹⁰ Arise, and depart! For this is not your resting place, because of uncleanness that destroys, even with a grievous destruction. ¹¹ If a man walking in a spirit of falsehood lies, saying, "I will prophesy to you of wine and of strong drink," he would be the prophet of this people. ¹² I will surely assemble all of you, Jacob. I will surely gather the remnant of Israel. I will put them together as the sheep of Bozrah, as a flock in the middle of their pasture. They will swarm with people. ¹³ He who breaks open the way goes up before them. They break through the gate, and go out. Their king passes on before them, with Yahweh at their head.

3

¹ I said, "Please listen, you heads of Jacob, and rulers of the house of Israel: Isn't it for you to know justice? ² You who hate the good, and love the evil; who tear off their skin, and their flesh from off their bones; ³ who also eat the flesh of my people, and peel their skin from off them, and break their bones, and chop them in pieces, as for the pot, and as meat within the cauldron. ⁴ Then they will cry to Yahweh, but he will not answer them. Yes, he will hide his face from them at that time, because they made their deeds evil." ⁵ Yahweh says concerning the prophets who lead my people astray—for those who feed their teeth, they proclaim, "Peace!" and whoever doesn't provide for their mouths, they prepare war against him: ⁶"Therefore night is over you, with no vision, and it is dark to you, that you may not divine; and the sun will go down on the prophets, and the day will be black over them. ⁷ The seers

shall be disappointed, and the diviners confounded. Yes, they shall all cover their lips, for there is no answer from God." **8** But as for me, I am full of power by Yahweh's Spirit, and of judgment, and of might, to declare to Jacob his disobedience, and to Israel his sin. **9** Please listen to this, you heads of the house of Jacob, and rulers of the house of Israel, who abhor justice, and pervert all equity, **10** who build up Zion with blood, and Jerusalem with iniquity. **11** Her leaders judge for bribes, and her priests teach for a price, and her prophets of it tell fortunes for money; yet they lean on Yahweh, and say, "Isn't Yahweh among us? No disaster will come on us." **12** Therefore Zion for your sake will be plowed like a field, and Jerusalem will become heaps of rubble, and the mountain of the temple like the high places of a forest.

4

1 But in the latter days, it will happen that the mountain of Yahweh's temple will be established on the top of the mountains, and it will be exalted above the hills; and peoples will stream to it. **2** Many nations will go and say, "Come! Let's go up to the mountain of Yahweh, and to the house of the God of Jacob; and he will teach us of his ways, and we will walk in his paths." For the law will go out of Zion, and Yahweh's word from Jerusalem; **3** and he will judge between many peoples, and will decide concerning strong nations afar off. They will beat their swords into plowshares, and their spears into pruning hooks. Nation will not lift up sword against nation, neither will they learn war any more. **4** But every man will sit under his vine and under his fig tree. No one will make them afraid, for the mouth of Yahweh of Armies has spoken. **5** Indeed all the nations may walk in the name of their gods, but we will walk in the name of Yahweh our God forever and ever. **6** "In that day," says Yahweh, "I will assemble that which is lame, and I will gather that which is driven away, and that which I have afflicted; **7** and I will make that which was lame a remnant, and that which was cast far off a strong nation: and Yahweh will reign over them on Mount Zion from then on, even forever." **8** You, tower of the flock, the hill of the daughter of Zion, to you it will come. Yes, the former dominion will come, the kingdom of the daughter of Jerusalem. **9** Now why do you cry out aloud? Is there no king in you? Has your counselor perished, that pains have taken hold of you as of a woman in travail? **10** Be in pain, and labor to give birth, daughter of Zion, like a woman in travail; for now you will go out of the city, and will dwell in the field, and will come even to Babylon. There you will be rescued. There Yahweh will redeem you from the hand of your enemies. **11** Now many nations have assembled against you, that say, "Let her be defiled, and let our eye gloat over Zion." ¹² But they don't know the thoughts of Yahweh, neither do they understand his counsel; for he has gathered them like the sheaves to the threshing floor. ¹³ Arise and thresh, daughter of Zion, for I will make your horn iron, and I will make your hoofs bronze. You will beat in pieces many peoples. I will devote their gain to Yahweh, and their substance to the Lord of the whole earth.

5

¹ Now you shall gather yourself in troops, daughter of troops. He has laid siege against us. They will strike the judge of Israel with a rod on the cheek. ² But you, Bethlehem Ephrathah, being small among the clans of Judah, out of you one will come out to me who is to be ruler in Israel; whose goings out are from of old, from ancient times. ³ Therefore he will abandon them until the time that she who is in labor gives birth. Then the rest of his brothers will return to the children of Israel. ⁴ He shall stand, and shall shepherd in the strength of Yahweh, in the majesty of the name of Yahweh his God. They will live, for then he will be great to the ends of the earth. ⁵ He will be our peace when Assyria invades our land and when he marches through our fortresses, then we will raise against him seven shepherds, and eight leaders of men. ⁶ They will rule the land of Assyria with the sword, and the land of Nimrod in its gates. He will deliver us from the Assyrian, when he invades our land, and when he marches within our border. ⁷ The remnant of Jacob will be among many peoples like dew from Yahweh, like showers on the grass, that don't wait for man nor wait for the sons of men. ⁸ The remnant of Jacob will be among the nations, among many peoples, like a lion among the animals of the forest, like a young lion among the flocks of sheep; who, if he goes through, treads down and tears in pieces, and there is no one to deliver. ⁹ Let your hand be lifted up above your adversaries, and let all of your enemies be cut off. ¹⁰"It will happen in that day", says Yahweh, "that I will cut off your horses from among you and will destroy your chariots. ¹¹ I will cut off the cities of your land and will tear down all your strongholds. ¹² I will destroy witchcraft from your hand. You shall have no soothsayers. ¹³ I will cut off your engraved images and your pillars from among you; and you shall no more worship the work of your hands. ¹⁴ I will uproot your Asherah poles from among you; and I will destroy your cities. ¹⁵ I will execute vengeance in anger and wrath on the nations that didn't listen."

6

1 Listen now to what Yahweh says: "Arise, plead your case before the mountains, and let the hills hear what you have to say. 2 Hear, you mountains, Yahweh's indictment, and you enduring foundations of the earth; for Yahweh has a case against his people, and he will contend with Israel. 3 My people, what have I done to you? How have I burdened you? Answer me! 4 For I brought you up out of the land of Egypt, and redeemed you out of the house of bondage. I sent before you Moses, Aaron, and Miriam. 5 My people, remember now what Balak king of Moab devised, and what Balaam the son of Beor answered him from Shittim to Gilgal, that you may know the righteous acts of Yahweh." 6 How shall I come before Yahweh, and bow myself before the exalted God? Shall I come before him with burnt offerings, with calves a year old? 7 Will Yahweh be pleased with thousands of rams? With tens of thousands of rivers of oil? Shall I give my firstborn for my disobedience? The fruit of my body for the sin of my soul? 8 He has shown you, O man, what is good. What does Yahweh require of you, but to act justly, to love mercy, and to walk humbly with your God? 9 Yahweh's voice calls to the city— and wisdom fears your name— "Listen to the rod, and he who appointed it. 10 Are there yet treasures of wickedness in the house of the wicked, and a short ephah that is accursed? 11 Shall I tolerate dishonest scales, and a bag of deceitful weights? 12 Her rich men are full of violence, her inhabitants speak lies, and their tongue is deceitful in their speech. 13 Therefore I also have struck you with a grievous wound. I have made you desolate because of your sins. 14 You shall eat, but not be satisfied. Your hunger will be within you. You will store up, but not save, and that which you save I will give up to the sword. 15 You will sow, but won't reap. You will tread the olives, but won't anoint yourself with oil; and crush grapes, but won't drink the wine. 16 For the statutes of Omri are kept, and all the works of Ahab's house. You walk in their counsels, that I may make you a ruin, and your inhabitants a hissing. You will bear the reproach of my people."

7

1 Misery is mine! Indeed, I am like one who gathers the summer fruits, as gleanings of the vineyard. There is no cluster of grapes to eat. My soul desires to eat the early fig. 2 The godly man has perished out of the earth, and there is no one upright among men. They all lie in wait for blood; every man hunts his brother with a net. 3 Their hands are on that which is evil to do it

diligently. The ruler and judge ask for a bribe. The powerful man dictates the evil desire of his soul. Thus they conspire together. 4 The best of them is like a brier. The most upright is worse than a thorn hedge. The day of your watchmen, even your visitation, has come; now is the time of their confusion. 5 Don't trust in a neighbor. Don't put confidence in a friend. With the woman lying in your embrace, be careful of the words of your mouth! 6 For the son dishonors the father, the daughter rises up against her mother, the daughter-in-law against her mother-in-law; a man's enemies are the men of his own house. 7 But as for me, I will look to Yahweh. I will wait for the God of my salvation. My God will hear me. 8 Don't rejoice against me, my enemy. When I fall, I will arise. When I sit in darkness, Yahweh will be a light to me. 9 I will bear the indignation of Yahweh, because I have sinned against him, until he pleads my case and executes judgment for me. He will bring me out to the light. I will see his righteousness. 10 Then my enemy will see it, and shame will cover her who said to me, "Where is Yahweh your God?" My eyes will see her. Now she will be trodden down like the mire of the streets. 11 A day to build your walls! In that day, he will extend your boundary. 12 In that day they will come to you from Assyria and the cities of Egypt, and from Egypt even to the River, and from sea to sea, and mountain to mountain. 13 Yet the land will be desolate because of those who dwell therein, for the fruit of their doings. 14 Shepherd your people with your staff, the flock of your heritage, who dwell by themselves in a forest. Let them feed in the middle of fertile pasture land, in Bashan and Gilead, as in the days of old. 15 "As in the days of your coming out of the land of Egypt, I will show them marvelous things." 16 The nations will see and be ashamed of all their might. They will lay their hand on their mouth. Their ears will be deaf. 17 They will lick the dust like a serpent. Like crawling things of the earth, they will come trembling out of their dens. They will come with fear to Yahweh our God, and will be afraid because of you. 18 Who is a God like you, who pardons iniquity, and passes over the disobedience of the remnant of his heritage? He doesn't retain his anger forever, because he delights in loving kindness. 19 He will again have compassion on us. He will tread our iniquities under foot. You will cast all their sins into the depths of the sea. 20 You will give truth to Jacob, and mercy to Abraham, as you have sworn to our fathers from the days of old.

The Book of Nahum

1

1 A revelation about Nineveh. The book of the vision of Nahum the Elkoshite. 2 Yahweh is a jealous God and avenges. Yahweh avenges and is full of wrath. Yahweh takes vengeance on his adversaries, and he maintains wrath against his enemies. 3 Yahweh is slow to anger, and great in power, and will by no means leave the guilty unpunished. Yahweh has his way in the whirlwind and in the storm, and the clouds are the dust of his feet. 4 He rebukes the sea and makes it dry, and dries up all the rivers. Bashan and Carmel languish. The flower of Lebanon languishes. 5 The mountains quake before him, and the hills melt away. The earth trembles at his presence, yes, the world, and all who dwell in it. 6 Who can stand before his indignation? Who can endure the fierceness of his anger? His wrath is poured out like fire, and the rocks are broken apart by him. 7 Yahweh is good, a stronghold in the day of trouble; and he knows those who take refuge in him. 8 But with an overflowing flood, he will make a full end of her place, and will pursue his enemies into darkness. 9 What do you plot against Yahweh? He will make a full end. Affliction won't rise up the second time. 10 For entangled like thorns, and drunken as with their drink, they are consumed utterly like dry stubble. 11 One has gone out of you who devises evil against Yahweh, who counsels wickedness. 12 Yahweh says: "Though they are in full strength and likewise many, even so they will be cut down and pass away. Though I have afflicted you, I will afflict you no more. 13 Now I will break his yoke from off you, and will burst your bonds apart." 14 Yahweh has commanded concerning you: "No more descendants will bear your name. Out of the house of your gods, I will cut off the engraved image and the molten image. I will make your grave, for you are vile." 15 Behold, on the mountains the feet of him who brings good news, who publishes peace! Keep your feasts, Judah! Perform your vows, for the wicked one will no more pass through you. He is utterly cut off.

2

1 He who dashes in pieces has come up against you. Keep the fortress! Watch the way! Strengthen your waist! Fortify your power mightily! 2 For Yahweh restores the excellency of Jacob as the excellency of Israel, for the destroyers have destroyed them and ruined their vine branches. 3 The shield of his mighty men is made red. The valiant men are in scarlet. The chariots

flash with steel in the day of his preparation, and the pine spears are brandished. 4 The chariots rage in the streets. They rush back and forth in the wide ways. Their appearance is like torches. They run like the lightnings. 5 He summons his picked troops. They stumble on their way. They dash to its wall, and the protective shield is put in place. 6 The gates of the rivers are opened, and the palace is dissolved. 7 It is decreed: she is uncovered, she is carried away; and her servants moan as with the voice of doves, beating on their breasts. 8 But Nineveh has been from of old like a pool of water, yet they flee away. "Stop! Stop!" they cry, but no one looks back. 9 Take the plunder of silver. Take the plunder of gold, for there is no end of treasure, an abundance of every precious thing. 10 She is empty, void, and waste. The heart melts, the knees knock together, their bodies and faces have grown pale. 11 Where is the den of the lions, and the feeding place of the young lions, where the lion and the lioness walked with the lion's cubs, and no one made them afraid? 12 The lion tore in pieces enough for his cubs, and strangled prey for his lionesses, and filled his caves with the kill and his dens with prey. 13"Behold, I am against you," says Yahweh of Armies, "and I will burn her chariots in the smoke, and the sword will devour your young lions; and I will cut off your prey from the earth, and the voice of your messengers will no longer be heard."

3

1 Woe to the bloody city! It is all full of lies and robbery—no end to the prey. 2 The noise of the whip, the noise of the rattling of wheels, prancing horses, and bounding chariots, 3 the horseman charging, and the flashing sword, the glittering spear, and a multitude of slain, and a great heap of corpses, and there is no end of the bodies. They stumble on their bodies 4 because of the multitude of the prostitution of the alluring prostitute, the mistress of witchcraft, who sells nations through her prostitution, and families through her witchcraft. 5"Behold, I am against you," says Yahweh of Armies, "and I will lift your skirts over your face. I will show the nations your nakedness, and the kingdoms your shame. 6 I will throw abominable filth on you and make you vile, and will make you a spectacle. 7 It will happen that all those who look at you will flee from you, and say, 'Nineveh is laid waste! Who will mourn for her?' Where will I seek comforters for you?" 8 Are you better than No-Amon, who was situated among the rivers, who had the waters around her, whose rampart was the sea, and her wall was of the sea? 9 Cush and Egypt were her boundless strength. Put and Libya were her

helpers. 10 Yet was she carried away. She went into captivity. Her young children also were dashed in pieces at the head of all the streets, and they cast lots for her honorable men, and all her great men were bound in chains. 11 You also will be drunken. You will be hidden. You also will seek a stronghold because of the enemy. 12 All your fortresses will be like fig trees with the first-ripe figs. If they are shaken, they fall into the mouth of the eater. 13 Behold, your troops among you are women. The gates of your land are set wide open to your enemies. The fire has devoured your bars. 14 Draw water for the siege. Strengthen your fortresses. Go into the clay, and tread the mortar. Make the brick kiln strong. 15 There the fire will devour you. The sword will cut you off. It will devour you like the grasshopper. Multiply like grasshoppers. Multiply like the locust. 16 You have increased your merchants more than the stars of the skies. The grasshopper strips and flees away. 17 Your guards are like the locusts, and your officials like the swarms of locusts, which settle on the walls on a cold day, but when the sun appears, they flee away, and their place is not known where they are. 18 Your shepherds slumber, king of Assyria. Your nobles lie down. Your people are scattered on the mountains, and there is no one to gather them. 19 There is no healing your wound, for your injury is fatal. All who hear the report of you clap their hands over you, for who hasn't felt your endless cruelty?

The Book of Habakkuk

1

1 The revelation which Habakkuk the prophet saw. 2 Yahweh, how long will I cry, and you will not hear? I cry out to you "Violence!" and will you not save? 3 Why do you show me iniquity, and look at perversity? For destruction and violence are before me. There is strife, and contention rises up. 4 Therefore the law is paralyzed, and justice never prevails; for the wicked surround the righteous; therefore justice comes out perverted. 5"Look among the nations, watch, and wonder marvelously; for I am working a work in your days which you will not believe though it is told you. 6 For, behold, I am raising up the Chaldeans, that bitter and hasty nation who march through the width of the earth, to possess dwelling places that are not theirs. 7 They are feared and dreaded. Their judgment and their dignity proceed from themselves. 8 Their horses also are swifter than leopards, and are more fierce than the evening wolves. Their horsemen press proudly on. Yes, their horsemen come from afar. They fly as an eagle that hurries to devour. 9 All of them come for violence. Their hordes face forward. They gather prisoners like sand. 10 Yes, they scoff at kings, and princes are a derision to them. They laugh at every stronghold, for they build up an earthen ramp and take it. 11 Then they sweep by like the wind and go on. They are indeed guilty, whose strength is their god." 12 Aren't you from everlasting, Yahweh my God, my Holy One? We will not die. Yahweh, you have appointed them for judgment. You, Rock, have established him to punish. 13 You who have purer eyes than to see evil, and who cannot look on perversity, why do you tolerate those who deal treacherously and keep silent when the wicked swallows up the man who is more righteous than he, 14 and make men like the fish of the sea, like the creeping things that have no ruler over them? 15 He takes up all of them with the hook. He catches them in his net and gathers them in his dragnet. Therefore he rejoices and is glad. 16 Therefore he sacrifices to his net and burns incense to his dragnet, because by them his life is luxurious and his food is good. 17 Will he therefore continually empty his net, and kill the nations without mercy?

2

1 I will stand at my watch and set myself on the ramparts, and will look out to see what he will say to me, and what I will answer concerning my complaint. 2 Yahweh answered me, "Write the vision, and make it plain on

tablets, that he who runs may read it. ³ For the vision is yet for the appointed time, and it hurries toward the end, and won't prove false. Though it takes time, wait for it, because it will surely come. It won't delay. ⁴ Behold, his soul is puffed up. It is not upright in him, but the righteous will live by his faith. ⁵ Yes, moreover, wine is treacherous: an arrogant man who doesn't stay at home, who enlarges his desire as Sheol; he is like death and can't be satisfied, but gathers to himself all nations and heaps to himself all peoples. ⁶ Won't all these take up a parable against him, and a taunting proverb against him, and say, 'Woe to him who increases that which is not his, and who enriches himself by extortion! How long?' ⁷ Won't your debtors rise up suddenly, and wake up those who make you tremble, and you will be their victim? ⁸ Because you have plundered many nations, all the remnant of the peoples will plunder you because of men's blood, and for the violence done to the land, to the city and to all who dwell in it. ⁹ Woe to him who gets an evil gain for his house, that he may set his nest on high, that he may be delivered from the hand of evil! ¹⁰ You have devised shame to your house by cutting off many peoples, and have sinned against your soul. ¹¹ For the stone will cry out of the wall, and the beam out of the woodwork will answer it. ¹² Woe to him who builds a town with blood, and establishes a city by iniquity! ¹³ Behold, isn't it from Yahweh of Armies that the peoples labor for the fire, and the nations weary themselves for vanity? ¹⁴ For the earth will be filled with the knowledge of Yahweh's glory, as the waters cover the sea. ¹⁵"Woe to him who gives his neighbor drink, pouring your inflaming wine until they are drunk, so that you may gaze at their naked bodies! ¹⁶ You are filled with shame, and not glory. You will also drink and be exposed! The cup of Yahweh's right hand will come around to you, and disgrace will cover your glory. ¹⁷ For the violence done to Lebanon will overwhelm you, and the destruction of the animals will terrify you, because of men's blood and for the violence done to the land, to every city and to those who dwell in them. ¹⁸"What value does the engraved image have, that its maker has engraved it; the molten image, even the teacher of lies, that he who fashions its form trusts in it, to make mute idols? ¹⁹ Woe to him who says to the wood, 'Awake!' or to the mute stone, 'Arise!' Shall this teach? Behold, it is overlaid with gold and silver, and there is no breath at all within it. ²⁰ But Yahweh is in his holy temple. Let all the earth be silent before him!"

3

¹ A prayer of Habakkuk, the prophet, set to victorious music. ² Yahweh, I

have heard of your fame. I stand in awe of your deeds, Yahweh. Renew your work in the middle of the years. In the middle of the years make it known. In wrath, you remember mercy. 3 God came from Teman, the Holy One from Mount Paran. Selah. His glory covered the heavens, and his praise filled the earth. 4 His splendor is like the sunrise. Rays shine from his hand, where his power is hidden. 5 Plague went before him, and pestilence followed his feet. 6 He stood, and shook the earth. He looked, and made the nations tremble. The ancient mountains were crumbled. The age-old hills collapsed. His ways are eternal. 7 I saw the tents of Cushan in affliction. The dwellings of the land of Midian trembled. 8 Was Yahweh displeased with the rivers? Was your anger against the rivers, or your wrath against the sea, that you rode on your horses, on your chariots of salvation? 9 You uncovered your bow. You called for your sworn arrows. Selah. You split the earth with rivers. 10 The mountains saw you, and were afraid. The storm of waters passed by. The deep roared and lifted up its hands on high. 11 The sun and moon stood still in the sky at the light of your arrows as they went, at the shining of your glittering spear. 12 You marched through the land in wrath. You threshed the nations in anger. 13 You went out for the salvation of your people, for the salvation of your anointed. You crushed the head of the land of wickedness. You stripped them head to foot. Selah. 14 You pierced the heads of his warriors with their own spears. They came as a whirlwind to scatter me, gloating as if to devour the wretched in secret. 15 You trampled the sea with your horses, churning mighty waters. 16 I heard, and my body trembled. My lips quivered at the voice. Rottenness enters into my bones, and I tremble in my place because I must wait quietly for the day of trouble, for the coming up of the people who invade us. 17 For even though the fig tree doesn't flourish, nor fruit be in the vines, the labor of the olive fails, the fields yield no food, the flocks are cut off from the fold, and there is no herd in the stalls, 18 yet I will rejoice in Yahweh. I will be joyful in the God of my salvation! 19 Yahweh, the Lord, is my strength. He makes my feet like deer's feet, and enables me to go in high places. For the music director, on my stringed instruments.

The Book of Zephaniah

1

1 Yahweh's word which came to Zephaniah, the son of Cushi, the son of Gedaliah, the son of Amariah, the son of Hezekiah, in the days of Josiah, the son of Amon, king of Judah. 2 I will utterly sweep away everything from the surface of the earth, says Yahweh. 3 I will sweep away man and animal. I will sweep away the birds of the sky, the fish of the sea, and the heaps of rubble with the wicked. I will cut off man from the surface of the earth, says Yahweh. 4 I will stretch out my hand against Judah and against all the inhabitants of Jerusalem. I will cut off the remnant of Baal from this place—the name of the idolatrous and pagan priests, 5 those who worship the army of the sky on the housetops, those who worship and swear by Yahweh and also swear by Malcam, 6 those who have turned back from following Yahweh, and those who haven't sought Yahweh nor inquired after him. 7 Be silent at the presence of the Lord Yahweh, for the day of Yahweh is at hand. For Yahweh has prepared a sacrifice. He has consecrated his guests. 8 It will happen in the day of Yahweh's sacrifice that I will punish the princes, the king's sons, and all those who are clothed with foreign clothing. 9 In that day, I will punish all those who leap over the threshold, who fill their master's house with violence and deceit. 10 In that day, says Yahweh, there will be the noise of a cry from the fish gate, a wailing from the second quarter, and a great crashing from the hills. 11 Wail, you inhabitants of Maktesh, for all the people of Canaan are undone! All those who were loaded with silver are cut off. 12 It will happen at that time, that I will search Jerusalem with lamps, and I will punish the men who are settled on their dregs, who say in their heart, "Yahweh will not do good, neither will he do evil." 13 Their wealth will become a plunder, and their houses a desolation. Yes, they will build houses, but won't inhabit them. They will plant vineyards, but won't drink their wine. 14 The great day of Yahweh is near. It is near and hurries greatly, the voice of the day of Yahweh. The mighty man cries there bitterly. 15 That day is a day of wrath, a day of distress and anguish, a day of trouble and ruin, a day of darkness and gloom, a day of clouds and blackness, 16 a day of the trumpet and alarm against the fortified cities and against the high battlements. 17 I will bring such distress on men that they will walk like blind men because they have sinned against Yahweh. Their blood will be poured out like dust and their flesh like dung. 18 Neither their silver nor their gold will be able to deliver

them in the day of Yahweh's wrath, but the whole land will be devoured by the fire of his jealousy; for he will make an end, yes, a terrible end, of all those who dwell in the land.

2

¹ Gather yourselves together, yes, gather together, you nation that has no shame, ² before the appointed time when the day passes as the chaff, before the fierce anger of Yahweh comes on you, before the day of Yahweh's anger comes on you. ³ Seek Yahweh, all you humble of the land, who have kept his ordinances. Seek righteousness. Seek humility. It may be that you will be hidden in the day of Yahweh's anger. ⁴ For Gaza will be forsaken, and Ashkelon a desolation. They will drive out Ashdod at noonday, and Ekron will be rooted up. ⁵ Woe to the inhabitants of the sea coast, the nation of the Cherethites! Yahweh's word is against you, Canaan, the land of the Philistines. I will destroy you until there is no inhabitant. ⁶ The sea coast will be pastures, with cottages for shepherds and folds for flocks. ⁷ The coast will be for the remnant of the house of Judah. They will find pasture. In the houses of Ashkelon, they will lie down in the evening, for Yahweh, their God, will visit them and restore them. ⁸ I have heard the reproach of Moab and the insults of the children of Ammon, with which they have reproached my people and magnified themselves against their border. ⁹ Therefore, as I live, says Yahweh of Armies, the God of Israel, surely Moab will be as Sodom, and the children of Ammon as Gomorrah, a possession of nettles and salt pits, and a perpetual desolation. The remnant of my people will plunder them, and the survivors of my nation will inherit them. ¹⁰ This they will have for their pride, because they have reproached and magnified themselves against the people of Yahweh of Armies. ¹¹ Yahweh will be awesome to them, for he will famish all the gods of the land. Men will worship him, everyone from his place, even all the shores of the nations. ¹² You Cushites also, you will be killed by my sword. ¹³ He will stretch out his hand against the north, destroy Assyria, and will make Nineveh a desolation, as dry as the wilderness. ¹⁴ Herds will lie down in the middle of her, all kinds of animals. Both the pelican and the porcupine will lodge in its capitals. Their calls will echo through the windows. Desolation will be in the thresholds, for he has laid bare the cedar beams. ¹⁵ This is the joyous city that lived carelessly, that said in her heart, "I am, and there is no one besides me." How she has become a desolation, a place for animals to lie down in! Everyone who passes by her will hiss and shake their fists.

3

1 Woe to her who is rebellious and polluted, the oppressing city! 2 She didn't obey the voice. She didn't receive correction. She didn't trust in Yahweh. She didn't draw near to her God. 3 Her princes within her are roaring lions. Her judges are evening wolves. They leave nothing until the next day. 4 Her prophets are arrogant and treacherous people. Her priests have profaned the sanctuary. They have done violence to the law. 5 Yahweh, within her, is righteous. He will do no wrong. Every morning he brings his justice to light. He doesn't fail, but the unjust know no shame. 6 I have cut off nations. Their battlements are desolate. I have made their streets waste, so that no one passes by. Their cities are destroyed, so that there is no man, so that there is no inhabitant. 7 I said, "Just fear me. Receive correction," so that her dwelling won't be cut off, according to all that I have appointed concerning her. But they rose early and corrupted all their doings. 8"Therefore wait for me", says Yahweh, "until the day that I rise up to the prey, for my determination is to gather the nations, that I may assemble the kingdoms to pour on them my indignation, even all my fierce anger, for all the earth will be devoured with the fire of my jealousy. 9 For then I will purify the lips of the peoples, that they may all call on Yahweh's name, to serve him shoulder to shoulder. 10 From beyond the rivers of Cush, my worshipers, even the daughter of my dispersed people, will bring my offering. 11 In that day you will not be disappointed for all your doings in which you have transgressed against me; for then I will take away out from among you your proudly exulting ones, and you will no more be arrogant in my holy mountain. 12 But I will leave among you an afflicted and poor people, and they will take refuge in Yahweh's name. 13 The remnant of Israel will not do iniquity nor speak lies, neither will a deceitful tongue be found in their mouth, for they will feed and lie down, and no one will make them afraid." 14 Sing, daughter of Zion! Shout, Israel! Be glad and rejoice with all your heart, daughter of Jerusalem. 15 Yahweh has taken away your judgments. He has thrown out your enemy. The King of Israel, Yahweh, is among you. You will not be afraid of evil any more. 16 In that day, it will be said to Jerusalem, "Don't be afraid, Zion. Don't let your hands be weak." 17 Yahweh, your God, is among you, a mighty one who will save. He will rejoice over you with joy. He will calm you in his love. He will rejoice over you with singing. 18 I will remove those who grieve about the appointed feasts from you. They are a burden and a reproach to you. 19 Behold, at that time I will deal with all those who afflict you; and I

will save those who are lame and gather those who were driven away. I will give them praise and honor, whose shame has been in all the earth. [20] At that time I will bring you in, and at that time I will gather you; for I will give you honor and praise among all the peoples of the earth when I restore your fortunes before your eyes, says Yahweh.

The Book of Haggai

1

1 In the second year of Darius the king, in the sixth month, in the first day of the month, Yahweh's word came by Haggai the prophet, to Zerubbabel the son of Shealtiel, governor of Judah, and to Joshua the son of Jehozadak, the high priest, saying, 2"This is what Yahweh of Armies says: These people say, 'The time hasn't yet come, the time for Yahweh's house to be built.'" 3 Then Yahweh's word came by Haggai the prophet, saying, 4"Is it a time for you yourselves to dwell in your paneled houses, while this house lies waste? 5 Now therefore this is what Yahweh of Armies says: 'Consider your ways. 6 You have sown much, and bring in little. You eat, but you don't have enough. You drink, but you aren't filled with drink. You clothe yourselves, but no one is warm; and he who earns wages earns wages to put them into a bag with holes in it.' 7"This is what Yahweh of Armies says: 'Consider your ways. 8 Go up to the mountain, bring wood, and build the house. I will take pleasure in it, and I will be glorified," says Yahweh. 9"You looked for much, and, behold, it came to little; and when you brought it home, I blew it away. Why?" says Yahweh of Armies, "Because of my house that lies waste, while each of you is busy with his own house. 10 Therefore for your sake the heavens withhold the dew, and the earth withholds its fruit. 11 I called for a drought on the land, on the mountains, on the grain, on the new wine, on the oil, on that which the ground produces, on men, on livestock, and on all the labor of the hands." 12 Then Zerubbabel the son of Shealtiel and Joshua the son of Jehozadak, the high priest, with all the remnant of the people, obeyed Yahweh their God's voice, and the words of Haggai the prophet, as Yahweh their God had sent him; and the people feared Yahweh. 13 Then Haggai, Yahweh's messenger, spoke Yahweh's message to the people, saying, "I am with you," says Yahweh. 14 Yahweh stirred up the spirit of Zerubbabel the son of Shealtiel, governor of Judah, and the spirit of Joshua the son of Jehozadak, the high priest, and the spirit of all the remnant of the people; and they came and worked on the house of Yahweh of Armies, their God, 15 in the twenty-fourth day of the month, in the sixth month, in the second year of Darius the king.

2

1 In the seventh month, in the twenty-first day of the month, Yahweh's word came by Haggai the prophet, saying, 2"Speak now to Zerubbabel the son of

Shealtiel, governor of Judah, and to Joshua the son of Jehozadak, the high priest, and to the remnant of the people, saying, 3'Who is left among you who saw this house in its former glory? How do you see it now? Isn't it in your eyes as nothing? 4 Yet now be strong, Zerubbabel,' says Yahweh. 'Be strong, Joshua son of Jehozadak, the high priest. Be strong, all you people of the land,' says Yahweh, 'and work, for I am with you,' says Yahweh of Armies. 5 This is the word that I covenanted with you when you came out of Egypt, and my Spirit lived among you. 'Don't be afraid.' 6 For this is what Yahweh of Armies says: 'Yet once more, it is a little while, and I will shake the heavens, the earth, the sea, and the dry land; 7 and I will shake all nations. The treasure of all nations will come, and I will fill this house with glory, says Yahweh of Armies. 8 The silver is mine, and the gold is mine,' says Yahweh of Armies. 9'The latter glory of this house will be greater than the former,' says Yahweh of Armies; 'and in this place I will give peace,' says Yahweh of Armies." 10 In the twenty-fourth day of the ninth month, in the second year of Darius, Yahweh's word came by Haggai the prophet, saying, 11"Yahweh of Armies says: Ask now the priests concerning the law, saying, 12'If someone carries holy meat in the fold of his garment, and with his fold touches bread, stew, wine, oil, or any food, will it become holy?'" The priests answered, "No." 13 Then Haggai said, "If one who is unclean by reason of a dead body touches any of these, will it be unclean?" The priests answered, "It will be unclean." 14 Then Haggai answered, "'So is this people, and so is this nation before me,' says Yahweh; 'and so is every work of their hands. That which they offer there is unclean. 15 Now, please consider from this day and backward, before a stone was laid on a stone in Yahweh's temple. 16 Through all that time, when one came to a heap of twenty measures, there were only ten. When one came to the wine vat to draw out fifty, there were only twenty. 17 I struck you with blight, mildew, and hail in all the work of your hands; yet you didn't turn to me,' says Yahweh. 18'Consider, please, from this day and backward, from the twenty-fourth day of the ninth month, since the day that the foundation of Yahweh's temple was laid, consider it. 19 Is the seed yet in the barn? Yes, the vine, the fig tree, the pomegranate, and the olive tree haven't produced. From today I will bless you.'" 20 Yahweh's word came the second time to Haggai in the twenty-fourth day of the month, saying, 21"Speak to Zerubbabel, governor of Judah, saying, 'I will shake the heavens and the earth. 22 I will overthrow the throne of kingdoms. I will destroy the strength of the kingdoms of the nations. I will overthrow the chariots and those who ride in them. The horses and their riders will come down, everyone by the sword of his brother. 23 In that day, says Yahweh of Armies, I will take you, Zerubbabel my servant, the son of Shealtiel,' says Yahweh, 'and will make you like a signet ring, for I have chosen you,' says Yahweh of Armies."

The Book of Zechariah

1

1 In the eighth month, in the second year of Darius, Yahweh's word came to the prophet Zechariah the son of Berechiah, the son of Iddo, saying, 2"Yahweh was very displeased with your fathers. 3 Therefore tell them, Yahweh of Armies says: 'Return to me,' says Yahweh of Armies, 'and I will return to you,' says Yahweh of Armies. 4 Don't you be like your fathers, to whom the former prophets proclaimed, saying: Yahweh of Armies says, 'Return now from your evil ways and from your evil doings;' but they didn't hear nor listen to me, says Yahweh. 5 Your fathers, where are they? And the prophets, do they live forever? 6 But my words and my decrees, which I commanded my servants the prophets, didn't they overtake your fathers?

"Then they repented and said, 'Just as Yahweh of Armies determined to do to us, according to our ways and according to our practices, so he has dealt with us.'" 7 On the twenty-fourth day of the eleventh month, which is the month Shebat, in the second year of Darius, Yahweh's word came to the prophet Zechariah the son of Berechiah, the son of Iddo, saying, 8"I had a vision in the night, and behold, a man riding on a red horse, and he stood among the myrtle trees that were in a ravine; and behind him there were red, brown, and white horses. 9 Then I asked, 'My lord, what are these?'" The angel who talked with me said to me, "I will show you what these are." 10 The man who stood among the myrtle trees answered, "They are the ones Yahweh has sent to go back and forth through the earth." 11 They reported to Yahweh's angel who stood among the myrtle trees, and said, "We have walked back and forth through the earth, and behold, all the earth is at rest and in peace." 12 Then Yahweh's angel replied, "O Yahweh of Armies, how long will you not have mercy on Jerusalem and on the cities of Judah, against which you have had indignation these seventy years?" 13 Yahweh answered the angel who talked with me with kind and comforting words. 14 So the angel who talked with me said to me, "Proclaim, saying, 'Yahweh of Armies says: "I am jealous for Jerusalem and for Zion with a great jealousy. 15 I am very angry with the nations that are at ease; for I was but a little displeased, but they added to the calamity." 16 Therefore Yahweh says: "I have returned to Jerusalem with mercy. My house shall be built in it," says Yahweh of Armies, "and a line shall be stretched out over Jerusalem."' 17"Proclaim further, saying, 'Yahweh of Armies says: "My cities will again overflow with prosperity, and Yahweh will again comfort Zion, and will again choose Jerusalem."'" 18 I lifted up my eyes and saw, and behold, four horns. 19 I asked the angel who talked with me, "What are these?" He answered me, "These are the horns which have scattered Judah, Israel, and Jerusalem." 20 Yahweh showed me four craftsmen. 21 Then I asked, "What are these coming to do?" He said, "These are the horns which scattered Judah, so that no man lifted up his head; but these have come to terrify them, to cast down the horns of the nations that lifted up their horn against the land of Judah to scatter it."

2

1 I lifted up my eyes, and saw, and behold, a man with a measuring line in his hand. 2 Then I asked, "Where are you going?" He said to me, "To measure Jerusalem, to see what is its width and what is its length." 3 Behold, the angel who talked with me went out, and another angel went out to meet him, 4 and said to him, "Run, speak to this young man, saying, 'Jerusalem will be inhabited as villages without walls, because of the multitude of men and livestock in it. 5 For I,' says Yahweh, 'will be to her a wall of fire around it, and I will be the glory in the middle of her. 6 Come! Come! Flee from the land of the north,' says Yahweh; 'for I have spread you abroad as the four winds of the sky,' says Yahweh. 7 'Come, Zion! Escape, you who dwell with the daughter of Babylon.' 8 For Yahweh of Armies says: 'For honor he has sent me to the nations which plundered you; for he who touches you touches the apple of his eye. 9 For, behold, I will shake my hand over them, and they will be a plunder to those who served them; and you will know that Yahweh of Armies has sent me. 10 Sing and rejoice, daughter of Zion! For behold, I come and I will dwell within you,' says Yahweh. 11 Many nations shall join themselves to Yahweh in that day, and shall be my people; and I will dwell among you, and you shall know that Yahweh of Armies has sent me to you. 12 Yahweh will inherit Judah as his portion in the holy land, and will again choose Jerusalem. 13 Be silent, all flesh, before Yahweh; for he has roused himself from his holy habitation!"

3

1 He showed me Joshua the high priest standing before Yahweh's angel, and Satan standing at his right hand to be his adversary. 2 Yahweh said to Satan, "Yahweh rebuke you, Satan! Yes, Yahweh who has chosen Jerusalem rebuke you! Isn't this a burning stick plucked out of the fire?" 3 Now Joshua was clothed with filthy garments, and was standing before the angel. 4 He

answered and spoke to those who stood before him, saying, "Take the filthy garments off him." To him he said, "Behold, I have caused your iniquity to pass from you, and I will clothe you with rich clothing." 5 I said, "Let them set a clean turban on his head." So they set a clean turban on his head, and clothed him; and Yahweh's angel was standing by. 6 Yahweh's angel solemnly assured Joshua, saying, 7"Yahweh of Armies says: 'If you will walk in my ways, and if you will follow my instructions, then you also shall judge my house, and shall also keep my courts, and I will give you a place of access among these who stand by. 8 Hear now, Joshua the high priest, you and your fellows who sit before you, for they are men who are a sign; for, behold, I will bring out my servant, the Branch. 9 For, behold, the stone that I have set before Joshua: on one stone are seven eyes; behold, I will engrave its inscription,' says Yahweh of Armies, 'and I will remove the iniquity of that land in one day. 10 In that day,' says Yahweh of Armies, 'you will invite every man his neighbor under the vine and under the fig tree.'"

4

1 The angel who talked with me came again and wakened me, as a man who is wakened out of his sleep. 2 He said to me, "What do you see?" I said, "I have seen, and behold, a lamp stand all of gold, with its bowl on the top of it, and its seven lamps on it; there are seven pipes to each of the lamps which are on the top of it; 3 and two olive trees by it, one on the right side of the bowl, and the other on the left side of it." 4 I answered and spoke to the angel who talked with me, saying, "What are these, my lord?" 5 Then the angel who talked with me answered me, "Don't you know what these are?" I said, "No, my lord." 6 Then he answered and spoke to me, saying, "This is Yahweh's word to Zerubbabel, saying, 'Not by might, nor by power, but by my Spirit,' says Yahweh of Armies. 7 Who are you, great mountain? Before Zerubbabel you are a plain; and he will bring out the capstone with shouts of 'Grace, grace, to it!'" 8 Moreover Yahweh's word came to me, saying, 9"The hands of Zerubbabel have laid the foundation of this house. His hands shall also finish it; and you will know that Yahweh of Armies has sent me to you. 10 Indeed, who despises the day of small things? For these seven shall rejoice, and shall see the plumb line in the hand of Zerubbabel. These are Yahweh's eyes, which run back and forth through the whole earth." 11 Then I asked him, "What are these two olive trees on the right side of the lamp stand and on the left side of it?" 12 I asked him the second time, "What are these two olive branches, which are beside the two golden spouts that pour the golden oil out

of themselves?" 13 He answered me, "Don't you know what these are?" I said, "No, my lord." 14 Then he said, "These are the two anointed ones who stand by the Lord of the whole earth."

5

1 Then again I lifted up my eyes and saw, and behold, a flying scroll. 2 He said to me, "What do you see?" I answered, "I see a flying scroll; its length is twenty cubits, and its width ten cubits." 3 Then he said to me, "This is the curse that goes out over the surface of the whole land, for everyone who steals shall be cut off according to it on the one side; and everyone who swears falsely shall be cut off according to it on the other side. 4 I will cause it to go out," says Yahweh of Armies, "and it will enter into the house of the thief, and into the house of him who swears falsely by my name; and it will remain in the middle of his house, and will destroy it with its timber and its stones." 5 Then the angel who talked with me came forward and said to me, "Lift up now your eyes and see what this is that is appearing." 6 I said, "What is it?" He said, "This is the ephah basket that is appearing." He said moreover, "This is their appearance in all the land— 7 and behold, a lead cover weighing one talent was lifted up—and there was a woman sitting in the middle of the ephah basket." 8 He said, "This is Wickedness;" and he threw her down into the middle of the ephah basket; and he threw the lead weight on its mouth. 9 Then I lifted up my eyes and saw, and behold, there were two women; and the wind was in their wings. Now they had wings like the wings of a stork, and they lifted up the ephah basket between earth and the sky. 10 Then I said to the angel who talked with me, "Where are these carrying the ephah basket?" 11 He said to me, "To build her a house in the land of Shinar. When it is prepared, she will be set there in her own place."

6

1 Again I lifted up my eyes, and saw, and behold, four chariots came out from between two mountains; and the mountains were mountains of bronze. 2 In the first chariot were red horses. In the second chariot were black horses. 3 In the third chariot were white horses. In the fourth chariot were dappled horses, all of them powerful. 4 Then I asked the angel who talked with me, "What are these, my lord?" 5 The angel answered me, "These are the four winds of the sky, which go out from standing before the Lord of all the earth. 6 The one with the black horses goes out toward the north country; and the white went out after them; and the dappled went out toward the south

country." 7 The strong went out, and sought to go that they might walk back and forth through the earth. He said, "Go around and through the earth!" So they walked back and forth through the earth. 8 Then he called to me, and spoke to me, saying, "Behold, those who go toward the north country have quieted my spirit in the north country." 9 Yahweh's word came to me, saying, 10"Take of them of the captivity, even of Heldai, of Tobijah, and of Jedaiah; and come the same day, and go into the house of Josiah the son of Zephaniah, where they have come from Babylon. 11 Yes, take silver and gold, and make crowns, and set them on the head of Joshua the son of Jehozadak, the high priest; 12 and speak to him, saying, 'Yahweh of Armies says, "Behold, the man whose name is the Branch! He will grow up out of his place; and he will build Yahweh's temple. 13 He will build Yahweh's temple. He will bear the glory, and will sit and rule on his throne. He will be a priest on his throne. The counsel of peace will be between them both. 14 The crowns shall be to Helem, to Tobijah, to Jedaiah, and to Hen the son of Zephaniah, for a memorial in Yahweh's temple. 15 Those who are far off shall come and build in Yahweh's temple; and you shall know that Yahweh of Armies has sent me to you. This will happen, if you will diligently obey Yahweh your God's voice.""""

7

1 In the fourth year of King Darius, Yahweh's word came to Zechariah in the fourth day of the ninth month, the month of Chislev. 2 The people of Bethel sent Sharezer and Regem Melech and their men to entreat Yahweh's favor, 3 and to speak to the priests of the house of Yahweh of Armies and to the prophets, saying, "Should I weep in the fifth month, separating myself, as I have done these so many years?" 4 Then the word of Yahweh of Armies came to me, saying, 5"Speak to all the people of the land and to the priests, saying, 'When you fasted and mourned in the fifth and in the seventh month for these seventy years, did you at all fast to me, really to me? 6 When you eat and when you drink, don't you eat for yourselves and drink for yourselves? 7 Aren't these the words which Yahweh proclaimed by the former prophets when Jerusalem was inhabited and in prosperity, and its cities around her, and the South and the lowland were inhabited?'" 8 Yahweh's word came to Zechariah, saying, 9"Thus has Yahweh of Armies spoken, saying, 'Execute true judgment, and show kindness and compassion every man to his brother. 10 Don't oppress the widow, the fatherless, the foreigner, nor the poor; and let none of you devise evil against his brother in your heart.' 11 But they refused

to listen, and turned their backs, and stopped their ears, that they might not hear. 12 Yes, they made their hearts as hard as flint, lest they might hear the law and the words which Yahweh of Armies had sent by his Spirit by the former prophets. Therefore great wrath came from Yahweh of Armies. 13 It has come to pass that, as he called and they refused to listen, so they will call and I will not listen," said Yahweh of Armies; 14 "but I will scatter them with a whirlwind among all the nations which they have not known. Thus the land was desolate after them, so that no man passed through nor returned; for they made the pleasant land desolate."

8

1 The word of Yahweh of Armies came to me. 2 Yahweh of Armies says: "I am jealous for Zion with great jealousy, and I am jealous for her with great wrath." 3 Yahweh says: "I have returned to Zion, and will dwell in the middle of Jerusalem. Jerusalem shall be called 'The City of Truth;' and the mountain of Yahweh of Armies, 'The Holy Mountain.'" 4 Yahweh of Armies says: "Old men and old women will again dwell in the streets of Jerusalem, every man with his staff in his hand because of their old age. 5 The streets of the city will be full of boys and girls playing in its streets." 6 Yahweh of Armies says: "If it is marvelous in the eyes of the remnant of this people in those days, should it also be marvelous in my eyes?" says Yahweh of Armies. 7 Yahweh of Armies says: "Behold, I will save my people from the east country and from the west country. 8 I will bring them, and they will dwell within Jerusalem. They will be my people, and I will be their God, in truth and in righteousness." 9 Yahweh of Armies says: "Let your hands be strong, you who hear in these days these words from the mouth of the prophets who were in the day that the foundation of the house of Yahweh of Armies was laid, even the temple, that it might be built. 10 For before those days there was no wages for man nor any wages for an animal, neither was there any peace to him who went out or came in, because of the adversary. For I set all men everyone against his neighbor. 11 But now I will not be to the remnant of this people as in the former days," says Yahweh of Armies. 12 "For the seed of peace and the vine will yield its fruit, and the ground will give its increase, and the heavens will give their dew. I will cause the remnant of this people to inherit all these things. 13 It shall come to pass that, as you were a curse among the nations, house of Judah and house of Israel, so I will save you, and you shall be a blessing. Don't be afraid. Let your hands be strong." 14 For Yahweh of Armies says: "As I thought to do evil to you when your fathers

provoked me to wrath," says Yahweh of Armies, "and I didn't repent, ¹⁵ so again I have thought in these days to do good to Jerusalem and to the house of Judah. Don't be afraid. ¹⁶ These are the things that you shall do: speak every man the truth with his neighbor. Execute the judgment of truth and peace in your gates, ¹⁷ and let none of you devise evil in your hearts against his neighbor, and love no false oath; for all these are things that I hate," says Yahweh. ¹⁸ The word of Yahweh of Armies came to me. ¹⁹ Yahweh of Armies says: "The fasts of the fourth, fifth, seventh, and tenth months shall be for the house of Judah joy, gladness, and cheerful feasts. Therefore love truth and peace." ²⁰ Yahweh of Armies says: "Many peoples and the inhabitants of many cities will yet come. ²¹ The inhabitants of one will go to another, saying, 'Let's go speedily to entreat the favor of Yahweh, and to seek Yahweh of Armies. I will go also.' ²² Yes, many peoples and strong nations will come to seek Yahweh of Armies in Jerusalem and to entreat the favor of Yahweh." ²³ Yahweh of Armies says: "In those days, ten men out of all the languages of the nations will take hold of the skirt of him who is a Jew, saying, 'We will go with you, for we have heard that God is with you.'"

9

¹ A revelation. Yahweh's word is against the land of Hadrach, and will rest upon Damascus— for the eye of man and of all the tribes of Israel is toward Yahweh— ² and Hamath, also, which borders on it, Tyre and Sidon, because they are very wise. ³ Tyre built herself a stronghold, and heaped up silver like the dust, and fine gold like the mire of the streets. ⁴ Behold, the Lord will dispossess her, and he will strike her power in the sea; and she will be devoured with fire. ⁵ Ashkelon will see it, and fear; Gaza also, and will writhe in agony; as will Ekron, for her expectation will be disappointed; and the king will perish from Gaza, and Ashkelon will not be inhabited. ⁶ Foreigners will dwell in Ashdod, and I will cut off the pride of the Philistines. ⁷ I will take away his blood out of his mouth, and his abominations from between his teeth; and he also will be a remnant for our God; and he will be as a chieftain in Judah, and Ekron as a Jebusite. ⁸ I will encamp around my house against the army, that no one pass through or return; and no oppressor will pass through them any more: for now I have seen with my eyes. ⁹ Rejoice greatly, daughter of Zion! Shout, daughter of Jerusalem! Behold, your King comes to you! He is righteous, and having salvation; lowly, and riding on a donkey, even on a colt, the foal of a donkey. ¹⁰ I will cut off the chariot from Ephraim and the horse from Jerusalem. The battle bow will be cut off; and he will

speak peace to the nations. His dominion will be from sea to sea, and from the River to the ends of the earth. 11 As for you also, because of the blood of your covenant, I have set free your prisoners from the pit in which is no water. 12 Turn to the stronghold, you prisoners of hope! Even today I declare that I will restore double to you. 13 For indeed I bend Judah as a bow for me. I have loaded the bow with Ephraim. I will stir up your sons, Zion, against your sons, Greece, and will make you like the sword of a mighty man. 14 Yahweh will be seen over them. His arrow will flash like lightning. The Lord Yahweh will blow the trumpet, and will go with whirlwinds of the south. 15 Yahweh of Armies will defend them. They will destroy and overcome with sling stones. They will drink, and roar as through wine. They will be filled like bowls, like the corners of the altar. 16 Yahweh their God will save them in that day as the flock of his people; for they are like the jewels of a crown, lifted on high over his land. 17 For how great is his goodness, and how great is his beauty! Grain will make the young men flourish, and new wine the virgins.

10

1 Ask of Yahweh rain in the spring time, Yahweh who makes storm clouds, and he gives rain showers to everyone for the plants in the field. 2 For the teraphim have spoken vanity, and the diviners have seen a lie; and they have told false dreams. They comfort in vain. Therefore they go their way like sheep. They are oppressed, because there is no shepherd. 3 My anger is kindled against the shepherds, and I will punish the male goats, for Yahweh of Armies has visited his flock, the house of Judah, and will make them as his majestic horse in the battle. 4 From him will come the cornerstone, from him the tent peg, from him the battle bow, from him every ruler together. 5 They will be as mighty men, treading down muddy streets in the battle. They will fight, because Yahweh is with them. The riders on horses will be confounded. 6"I will strengthen the house of Judah, and I will save the house of Joseph. I will bring them back, for I have mercy on them. They will be as though I had not cast them off, for I am Yahweh their God, and I will hear them. 7 Ephraim will be like a mighty man, and their heart will rejoice as through wine. Yes, their children will see it and rejoice. Their heart will be glad in Yahweh. 8 I will signal for them and gather them, for I have redeemed them. They will increase as they were before. 9 I will sow them among the peoples. They will remember me in far countries. They will live with their children and will return. 10 I will bring them again also out of the land of Egypt, and gather

them out of Assyria. I will bring them into the land of Gilead and Lebanon; and there won't be room enough for them. 11 He will pass through the sea of affliction, and will strike the waves in the sea, and all the depths of the Nile will dry up; and the pride of Assyria will be brought down, and the scepter of Egypt will depart. 12 I will strengthen them in Yahweh. They will walk up and down in his name," says Yahweh.

11

1 Open your doors, Lebanon, that the fire may devour your cedars. 2 Wail, cypress tree, for the cedar has fallen, because the stately ones are destroyed. Wail, you oaks of Bashan, for the strong forest has come down. 3 A voice of the wailing of the shepherds! For their glory is destroyed—a voice of the roaring of young lions! For the pride of the Jordan is ruined. 4 Yahweh my God says: "Feed the flock of slaughter. 5 Their buyers slaughter them and go unpunished. Those who sell them say, 'Blessed be Yahweh, for I am rich;' and their own shepherds don't pity them. 6 For I will no more pity the inhabitants of the land," says Yahweh; "but, behold, I will deliver every one of the men into his neighbor's hand and into the hand of his king. They will strike the land, and out of their hand I will not deliver them." 7 So I fed the flock to be slaughtered, especially the oppressed of the flock. I took for myself two staffs. The one I called "Favor" and the other I called "Union", and I fed the flock. 8 I cut off the three shepherds in one month; for my soul was weary of them, and their soul also loathed me. 9 Then I said, "I will not feed you. That which dies, let it die; and that which is to be cut off, let it be cut off; and let those who are left eat each other's flesh." 10 I took my staff Favor and cut it apart, that I might break my covenant that I had made with all the peoples. 11 It was broken in that day; and thus the poor of the flock that listened to me knew that it was Yahweh's word. 12 I said to them, "If you think it best, give me my wages; and if not, keep them." So they weighed for my wages thirty pieces of silver. 13 Yahweh said to me, "Throw it to the potter—the handsome price that I was valued at by them!" I took the thirty pieces of silver and threw them to the potter in Yahweh's house. 14 Then I cut apart my other staff, Union, that I might break the brotherhood between Judah and Israel. 15 Yahweh said to me, "Take for yourself yet again the equipment of a foolish shepherd. 16 For, behold, I will raise up a shepherd in the land who will not visit those who are cut off, neither will seek those who are scattered, nor heal that which is broken, nor feed that which is sound; but he will eat the meat of the fat sheep, and will tear their hoofs in pieces. 17

Woe to the worthless shepherd who leaves the flock! The sword will strike his arm and his right eye. His arm will be completely withered, and his right eye will be totally blinded!"

12

1 A revelation of Yahweh's word concerning Israel: Yahweh, who stretches out the heavens and lays the foundation of the earth, and forms the spirit of man within him says: 2"Behold, I will make Jerusalem a cup of reeling to all the surrounding peoples, and it will also be on Judah in the siege against Jerusalem. 3 It will happen in that day that I will make Jerusalem a burdensome stone for all the peoples. All who burden themselves with it will be severely wounded, and all the nations of the earth will be gathered together against it. 4 In that day," says Yahweh, "I will strike every horse with terror and his rider with madness. I will open my eyes on the house of Judah, and will strike every horse of the peoples with blindness. 5 The chieftains of Judah will say in their heart, 'The inhabitants of Jerusalem are my strength in Yahweh of Armies their God.' 6 In that day I will make the chieftains of Judah like a pan of fire among wood, and like a flaming torch among sheaves. They will devour all the surrounding peoples on the right hand and on the left; and Jerusalem will yet again dwell in their own place, even in Jerusalem. 7 Yahweh also will save the tents of Judah first, that the glory of David's house and the glory of the inhabitants of Jerusalem not be magnified above Judah. 8 In that day Yahweh will defend the inhabitants of Jerusalem. He who is feeble among them at that day will be like David, and David's house will be like God, like Yahweh's angel before them. 9 It will happen in that day, that I will seek to destroy all the nations that come against Jerusalem. 10 I will pour on David's house and on the inhabitants of Jerusalem the spirit of grace and of supplication. They will look to me whom they have pierced; and they shall mourn for him as one mourns for his only son, and will grieve bitterly for him as one grieves for his firstborn. 11 In that day there will be a great mourning in Jerusalem, like the mourning of Hadadrimmon in the valley of Megiddo. 12 The land will mourn, every family apart; the family of David's house apart, and their wives apart; the family of the house of Nathan apart, and their wives apart; 13 the family of the house of Levi apart, and their wives apart; the family of the Shimeites apart, and their wives apart; 14 all the families who remain, every family apart, and their wives apart.

13

1"In that day there will be a fountain opened to David's house and to the inhabitants of Jerusalem, for sin and for uncleanness. 2 It will come to pass in that day, says Yahweh of Armies, that I will cut off the names of the idols out of the land, and they will be remembered no more. I will also cause the prophets and the spirit of impurity to pass out of the land. 3 It will happen that when anyone still prophesies, then his father and his mother who bore him will tell him, 'You must die, because you speak lies in Yahweh's name;' and his father and his mother who bore him will stab him when he prophesies. 4 It will happen in that day that the prophets will each be ashamed of his vision when he prophesies; they won't wear a hairy mantle to deceive, 5 but he will say, 'I am no prophet, I am a tiller of the ground; for I have been made a bondservant from my youth.' 6 One will say to him, 'What are these wounds between your arms?' Then he will answer, 'Those with which I was wounded in the house of my friends.' 7"Awake, sword, against my shepherd, and against the man who is close to me," says Yahweh of Armies. "Strike the shepherd, and the sheep will be scattered; and I will turn my hand against the little ones. 8 It shall happen that in all the land," says Yahweh, "two parts in it will be cut off and die; but the third will be left in it. 9 I will bring the third part into the fire, and will refine them as silver is refined, and will test them like gold is tested. They will call on my name, and I will hear them. I will say, 'It is my people;' and they will say, 'Yahweh is my God.'"

14

1 Behold, a day of Yahweh comes, when your plunder will be divided within you. 2 For I will gather all nations against Jerusalem to battle; and the city will be taken, the houses rifled, and the women ravished. Half of the city will go out into captivity, and the rest of the people will not be cut off from the city. 3 Then Yahweh will go out and fight against those nations, as when he fought in the day of battle. 4 His feet will stand in that day on the Mount of Olives, which is before Jerusalem on the east; and the Mount of Olives will be split in two from east to west, making a very great valley. Half of the mountain will move toward the north, and half of it toward the south. 5 You shall flee by the valley of my mountains, for the valley of the mountains shall reach to Azel. Yes, you shall flee, just like you fled from before the earthquake in the days of Uzziah king of Judah. Yahweh my God will come, and all the holy ones with you. 6 It will happen in that day that there will not be light, cold, or frost. 7 It will be a unique day which is known to Yahweh— not day, and not night; but it will come to pass that at evening time there will

be light. 8 It will happen in that day that living waters will go out from Jerusalem, half of them toward the eastern sea, and half of them toward the western sea. It will be so in summer and in winter. 9 Yahweh will be King over all the earth. In that day Yahweh will be one, and his name one. 10 All the land will be made like the Arabah, from Geba to Rimmon south of Jerusalem; and she will be lifted up and will dwell in her place, from Benjamin's gate to the place of the first gate, to the corner gate, and from the tower of Hananel to the king's wine presses. 11 Men will dwell therein, and there will be no more curse; but Jerusalem will dwell safely. 12 This will be the plague with which Yahweh will strike all the peoples who have fought against Jerusalem: their flesh will consume away while they stand on their feet, and their eyes will consume away in their sockets, and their tongue will consume away in their mouth. 13 It will happen in that day that a great panic from Yahweh will be among them; and they will each seize the hand of his neighbor, and his hand will rise up against the hand of his neighbor. 14 Judah also will fight at Jerusalem; and the wealth of all the surrounding nations will be gathered together: gold, silver, and clothing, in great abundance. 15 A plague like this will fall on the horse, on the mule, on the camel, on the donkey, and on all the animals that will be in those camps. 16 It will happen that everyone who is left of all the nations that came against Jerusalem will go up from year to year to worship the King, Yahweh of Armies, and to keep the feast of booths. 17 It will be that whoever of all the families of the earth doesn't go up to Jerusalem to worship the King, Yahweh of Armies, on them there will be no rain. 18 If the family of Egypt doesn't go up and doesn't come, neither will it rain on them. This will be the plague with which Yahweh will strike the nations that don't go up to keep the feast of booths. 19 This will be the punishment of Egypt and the punishment of all the nations that don't go up to keep the feast of booths. 20 In that day there will be inscribed on the bells of the horses, "HOLY TO YAHWEH"; and the pots in Yahweh's house will be like the bowls before the altar. 21 Yes, every pot in Jerusalem and in Judah will be holy to Yahweh of Armies; and all those who sacrifice will come and take of them, and cook in them. In that day there will no longer be a Canaanite in the house of Yahweh of Armies.

The Book of Malachi

1

¹ A revelation, Yahweh's word to Israel by Malachi. ²"I have loved you," says Yahweh. Yet you say, "How have you loved us?" "Wasn't Esau Jacob's brother?" says Yahweh, "Yet I loved Jacob; ³ but Esau I hated, and made his mountains a desolation, and gave his heritage to the jackals of the wilderness." ⁴ Whereas Edom says, "We are beaten down, but we will return and build the waste places," Yahweh of Armies says, "They shall build, but I will throw down; and men will call them 'The Wicked Land,' even the people against whom Yahweh shows wrath forever." ⁵ Your eyes will see, and you will say, "Yahweh is great—even beyond the border of Israel!" ⁶"A son honors his father, and a servant his master. If I am a father, then where is my honor? And if I am a master, where is the respect due me?" says Yahweh of Armies to you priests who despise my name. "You say, 'How have we despised your name?' ⁷ You offer polluted bread on my altar. You say, 'How have we polluted you?' In that you say, 'Yahweh's table is contemptible.' ⁸ When you offer the blind for sacrifice, isn't that evil? And when you offer the lame and sick, isn't that evil? Present it now to your governor! Will he be pleased with you? Or will he accept your person?" says Yahweh of Armies. ⁹"Now, please entreat the favor of God, that he may be gracious to us. With this, will he accept any of you?" says Yahweh of Armies. ¹⁰"Oh that there were one among you who would shut the doors, that you might not kindle fire on my altar in vain! I have no pleasure in you," says Yahweh of Armies, "neither will I accept an offering at your hand. ¹¹ For from the rising of the sun even to its going down, my name is great among the nations, and in every place incense will be offered to my name, and a pure offering; for my name is great among the nations," says Yahweh of Armies. ¹²"But you profane it when you say, 'Yahweh's table is polluted, and its fruit, even its food, is contemptible.' ¹³ You say also, 'Behold, what a weariness it is!' And you have sniffed at it", says Yahweh of Armies; "and you have brought that which was taken by violence, the lame, and the sick; thus you bring the offering. Should I accept this at your hand?" says Yahweh. ¹⁴" But the deceiver is cursed who has in his flock a male, and vows and sacrifices to the Lord a defective thing; for I am a great King," says Yahweh of Armies, "and my name is awesome among the nations."

2

¹"Now, you priests, this commandment is for you. ² If you will not listen, and if you will not take it to heart, to give glory to my name," says Yahweh of Armies, "then I will send the curse on you, and I will curse your blessings. Indeed, I have cursed them already, because you do not take it to heart. ³ Behold, I will rebuke your offspring, and will spread dung on your faces, even the dung of your feasts; and you will be taken away with it. ⁴ You will know that I have sent this commandment to you, that my covenant may be with Levi," says Yahweh of Armies. ⁵"My covenant was with him of life and peace; and I gave them to him that he might be reverent toward me; and he was reverent toward me, and stood in awe of my name. ⁶ The law of truth was in his mouth, and unrighteousness was not found in his lips. He walked with me in peace and uprightness, and turned many away from iniquity. ⁷ For the priest's lips should keep knowledge, and they should seek the law at his mouth; for he is the messenger of Yahweh of Armies. ⁸ But you have turned away from the path. You have caused many to stumble in the law. You have corrupted the covenant of Levi," says Yahweh of Armies. ⁹"Therefore I have also made you contemptible and wicked before all the people, according to the way you have not kept my ways, but have had respect for persons in the law. ¹⁰ Don't we all have one father? Hasn't one God created us? Why do we deal treacherously every man against his brother, profaning the covenant of our fathers? ¹¹ Judah has dealt treacherously, and an abomination is committed in Israel and in Jerusalem; for Judah has profaned the holiness of Yahweh which he loves, and has married the daughter of a foreign god. ¹² Yahweh will cut off the man who does this, him who wakes and him who answers, out of the tents of Jacob and him who offers an offering to Yahweh of Armies. ¹³"This again you do: you cover Yahweh's altar with tears, with weeping, and with sighing, because he doesn't regard the offering any more, neither receives it with good will at your hand. ¹⁴ Yet you say, 'Why?' Because Yahweh has been witness between you and the wife of your youth, against whom you have dealt treacherously, though she is your companion and the wife of your covenant. ¹⁵ Did he not make you one, although he had the residue of the Spirit? Why one? He sought godly offspring. Therefore take heed to your spirit, and let no one deal treacherously against the wife of his youth. ¹⁶ One who hates and divorces", says Yahweh, the God of Israel, "covers his garment with violence!" says Yahweh of Armies. "Therefore pay attention to your spirit, that you don't be unfaithful. ¹⁷ You have wearied Yahweh with your words. Yet you say, 'How have we wearied him?' In that

you say, 'Everyone who does evil is good in Yahweh's sight, and he delights in them;' or 'Where is the God of justice?'

3

1"Behold, I send my messenger, and he will prepare the way before me! The Lord, whom you seek, will suddenly come to his temple. Behold, the messenger of the covenant, whom you desire, is coming!" says Yahweh of Armies. 2"But who can endure the day of his coming? And who will stand when he appears? For he is like a refiner's fire, and like launderers' soap; 3 and he will sit as a refiner and purifier of silver, and he will purify the sons of Levi, and refine them as gold and silver; and they shall offer to Yahweh offerings in righteousness. 4 Then the offering of Judah and Jerusalem will be pleasant to Yahweh as in the days of old and as in ancient years. 5 I will come near to you to judgment. I will be a swift witness against the sorcerers, against the adulterers, against the perjurers, and against those who oppress the hireling in his wages, the widow, and the fatherless, and who deprive the foreigner of justice, and don't fear me," says Yahweh of Armies. 6"For I, Yahweh, don't change; therefore you, sons of Jacob, are not consumed. 7 From the days of your fathers you have turned away from my ordinances and have not kept them. Return to me, and I will return to you," says Yahweh of Armies. "But you say, 'How shall we return?' 8 Will a man rob God? Yet you rob me! But you say, 'How have we robbed you?' In tithes and offerings. 9 You are cursed with the curse; for you rob me, even this whole nation. 10 Bring the whole tithe into the storehouse, that there may be food in my house, and test me now in this," says Yahweh of Armies, "if I will not open you the windows of heaven, and pour you out a blessing, that there will not be enough room for. 11 I will rebuke the devourer for your sakes, and he shall not destroy the fruits of your ground; neither shall your vine cast its fruit before its time in the field," says Yahweh of Armies. 12"All nations shall call you blessed, for you will be a delightful land," says Yahweh of Armies. 13"Your words have been harsh against me," says Yahweh. "Yet you say, 'What have we spoken against you?' 14 You have said, 'It is vain to serve God,' and 'What profit is it that we have followed his instructions and that we have walked mournfully before Yahweh of Armies? 15 Now we call the proud happy; yes, those who work wickedness are built up; yes, they tempt God, and escape.' 16 Then those who feared Yahweh spoke one with another; and Yahweh listened and heard, and a book of memory was written before him for those who feared Yahweh and who honored his name. 17 They shall be mine," says Yahweh of Armies, "my own possession in the day that I make. I will spare them, as a man spares his own son who serves him. 18 Then you shall return and discern between the righteous and the wicked, between him who serves God and him who doesn't serve him.

4

1"For behold, the day comes, burning like a furnace, when all the proud and all who work wickedness will be stubble. The day that comes will burn them up," says Yahweh of Armies, "so that it will leave them neither root nor branch. 2 But to you who fear my name shall the sun of righteousness arise with healing in its wings. You will go out and leap like calves of the stall. 3 You shall tread down the wicked; for they will be ashes under the soles of your feet in the day that I make," says Yahweh of Armies.

4"Remember the law of Moses my servant, which I commanded to him in Horeb for all Israel, even statutes and ordinances.

5 Behold, I will send you Elijah the prophet before the great and terrible day of Yahweh comes. 6 He will turn the hearts of the fathers to the children and the hearts of the children to their fathers, lest I come and strike the earth with a curse."

Made in the USA
Las Vegas, NV
11 March 2025

4559ef96-b135-4b7f-a2d5-18c510a995d8R01